THE SHAWINIGAN FOX

HOW JEAN CHRÉTIEN DEFIED
THE ELITES AND RESHAPED CANADA

BY BOB PLAMONDON

great river media inc.

The Shawinigan Fox : How Jean Chrétien Defied the Elites and Reshaped Canada
By Bob Plamondon
Great River Media
Copyright @ 2017 by Bob Plamondon

Library and Archives Canada Cataloguing in Publication

Plamondon, Bob, author
The Shawinigan Fox / Bob Plamondon

ISBN 978-1-7750981-1-9

Great River Media Inc.
Suite 500 - 250 City Centre Ave
Ottawa, ON
K1R 6K7
www.greatriver.ca

Book design: Lisa Georges
Printed and bound in Canada

TABLE OF CONTENTS

PREFACE

Despite his electoral record and his success in slaying the deficit, stimulating the economy, fighting back the forces of separatism, and keeping Canada out a disastrous and ill-conceived military conflict, few historians are willing to put Jean Chrétien on the list of Canada's great prime ministers.

Historian Michael Bliss wrote that Chrétien was moderately competent and only moderately corrupt. Author Peter C. Newman described Chrétien's time in office as a baleful and listless administration — an interregnum — without a defining legacy.

Jean Chrétien has often been portrayed as a smalltown hick who stumbled his way to the top through luck and persistence. He won three majorities without breaking a sweat because of a civil war within conservative ranks. Chrétien balanced the books on the back of Brian Mulroney's GST. And it was Mulroney's North American Free Trade Agreement, not Chrétien's economic policies, that spurred Canadian investment and jobs. Indeed, Chrétien benefited from the very trade deal that he had campaigned against in the 1993 election.

According to Ottawa lore, federal bureaucrats bristled at the simpleton residing at 24 Sussex Drive, a man who was said to govern by slogans and refused to read any memo that was longer than a single page. As English comedians mocked his thick accent, critics in Québec cringed at how he mangled the French language and accused him of selling out to English Canada, calling him Québec's "Uncle Tom."

Chrétien, it was widely believed, was incapable of geopolitical insight. Sure, he made the right call in keeping Canada out of the Iraq war, but he did it for the wrong reasons. How was he to know that the Bush administration would ineptly manage Iraq in the aftermath of deposing Saddam Hussein?

Many Liberals gave Paul Martin, rather than Chrétien, credit for the Liberal government's achievements. Martin was considered the brains behind the operation, the star-prime-minister-in-waiting who was forced to bide his time until his aging predecessor finally surrendered the reins of power. Martin's strongest supporters were so convinced that he would do a better job that they ultimately launched a mutiny against Chrétien.

An in-depth analysis of Chrétien's performance shows that lurking beneath his plain-spoken manner and folksy charm were a deep intelligence, strong leadership skills, and highly tuned political instincts. Chrétien may not have articulated a grand vision, but he focused on what mattered to Canadians in their day-to-day lives. He fixed intractable problems, some of which had persisted for generations, and he made difficult and sometimes controversial decisions that time has proven to be prescient.

Following the near-loss in the 1995 Québec referendum, Chrétien changed the rules of the separation game. At the time, few thought the passage of the Clarity Act would end well. Many in Chrétien's cabinet were frozen by fear and anxiety. The separatists initially rejoiced at the provocation and the new legal path that Chrétien had given them to fulfill their ambitions. In hindsight, however, the Clarity Act has been revealed as a powerful stroke. When Chrétien left office, the country was more united than it had been in 50 years.

Under Chrétien, Canada went from a fiscal basket case to an international role model in economic management. As Canada's most fiscally conservative prime minister, he fundamentally shrank government and paid down debt. And it was not a quick fix. Once Chrétien balanced the books, the federal government rattled off 11 consecutive surpluses. The credit has often gone to Paul Martin, but it was Chrétien who did the heavy lifting in cabinet and who actively managed the public accounts. Government investments, when they came, turned a brain-drain into a brain-gain. On international trade, Chrétien happily played the role of Canada's salesman-in-chief.

Those who pressured Chrétien to send Canadian troops to Iraq in 2003 to depose the tyrant Saddam Hussein — including the president of the United States, the prime minister of the United Kingdom, the Canadian business establishment, the official Opposition, and senior members of his cabinet — found that the prime minister could not be intimidated. He defied expectations by staying out of the war, a move that saved lives and put Canada on the right side of history.

Chretien was an intuitive politician who made few mistakes in his 40 years of public service. Controversies, such as the sponsorship scandal, were rare. Little of what Chretien did for Canada has been undone by his successors.

There is much to learn from Chrétien's leadership style and his approach to the issues. Despite coming to office with more experience around the cabinet table than any of his predecessors, Chrétien had few pre-determined policy pre-scriptions. His brand of populism was anything but superficial, rooted more in optimism than fear and more in strengthening public institutions than taking them down. He understood that confident citizens invested in themselves and their future.

Chrétien resisted ideology and wisely evolved his thinking and positions over time. He trusted that the people of Canada would almost always point him in the right direction. And while he stood up for the underdog and the disadvan-taged, he was no bleeding heart.

He made Canadians laugh and feel good about the country. Chrétien took his job more seriously than he did himself. He did not get mired in detail and managed only those issues that cut across departments, such as government finances and national unity. He had a knack for boiling down issues to their essence. His need for order and timeliness was legendary, which he connected with his inclination to be decisive. Chrétien's restriction on memo length, he said, was only a problem for those who didn't know what they were talking about. For a man who was thought to be flippant, he was as clever and cunning as a fox.

Paul Martin, meanwhile, was widely thought to be the Liberal party's stron-gest asset, the consigliere who steered Chrétien toward fiscal rectitude, the star attraction at many campaign events. In a period when Chrétien faced few challenges from the opposition, journalists often cast their eyes forward to when Martin would eventually replace Chrétien, predicting sweeping majority governments and a time of great change and opportunity.

What they overlook is that it was Martin who wobbled at times on spending cuts, failed to speak out against the Iraq war, was jittery about critical national unity matters, and irresolute about major policy decisions. Martin did little that was not examined through the lens of his ambition to replace Chrétien as prime minister.

Enough time has passed to allow for a thorough assessment of this critical time in Canadian history, when the country avoided financial ruin, faced major foreign policy choices, and survived a national unity crisis. Time has also liberated those who were closest to the action — the cabinet ministers, political staff, strategists, high-ranking bureaucrats, and provincial premiers who were interviewed for this book — to speak their minds and reveal the secrets of what happened behind the scenes, including the feud between Chrétien and Martin.

"GODDAMN CHRÉTIEN"

In the final few days before the 1995 federal budget, Paul Martin was angry enough to seriously consider resigning as finance minister. He pulled industry minister John Manley and trade minister Roy MacLaren aside. "Goddamn Chrétien," Martin said to his cabinet colleagues. "One of the two of you may end up being minister of finance."

The issue was a proposed cut to seniors' benefits. Martin believed that he had to chop at least one major social program to not only meet the government's fiscal targets but to restore his personal credibility after the bad reviews of his debut budget in 1994. Martin figured he had one more shot as finance minister, "but that was it."[1]

Martin wrote in his memoirs that he fought the prime minister to get the cuts he wanted and that his confrontations with Chrétien left emotional scars that never fully healed. It was the beginning, Martin said, of a growing distance between them, a gulf that continued to widen throughout the remainder of their political careers.

But according to key bureaucrats who worked on the budget, if there were any jitters over departmental spending cuts they came from Martin, not Chrétien. A senior bureaucrat involved in the spending review exercise observed that the minister most likely to balk at serious cuts was Martin.

> Martin wobbled on the spending cuts when pressured. Ministers would go to him to get cuts reversed and he would go to bat for them. Martin was never a hawk. He did not have the drive to resist pressure. As we were working to hit our targets he took us backward. We used to ask him, 'Whose side are you on?'

The bureaucrat also observed that when Martin met with officials to review the proposed cuts, he was "unbelievably nervous." Martin did not like to disappoint his cabinet colleagues and was worried about how decisions might affect his future leadership ambitions. One minister took a dispute over a budget cut to Martin and after a two-hour "bare-knuckle" fight, the cut was scaled back by 25 per cent.[2]

This was inconsistent with the image Martin tried to promote – a finance minister who boasted that "hell and high water" would not budge him from his goal – and it was an early indication of Martin's struggle to balance competing priorities. Indeed, historian Michael Bliss wrote that Martin was, at heart, an economic interventionist as well as a tax-and-spend liberal. "The business community and those who see him only as a deficit fighter are mistaken," said Bliss. Reflecting on Martin's career as finance minister, Bliss said he was much further to the left than the business world thought he was.[3]

Chrétien was certainly committed to restraint, telling his staff and the media that he was prepared to be prime minister for only one term if that's what it took to restore fiscal sanity.[4] Other members of the cabinet understood Chrétien's resolve. Industry minister John Manley said there was no use in complaining to the prime minister about cuts to his department. "Chrétien was the man with the steel rod up his spine," Manley said. "He was inflexible."[5] Manley also advised Martin that his future political success was tied to his battle with the deficit: "Martin had to succeed in that. I assumed he would be the next leader and I genuinely wished him well."

Martin had settled on combining the seniors' benefits which were then distributed separately to husbands and wives into a single payment. That payment would then be taxed back from high-income families. The cut was supported by the deputy minister of finance, David Dodge, who thought it would be difficult for the government to cut into provincial social transfer payments without also paring back federal benefits. Chrétien thought it was ridiculous that Martin was motivated by a desire to burnish his image on Bay Street. The prime minister was not going to cut a seniors' program to improve Martin's reputation.

Chrétien's political instincts told him that tampering with senior benefits would have a catastrophic effect on the approaching Québec referendum. Chrétien discussed Martin's proposal with some old family friends who were aghast at the idea for other reasons. They told the prime minister that the monthly government cheque was the only money controlled by women who had been at home all their lives. "After thirty or forty years of begging their husbands for every cent," Chrétien was told, "they can buy themselves a new hat or take a friend out for cake and coffee without answering to anybody."[6] It was classic kitchen-table politics and Chrétien recognized that tampering with the benefit would take the government into dangerous territory. It reminded Chrétien of the time his wife told him in 1973 not to change the family allowance system. "Jean," Aline said, "if you touch that you will be in trouble. This is the only money some women in Shawinigan have got for themselves."[7]

There was always an expert who would make a theoretical argument in favour of a particular economic policy that left aside the reality of basic human behaviour. But from her perch in cabinet, Anne McLellan observed that it was normal for the prime minister to reach out to ordinary Canadians for advice: "He listened to people in his riding, when he went home, his caucus, his cabinet, his advisors, and to people around the world. He would pick up the phone and talk to people. He would take in what he had heard, he would analyse it and then reach a conclusion."

Venting to Manley and Maclaren, Martin pressed his case: "We have to put something in the budget for the elderly. The elderly have to contribute. There is no other way. And he won't let me have it." Beyond the politics, Chrétien saw no need to gut a social program since the draft budget had already hit the government's fiscal targets. The Privy Council Office supported Chrétien's view on the numbers: the cut to Old Age Security was simply not needed for the budget math to work. A senior bureaucrat involved in the budget negotiations heard Chrétien tell Martin that they should leave well enough alone and that they had a good package that Canadians would accept.

The week before the budget was to be delivered, Martin told his inner circle and the Clerk of the Privy Council that if he didn't get what he wanted, he would resign. The threat was never reported by the media, so the government avoided what could have become a major crisis. It was, according to the prime minister's communications director Peter Donolo, a case of the finance minister acting like a prima donna. Chrétien asked the Privy Council Office to give him advice on who could deliver the budget should Martin resign.

Rather than face Chrétien directly, Martin sent Peter Nicholson, a visiting departmental economist, to 24 Sussex Drive to make his final pitch and deliver his ultimatum.[8]

Chrétien recalled how Michael Wilson, Mulroney's finance minister, had to back away from a budget plan to partially de-index seniors' benefits from inflation in 1985. A pivotal moment came for Mulroney when he was accosted by an elderly protester, Solange Denis, who told him he was a liar because he had once called social programs a "sacred trust." She dismissed Mulroney with the memorable phrase, "You lied to us .... You made us vote for you and then goodbye Charlie Brown." Chrétien wanted no part of a policy from which he might later have to retreat.

Martin even went so far as to speak with Solange Denis in 1995. She agreed that under the circumstances a cut in seniors' benefits was necessary. But Chrétien wouldn't budge. And Martin's offer to resign didn't faze him. "Really?" Chrétien said to Martin's emissary. "You know, it's been the dream of my life to be my own minister of finance. I'd be happy to read the budget speech myself."[9] Eddie Goldenberg, Chrétien's most important political advisor, said it was his way of making the point that there was only one prime minister.

According to David Dodge, the prime minister was more optimistic about the economy and government revenues than the department of finance was. The "compromise" on which Martin hung his hat was that Chrétien agreed he would revisit the issue the following year if finances were not improving. "It was simply a face-saving measure for Martin," said Manley.

Realistically, the compromise meant nothing since all issues are open for debate when a budget is prepared. "The prime minister did not make a commitment," said Dodge, "but asked us to go away and come back with something he could sell. We spent a lot of time – a great deal of time – the following year trying to work out a more sophisticated way to deal with seniors' benefits. But when we got to the 1996 budget we started to see that we were not going to have the same fiscal difficulties." In other words, Chrétien's fiscal projections were correct. Martin climbed down from his skirmish with Chrétien in the 1995 budget, although he admitted, "Having won so many battles I found it hard to lose on this one."[10]

On one issue, Martin never won. Every year they were in government together, Chrétien and Martin made a bet on the size of the deficit or surplus. Every single time, Chrétien won the bet. Indeed, Martin once acknowledged that he owes Chrétien $700 as a result of the wagers, a debt he has never paid.[11] "Quite frankly, I don't know why you aren't paying me because I have no intention of cashing your cheque," Chrétien told Martin. "I'm going to frame it and put it on my wall."[12]

THE FOX AND THE BADGER

Fate placed Jean Chrétien and Paul Martin Jr. on a path where they were destined to clash. In their relationship Martin was the badger and Chretien was the fox.

Jean Chrétien was born on January 11, 1934, the eighteenth of 19 children born to Wellie and Marie Chrétien. While he shared a birthday with Canada's founding Conservative prime minister, Sir John A. Macdonald, there was never any doubt that Chrétien would be a Liberal.

Wellie passed on his love of politics and fierce Liberal partisanship to his son. He brought Jean with him to political events, instilling both a civic responsibility and a desire to win.[1] At the age of 14, Jean handed out 12-ounce bottles of whiskey in exchange for votes. The following year he shook the hand of Prime Minister Louis St. Laurent and debated politics at the poolroom near his home.

The Chrétien family had earned a reputation among the political powerbrokers in the province as staunch Liberals. When Union Nationale premier Maurice Duplessis first met Jean Chrétien, he called the teenager "a damn rouge." In turn, Chrétien made political speeches in the mill cafeteria denouncing Duplessis.

The Duplessis government, which ruled Québec for a total of 18 years, ending in 1959, was immensely powerful and actively sought to intimidate its opponents. In the 1952 provincial election, the party targeted Chrétien's home riding, which was then held by a Liberal. Duplessis warned voters that if they did not return a member of his party, they would not get the bridge they wanted. In speeches in support of his local Liberal candidate, Chrétien proclaimed, "I will cross the river swimming, but I will never cross the river on my knees."[2]

When Chrétien spoke with his father about the possibility of studying architecture, Wellie steered his son to study the law, not as a career but as a path to public office.[3] Politics was not only a calling but a place where Chrétien confronted his anxieties: "Some people find it hard to believe, but I've always had an inferiority complex"[4] But that insecurity fuelled his desire to prove himself. Politics, for Chrétien, was a place where he could fight for, and win, validation.

In his personal and professional life, he was anything but flashy. He worked long hours, wore inexpensive suits, drove a small car, and he socialized little. He also kept a close watch over his family and business finances. Despite having the means to live wherever he wanted in his hometown, he chose the working-class neighbourhood of Shawinigan North. His personal attachment was to the lower and middle-class.

As a lawyer, Chrétien chose to line up on the union side of the labour-management table where he advocated for improvements in working conditions and wages. "That was very much my desire," Chrétien wrote. "My social ambition was to be on the populist side, not the side of business."[5]

When Chrétien first thought about running for federal parliament in his mid-20s, there was little hope for an opening in his home riding. The sitting Liberal MP, Joseph-Adolphe Richard, who had held the seat since 1949, looked like he would stay put for many elections to come. Chrétien did not want to challenge the incumbent Liberal, but an upsurge in the vote for the Social Credit in Québec in the 1962 election unexpectedly gave Richard his walking papers.

The newly elected Social Credit MP, Gérard Lamy, assumed he was in solid shape going into the 1963 election. In 1962, he had nearly double the Liberal vote. Chrétien, then 29, won the Liberal nomination, but was the clear underdog in the general election. Lamy boasted that being the father of 15 children gave him the requisite experience to represent the riding. Chrétien, a recent law school graduate, argued that the constituency needed a legislator, not a reproducer.

But even Liberals thought Chrétien had little chance of winning. To energize his team, Chrétien put his money where its mouth was with a series of five-dollar bets that he would come out on top on election day. The bravado, backed up by wagers from other supporters, made people think twice.

Two weeks before the election, Chrétien debated his opponent in front of a crowd packed with his own supporters. After they started heckling the incumbent, Chrétien intervened. "Ladies and gentlemen," Chrétien pleaded, "Mr. Lamy is your Member of Parliament. Will you listen to him, please?" Then he added, "In two weeks no one will have to listen to him anymore."[6] Chrétien showed that he belonged on the stage and could not be intimidated.

Chrétien was a natural at the game and learned early on that it was better to make friends on the campaign trail than impress them with academic arguments or theories. Chrétien wrote that the art of engaging a voter is a talent that some people are born with. "If you make the voter feel happy or comfortable, you'll get his vote. If you're pushy or tense or clumsy or self-satisfied, you'll lose that vote forever."[7]

By the end of the campaign over $17,000 had been wagered on the outcome of the election, including a single bet of $5,000 made on the eve of the vote by a local businessman. Chrétien and his family members covered all bets. Chrétien won with room to spare, receiving 16,358 votes; slightly less than 50 per cent of the total vote, but 1,944 votes ahead of his main opponent.

When he came into politics, Chrétien placed himself on the left wing of the Liberal party. He claims never to have had any great interest in making money and happily substituted his $30,000 income as a practicing lawyer for $10,000 to serve as an MP. But he was always interested in the economy. When Chrétien arrived in Ottawa he volunteered to sit on the House of Commons banking and finance committee, an unusual request for an MP from Québec of that time. Economic matters were then thought to be the purview of Anglophone politicians.

Chrétien got his first taste of the government's accounts under the tutelage of Mitchell Sharp. First elected to Parliament along with Chrétien in 1963, Sharp had the look of a patrician. Although he had grown up in a working-class family in Winnipeg, he studied at the London School of Economics and rose through the ranks of the public service to become deputy minister to the minister of industry and commerce. After Sharp became Lester Pearson's minister of finance in 1965, he asked that Chrétien be appointed his parliamentary secretary.

Under Sharp's guidance, Chrétien jettisoned some of his left-wing thinking and adopted a more employer-friendly outlook. But as he followed Sharp around

Ottawa, Chrétien readily admitted he was a fish out of water. At the end of one meeting with senior officials from the Department of Finance and the Bank of Canada, Sharp reminded Chrétien of the confidential nature of the subject matter being discussed: "Don't be worried, Mitchell," Chrétien responded. "I didn't understand a bloody thing."[8] The political and intellectual partnership that Sharp and Chrétien formed endured for 40 years until Chrétien retired from public life.[9]

Chrétien thought he would be in Ottawa for ten years before being appointed a judge for Québec City. He even enrolled in a postgraduate course at the University of Ottawa law faculty while serving as an MP. But the thought of a career after politics did not quell his ambition to stand out among his parliamentary colleagues. Soon after arriving in Ottawa he set his sights on the front benches of the Pearson government. To show he could play on the national stage, Chrétien established a network of MPs from across the country. This not only helped him to improve his English but also built up his reputation as a hard worker and a team player. For inspiration, he put up a picture of John and Robert Kennedy in his office.[10]

Chrétien had no illusions about the vagaries of politics and recognized there was a greasy pole that must be climbed to get to the top. In his first autobiography, he recounted how some backbench members of the Liberal government would pass notes to opposition Progressive Conservative members hoping to help them embarrass the minister so that a slot might open up for one of them.[11]

The House of Commons was, at that time, a difficult environment for unilingual francophones. It was a place where most of the spoken French came from maintenance workers, not Parliamentarians. Chrétien could only read a bit of English and there were no language teachers on Parliament Hill. To improve his English skills he read magazines, such as *Time* and *Newsweek*. He recalled that he made many mistakes in his second language, but that Canadians were sympathetic to his challenge. When he took formal language training his teacher refused to correct his accent. "When I turn on the radio and you're speaking, I know it's you. You have to keep it."[12] Chrétien later remarked that only he and actor Maurice Chevalier had to practise to keep their French accent when speaking English. Chrétien's teacher was playing to his strengths as a man of the people.

Chrétien was a rising star within his party, so much so that in 1964 the provincial Liberals in Québec asked him to quit federal politics to run in his home province. "Jean," said Liberal cabinet minister René Lévesque, a future Parti Québecois premier, "you have no future in Ottawa. Because in five years Ottawa will not exist for us."[13] Chrétien discussed the offer with Prime Minister Pearson and with his closest advisors, most of whom encouraged him to make the leap. Chrétien stayed put: "I'm 30 years old, I'm chairman of the justice committee of the House of Commons, and I'm beginning to be known."

Despite being a backbencher, Chrétien did not hesitate to offer his opinions. When Pearson thought he could convert his minority into a majority government in 1965, Chrétien advised him not to call an election. The Tories ended up picking up seats, though the Liberals held on to its minority government. This was the election that brought Pierre Trudeau into the Pearson government.

With new talent coming out of Québec, the prospects of Chrétien being given a cabinet post had dimmed. To lessen the blow Pearson told him that he hoped one day he would become the first French-Canadian minister of finance, something Trudeau eventually made a reality.[13]

Once in cabinet, Chrétien's economic outlook veered once again to the right. As Treasury Board minister, he took pride in being called "Dr. No" by his cabinet colleagues. As Canada's first Francophone finance minister he chastised his Liberal predecessors for not keeping a tighter hold on the public purse.

In Trudeau's government, Chrétien was a role player who was given difficult portfolios at points of crisis. He went to Finance when inflation and the deficit were out of control, to Justice when the Constitution needed a miracle worker and to Energy when the West was infuriated by the National Energy Program. As energy minister, he didn't hesitate to enact policy changes that reflected poorly on his predecessors.[15] It was a difficult file to handle, one that his colleague Eugene Whelan described as "shit." Chrétien replied, "Yeah, it's shit. I know it's shit. And you know what happens when there's shit. They say, 'Hey, Jean, here's the shovel.'"[16]

Chrétien was devastated when he lost the 1984 leadership race and John Turner succeeded Trudeau as prime minister. It would be the only vote he ever lost. And six years and two federal elections later, he was ready for another run for the Liberal leadership. This time, his primary challenger was Paul Martin.

POLITICAL AMBITION WAS INSTILLED in Paul Martin Jr. at an early age. His father, Paul Martin Sr., a respected Member of Parliament and minister of the Crown, attempted to win the leadership of the Liberal party on three occasions. In 1948, he withdrew before the first ballot vote in the contest where Louis St. Laurent became Liberal leader and prime minister. In 1958, Lester B. Pearson took 77 per cent of the first-ballot votes compared with just 22 per cent for Martin. In 1968, Martin withdrew after picking up only 11 per cent on the first ballot.

In the 1958 contest for the Liberal leadership, Jean Chrétien supported Paul Martin Sr. He had no intention of supporting the anglophone from Windsor, Ontario, but when he saw the forces that were lining up with the front runner, Chrétien sided with the underdog.[17]

Paul Martin Sr. was known to represent the progressive or left-wing faction of the Liberal party. He is given some credit for being the father of medicare because of his role in implementing hospital insurance. C.D. Howe, a senior minister in the Liberal governments during the 1940s and 1950s, was reported to have referred to Paul Martin Sr. as "my young Communist friend."[18] According to Don Drummond, who served as the younger Martin's associate deputy minister of finance, the apple did not fall too far from the tree. "I think he is very much his father's son," said Drummond. "People paint a picture of him as an ultra-fiscal conservative. I don't think he is."[19]

There is no denying Paul Martin Sr. his place in history. He is one of only nine individuals to be granted the title "Right Honourable" without becoming prime minister, governor general or chief justice of the Supreme Court. Paul Martin Jr. was inspired by his father's dedication to public service and was committed to the ideals he espoused. "No one has had one-tenth the influence on Paul that his father has," said John English, a historian and Liberal MP under Chrétien. "I have never seen a relationship so intense and so deep between a father and a son as those two."

The younger Martin was powerfully motivated to reach the office that his father had long sought but never achieved. *The Economist* wrote that this was how the younger Martin intended to redress history.[20] On the day he was sworn in as prime minister, Martin held the flag that had flown on Parliament Hill the day his father passed away.

The younger Martin grew up surrounded by big ideas and a cast of political characters. But he claims, perhaps understating his ambition, that his first love was not politics.[21] He began his professional career in the executive suite at Power Corporation. Before that, he had worked as a field officer with the World Bank, and with the United Nations.[21] Martin's mentor was not a politician but a man who crossed the line between business and public service. Maurice Strong was the CEO of Power Corporation when he picked Martin as his executive assistant. Martin said he knew nothing about business at the time or had much passion for its aims.[23] Power Corporation was known to hire and court political figures, and hiring the son of Paul Martin Sr. fit with this strategy. Strong told Martin that if he wanted to have a career in politics he first needed to understand how business worked.

Paul Martin Jr. is described as someone who was born on third base. "I still remember my first business lunch," recalled Martin, "realizing that the bill was about what Sheila and I normally spent on groceries for a month! I entered the corporation at what I later realized was a pretty rarefied level."[24] Martin progressed through the ranks of Power Corporation and in 1973 he was given the helm at Canada Steamship Lines, a Power Corp. subsidiary. At the time, the company was struggling with labour relations, so Martin hired a hotshot Montreal lawyer named Brian Mulroney to calm the waters.[25] When Power Corporation made a takeover bid for Canadian Pacific Railway, the Competition Bureau made the holding company choose between owning a rail line and a shipping business. In June 1981, Power Corporation CEO Paul Demarais instructed Martin to find a buyer for Canada Steamship Lines. Martin didn't want to find a buyer; he wanted to own the company himself.[26] Martin wrote that he borrowed almost every penny of the $180 million it took to buy the company. It was a wise investment, making Martin spectacularly wealthy and well positioned for a career in politics.

Martin wrote in his memoir that he was not a political animal. But few observers were surprised when he ran for Parliament in 1988. When the CBC profiled Martin they dubbed him a saviour for the party, especially in Québec.[27] Chrétien, who had stepped away from politics after John Turner became Liberal leader, advised Martin to run in a Windsor, Ontario riding. That's where Martin was born and where his father had served as a member of Parliament. And, thinking well ahead, Chrétien suggested that Martin would be better positioned to succeed him by running in an Ontario riding to follow the long-standing Liberal tradition of alternating between English and French leaders.[28]

Martin claimed that he did not enter politics with the ambition of becoming prime minister. "I wanted to be the C.D. Howe of my generation," wrote Martin, "using my understanding of business and the larger economy to build a Canada that could take on the economic giants outside our borders. It was that dream that initially led me to fix on becoming Minister of Industry."[29] But the professed lack of ambition did not square with what was going on behind the scenes. Sheila Copps said that a Martin surrogate called her in 1984, on the day she was first elected to Parliament, to set up a meeting with Martin. Copps said that Martin told her that he wanted to pursue the twin objectives of becoming a member of Parliament and then prime minister.

Martin was a lifelong Liberal, but he was uncomfortable with the direction his party had taken over the 1970s and early 1980s:

> It was clear that the global economy was changing fundamentally. The days of easy economic growth, abundant job creation, and low inflation were behind us. But like a lot of governments around the world, Canada was slow to recognize what was happening. The economy was stalled but inflation continued apace, and a new term, stagflation, was coined. Many people in power apparently believed that Ottawa could spend its way out of economic difficulties, and all that borrowed money would be easily handled in the next upturn.[30]

John Turner's opposition to free trade with the United States cast Martin further adrift.[31] But he did serve on the board of directors of the Canadian Development Institute, a Crown corporation that was the investment arm of the Canadian government, mandated to make investments in key sectors of the Canadian economy.[32] He also affirmed his support for economic nationalism at a Liberal youth convention in November 1982 where he praised the thrust of the National Energy Program and the Foreign Investment Review Agency.[33]

While running in the 1988 election, Martin was described in the press as a "hot property" and a potential future Liberal leader. Political observers viewed Martin's family legacy, experience in the business world, and dedication to Third World interests as a potent combination. In the campaign, he spoke in broad policy strokes about societal change and national competitiveness, deflecting questions about his ultimate political ambition.

His résumé aside, questions were raised about whether Martin could perform in the political arena. Shortly after he won his seat in 1988, a report in the *Ottawa Citizen* suggested that Martin lacked the cutthroat instincts needed in Ottawa.[34] The early reviews were that he was thin-skinned and awkward. He could articulate grand visions, it was reported, but had difficulty making decisions. All the same, he had no difficulty in deciding what to do when the leadership of the Liberal party came up for grabs in 1990.

After Chrétien defeated Martin in the 1990 leadership race, they struck an uneasy partnership that formed the backbone of the Liberal government that began in 1993. That tense but often productive alliance ended when Martin effectively resigned as finance minister, not in 1995 as he had originally threatened, but in 2002, to launch a direct campaign to dethrone Chrétien.

Throughout the 1990s, it was a widely held perception among opinion columnists and within the upper ranks of the Liberal party that Martin would be a more thoughtful and credible prime minister than Chrétien. But the record tells a different story from the prevailing wisdom about both men. It also demonstrates the importance of the time: Canada's prosperity, unity and its place in the world in the 21st century were established by several key decisions made by the Chrétien government between 1993 and 2003. Other choices with very different outcomes might have been made if the Liberals had voted differently in the leadership race of 1990.

THE NATION

MEECH LAKE

Canadian unity was the cause of Jean Chrétien's political life.[1] He believed that if Québec were to separate, Canada would ultimately be absorbed into the United States and that it would only be a matter of time before an isolated Republic of Québec would follow suit.[2]

Growing up, Chrétien was taught by his father that Canada was the protector of Québec's culture and the French language. The threat to the French fact in North America, he was told, was not Canada but the United States.

Wellie Chrétien was not just loyal to Canada out of convenience. He was among the 28 per cent of Québecers, including anglophones, who voted yes in the conscription referendum during the Second World War. Wellie had three draft-eligible sons at the time. He told his sons that there would be no conscripts in his household and insisted they volunteer for service. Two were rejected, one because he was a medical doctor who was needed in his community and another who had specialized skills that were essential to the operation of a local plant. Wellie's only eligible son served overseas and became a captain in the artillery. Wellie proudly displayed a star in the window of his home signifying a family member was serving his country at a time of war. Marie Chrétien knitted socks for the troops overseas. The Chrétien household was proud to be Canadian.

Given his father's influence, it's not surprising that Jean Chrétien was attracted to federal politics even though he spoke next to no English. After moving to Ottawa to serve as an MP from Québec, Chrétien took his family by train to Vancouver. It was his first time in Western Canada and he fell in love with the vastness of the country, especially the majesty of the Rocky Mountains. He was impressed that a Quebecer with halting English was so warmly received right across the country.

When given the opportunity to offer his solution to Canada's unity challenge, Chrétien said that Québec's cultural and linguistic aspirations would not be met by a rigid centralizing form of federalism. In his maiden speech in the House of Commons in 1963, Chrétien argued for federal flexibility in response to Québec's demands for more powers:

> [Québec] may wish to be more independent from Confederation than in the past. The government of the province must be given the means to solve its own problems. The federal government will have to adopt laws on biculturalism that are adequate and recognize, on a national scale, that during the next 100 years, Canada, the country where there are two languages and two cultures, will be different from the United States.

His first memorable accomplishment as a backbench MP was spearheading the passage of a private members' bill that changed the name of TransCanada Airlines to the bilingual Air Canada. Then, as now, it was unusual for a private member's bill to pass and it took some deft footwork on Chrétien's part to snake his bill through the House of Commons when some Tory members were opposed.

After navigating an array of the more difficult files for Pierre Trudeau, Chrétien became Trudeau's point man on all sensitive matters concerning Québec. This included taking the federal lead in the 1980 Québec referendum and in the ensuing negotiations aimed at patriating the constitution from the British Parliament. Trudeau's preference for a strong central government did not align with Chrétien's inclinations, but he respected the way in which Trudeau confronted Québec separatists.

Part of Chrétien's challenge in Québec was dealing with intellectuals from the province who did not respect a street-smart but unsophisticated politician from Shawinigan. Provincial politicians and editorial writers from Québec thought Chrétien was an inarticulate hick who lacked the cerebral heft and sophistication to represent them on the national stage. But Chrétien was not insecure, and took delight in being underestimated and demeaned because he identified with the common man.

Chief among his detractors was Claude Ryan, then editor of the widely-respected newspaper *Le Devoir* and later leader of the Québec Liberal party. Ryan led the No forces in the 1980 Québec referendum on sovereignty-association. Ryan showed his disdain for Chrétien by showing up late for meetings and by dismissing his point of view. Where Ryan was logical and studious, Chrétien was emotional and patriotic. For the referendum, Ryan proposed the slogan, "Mon non est Québecois" while Chrétien pitched "Non, Merci." As Ryan would later find out from Chrétien and Trudeau, in a referendum campaign emotions matter.

Chrétien had never felt as much pressure as he did during the 1980 referendum, and said it was more stressful than being minister of finance: "Normally I leap with pleasure at new challenges – the bigger the better – but this one frightened me." He lost 15 pounds off an already slim frame. Yet, when the No side won the referendum, Chrétien was in no mood to celebrate, saying he took no pride in destroying other people's dreams. As it was, Ryan refused to let Chrétien speak from the podium on referendum night because, in Ryan's estimation, he had already "stolen enough of the show."[3]

WITH MOMENTUM ON THE side of federalists, Trudeau asked Chrétien to lead his fight to patriate the constitution. Ever the loyal soldier, Chrétien immediately accepted the challenge that had confounded Canadian governments since efforts were first made in the 1920s. Whenever a made-in-Canada constitution was close to reality, one or more provincial governments — most often, Québec — would get cold feet.

Chrétien was not keen to pick up the constitutional file because he didn't think changing the constitution would solve the nation's problems. In every cabinet post, he held that his approach was to deliver practical results, saying "I have been in government too long to be impressed by editorials and abstract theories."[4]

Grand visions were Trudeau's shtick. Few in Trudeau's cabinet had the skills to take on the challenge so Chrétien was given the nod. Despite his eagerness to serve, Chrétien drew the line when Trudeau proposed a national referendum to settle the constitutional question: "I won't be putting on my running shoes again for you. I've had enough of villages divided, French against English. A national referendum will be worse."[5]

Trudeau succeeded in obtaining a constitutional deal, although it was marred by the absence of the Québec premier's signature. Chrétien's deal-making skills led to the agreement that he took to Trudeau for approval. Trudeau agreed, but was upset that the package included a notwithstanding clause allowing the provinces and the federal Parliament to override many elements of the Charter of Rights and Freedoms. Unlike Trudeau, Chrétien saw nothing wrong with the notwithstanding clause since it gave democracy a check and balance on court rulings. He said he would have no problem if the government of the day used the notwithstanding clause to prevent the spread of discrimination or if images of child pornography were given court protection.[6] In other words, if the courts got something fundamentally wrong the elected representatives could prevail.

Trudeau is known as the architect of the Constitution Act and Chrétien is considered the builder, but this was not always the case. It was Chrétien who told Trudeau he would consider the constitution to be a failure unless it included the right for Canadians to educate their children in either English or French. For Chrétien, it was personal. His connection to the issue was through his mother's extended family that had grown up in Alberta under a unilingual English education system. Chrétien knew that it was impractical to create a school for a single child, so the right was extended to communities where numbers warranted.

Chrétien recognized the damage that could result from leaving Québec constitutionally isolated. In the weeks following the 1980 constitutional conference, Chrétien persuaded Trudeau to accept a modest amendment giving Québec fiscal compensation when it opted out of amendments that affected culture and education.

As far as Chrétien was concerned, the constitutional file was closed when the Queen signed the Charter on Parliament Hill on April 17, 1982.

AT A 1984 CAMPAIGN stop in Sept Isles, Québec, Brian Mulroney promised that a Progressive Conservative government would revise the Constitution so that the Québec National Assembly would give its consent with "honour and enthusiasm." Mulroney won that election, and along with it a mandate to pursue constitutional change.

For its part, the Québec government of Robert Bourassa identified five conditions to be met before a constitutional package would be placed before the

National Assembly for ratification. These were:

1.   A veto over constitutional amendments,

2.   A role in the appointment of Supreme Court judges,

3.   Increased powers over immigration,

4.   Limitations on federal spending power in areas of provincial jurisdiction, and

5.   Constitutional recognition of Québec as a distinct society.

Gordon Robertson, the most senior civil servant advising Pearson and Trudeau on constitutional matters, said the five conditions were the most moderate proposals to emerge from any Québec government since the Victoria constitutional conference of 1971. Negotiations ensued and a unanimous deal was reached by the prime minister and all provincial premiers at Meech Lake in 1987. The accord was subject to ratification by the federal Parliament and all provincial legislatures.

Trudeau, then in retirement, thought Meech Lake would have weakened the federal government to the point where Canada ceased to exist as a nation. The Liberal caucus, then under the leadership of John Turner, split over the issue. Those loyal to Trudeau and his vision were unwilling to accept the leadership of his successor on the matter. Turner said this was more than just a policy disagreement: "Trudeau intervened and caused great divisions in the party. He did not clear it with me first and he didn't talk to me."

The Meech Lake Accord had a ratification deadline of June 23, 1990. After Turner announced his resignation in May 1989, the accord became fodder in the ensuing Liberal leadership campaign. Chrétien, the clear frontrunner for the leadership, could have done without the constitutional drama. It did not help that the deadline to ratify the accord landed on the same weekend as the Liberal leadership convention. As the deadline for ratification approached, three provinces — New Brunswick, Manitoba, and Newfoundland — needed to gain approval.

Three of Chrétien's key political advisors informed Mulroney's chief of staff that they were "absolutely sure" an endorsement for Meech was imminent.[7] In the spring of 1990, at the home of Senator Leo Kolber, Chrétien mused with

Trudeau about the impact that the defeat of Meech would have on a future Québec referendum. Trudeau responded that if Chrétien supported Meech he would personally campaign against him for the Liberal leadership. Mulroney contends that it was that threat that caused Chrétien to back away from endorsing Meech.[8]

The other major Liberal leadership candidate, Paul Martin, had arranged a private lunch with Trudeau before the leadership race got underway. When the subject of Meech Lake came up, Martin argued that the clause describing Québec as a distinct society simply reflected reality and did not provide an increase in powers. Trudeau told Martin he was wrong. "No, Mr. Trudeau," responded Martin, "you are wrong."

Martin said he supported Meech Lake because it incorporated a fundamental recognition of Québec's place in Canada and remedied a flaw in the 1981 patriation of the Constitution. Martin claims that he sent emissaries to the Chrétien organization to seek an agreement to try to keep the accord on the back burner during the leadership race, but was rebuffed. Eddie Goldenberg said this never happened. Martin also claims Chrétien used Meech Lake as a wedge issue: "Jean Chrétien clearly believed that it was to his advantage [to keep Meech Lake visible], and he played the issue out till almost the end when he had secured his support in English Canada. Then, suddenly, he decided that the debate was not working to his advantage, particularly in Québec, and that it should stop."[9] But Martin biographer John Gray wrote that Martin was equally intent on using Meech Lake to win the leadership. He concluded that his path to victory would be enhanced by scooping up delegates in Québec based on his pro-Meech position.[10] It was a miscalculation: rank and file Liberal members in Québec were not nationalists and sided more with Pierre Trudeau's stance on Meech.

At a Liberal leadership debate in Winnipeg, Chrétien reiterated his concerns about the supremacy of the Charter while Martin responded by calling Chrétien Trudeau's puppet and saying that "it was time to start looking to the future."[11] The battle lines were drawn, with Meech Lake serving as the blow torch to heat up the differences between the candidates.

At another leadership event in Montreal, Martin supporters who had been bussed in from Ontario harangued Chrétien and taunted him by shouting "vendu" and "Judas." Martin said he did not think much of the matter until later when he was told that Chrétien had taken offence. He said that Chrétien had allowed the memory of this event "to turn into a bitter shrine."[12] On this point Martin was correct. Chrétien recalls it as one of the lowest moments of the campaign and his career.[13] After Martin lost the leadership race he did little to reconcile with Chrétien. He did not apologize for the insult and the wound only festered with Chrétien.

Richard Mahoney, a key Martin advisor, said there were excesses in the leadership campaign that were unhelpful: "A winner-take-all at the riding level made for a very acrimonious contest. Some of our young supporters went over the top. If I could erase that I would. To this day, I believe Mr. Chrétien believes that (the protest) was planned, but it wasn't. I don't think Mr. Chrétien ever forgave Mr. Martin for that."

In his memoirs, Martin acknowledged that the divisions and future rancour over the demise of Meech haunted the Liberal party for more than a decade:

> By stoking the fire of opposition to Meech Lake in English Canada, [Chrétien] was compounding the difficulties the Liberal party already had in confronting the separatist push in Québec in the coming election. This is why I wanted him to agree to a nonaggression pact over the issue, if not to change his opposition to the accord. Instead, he ratcheted up the volume.[14]

Eddie Goldenberg accused Martin of being disingenuous: "Martin told me at the Montebello resort that he was against the Meech Lake Accord but would support it publicly to gain favour in Québec. He said he knew it would not go through so he made a political calculation. He didn't understand what was at stake." At an informal meeting of leading Liberals — known as the Grindstone Group — Martin was described as dithering when he spoke about the Meech Lake Accord. *Globe and Mail* columnist Hugh Winsor wrote that no one knew what Martin was talking about.[15]

Chrétien met secretly with Mulroney's team to help get Meech passed by dealing with the contentious aspects of the accord.[16] The key points were: the federal government's role in promoting linguistic duality and the subordination of Québec's distinct society to the Charter of Rights.[17] Chrétien claims that he consulted widely on Meech Lake. "I listened to the arguments; I tried through intermediaries to help work out a compromise. In the end," he said, "it was beyond saving." Regardless, he understood that he would be demonized in Québec for not providing full-throated support for Meech Lake.[18]

Jean Charest, who co-chaired a Parliamentary committee to recommend options to get Meech ratified, saw Chrétien in a more positive light:

> He was very pragmatic and wanted to see a positive outcome. But it wasn't the issue he wanted to be identified with. In a pragmatic way, he was hoping it could be resolved so he could move on to other matters. But he did not have much ability to control the outcome. He certainly did not control Pierre Trudeau or (Newfoundland premier) Clyde Wells.

While Chrétien may not have stuck his neck out on Meech, Eddie Goldenberg thought that was because his boss never liked what Meech Lake represented: "His issue was who spoke for Canada? He saw it as a weakening of the federal government. If you give in a bit to the provinces, then what's next? He certainly did not want Supreme Court judges to be appointed by the provinces. He was very happy that it didn't go through."

The day Chrétien won the leadership and the Meech Lake Accord died, many Liberal MPs and other delegates donned black armbands. One MP, Jean Lapierre, said he did not for one minute want to have an association with Chrétien, "who is now the shame of most Québecers."[19] Mulroney predicted that because of the role that Chrétien and other Liberals played in the demise of Meech Lake, there would never be a Liberal government elected in his lifetime and that Chrétien would not win a seat in Québec. After becoming leader, Chrétien ran in a by-election in New Brunswick rather than in his home province.[20]

THE NEXT ROUND OF constitutional negotiations concluded in Charlottetown, PEI in 1992. The resulting accord was endorsed by all political parties in the House of Commons, all provincial governments, First Nations groups, and, in the early days, public opinion polls. Unlike Meech Lake, it was the people of Canada who determined the fate of the Charlottetown Accord in a national referendum on October 26, 1992.

Once again Pierre Trudeau became its most visible detractor, which put him in conflict with Chrétien. Chrétien met with Trudeau at a private dinner in a suite at the Royal York Hotel in Toronto, where they sought common ground. Trudeau argued that the phrase "distinct society" gave Québec strong powers to discriminate against the English. Chrétien countered that the term had only symbolic significance. "Jean, there are no words that mean nothing," Trudeau replied. Chrétien admitted that he didn't know too many such words, but in this case, he told Trudeau he had it wrong.[21]

Although Chrétien had encouraged Mulroney to hold the referendum, he kept a low profile during the campaign, especially in Québec.[22] Voters rejected the Charlottetown Accord nationally by a vote of 54 to 46 per cent. The Accord passed in New Brunswick, Newfoundland, Ontario, and PEI, but failed in Nova Scotia, Québec, and in all four western provinces.

Chrétien would have preferred that Mulroney avoid the constitutional issue altogether. "Having barely survived the battles over patriation and the Charter of Rights as Trudeau's minister of justice, I thought Mulroney was wrong to have reopened the constitutional file," he said. "I felt the Meech Lake Accord was more symbolic than real."[23] Chrétien suggested Mulroney might have survived to fight and win a third term if he hadn't put the country in a constitutional pressure cooker.[24]

By the time the 1993 election rolled around, Chrétien had had enough of constitutional battles. To one voter he said, "If you want to talk about the constitution, don't vote for me."[25] And many Québecers did not. In fact, the Bloc Québécois, a party intent on separating Québec from Canada, led by Lucien Bouchard, took 54 of Québec's 75 seats, then, ironically, became Her Majesty's Loyal Opposition. This new political force not only represented Québec's interest in the House of Commons but also worked from its beachhead in Ottawa to create the conditions for Québec to become a sovereign state.

With the Meech Lake and Charlottetown Accords behind him, Chrétien came into office in November 1993 hoping that constitutional wrangling would remain dormant for many years to come. But the grief in Québec over both the patriation of the constitution and the demise of Meech Lake remained a potent political timebomb. This took on new meaning on September 12, 1994, when Parti Québecois leader Jacques Parizeau was elected premier of Québec with a commitment to hold a referendum on sovereignty.

Prominent Québec-based columnist Chantal Hébert wrote that Chrétien would be hard-pressed to overcome the perception that he was unfriendly to Québec's aspirations, suggesting there was an anybody-but-Chrétien tide rising in the lead-up to the 1993 federal election, not just among the separatists.

> Many outside Québec assume that the nationalists make up the bulk of those who detest Chrétien. But to just as many federalists in Québec, there is no doubt that a majority Chrétien government in Ottawa would be the single greatest asset to the Parti Québecois in an ensuing provincial election ... In Québec, a [March 1993] poll showed that more than 40 per cent thought Campbell would make a good prime minister. Less than one in 10 thought the same of Chrétien. His image is so bad that Liberal insiders concede there is a strong probability he will not regain his St-Maurice seat in the next election.[26]

Chrétien won his seat in his home Québec riding in the 1993 general election, earning 54 per cent of the vote to 40 per cent for his Bloc Québécois opponent. The Liberals won 19 seats in Québec, a gain of 7 from the previous general election. Clearly, Chrétien was not the spent force in Québec that many had predicted.

1995 REFERENDUM

On December 6, 1994, draft legislation was introduced in the Québec National Assembly that positioned Québec as a sovereign nation and declared the premier of Québec as the prime minister of a country. It was a bold launch to a referendum campaign in which the following question would be on the ballot:

> Do you agree that Québec should become sovereign after having made a formal offer to Canada for a new economic and political partnership within the scope of the bill respecting the future of Québec and of the agreement signed on June 12, 1995?

Chrétien's cabinet colleagues were panic-stricken by the coalition of forces that had assembled behind Jacques Parizeau. Some ministers argued that the government should change course from the planned 1995 austerity budget to show Québecers that federalism remained a profitable enterprise. Chrétien thought the best argument for national unity was a competent and effective federal government that delivered a high quality of life to all Canadians. He recognized that economic mismanagement and a growing national debt had harmed the nation and its unity, and thought Québecers would be more impressed with Canada if the country had a strong balance sheet. Chrétien believed that running an honest and open government while creating good paying jobs would impress Québecers more than trying to buy their support on borrowed money. He told his team not to worry: he had beaten the separatists before and he would do it again.

One argument coming out of Québec was that there was no place for francophones in an English-dominated nation. But there was no shortage of examples to demonstrate Québec's growing influence in Ottawa. This included not only the prime minister but his chief of staff, the governor general, the chief justice of the Supreme Court, the Clerk of the Privy Council, the minister of foreign affairs, and the Canadian ambassador to the United States. The prime minister boasted that the most important daily meeting in the country, the one involving himself, his chief of staff, and the Clerk of the Privy Council, was conducted in French. Chrétien wondered how anyone could claim discrimination and oppression against Québecers when they had such powerful roles in the affairs of state.[1]

The opinion polls showed that federalists were in a stronger position in 1995 than they had been going into the 1980 referendum campaign, when they won with 60 per cent of the vote. But winning was not certain. That's why Reform Party leader Preston Manning wanted Chrétien to show Québec some tough love. He pushed Chrétien to come up with a Plan B in the event the No side lost, even if only by a single vote. Chrétien thought Manning was being irresponsible, saying even the Roman Catholic Church required two-thirds of cardinals to elect a pope. Most corporations, unions, even the Reform Party, required a two-thirds majority to change their charters. So why tell Québecers they could make an irrevocable decision without a significant majority? Chrétien suspected that Manning knew he could never become prime minister of Canada because of his party's lack of support in Québec, and, as a result, "he wouldn't have been terribly sorry to see it leave the federation."[2]

While Chrétien was trying to make the case for Canada, Preston Manning wanted to box him into a tight corner. He asked the prime minister in the House of Commons to declare that a Yes vote meant separation and a No meant federalism.

The editorial writers at the federalist Montreal Gazette called Manning's musings dangerous claptrap and potentially damaging to national unity. They supported the prime minister's view that Canada could not be destroyed by a slim separatist victory on a confusing question:

> Mr. Chrétien would be irresponsible to make the commitment Mr. Manning seeks ...While claiming to be a federalist, Mr. Manning and his party's policies have become the unwitting ally of the separatists and the Bloc Québécois. If Mr. Manning ever hopes to be a credible voice for Canada in the unity debate, he will have to be more than an unwitting stooge for those who would destroy the country.[3]

Manning told authors Chantal Hébert and Jean Lapierre that he had met with representatives of separatist forces in Québec to plot a course of action should they win the referendum. Even with a 50.1 per cent Yes vote on a convoluted question, Manning said he would call for talks to negotiate Québec's secession.[4] Manning said that western members would have withdrawn from Parliament following a Yes vote, because "it would have been considered illegitimate."

Chrétien believed that Canada could not be broken up so easily: "If the Reform Party had left the House, I would have had an easier time. You are legitimate until you quit. Manning might have dreamt about becoming prime minister once Québec is gone. But I had a majority government."[5]

It was one thing for Manning to game out within his closed circle of advisors what he might do if the referendum went the wrong way for federalists. But it was quite another to sit down with Québec separatists and offer encouragement. If a Yes vote materialized, and there was a battle over the legitimacy of the referendum, Manning would likely have sided with Jacques Parizeau's interpretation of the results. Eddie Goldenberg called Manning's conduct shameful and almost at the level of treason.

Going into the referendum campaign, Chrétien was advised by provincial Liberals not to take an active role, in part because his initial opposition to Meech Lake would be used against him.[6] It did not help that during the 1990 Liberal leadership campaign, Paul Martin had told Chrétien that he did not understand that Québec could no longer be pushed around. Even within the federal Liberal caucus, federalist forces were not unified.

One of the arguments Chrétien wanted to make was that if Québec could separate from Canada so too could communities separate from Québec. Polls showed that much of the Island of Montreal and many Indigenous communities would choose overwhelmingly to remain in Canada.[7] But that argument was too provocative for Québec Liberal leader Daniel Johnson's team on the ground in Québec. It bothered Chrétien that the No forces were being timid, but with a 55 to 45 per cent federalist lead in the opinion polls, he was not prepared to break ranks to argue the point.[8]

Chrétien ridiculed Jacques Parizeau's assertion that Québec could divorce itself from Canada but remain partners at the same time. "For me, that was like a man asking his wife if he could take a mistress during the week and still come home on weekends. The odds of her saying yes weren't great."[9] Chrétien's pre-referendum strategy was low key: "Some say I have no strategy to resolve the problem. But I have a good and clear strategy: it's faith in Canada. If we provide a good, honest, hard-working government, everybody will want to remain in Canada." Besides, he thought, the constitution did not permit the separation of a province, so there were no legal means for Parizeau to accomplish his goal. However, this was a position Chrétien did not express publicly.

Allan Rock found it bizarre that the strategy was to sideline Chrétien during the referendum:

> The brain trust led by Daniel Johnson only invited certain federal ministers to help out in the back room. But they did not want the prime minister front and centre, thinking he would not be an asset to the campaign. They wanted to run this themselves, which turned out to be a catastrophic mistake. They were so completely incompetent.

But it's clear that Chrétien remained a lightning rod in the referendum. Mario Dumont, leader of the Action démocratique, joined with the Yes forces because he said being on the same side as Jean Chrétien was impossible: "People in Québec wanted change. The Chrétien camp was not proposing any change … The offer was status quo or shut up."[10]

Chrétien aside, many federal cabinet ministers thought the federal government's absence in the referendum campaign was an abdication of responsibility. David Collenette, the minister of transport, said that voters in his constituency elected him to be their representative on all issues affecting the country, including Québec's place in Canada: "Being 10 points ahead was no excuse for us staying on the sidelines."

What was most important, said Eddie Goldenberg, was for Chrétien not to act in a way that would risk breaking the coalition of federalist forces that was, according to Québec law, led by the provincial Liberal leader Daniel Johnson:

> Chrétien had wanted to be in it from the beginning. He wanted to make it an emotional campaign based on an emotional attachment to Canada. It was like holding a horse back because he wanted to enter the fray. With three weeks to go we were up by 10 percentage points in the polls and it looked like there was no need for us to intervene.

It was a rare instance where Chrétien set his instincts aside. What he did not anticipate — indeed, what no one anticipated — was how the poll numbers would abruptly change when Jacques Parizeau announced that after a Yes victory, Lucien Bouchard of the Bloc Québeécois would serve as Québec's chief negotiator.

Bouchard was far more charismatic than Parizeau and had achieved a secular sainthood status in Québec after having his leg amputated and almost dying in a battle with necrotizing fasciitis, or flesh-eating disease, in December 1994. Federalists thought Bouchard's mid-campaign promotion was an act of desperation by the Yes side, and their initial reaction was to laugh it off.[11] But as Chrétien later observed, "When one campaigns with a cane, it works."[12]

John Rae, an advisor to Chrétien going back to the late 1960s, was the federal lead for the referendum campaign. Like most on his team, Rae had thought that the 1995 referendum would produce a result like the 1980 outcome. But it was his job to call the prime minister at midnight on October 19 with bad news: "I'm sorry I have to tell you the numbers have been reversed. We have a lot of work ahead of us." The 55–45 margin that once favoured the No side had suddenly become the margin for the Yes campaign. The prime minister told Rae to remain calm: "We have to work much harder. But first, let's get a good night's sleep." Then Chrétien added: "Ne lâche pas:" "keep on going."

Chrétien went on a war footing. It was a familiar reaction. Chrétien never backed down from a fight. If he couldn't win by brute force and raw guts, he would outmanoeuvre his foes. In one encounter in his youth, he feigned a sheepish retreat from a bully's taunt before using the element of surprise to get on top of his stronger foe and pummel him into submission.[13] It was an underhanded tactic, but also showed a desire to win by any means.

Federalist forces were stumped on how to turn the momentum around.[14] Chrétien had experience jousting with Bouchard in the House of Commons and had never treated him with kid gloves. "It's all right for you (to support separation)," the prime minister challenged Bouchard in the House of Commons. "Both your kids have dual citizenship because their mother is an American. So, if things don't work out so well for Québec I guess they can always move to the United States. So it's pretty safe for you, but your buddies in Lac Saint Jean don't have the same flexibility."[15]

According to Brian Mulroney, Lucien Bouchard's first decision was to throw the studies that Jacques Parizeau's team were using to show how Québec stood to gain financially from separation in the wastebasket. He said the only question was Pierre Trudeau and Jean Chrétien's treason and betrayal of Québec in patriating the Constitution without Québec's signature. Chrétien found it a bit rich to be called a traitor to Québec by Bouchard, someone who had changed political parties four times in his life.[16]

Paul Martin gave a speech in Québec City on October 17 in which he warned that an independent Québec might find itself excluded from NAFTA, with the resulting impact being a potential loss of one million Québec jobs. It was an absurd suggestion given that Canada and the US were seeking to expand trade around the world. Why would Canada not want to trade with Québec? The negative press had Martin calling Québec journalists to get them to tone down their critiques of his intervention.[17] Martin was marginalized for the remainder of the campaign.

A desperate Chrétien called President Bill Clinton for help. "You know, Jean," Clinton observed, "it would be a terrible tragedy for the world if a country like Canada were to disappear." Four days later Clinton responded to a question about the referendum that his staff had planted with a Canadian reporter. "I can tell you that a strong and united Canada has been a wonderful partner for the United States and an incredibly important and constructive citizen throughout the entire world," Clinton said.[18] Clinton had previously supported the cause of Canadian unity in an address to Parliament in February. "Canada stands as a model in how people of different cultures can work together in peace, prosperity and mutual respect." All MPs gave the president a standing ovation except for the members of the Bloc Québécois, who sat on their hands. Lucien Bouchard said there was nothing in the diplomatic code that compelled him to stand for something he did not want to hear. When asked to respond to Bouchard's comments, Clinton said, "I think they got the message."

On the other side of the question was President Jacques Chirac of France. In reply to a question from CNN's Larry King, Chirac said that the government of France would recognize the independence of Québec if its citizens voted to separate from Canada. On the question of the strength of the vote, he noted that France had joined the European Union after a referendum vote with just 52 per cent in favour.

Chrétien admonished Chirac a few weeks after the referendum at the Francophonie summit, asking Chirac if he would like it if Chrétien showed up in Paris and shouted: "Long live a free Corsica!"[19] Chrétien also told Chirac that Canada was the only country in the world where the number of people speaking French was increasing. Chrétien said he was confident that the government of France would not recognize Québec as sovereign unless that was the determination of the government of Canada.

With a little over a week before the referendum vote, and with the No forces in a funk, Chrétien set aside a failing campaign strategy. He decided to speak to Québecers' hearts rather than their wallets. But he understood that he was weighed down by his role in the patriation of the Constitution and the defeat of Meech Lake.[20] Bouchard had no hesitation in calling the prime minister, "The assassin of Meech Lake."

A few weeks earlier, Chrétien had told his staff that he would not make promises that he could not keep. "I won't promise constitutional change. I don't want to create the expectation that Trudeau, rightly or wrongly, created in 1980 at the Paul Sauvé Arena, and then find I'm not able to deliver. In the long run, that would be disastrous for the unity of the country."[21]

A Université de Montréal professor, Stéphane Dion, warned federalist forces that promising distinct society recognition, while great for Québec, could backfire if he could not get the other provinces onside.[22] Dion had also argued that it was a mistake not to let Pierre Trudeau speak during the referendum campaign. He said that the way separatists demonized patriation without the No forces responding made it difficult for nationalists to vote No with pride. But Dion was also worried that Trudeau would equate a strong Canada with a strong federal government.[23]

Chrétien held to the "no new promises" line and said as much while he was visiting the United Nations the week before the vote. The problem was that he said this on the same day that the leader of the No campaign, Daniel Johnson, suggested that constitutional changes were possible. The media reported that federalist forces were in disarray. Federalists in Québec pleaded with the Chrétien government to give them something they could use to demonstrate it was willing to respond to the province's cultural and linguistic concerns.[24]

With the polls showing the Yes campaign was headed for victory, Chrétien set aside his pride and his plan by offering concrete concessions to Québec. The prime minister promised to return to Québec its historic veto over constitutional changes (or at least he would try to persuade provincial premiers to accept the concession as a necessary step to keep the country intact.)[25] Chrétien had a more difficult time reconciling himself with the idea of the recognition of Québec as a distinct society, but it was a gesture he was prepared to offer to keep Québec in Canada:

> Most Canadians were still highly suspicious that distinct society meant special powers for the government of Québec, and though I remained more concerned that these words might lead to a disappointment by meaning too little in practice, there was also a risk that, by addressing the issue now, I might look as though I was undergoing a deathbed conversion, out of weakness or despair. The phrase had become an important symbol for many Québecers, however, and if it was what they needed to feel more respected and comfortable within Canada, it wasn't much of a problem for me to offer it to them.

When Chrétien phoned Pierre Trudeau to warn him that he was about to concede on the distinct society issue, he found the former prime minister as nervous as every other federalist about the polls. "You're in charge," Trudeau told Chrétien. "Do what you think you have to do."[26]

Chrétien's willingness to offer Québec additional powers near the end of the campaign was an admission that his initial plan was flawed. As the boxer Mike Tyson once said, everyone has a plan until they are punched in the face. In the end, winning was more important than sticking to a plan.

Mulroney and many other Québec federalists lamented that if Meech Lake had passed in 1990 there would have been no referendum in 1995. They remembered the pitch Mulroney had made to the Newfoundland legislature in June 1990 as they were about to hold a vote re-ratify the Meech Lake Accord: "If Mr. Parizeau gets a chance to have a referendum ... on referendum night one thought is going to go through your mind ... Do you mean to tell me that we could have avoided all this through Meech Lake?" The premier of Newfoundland, Clyde Wells, cancelled the planned vote on Meech, and now, in 1995, the Québec referendum was too close to call.

In Bouchard's key television address in the days before the vote, he held up a newspaper from November 1981, showing Trudeau and Chrétien laughing during a break in the constitutional talks. The Bloc Québécois leader claimed the two men were laughing at Québec while they stabbed the province in the back. Many Québec politicians said that Chrétien had orchestrated "the night of the long knives" by negotiating with all the other provinces while Québec's representatives slept in their hotel rooms. This infuriated Chrétien, who called it "the crudest stunt I have ever seen in Canadian politics."[27] But the prime minister worried that Québecers would treat the referendum the way a union treats a strike vote and give their negotiators a strong hand when they went to the bargaining table.

John Rae said the vote was based on a misunderstanding of federalism, but the vote was well-timed by Parizeau: "There were bad feelings about Meech, bad feelings about the high interest rates and high unemployment, bad feelings about the Mulroney government."

Chrétien told Québecers that the referendum was not a negotiation, it was a divorce. In delivering this message he used his best acting skills since he meant not a word of it. There was no doubt in Eddie Goldenberg's mind that his boss would never accept a Yes vote to an ambiguous question as a mandate to separate.[28] Chrétien told him as much: "Let's do everything it takes to win this week. If we still lose, I won't be deterred from making the argument that the question was too unclear to be taken as a mandate to separate."[29] Goldenberg's view was that if the prime minister did not say it was a vote for separation, then the federalists might have lost and the country would have been thrown into turmoil. "It was safer to up the stakes and win than to downplay the stakes and lose. If we lost, we would worry about that later on." Chrétien's cabinet colleagues were not so sure. They wondered how Chrétien could reverse course if the Yes side won by saying it was a trick question.[30]

On October 24, Chrétien spoke at a rally at the Verdun Arena to an overflow crowd of 12,000 supporters. The traffic going to the arena was at a standstill so Chrétien and his entourage walked the last few blocks to the arena. John Rae lightened the moment by whistling the "Colonel Bogey March" as a reminder that they were headed into a battle.

It was Chrétien's opportunity to say that a No vote was, in fact, a vote for change. He promised his support for Québec to be recognized as a distinct society and for Québec's constitutional powers to remain untouched without its consent:

I have listened to my fellow Québecers throughout this campaign say-ing that they are deeply attached to Canada. But they've also been say-ing that they want to see this country change and evolve toward their aspirations. They want to see Québec recognized as a distinct society within Canada by virtue of its language, culture and institutions. I've said it before and I'll say it again: I agree. I have supported that posi-tion in the past, I support it today, and I will support it in the future, whatever the circumstances ... We will be keeping open all the other paths for change, including the administrative and constitutional paths. Any changes in constitutional jurisdiction for Québec will only be made with the consent of Québecers.

Chrétien concluded on a more emotional level, telling his supporters that French is spoken in North America only because Québec is part of Canada. The speech was referred to in the media as a Hail Mary pass. Chrétien was famished after it was over and asked his driver to locate the nearest Harvey's so he could eat a burger. But the restaurant had just closed and the staff refused to reopen to serve the prime minister. It was not a good sign.[31]

While Chrétien did not want to speak publicly about a Plan B, contingency plans for a Yes vote were being made behind the scenes in Ottawa by top bu-reaucrats in the Privy Council. Wayne Wouters and Mike Horgan had spent several months working on a plan, although given the early survey results it was initially difficult for them to imagine the circumstances under which the briefing material for a Yes vote would be relevant. Chrétien declined to be briefed on the contents of the binder. Chrétien's thinking was when you are in the seventh game of the Stanley Cup final there is no point in thinking about what you would do if you lose.

Paul Martin was concerned about a possible run on the Canadian dollar and a weakening of the nation's financial institutions. With a significant amount of government debt in short-term securities, a spike in interest rates would in-crease the carrying charges, the last thing the country needed while still mired in deficits.[32] The finance department was ready to inject money in the form of loans to banks if a Yes vote caused panic in the markets.

David Collenette said the defence department went further than most in thinking ahead, but that it was not appropriate to take sides or tamper with democracy. "There must be a preservation of order," said Collenette, "but the moment it takes sides the military destroys its credibility." He went on:

> As minister of defence I had duties and responsibilities that went beyond my loyalty to the government of the day, but to the country. I'm very comfortable that I discharged my duties to the country as the minister of defence. I had limited jurisdiction, but wanted to make sure on the day after the referendum that we were ready. The question would have been less about what we thought should be done but what we had already done. There was much made of the CF18s leaving Bagotville to participate in a military exercise in Virginia.

It's easy to read between the lines that the military was only too happy to latch on to military exercises that took CF18s out of Québec.

As THE REFERENDUM DATE neared, Brian Tobin, a senior cabinet minister from Newfoundland, decided he could no longer sit on the sidelines:

> Here we are facing at the very least a possible constitutional crisis in a week's time, and [people] were behaving as though everything was normal. And it's not. The notion that people in some other parts of Canada should be told to stay home because the question of separation is an exclusive debate for Québecers was unacceptable, and it had been a mistake for the federal government to accept a separatist's rules. I refuse to acknowledge that a sovereignist government should frame the question, shape the debate and tell the rest of Canada it was none of our business.[33]

Tobin asked if there were any scheduled events that might be appropriate for those across the country to attend and demonstrate their love of country. The chosen event was a planned business rally to be held that Friday at Place du Canada in Montreal. After Tobin made some calls, the airlines cut their fares by up to 90 per cent and VIA Rail gave a discount of up to 60 per cent. Rather than the 5,000 people the event was intended to attract, close to 100,000 made the trek from across Canada. This included about 15,000 Ottawa-area residents that had been assembled by Liberal MP Mauril Belanger.

The rally played differently on English and French media. Carried live, the CBC broadcast team led by Don Newman stopped talking when the Canadian national anthem was played. Newman looked over at the booth for Radio Canada, the CBC's French counterpart, where the broadcast continued to talk while *O Canada* was sung.

It was unclear if the last-minute federalist pleas were too little and too late. Polls conducted for the CBC had the Yes side with a one-point lead. In an emotional address to his caucus that day, Chrétien had tears streaming down his face while his colleagues sought to console him.

ON REFERENDUM NIGHT, CHRÉTIEN predicted a federalist win by 1 per cent. With a 93.5 per cent turnout, the No forces eked out a victory – 50.6 per cent to 49.4 per cent.

In the aftermath, Chrétien was asked what he would have done had the Yes side prevailed. His answer was simple and curt: "I did not debate, and will never debate, what I would have done if the Yes side had won."[34]

But, behind the scenes, cabinet ministers felt they had a duty to think about the consequences of a Yes vote. This included the Justice Minister Allan Rock:

> On the weekend before the vote, I called a meeting at my office to which I invited a number of people to plan for how we might react and respond if things went the wrong way. It was done quietly. We canvassed a whole bunch of options and after much anxious conversation we decided that the only safe course in such a circumstance was to go to the Supreme Court with a reference that I would make, asking the court's direction as to how the matter should be managed. It turned out that's what we did that anyway, some months later.

While most senior bureaucrats in the PCO thought Allan Rock was simply doing his job, Eddie Goldenberg was less pleased with Brian Tobin, who had organized a meeting in the private room of an Ottawa-area restaurant in the days before the vote. Tobin's view was that federal Parliamentarians from Québec, including Chrétien, could not negotiate with provincial Parliamentarians on the terms of succession. No ministers from Québec were invited to Tobin's meeting. Tobin explained his thinking on the meeting to author Chantal Hébert:

> At that time, the key folks who were to have had responsibilities to negotiate were all Québecers. But there was a simple reality that Québeckers

. would have to face in the event of a Yes vote and it is that the notion that there would be a bunch of Québecers negotiating with a bunch of Québecers is false ... The negotiation would be done, the dialogue would be done, by folks who were looking in an unvarnished way at the interests of both sides.[35]

Some in the Prime Minister's Office thought the meeting had the air of a conclave where one of the participants would end up as prime minister. But if it was an act of disloyalty it was done with good intentions, and not primarily motivated by a desire to see a change in leadership. Eddie Goldenberg said it was only a few years after the fact that he was told what had transpired: "I didn't like what I read about it. As a cabinet minister, you have a duty to tell the PM what you are about to do. I doubt anyone who participated would be proud of what was done."

Chrétien said that when he heard about the meeting he was not particularly concerned, adding that had they all resigned it would have been another matter altogether. Chrétien had more important issues to deal with at the time than worrying about a ministerial brainstorming session.

Rock said that he never doubted Chrétien's ability to lead the negotiations on behalf of the Government of Canada or to manage the situation: "I know there were some who said it couldn't be a leader from Québec, and others said this particular leader, having been in government when the referendum was lost, did not have the moral authority. I don't accept either of those propositions."

It stretched credulity to suggest Chrétien would have lost legitimacy because he was from Québec. He had been in the federal Parliament for much of the previous 30 years and had travelled the country more than any other politician. He had won a national mandate in 1993, including 99 of Ontario's 100 seats. The issue would not have been that he was from Québec but that he was prime minister when Québecers voted to fundamentally change their relationship with Canada, or perhaps even to separate.

It's an open question whether a different prime minister would have delivered a better or worse result for federalist forces on referendum night. There is a lot of blame to go around. We could blame Pierre Trudeau for patriating the constitution without Québec's signature. We could blame Brian Mulroney for reopening the constitution rather than letting sleeping dogs lie. We could blame Newfoundland premier Clyde Wells for his decisive role in defeating Meech Lake. We could blame Jacques Parizeau for asking a trick question. And we could blame Chrétien for not anticipating and preparing for what turned out to be a razor-thin referendum vote.

What had looked to be a significant federalist victory a few weeks before the vote turned in favour of the separatists virtually overnight. At the time, federalists on the ground in Québec did not expect that Bouchard's arrival was much to worry about. The editorial writers at the *Montreal Gazette* said Bouchard was simply a better salesman.[36] Jeffrey Simpson wrote that the separatists had turned to their most credible voice, perhaps their only credible voice.[37]

When the tide turned, Chrétien had little time to react, but he did not sit on his hands. The prime minister threw everything he could at the referendum—drawing on his reputation and reversing long-standing positions — to move the vote his way. Had he lost the vote, Chrétien is unlikely to have survived in office. More important, it would have been chaos for Canada.

There is one key question that the Monday morning quarterbacks rarely ask. Even if the federal forces had anticipated that Bouchard would be elevated mid-campaign, what might they have done about it beforehand? Certainly, no one would have predicted such a monumental shift in voting intentions. By passing the negotiation baton to Bouchard, Parizeau effectively surrendered his leadership, an astonishing move for someone with such a monumental ego.

Had the separatist forces thought this would change the game in their favour, they would have done it much earlier. In fact, had the polls been close mid-campaign, it's unlikely that the Bouchard card would ever have been played. In their book *The Morning After: The 1995 Québec Referendum and the Day that Almost Was*, authors Chantal Hébert and Jean Lapierre reveal the extent to which Parizeau and Bouchard were on different pages during the referendum campaign. Their change in tactics was unplanned, almost slapdash. In fact, the Yes forces were deeply divided on the meaning of a victory. Would it be the first inevitable step to outright separation? Or would it be a strong bargaining position from which to gain more powers for Québec? A Yes vote would have thrown Québec and Canada into bedlam. The Canadian dollar would have fallen, stock markets would have crashed, and investment into Québec would have dried up.

Chrétien believed that many Québecers were voting yes simply to give their provincial government a strong hand in negotiating a better deal from Ottawa. He wanted to make it more difficult for them to take that risk. It was Chrétien who said that a Yes vote was a vote for separation. But if the federalists had come up short, Chrétien had a plan that has never been revealed, until now. First, he would have reneged by saying that the referendum question was unclear and that there was nothing in the Canadian constitution that contemplated separation. Québec sovereignists would undoubtedly have used Chrétien's words in the referendum campaign against him. Jacques Parizeau would likely have continued to implement his project, seeking recognition from foreign governments and dismantling links with the federal government.

At that point Chrétien would not argue with mere words. He would need a game-changer. His plan was to move quickly, within a month or so, to ask Québecers another question in another referendum: Do you want Québec to separate from Canada? If those voting yes had a clear majority — not just 50 per cent plus one but some unspecified threshold — he planned to hold a national referendum on what position the federal government should take.

Chrétien was not prepared to see the country break up on a trick question and a narrow margin of support. But he was prepared to ask Québecers a direct question and live with the result. He had no doubt that if the question was clear and binary — leave or stay — that Canada would never lose.

When the polls turned against him, Chrétien did what prime ministers like Macdonald and Laurier had done when opposing forces were trying to tear the country apart. They fought. They compromised. They did what was necessary to keep Canada united.

CLARITY

The referendum was a near-death experience for Chrétien, one that he was determined Québec and Canada would never experience again. He needed no time for reflection and went to work the day after the vote to make good on the promises he had made during the campaign. But much of what he had pledged he could not deliver on his own. The constitutional amendments he proposed required the consent of seven provinces representing at least 50 per cent of the population.

His first stop was a secret breakfast meeting with Ontario Premier Mike Harris, where he asked Harris to support an amendment that would give a constitutional veto to Ontario, Québec, Atlantic Canada, and the western provinces. He also sought an amendment that would recognize Québec as a distinct society. Harris would have none of it. With Ontario just coming out of a recession, Harris was unwilling to spend his time and political capital on the constitution.

While stymied by the provinces, Chrétien wanted to show Québecers his promises meant something. Within days of the referendum he instructed his justice minister, Allan Rock, to immediately introduce a Parliamentary resolution affirming that Québec was a distinct society within Canada.[1] Rock said this was not a good idea:

> I understood why it was important to respond to his commitments, but I suggested we take time to consider the implications. But the prime minister wanted to proceed immediately. I met with a constitutional advisor in my department and we both came to the conclusion that the matter should not be rushed. It was not just distinct society; we had to deal with the regional veto and manpower training. We needed a coherent approach.

Rock spoke with the prime minister's chief of staff, Jean Pelletier, about his concerns. Within the hour, Pelletier said the government would set up a cabinet committee to formulate an action plan. It took only a few weeks for the committee to complete its work.

Rock reported to cabinet with a recommendation that the federal government should establish the rules of the game in advance of another referendum. "We can never again put ourselves on the sidelines while a separatist government in Québec has the puck and is skating up and down the rink at will. We have to be on the ice, we have to establish blue lines, we have to have someone with a whistle, and we have to make this an organized contest." Chrétien agreed, saying he would never allow the country to again endure a crooked contest with a crooked question.

Rock was asked to bring a bill to Parliament affirming that Québec was a distinct society and that all regions of Canada should have a constitutional veto.[2] Before introducing the bill, Chrétien asked Progressive Conservative leader Jean Charest for his views:

> The prime minister informed me that he had two pieces of legislation ready, one to recognize Québec as a distinct society and the other on regional vetoes. I was opposed to both and told him why. I thought it would be seen as insignificant and a second-place prize for Québec. He said he would sleep on it. He called me at 6:00 a.m. the next morning and said he was going ahead. I criticized him, but it was very revealing of his style. He sincerely listened and we sincerely disagreed.

The bill was presented before the Christmas break, less than two months after the referendum vote. Initially, the bill placed British Columbia within the western contingent of provinces. But, given its growth in population and its economic clout, BC demanded a veto of its own. Ultimately, for political reasons, Chrétien agreed. The problem with the legislation was that its significance was only symbolic. Because it did not have the clout of a constitutional amendment, the provisions of the law did not bind future federal governments.

Although Chrétien was moving quickly after the narrow result in the referendum, he didn't enjoy the confidence of many of the nation's opinion leaders. The editor-in-chief of *The Globe and Mail*, William Thorsell, wrote about eminent Canadians attempting to educate the prime minister. "Men and women of great intelligence and good will wanted to rally to Canada's cause after that harrowing 'victory,' but found the prime minister inaccessible and defensive again, afraid that accepting their counsel would crack his fragile pretence to authority, if not power."[3]

For his part, Chrétien was intent on enacting substantive measures to bolster federalist support in Québec. To that end, he established a ministerial working group to come up with ideas, such as ways to reduce internal trade barriers and to promote Canada as an economic and social union. While the authority to eliminate interprovincial trade barriers rested with the federal government under the British North America Act, this power had been diluted by a number of court rulings. Provinces endorsed the principle of free trade within Canada, but Chrétien was frustrated that they remained captive to groups who were looking out for their own self-interest.[4]

In July 1994, the Chrétien government and the provinces reached a modest agreement on internal trade, covering government procurement as well as the movement of goods, labour, and professional employees across provincial borders. The elements of the deal mirrored a provision in the failed Charlottetown Accord. The agreement had little teeth and many of the barriers remained intact.

On December 1, 1995, the Reform Party made its contribution to the discussion by releasing a paper titled "20 Realities of Secession."[5] One proposal was that the smallest municipality, regardless of location, could choose to remain in Canada. Another was that an independent Québec would be allocated its proportionate share of the national debt based on population. Even if the governments of Québec and Canada agreed to a separation agreement, the Reform Party proposed that the deal would have to be approved by a national referendum.

In the 1996 Speech from the Throne, the Chrétien government committed to restricting federal spending power in areas of provincial jurisdiction, withdraw the federal presence in forestry and mining, and establish a new partnership with the provinces on a range of matters such as labour training, environmental management, tourism, social housing, and freshwater fish. These proposals were counter to the traditional Liberal penchant for a strong central government, but this was more in line with the vision Chrétien had articulated in his maiden speech in the House of Commons in 1963.

The provincial premiers, minus Lucien Bouchard, met in Calgary on September 14, 1997, and concluded a declaration that acknowledged the "unique character of Québec society." This gesture fell short of the "distinct society" language of the Meech Lake Accord. The declaration acknowledged the Québec government's duty to promote the use of the French language while supporting the province in sustaining its culture and civil law traditions. At the same time, the premiers declared that no province could possess powers that were not enjoyed by all. The declaration was largely dismissed in Québec as irrelevant.

In February 1999, Chrétien signed a Social Union Accord with the provinces that affirmed provincial jurisdiction over social programs without abandoning the power of the federal government to implement national initiatives. It was, to a large degree, consistent with the spirit of the Meech Lake Accord. With this agreement, the federal government committed not to introduce new national social programs without the agreement of at least six provinces. Although Bouchard refused to sign the accord, his government nonetheless cashed $6.5 billion in federal cheques for social programs. Chrétien boasted that the agreement was proof that federalism could adapt to new circumstances without changing a word of the Constitution.[6]

The editorial writers at *The Globe and Mail* gave the accord two thumbs up, saying it would improve health care and education by reducing ambiguities in the Constitution and strife among governments. "On those grounds," they wrote, "the Social Union signals a new willingness between the federal and provincial governments to deal with each other in a mature and co-operative fashion to negotiate and deliver appropriate and diverse social programming for all Canadians."[7]

Beyond power-sharing with the provinces, the cabinet committee on national unity also recommended that the federal government increase its profile and presence in Québec. Thus was born the federal sponsorship program, a scheme we will cover later that achieved the opposite of its intended purpose.[8]

CHRÉTIEN BROUGHT NEW FACES from Québec into his government, notably Lucienne Robillard, who had served in the Liberal cabinet of Québec premier Robert Bourassa. But he felt the need for more bench strength. Within weeks of the referendum, Aline Chrétien saw a university professor from the

Université de Montréal defending federalism on television. She called her husband to the living room to catch a glimpse of the show.

Without telling anyone on his staff, Chrétien arranged for Stéphane Dion to meet him at 24 Sussex Drive on a blustery November weekend. Dion, who earned his PhD from the Institut d'Études Politiques de Paris, was not what the prime minister was expecting. "When he showed up wearing heavy boots and a toque, covered in snow and caring a knapsack on his back, I thought to myself, 'Oh my God, what have I got myself involved with?'"

The conversation went well so Chrétien offered Dion a seat in his cabinet as minister of intergovernmental affairs with responsibility for the unity file. Given Dion's lack of experience in elected politics, or in the Liberal party, it was a big risk. Like Lucien Bouchard, whom Mulroney had summoned to serve in his Progressive Conservative cabinet without first being elected, Dion had been a sovereigntist who voted for the Parti Québecois in 1976. It was only in the aftermath of the demise of Meech Lake that Dion became a committed federalist.

Initially, Dion declined Chrétien's offer, suggesting that his academic skills and interests would not translate well into the world of politics. But as Dion warmed to the idea he pressed Chrétien to consider adding Pierre Pettigrew to his list of new recruits. Pettigrew had credibility as a business consultant and government adviser. By March of 1996, Dion and Pettigrew had won seats in the House of Commons that Chrétien had vacated by appointing Shirley Maheu to the Senate and André Ouellet to the chair of Canada Post.[9]

The editorial writers at the *Ottawa Citizen* saw the Dion appointment as a dangerous manoeuvre by a scrappy prime minister. They wrote that Dion inspired the "suicidal strategy" of the federalist camp during the referendum. "Chrétien is clearly pursuing his war to the bitter end with the 'separatists' but he is also declaring it to his former Québec Liberal allies, who want to begin reflection on the Constitution again and who firmly believe in the integrity of Québec's territory." Dion shared Chrétien's view that if Québec could separate from Québec then communities in Québec should be free to join Canada. "Dogmatic federalism which led Canada to the brink of a breakup," wrote the *Citizen*, "is well on its way to pushing it over the edge."[10]

Chrétien had formed a bond with Dion. Despite his view that a prime minister cannot afford to be friends with any of his ministers or staff because one day they may have to be bumped, he made an exception for Dion.[11] Those close to the prime minister believe the bond was established over the vitriol both had faced in Québec by nationalists who had put them in the category of Uncle Toms. In *La Presse*, Dion had regularly appeared in the editorial page cartoon as a rat.[12]

THE RULES OF THE referendum game, at least as far as the federal government was concerned, had never been spelled out. Brian Mulroney thought a certain amount of ambiguity was helpful and that it was unwise to put in place measures that would give Québec or any other province a clear path to leaving the country. We can only wonder, for example, how Alberta might have voted on a separation question when the National Energy Program was implemented in the early 1980s. Mulroney preferred the flexibility to be able to move the goalposts based on the circumstances of the day.

In a succession of three open letters to Lucien Bouchard, Dion made the legal argument for Canada on how a future referendum could be conducted. He argued that there was no precedent in international law that Québec could rely on to advance its aim of independence. In other words, it could do nothing unilaterally. Then Dion contended that a 50 per cent plus one vote was not legitimate by international standards. Finally, he asserted that Québec's borders should not be presumed to be inviolable.

But how and when to lay down these rules? At the time, Québec lawyer and former separatist Guy Bertand had sought an injunction to prevent the 1995 referendum from taking place because it violated his Charter rights. After the referendum was held, Bertrand went before the courts to request that no further referendums be allowed based on the precepts of international law. While Bertrand's case was destined to land before the Supreme Court, Allan Rock said he could short-circuit the process and get the court to rule on the key questions that were already before the lower courts:

> We intervened in the Bertrand court case because the Attorney General of the Government of Québec said in the litigation that the Canadian constitution had nothing to do with the process by which Québec will become sovereign. I said we cannot stand by and listen to that nonsense.

I said to the prime minister we could wait 35 years before this case gets to the Supreme Court or we could make the reference and get the court's attention immediately. I recommended we pursue a reference and the prime minister agreed.

The leader of the Progressive Conservative Party, Jean Charest, thought the reference was a mistake: "I thought it was a Plan B when we needed a Plan A. Chrétien was very tough in the House of Commons, accusing me of being disloyal. We were both inclined to excessive partisanship, but there was mutual respect because we both knew we were doing what we thought was best for Canada."

Lucien Bouchard took the view that the federal government had no role in or jurisdiction over how a province might decide its own future. In other words, the Canadian constitution held no powers over a province that was determined to secede.

The *Ottawa Citizen* tried to discourage Chrétien from taking the secession question to the court:

> It is hard to imagine how quarrelling in court about the legalities of separation could serve the cause of Canadian unity ... That is to say, an action chosen by the Québec government to achieve independence would not be judged chiefly by its legality. It would be judged by its legitimacy ... Whatever the motives, a federal reference to the Supreme Court seems bound to fail.[13]

Chrétien disagreed. "I wanted to establish once and for all that separation was a legal issue, not just a political one, subject to the Constitution of Canada. I especially wanted to clear away the separatists' myth that Québec had the right to self-determination under international law." That law, which contemplates secession from a country, does so only in circumstances of oppression or subjugation. These conditions, argued Chrétien, were not the modern-day reality of Québec.[14]

The three questions the federal government asked the Supreme Court were:

1. Under the Constitution of Canada, does the Government of Québec have the right to secede from Canada unilaterally?

2. Under international law, does the Government of Québec have the right to secede from Canada unilaterally?

3. If there is a conflict between the constitution and international law, which prevails in Canada?

On August 20, 1998, the Supreme Court rendered its verdict. The answers to questions one and two were no: there was no right to secession under Canadian or international law. That made the third question irrelevant. The court went further by declaring that any referendum on separation would have to be "free of ambiguity, both in terms of the question asked and in terms of support it generates." That meant more than 50 per cent plus one.[15]

Chrétien claimed victory, but he wanted more. After the Supreme Court determined the constitutional limitations, Chrétien said it was now up to elected politicians to determine what constitutes a clear question and a clear majority. In other words, he would not allow a single provincial government that was intent on separation to set out rules in its own favour.

There was a debate within the Liberal government as to whether the threshold for a separation vote should be specified. Those in the Privy Council Office argued for a clear number. The view in the Justice Department was that it should be up to the Parliament of the day to make the call.[16] Either way, this was uncharted territory for the federal government.

Other than a few speeches during two referendum campaigns, the federal government had never taken an official or legislated position on provincial separation. When the idea of a bill on secession referendums was presented to cabinet there was no consensus.

Chrétien later wrote that Paul Martin was opposed to legislation because he thought it would be like waving a red flag in front of a bull. Martin acknowledged that he was worried that federal legislation would undermine the authority of the Supreme Court and its traditional role of resolving disputes between the federal and provincial governments. Authors Chantal Hébert and Jean Lapierre wrote that getting a handle on Martin's thinking on the issue was like to trying to "hold a slippery fish with bare hands."[17] Susan Delacourt wrote that Martin was uncomfortable throughout the Clarity bill discussions knowing that his block of Quebec support was strongly against it.[18] Ultimately, however, Martin agreed to support whatever decision came out of cabinet.[19]

Eddie Goldenberg said that Martin liked the principle of issuing clear rules but did not think legislation was the best approach: "He thought if we did proceed it should be after a Parti Québecois convention, but he was all over the map."

Allan Rock acknowledged the nervousness that permeated the cabinet table when he brought the bill forward for discussion:

> I recognized the risks but I was strongly in favor of moving to adopt the Clarity Act as soon as possible. The lesson we had learned from 1995 was that there is never a good time to raise these subjects. It's always difficult and provocative. But there are dangers in remaining silent. While it may provide momentary comfort, is it can also entail long-term jeopardy.

Rock was one of the few ministers to strongly advocate for legislation. Pierre Trudeau told Chrétien he was worried about how Québecers would react. "People are telling me that this is very dangerous, Jean. Are you sure it won't wake the sleeping dog?" Chrétien replied that no one could say for certain what would happen.

An interminable debate ensued at cabinet. The prime minister is often de-scribed as the first among equals in Parliament. In this case, Chrétien decided to resolve the matter, telling his cabinet that there was a large consensus to do something, but nobody seemed to know what. "So I will do it for you," he said.[20] As Andrew Jackson is quoted as saying, one man with courage makes a ma-jority. Chrétien was sufficiently worried about the reaction that he had the bill introduced in the winter when it was tougher to demonstrate in the streets.[21]

Chrétien was sensitive to public reaction. He worried that risk-adverse public servants would slow down the development and passage of the bill. That's why he excluded all bureaucrats from the key meetings when the federal strategy was discussed. The bill was intended to state emphatically that a referendum required a clear question. But the title proposed by the justice department was anything but clear. It was called "An Act to give effect to the requirement for clarity as set out in the opinion of the Supreme Court of Canada in the Québec secession reference." Chrétien intervened and renamed it the Clarity Act.

When the bill landed in the House of Commons on December 13, 1999, the Bloc Québécois was outraged. Joe Clark, leader of the Progressive Conservative Party, also opposed the bill because he thought the legislation would inflame Québecers. The NDP sided with the government. Initially, the Reform Party

CLARITY

opposed the bill, but ultimately changed course, in part because they had been advocating for similar legislation for several years.

While Paul Martin hesitated before offering his support, one of his key advisors, Scott Reid, wrote in the *National Post* that the Clarity Act and its requirement for a clear majority would backfire. By demanding a super-majority, Reid argued, Québecers might feel free to cast strategic yes ballots.[22]

The Clarity Act passed third reading in the House of Commons on March 15, 2000. After much debate in the Senate, the upper chamber passed the bill, paving the way for royal assent on June 29. The Québec government responded the following December by passing the Fundamental Rights Act, endorsed by all political parties in the National Assembly, specifying that a simple majority vote would be sufficient to separate Québec from Canada. It also stipulated that Québec's territorial integrity was inviolable. While the statute affirmed that French was the official language of the province, there was also a reference to respecting minority rights, including "aboriginal and treaty rights of the aboriginal nations of Quebec."[23]

The first real test of the Clarity Act came in the 2000 federal election when Jean Chrétien had to defend his decision to Québec voters. In that contest, the Liberals increased their seat total in Québec from 26 to 36 and finished in a virtual tie with the Bloc Québécois in the popular vote. Three months later, Lucien Bouchard resigned as Québec premier.

Chrétien said that the risks he took on with the Clarity Act reminded him of a quote from Voltaire: "I did something, and that was my best work."[24] To the surprise of many, polls revealed that the federal law was accepted within mainstream Québec.

Many separatists, like Jacques Parizeau, said they would simply ignore the legislation. A more militant separatist, Pierre Bourgault, accepted the federal law and readied himself for battle:

> The little terrorist from Shawinigan, with what he considers a brutal law aimed at frightening Québecers into submission, will soon find out that his bomb will explode in his hands. Mr. Chrétien's project forces the federal government, for the first time in our history, to admit that Canada is divisible. It is music to our ears.[25]

Chrétien contends that most Québecers thought the law was fair.[26] Conrad Black saluted the Clarity Act and what it represented:

> The long era when Québec could threaten the viability of the whole country was almost over, as long as Canada would enforce the Clarity Act and the Supreme Court decision that it entrenched … It liberated the country from a spectre of French-English division which had haunted it for 40 years and lurked for two centuries before that.[27]

Even though the NDP supported the Clarity Act at the time, they advocated a different position in 2005, passing a declaration at a party convention in Sherbrooke that 50 per cent plus one vote was sufficient on a clear separation question. NDP leader Jack Layton trumpeted the declaration across Québec, which he said helped his party make a breakthrough in the 2011 election, winning 59 of the province's 75 seats. The NDP did not advocate for separatism, but for a principle that they thought was consistent with the tenets of democracy. On that score, it could point to Newfoundland, which had joined Confederation following a referendum that was settled by a vote with just 53 per cent in favour.

In the 2015 election, Liberal leader Justin Trudeau contended that the Sherbrooke Declaration put the NDP offside with the both the Clarity Act and the Supreme Court. In that election, the Liberals won 40 seats in Québec, while the NDP was reduced to 16.

THERE WAS NO CERTAINTY in 2000 that Chrétien's gamble with the Clarity Act would pay off. The reaction of Québecers was difficult to predict and the odds of success were impossible to calculate. There were no former prime ministers who thought Chrétien was doing the right thing. But having been traumatized by the 1995 referendum, Chrétien would not let the fight come to him. If there was going to be a scrap, Chrétien would not battle on the terms of others.

When others were unsteady, Chrétien's gut told him that Québecers would never turn their backs on their history and that they would stick with the country, which respected and defended minority language rights.

Since the Clarity Act was passed, the polls suggest that Québec's attachment to Canada has only strengthened. But this is not entirely due to Chrétien's courage. Other factors include Québec's changing demographics, a stronger and better managed Canada, the downloading of authority to the provinces, and a federal government that respected provincial jurisdiction. On many of these factors, Chrétien can claim credit.

Canadian historian Michael Bliss suggested that the impact of the Clarity Act is somewhat overstated. "The main effect," Bliss wrote, "was to bolt the barn door after the exhausted horse had gone to sleep in its stall."[28] Lawrence Martin, on the other hand, predicted that the Act would eventually be regarded by historians as one of Chrétien's major achievements, in large part because he outsmarted Québec separatists.[29]

Chrétien did what he had to do to win the referendum. He did what he could in its aftermath to show that Canada loved and respected Québec. He sought to prove to Québecers that Confederation was the best place to protect the French language and culture. And if Québecers wanted out of Canada, Chrétien gave them a clear path; a path he believed they would never take. Chrétien was not only on the right side of history; he made history.

MONEY MATTERS

DEFICIT SLAYER

When Chrétien came to power, the federal government had run 23 consecutive deficits and its balance sheet was burdened with close to $500 billion in accumulated debt. The financial condition of the government was at a breaking point and the consequences of inaction were severe. Chrétien argued that the country had reached a critical point, at which 25-year-old brokers with red suspenders would "drive down our currency, push up our interest rates, and compel the global financiers to step in and take charge of our spending decisions in exchange for a loan."[1]

Governments in Canada and around the world grew in the 1970s, but they did so by taking on debt, not by raising taxes. Chrétien held critical economic positions during this period — he was president of the Treasury Board; minister of Industry, Trade, and Commerce; and minister of Finance. But he was uncomfortable with his government's big-spending and big-deficit ways. As Trudeau's finance minister, he resisted calls from within the Liberal caucus to deliver a big-spending budget to buy votes in the 1979 election. As a result, some Liberals blamed Chrétien and his tight-fisted ways for losing power to the Progressive Conservatives under Joe Clark.

When Clark bungled his government's 1979 budget, the Liberals unexpectedly found themselves back in power after only a nine-month reprieve. Trudeau gave Chrétien responsibility for the constitutional file, so he had little or no sway over economic and fiscal policy at a time when federal spending and the deficit were soaring to post-war highs.

When Brian Mulroney was elected in 1984, he said he would hand out pink slips and running shoes in Ottawa. He made progress in his first term in office, turning a $12-billion-dollar operating deficit into a $7.6 billion operating surplus. Over his nine years in office, government revenues exceeded operating costs by $55 billion. But federal finances were weighed down by interest costs on the accumulated national debt, turning those operating surpluses into structural deficits. In his final year in office, Mulroney's operating surplus was $2 billion, which barely made a dent in the $40 billion interest bill.

For Chrétien's predecessors, there was always a reason — or an excuse — why the forecasted bottom line never met projections. Disappointment — or worse, cynicism — had been the reality for a succession of finance ministers.

In the 1993 election, Prime Minister Kim Campbell offered no hope that the budget could be balanced in the near term. When she did talk about her approach to deficit management her numbers didn't add up. Preston Manning proposed a bold plan to eliminate the deficit in three years. At the time, he was thought to be either delusional or naïve, but at least he had a plan.

Other developed nations were facing deficits in 1993, but Canada had earned its place near the bottom of the G7 barrel. Only Italy was in a tougher spot than Canada. Scott Clark, then associate deputy finance minister, was heard to say, "Thank God that Italy was there."[2]

Better than just beating Italy, Chrétien came up with an idea that would make Canada appear to be respectable by international standards. He proposed that Canada set a goal of exceeding the deficit-to-GDP target set for European countries under the 1992 Maastricht Treaty — the treaty that established the euro as a common currency. That meant that Canada would have to cut its relative deficit — then at 5.5 per cent of GDP — nearly in half. Some critics pointed out that the 3-per-cent-of-GDP European deficit target included national and sub-national governments — in other words, federal and provincial governments — but none of Chrétien's political opponents wanted to argue a point that would confuse voters.

Compared with the Tories, who had failed to tame the deficit, and the Reform Party, with its harsh-sounding zero-in-three plan, Chrétien's middle-of-the-road approach seemed reasonable to voters. But a rallying cry around meeting a 3 per cent deficit-to-GDP target made for a poor bumper sticker. Voters wanted passion and hope, not a dreary accounting lesson. So, in the campaign, Chrétien talked about cutting some of the Tories more controversial spending plans, such as new military helicopters and a luxurious plane for the prime minister's travel.

While the Liberal platform may have pitched the most realistic deficit-reduction plan, the editorial writers at *The Globe and Mail* didn't believe a word of it:

> After nine years in Official Opposition [Liberals] offer a program best described as bourbon economics. They have learned nothing and forgotten nothing. It's clear that a majority Liberal government would make no serious attempt to rescue the nation's finances. Indeed, it's a safe bet the Liberals would not get the deficit below $30 billion... The Liberals' expressed willingness to let inflation rise again only guarantees the country will have to endure another recession before long.[3]

To get to his 3 per cent target, Chrétien needed to find a combination of spending cuts or additional tax revenue that totalled $20 billion. As a fiscal conservative at heart, Chrétien was not prepared to make the case for higher taxes or larger government. And despite what he called his natural optimism, he wrote that there were days when he didn't believe that he could meet his 3 per cent deficit target in one term in office.[4] But he did better than that. He reached his goal, in three years, not four. And by the time Chrétien headed to the polls in 1997, the budget was nearing balance for the first time in 26 years. This meant that revenues not only covered program spending, they also covered the $40 billion the government was paying out in interest costs.

When Chrétien took over from the Tories, the federal government provided $1.18 worth of services for every dollar of revenue collected. Add interest cost into the mix and $1.43 went out the door for every dollar that came in. That might have been a good deal for those on the receiving end of government largesse, but not for the next generation of Canadians, who would be forced to pick up the tab. When the books were balanced in 1997 it was because the federal government provided only $0.71 worth of services for every dollar of revenue collected. The remainder covered interest costs.

The conventional wisdom is that the turnaround in government finances was due to Brian Mulroney's work in implementing the North American Free Trade Agreement (NAFTA) and the introduction of the Goods and Services Tax (GST). Mulroney liked to say that his ministers tilled and planted the garden while Jean Chrétien got to pick the flowers.[5] However, while Mulroney's initiatives were important planks in Canada's economic turnaround, they weren't the main reasons the federal budget went from deficit to surplus.

The budget was balanced because of deep and unprecedented spending cuts. In Chrétien's first term in office, taxes as a share of GDP rose a modest 1.1 percentage points while operating spending declined by 3.8 points. In other words, for every dollar that taxes rose, there was close to $4 in spending cuts.

SPENDING WAS SLASHED WHILE REVENUES HELD STEADY

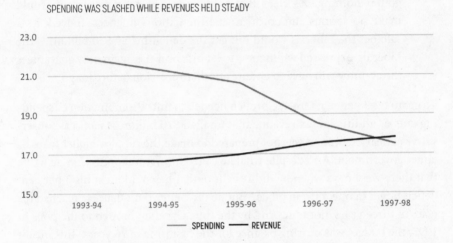

Once the budget was balanced in 1997–98 Chrétien kept going. In other words, even after the books were in surplus the size and reach of government remained on a steady downward track relative to the size of the economy.

SPENDING DID NOT RISE AFTER THE BUDGET WAS BALANCED

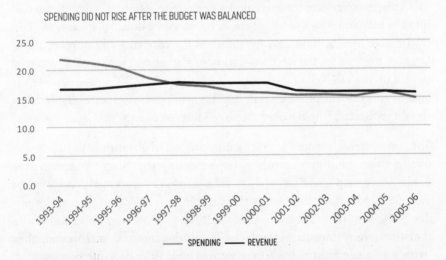

Chrétien never returned to deficit after the first surplus was recorded. In fact, he began a string of 11 consecutive surpluses, broken only in 2008–09 under the Conservative government of Stephen Harper.

CHRÉTIEN BEGAN STRING OF 11 CONSECUTIVE SURPLUSES

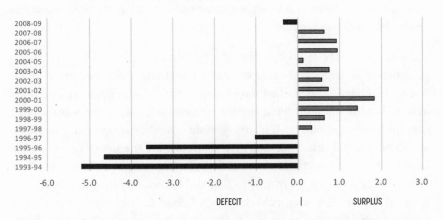

Having stopped the red ink from flowing, Chrétien had to deal with an even more important fiscal issue. The government's relative debt load had nearly tripled over the 20 years before Chrétien became prime minister. At first, the modest surpluses under Chrétien did not make much of a dent in the massive debt. It was only after a sustained period of economic growth and a string of consecutive surpluses that the debt load eased to more traditional levels relative to GDP.

FEDERAL DEBT WAS CUT IN HALF

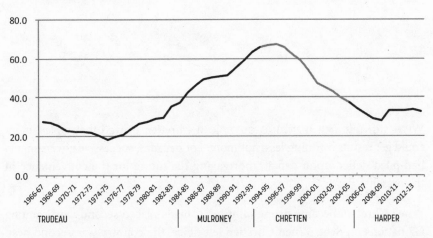

Fortunately, worldwide interest rates fell in the early 1990s. This, combined with a lower level of debt, helped to reduce the bite that interest costs took out of the federal budget, going from a high of 30 per cent of spending when Chrétien came into office to 19 per cent when he left.

Not only was debt reduced, but a greater percentage of our borrowing was funded by Canadian sources.

If interest costs are excluded from the calculations, the difference between government revenues and expenses makes Chrétien's numbers even more remarkable. Pierre Trudeau had amassed $54 billion in cumulative operating deficits, leaving not a nickel to pay the interest on the debt that was amassed over his 15 years in office. Mulroney recorded cumulative operating surpluses of $55 billion, but this came nowhere near covering the interest costs on the federal debt. Jean Chrétien's cumulative operational surpluses came in at $418 billion. After covering his own spending and the interest costs attributable to his predecessors, Chrétien paid down $66 billion in debt from its peak. The last time debt had been reduced was 1969, and that was by only $140 million.

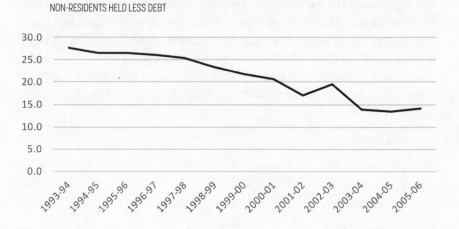

NON-RESIDENTS HELD LESS DEBT

WITH SIGNIFICANT SPENDING CUTS, Jean Chrétien proved that government could get results by doing less, not more. For decades, successive governments had piled deficit upon deficit, mortgaging the future for the convenience of the present.

When Chrétien became prime minister, Canada placed second worst among G7 nations on debt. When Chrétien left office, the country was second best. But not every historian sang the praises of the Liberal government. Historian Michael Bliss wrote that a more economically astute finance minister from another party might have acted earlier and more forcefully than Paul Martin.[6]

Chrétien wrote that balancing the budget without having started a revolution or triggering an economic recession was one of his proudest accomplishments. It was ironic that in balancing the books, Jean Chrétien accomplished what his Progressive Conservative predecessor could not. Conventional wisdom is that Conservatives tend to be prudent economic managers and the most disciplined when it comes to controlling government spending. While the Mulroney government is credited for making key structural changes in the economy, it did not have the stomach to impose the sort of spending cuts that Chrétien implemented.

The question no one has fully answered is, how did a Liberal reduce the size of government in a way that a Progressive Conservative could not?

DR. NO

Chrétien's first crack at an economic portfolio came in 1974 when he was appointed president of the Treasury Board — the department that approves or rejects the government's spending plans. When he landed in the job, government spending had been increasing each year at the rate of 25 per cent or more. He took his job seriously, so much so that his cabinet colleagues called him "Dr. No."[1] He took the nickname as a compliment.

Growth in the number of public servants was cut in half in his first year on the job and cut in half again in his second year.[2] When he was approached by the minister of finance about finding $500 million in savings, Chrétien came back with $1.7 billion. But not everyone was happy with the belt-tightening. The agriculture minister, Eugene Whelan, had milk poured over his head in 1976 by dairy farmers who protested government inaction on dairy subsidies.

In September 1977, Chrétien became the first francophone minister of finance. As he started his new job, Chrétien candidly remarked that his Liberal colleagues who preceded him in finance had done the country no favours with big spending increases and large deficits. "With the great advantage of hindsight," Chrétien observed in his 1978 budget speech, "we can see that we did not always use our good fortune wisely."[3] It was an early indication that Chrétien was prepared to spend his political capital before spending taxpayer money.

WHEN CHRÉTIEN BECAME PRIME minister in 1993, there was no appetite in the country for new taxes. He couldn't reduce interest costs and he had no mandate to cut entitlements like unemployment insurance, seniors' benefits. and children's' programs.

Chrétien's easiest cut — at least politically — was to cancel the previous Conservative government's $6 billion purchase of 43 EH-101 helicopters. But that decision was more about short-term politics than long-term savings. The contract cancellation led to higher annual maintenance costs for the existing fleet and a one-time penalty of $500 million.[4]

In another political move, the government also paid a penalty to cancel a contract negotiated by the Mulroney government to manage Toronto's Pearson Airport. Liberal cabinet minister Doug Young called the airport's privatization the biggest rip-off in Canadian history. Chrétien tried to legislate a provision that would deny the private contractors the ability to sue for damages, but that bill never made it through the Senate. In the end, the government coughed up $60 million just to walk away from the deal.

To show he meant business, Chrétien reduced the size of cabinet from 40 to 23 members and scaled back ministerial budgets for political assistants. The message to the bureaucracy was that if politicians could cut back on their spending then so could public servants. Chrétien added to the symbolism by having his newly sworn-in cabinet whisked away in minibuses rather than limousines.[5]

Also symbolic was Chrétien's refusal to fly in the plane that Mulroney had commissioned for the prime minister's travel. During the 1993 election campaign, Chrétien dubbed the aircraft "Air Farce One" and the "Flying Taj Mahal." The Airbus was already cleared for take-off so there were no cost savings to be had by leaving it on the ground. After the election, Chrétien directed government officials to put the plane up for sale, but ultimately the military used the aircraft to ship cargo and deploy troops.[6] Chrétien used the plane only on a few occasions, remarking that it felt more like riding in a Winnebago than flying in the lap of luxury.[7]

Once in office, some reporters had begged Chrétien to use the more modern and comfortable plane. But after he had ridiculed Mulroney's regal tastes, Chrétien saw political peril. Chrétien told the media he would use the plane if they didn't give him hell for it: "If you insist, fine. Just send me a petition and I'll agree."[8] They never did. Later Chrétien admitted his decision may have been short-sighted. In his first international meeting at the 1993 Asia-Pacific summit, he arrived on a small-scale Challenger aircraft, which pulled up beside the Boeing 747s of both the president of the United States and the president of the Philippines. In his memoirs, he sheepishly acknowledged, "I might have gone a bit overboard as opposition leader in criticizing Brian Mulroney's imperial style, which turned out to be quite modest compared to that of most heads of government."[9] But Chrétien believed that Canadians didn't like flashy displays. His communications director, Peter Donolo, boasted that the prime minister ran a "Chevrolet government."

While Chrétien saved on travel costs, his wife, Aline, cut back on the budget that Mila Mulroney had used to maintain an office.[10] Not only was the staff cut at the prime minister's residence at 24 Sussex, but when the National Capital Commission wanted to spend $150,000 to fix the dilapidated 50-year old cedar shingle roof, and another $200,000 to install an emergency power generator, Chrétien put the brakes on the much-needed repairs.[11] It was penny-wise and pound-foolish, but it was the sort of short-sighted symbolism that was emulated by his successor, Stephen Harper. It's hard to imagine the Americans allowing the White House to deteriorate to the point of becoming unhealthy and unsafe.

IF THE SYMBOLIC MOVES didn't always pay a fiscal dividend, they certainly had an impact on all who were watching. Brian Tobin described an early meeting of the Liberal government's inner circle by saying, "He dropped a bomb in cabinet." Tobin continued, "He was deadly serious about eliminating the deficit and we all said, 'Yes, prime minister' even if we didn't believe it." While Tobin was convinced, the editorial writers at The Globe and Mail were not. The day after Chrétien was sworn in as prime minister they predicted the government's resolve to meet their deficit targets would quickly fade:

> The Liberals will probably spend the first several years of their mandate avoiding the tough economic choices demanded by the public interest. They will borrow too much — and foreign lenders will let them. They will change too little — and Canadian voters will thank them. And five years from now, as pressures created by the public debt and interest charges become unbearable, the days of reckoning will be harder and darker than they might have been.[12]

The first crack at changing the nation's fiscal direction was the 1994 budget. In his budget speech, Paul Martin delivered a strong dose of rhetoric, but only a tincture of action. He said that Canadians were fed up with Ottawa not being able to get a grip on its finances. He promised to implement fundamental change so that our public finances would be in order, not in ruins: "The days of government simply nibbling at the edges are over … Our task is to put an end to drift."

While the government affirmed its fiscal targets from the election campaign, there was no plan to reach them. Modest changes were proposed to make unemployment insurance less attractive for those who quit their jobs or were terminated for misconduct. Minor cuts were proposed to provincial transfers. A signal was sent that major reductions in defence spending were coming.

The budget was replete with allusions to a new era of financial management. Martin promised that over the coming years there would be five dollars in cuts for every dollar raised in new revenues, but he didn't provide any details. When he declared that the last thing business needed was another government program he was hoping that Canadians would conclude he was more conservative than his Progressive Conservative predecessor:

> What [Canada] needs are lower taxes — relief from taxes that stand in the way of hiring and growth. What they do need is access to capital so that they can grow and create jobs. What they do need is a government that gets off their backs, and stops burdening them with unnecessary regulations and red tape.

Yet, at the same time, the budget included a host of new spending programs that totalled some $7.5 billion. The government wanted to have it both ways: talk tough on spending while also opening the taps on government-sponsored employment programs.[13] Reform Party leader Preston Manning said that Chrétien had turned his party's famous 1993 Red Book election platform into the "Red Ink Book."[14]

The nation's financial and corporate leaders saw little concrete action on the looming fiscal crisis and doubted Chrétien and Martin were the slightest bit serious about the government's deficit targets. Senior Ottawa bureaucrats had also concluded that little had changed from the Mulroney administration, meaning there was a lot of talk about the deficit, but not much action.[15] Martin complained that he simply felt rushed. "We came in with 60 days to do the first budget. [We] didn't know the books and didn't know how to go about it."[16]

Alain Dubuc of *La Presse* wrote that the budget was the product of a government that had yet to find itself: "If the budget doesn't hurt, it's essentially because it doesn't contain the steadfastness and determination that the crisis in public finances demanded and gives no sense that a turnaround is being undertaken." *The Globe and Mail* concluded, "In its ambivalence, shambling and shuffling, this government has forfeited its first year." [17]

ABOUT ONE MONTH AFTER his budget speech, Martin realized that he had blown it. He signalled that he had heard the criticism when he delivered the fall 1994 economic update. To ensure there was no mistake about his newfound resolve, he declared the government would meet its deficit reduction plans "come *Hell or High Water*." The expression stuck to Martin, so much so that he used it as the title of his autobiography.

Not impressed by Martin's rhetoric, in early 1995 the *Wall Street Journal* published an opinion piece that labelled Canada a fiscal basket-case:

Mexico isn't the only U.S. neighbour flirting with the financial abyss. Turn around and check out Canada, which has now become an honorary member of the Third World in the unmanageability of its debt problem. If dramatic action isn't taken in next month's federal budget, it's not inconceivable that Canada could hit the debt wall and, like Britain in the 1970s or New Zealand in the 1980s, have to call in the International Monetary Fund to stabilize its falling currency." [18]

The damning assessment in a highly influential publication had a significant impact and became a turning point for the government. There was nervousness at the finance department when Canadian bonds were almost shunned at a routine auction. [19] A country that can't renew its debt when it comes due is a bankrupt state.

In early 1995, markets were demanding a premium to buy Canadian government bonds. The spread between Canadian and American three-month treasury bills, which was non-existent in early 1993, had risen to almost a full percentage point by December 1994. [20] Martin knew that without creditor confidence the Bank of Canada would have no choice but to increase interest rates, and that would throw the government's budget projections further out of whack. [21]

The deputy minister of finance, David Dodge — who would later become the governor of the Bank of Canada — was grateful for the *Wall Street Journal* article, calling it a "seminal event."[22] But it was not just Canada that was under fiscal pressure. At that time, Mexico was facing a currency devaluation that led to a flight of capital out of the country, revealing that a nation that lost control of its debt gave up its ability to make economic decisions. Dodge said that without the peso crisis, Chrétien and Martin would have lost a lot of ground with ministers who were resisting spending cuts. Martin made the point to his Liberal colleagues that without deep cuts in spending, Canada's economic sovereignty and basic social programs were at risk.

BY MID-1994 FEDERAL bureaucrats had finally taken note of the shift in the government's resolve and in public opinion. Previously, government-wide attempts to cut spending were led from the finance department, or from a star chamber involving Finance, the Treasury Board Secretariat, and the Privy Council Office. But all these efforts had failed. Chrétien determined that the problem was sufficiently severe that a new approach was needed. He put the Privy Council Office in charge of program review and appointed a minister, Marcel Massé, to lead an ad hoc committee of seven ministers to complete the spending control exercise. Massé's committee sifted through every proposed spending cut, although social programs and transfers to the provinces were beyond the scope of their mandate.

Wayne Wouters, who was a senior PCO bureaucrat at the time, was told by his former colleagues at the Department of Finance that the PCO process was doomed to fail and that they were ready to come to the rescue, "as we always have." At first, finance officials refused to cooperate with the program-review exercise. Sharing the budget-making stage with other departments was a blow to their pride.[23]

Wouters acknowledged that it was a huge risk for the PCO to take the lead. A small PCO team developed targets, cutting most departments by between 10 and 25 per cent. It was left up to individual departments to determine how they would implement the cuts.

Chrétien's stroke of genius was to populate the committee with cabinet ministers known to be big spenders. His thinking was that if he put the fiscal hawks in the lead that the more progressive members of cabinet would man the barricades and fight the cuts. Chrétien knew it would have been difficult for a business-friendly minister like John Manley, who was not on the committee, to complain about harsh treatment when it was being imposed by a group who were otherwise inclined to increase departmental budgets. The left-leaning ministers who were at the table — and who had already accepted the cuts in their own departments — were in a strong position to demand more of others. As Manley described it, committee members got Stockholm Syndrome by fulfilling a mandate that was contrary to their leanings.

Chrétien would occasionally meet with committee members to thank them for their work, noting that he knew it wasn't easy to disappoint their colleagues. But just in case they felt secure and self-satisfied, he reminded them that if it was too tough, "I can always find new committee members to do the work."

Brian Tobin, who served on the committee, said the prime minister did a great job of keeping the committee focused on delivering results: "The fiscal discipline of any government starts and ends with the prime minister or premier. It takes the leader's direction to hold the line on spending." Tobin said that Martin as supported the goals and objectives of the committee, but did not sit in on the meetings: "We did not report to Paul Martin; we reported to the PM. The guy who provided the vision, the goals, the discipline was Jean Chrétien."

WHILE THE 1994 BUDGET was, as they say, all sled and no dog, the 1995 effort deserved a place in the federal budget hall of fame.

In his budget speech, Martin acknowledged what economic analysts had been warning following his feeble 1994 effort: that the government was not on track to reach its targets. "Unless direct action is taken now," Martin warned, "we could face shortfalls of $5 billion from our deficit target in 1995–96 and $10.6 billion the year after." Failing to meet fiscal targets was a story that Canadians were used to hearing from finance ministers.

Getting the government back on track meant chopping $13.4 billion in planned spending. Martin's path to reaching a 3-per-cent deficit-to-GDP target was to reduce the size of government by 19 per cent over three years, slash the public service by some 45,000 positions, and cut provincial transfer payments.

Martin argued that the 4.4 per cent reduction in support to provinces was small potatoes compared with the 7.3 per cent slice that was being taken out of federal operations.[24] When people complained about how the cuts would impact healthcare, Chrétien didn't blink. He pointed out that Canada spent more on health care as a share of GDP than many European countries that also offered universal coverage. He told the provinces that if they wanted more flexibility and control of the system to help manage costs they could have it, but with fewer federal dollars. This was not the vision advanced by his Liberal predecessors, who set the federal contribution at 50 per cent of healthcare spending, but with strings attached.

It helped that Chrétien didn't appear to enjoy gutting government programs. "I've been around a long time," he said. "It's no pleasure at all. I'm not a doctrinaire right-winger. I'm a Liberal, and I feel like a Liberal, and it's painful. But it's needed."[25] In the same way that the hawkish anti-communist Richard Nixon could open up diplomatic relations with China without appearing weak, Jean Chrétien could cut government spending without appearing heartless. The implication, to offer the contrast, was that conservatives enjoyed slicing and dicing government programs.

Reform Party leader Preston Manning lamented the 1995 budget as a lost opportunity. He warned that unless drastic measures were taken, old-age security, social assistance, equalization, and basic health care were at risk. Manning wanted deeper spending cuts, including taking $15 billion from social programs. Manning said the day of reckoning was coming and that the government had missed its one chance to turn the tide on financial recklessness: "This budget is dishonest, it is cowardly and it is hypocritical, and it does not do the job it is supposed to do for Canadians."[26] This was the sort of criticism that Martin had predicted and feared after he lost his battle with Chrétien to cut funding to seniors.

The left-leaning nationalist Maude Barlow called it "the beginning of the Americanization and the privatization of our social security system."[27] The reliably right-wing National Citizens' Coalition said the budget failed to deal with the fundamental problem of a government that was spending too much money. To Chrétien, being criticized from the left and right told him the budget was on safe ground. More importantly, the financial markets reacted positively to the budget and the prospect of a financial crisis was significantly diminished.

The Globe and Mail wrote that while Martin was a year late in bringing out the knife, the 1995 spending cuts were judicious. Still, the editorial writers predicted that the government's resolve was weak and that the country would still have a fiscal crisis on its hands during the next election cycle.[28]

Perhaps the peskiest budget critics came from within Liberal ranks. Martin received a phone call from the two most senior officials in the finance department, David Dodge and Don Drummond, who claimed that Liberal caucus members from the Ottawa area had the ear of the prime minister. The decision to freeze public-sector salaries was the issue. Martin worried that Chrétien would wobble. As he put it in his memoirs, "He did not see the need for attacking the deficit as aggressively as I was prepared to do."

But in the same breath, Martin said Chrétien was determined not to undermine him the way he had been undermined by Pierre Trudeau. The incident Martin had in mind followed the 1978 Bonn Economic Summit where Trudeau was told that Canada's rampant spending increases and large deficits were causing more harm than good. Shortly after returning home, Trudeau abruptly appeared on national television to announce $2.5 billion in spending cuts. But he had not bothered to discuss the matter with his finance minister, Jean Chrétien. When Eddie Goldenberg heard about the cuts he called Chrétien to see what he thought of Trudeau's speech. "What speech?" said Chrétien.[29]

The Clerk of the Privy Council had warned Trudeau he was making a mistake. Trudeau said he thought Chrétien was on holidays at his cottage and did not want him disturbed.[30] Trudeau later claimed his principal secretary was supposed to call Chrétien, which never happened. More likely Trudeau simply wanted to have his way without the bother of dealing with Chrétien, or as he said in his memoirs, "Sometimes you just have to move."

Chrétien considered resigning, but ultimately chose to stay. "I was made to look like a fool," he wrote in his autobiography.[31] The day after the announcement was made, Chrétien called Trudeau to "give him hell" and to tell him his actions were "stupid." When Chrétien and his deputy were asked by the press to explain where the cuts were going to come from they had no good answers to give, exacerbating the perception that the unsophisticated Chrétien was ignorant, incompetent, or both.

Trudeau thought Chrétien was a good soldier who would remain loyal.[32] He later said that Chrétien knew his limitations, "which is more than most of us."[33] Chrétien stayed in Trudeau's cabinet because he feared that the resignation of the first French-Canadian minister of finance would be used by the Parti Québecois government of René Lévesque to further its cause.[34]

This incident tarnished Chrétien in many ways, but it was also instructive. The lesson he learned was that a prime minister must never undermine one of his ministers, especially not the minister of finance. This, more than anything else, helps to explain why Paul Martin was given a wide berth to manage the finance portfolio. There were only a few occasions when Chrétien overruled Martin on policy, and it was almost always done behind closed doors.

THE POPULAR NOTION PERSISTS that Martin was the economic genius while Chrétien was an economic simpleton. The evidence proves otherwise. From his seat in the prime minister's office, Chrétien kept a close eye on the government's books. He is probably the only prime minister to have taken pleasure in reading the monthly updates on the government's financial accounts.[35] When the format of the *Fiscal Monitor* was revised one month, the deputy minister of finance was astounded when the prime minister called to ask why. Chrétien was also upset when he detected that the industry department had changed how the unemployment rate was calculated.

It was not unusual for Chrétien to play with mathematical problems in his spare time or when he had trouble sleeping at night. Eddie Goldenberg said that Chrétien made macroeconomic calculations in his head and knew the numbers better than both the minister and the deputy minister of finance. Chrétien even kept his eye open for errors made by low-level bureaucrats. In preparing for a conference on federal–provincial relations, Goldenberg recalled Chrétien asking if it was his job to point out that there was an adding error in one of the documents. "Most prime ministers would assume that the department of finance and the Privy Council Office would have checked that sort of thing, but the error was immediately evident to Mr. Chrétien."

Finance and PCO bureaucrats agreed that Chrétien was always more comfortable and confident than Martin on the numbers. At one point, Chrétien began to distrust the financial projections that were coming out of the finance department. In response, the Privy Council Office set up an operation they called "Finance North" to come up with their own financial projections. When he heard about this Martin fumed: "What are you trying to do?" Martin asked PCO officials, "Undermine me?" The numbers produced by PCO were sufficiently different from finance department data that it created nervousness in the system. In fact, the PCO modified their projections somewhat as a defensive measure, not because they thought they were wrong but they didn't want to make their Finance cousins look bad.

All the while, members of the Canadian media accepted the fiction that Martin was the one pulling the financial strings and that Chrétien was his puppet. Respected journalist Susan Delacourt observed that Martin was seen as the "senior partner, if not the brains of the operation."[36] If that bothered Chrétien he didn't say so. He was happy to let his ministers look good. A senior bureaucrat in the PCO observed that it was Chrétien who provided the leadership on the tough decisions: "Every time there was pressure on Martin it was Chrétien who held firm on the cuts. Martin would have let a lot of this unravel because he wanted to keep up his relationships with ministers."

ENCOURAGED BY THE GOOD PRESS and public reaction to their 1995 budget, Chrétien and Martin stayed the course in 1996. Chrétien started to talk about how a "vicious circle" of rising debt and poor economic results was being replaced by a "virtuous circle" in which lower spending produced lower deficits, which in turn produced lower interest rates, which reduced unemployment, which spurred economic growth.[37]

Chrétien insisted that no minister could bring forward a spending proposal unless they had offsetting spending cuts or another form of financing. "It put tremendous discipline into the system where we saw very few proposals come forward," observed one senior bureaucrat. "The pipeline of new ideas shrunk from billions to hundreds of millions."

Martin affirmed that the attack on the deficit was irrevocable and irreversible. He committed to going beyond the 3 per cent deficit-to-GDP target with a new goal: a balanced budget and a steadily declining debt-to-GDP ratio. Doubling down on his "*Hell or High Water*" pledge. Martin declared, "Nothing, I repeat nothing, will cause this government's conviction to change."

But even Martin was surprised at the speed of the turnaround:

> After the 1995 budget, interest rates fell faster than anyone expected, which made it less costly to service the debt and easier to meet our fiscal targets. As investors saw that we were serious about meeting, and soon exceeding those targets, it took a further premium off interest rates, which in turn made it easier for us to restructure our debt.[38]

Financial markets had become accustomed to governments falling short of the mark, but with Chrétien and Martin there were only upside surprises. The 1996 budget revealed that the deficit targets set in the Liberal Red Book — and affirmed in the 1994 and 1995 budgets — would be exceeded. To ensure there was sufficient cushioning in the budget, even in the event of an economic downturn, a built-in contingency reserve was established that could not be touched to fund new programs. Unused contingency funds would be applied directly to the national debt.

The government pledged further cuts to bring federal spending down to 12 per cent of GDP by 1998–99. That was a long way down from a peak of almost 21 per cent during the Trudeau years, and the 17 per cent that Chrétien had inherited from Mulroney. Federal spending had not been that low in 50 years.

The Liberal government under Chrétien was looking conservative in both tone and substance. Chrétien was proud that he had managed to cut both program spending and the federal bureaucracy without much rancour, a fact he attributed to setting fiscal targets that the country supported.[39] Chrétien also had enough goodwill on the table for Canadians to accept that an old Liberal like him wouldn't mess with social programs "just for the fun of it."[40]

To GIVE SOME CONTEXT to the financial turnaround, Chrétien went in a completely different direction from Trudeau and was more than twice as effective as Mulroney at controlling spending.

The Americans also reduced federal spending, but were not as aggressive as Canada. As a result, the relative gap in spending as a per cent of GDP between the two countries narrowed considerably.

FEDERAL DEBT WAS CUT IN HALF

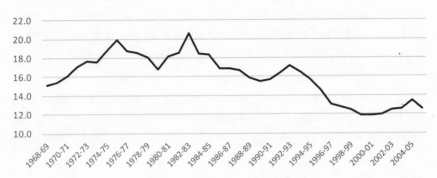

A MAJOR CRITICISM OF Chrétien and Martin's belt-tightening was that it was really a downloading of responsibility to the provinces. Chrétien's critics say federal cuts led to drastic changes in how provinces delivered health care and education.

SPENDING DECLINED FASTER IN CANADA THAN IN THE US

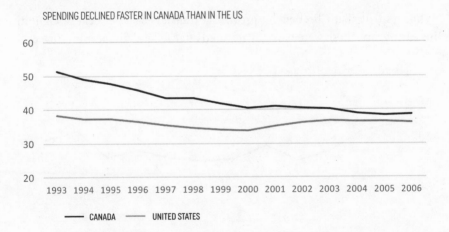

Ontario premier Bob Rae thought Chrétien was headed in the wrong direction by reducing provincial transfers. "It did not come as a total shock," Rae said. "But it was still devastating. We were determined in Ontario to weather those cuts." Coming out of an economic recession, Rae supported Chrétien's proposed infrastructure program. But this one-time money did nothing to help the provinces, which were looking for predictable and sustainable transfers from the federal government. Despite federal cuts, Rae maintained Ontario's spending on social programs and government services. But he noted that his successor, Mike Harris, used federal tightening as an excuse to cut welfare payments by 18 per cent: "The people who paid the price were those at the low end of the scale."

Rae understood that the federal government had to tighten its belt and provincial transfers could not be left untouched. But his view — one shared by some in the federal cabinet — was that the pendulum had swung too far and the cuts went too deep.

Although Chrétien made life difficult for the premiers by reducing transfers, he experienced little personal animosity for his decisions. Rae credits the prime minister's personal qualities and the friendships he had established over the years with premiers for keeping provincial griping to a minimum. Besides, Rae acknowledged, the premiers knew that fixing federal finances was an urgent priority.

While it's true that Chrétien cut provincial transfers as a per cent of GDP in his early years, these were partially restored after federal finances improved.

TRANSFERS TO PROVINCES FELL THEN ROSE

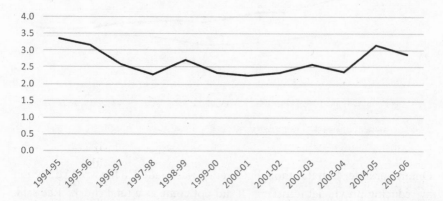

In the 1997 election campaign, Chrétien was put on the defensive by opposing party leaders in the televised debate for "putting the health of Canadians at risk" by slashing provincial transfers. Chrétien countered that front-line health care was a provincial responsibility and how they chose to spend money, and respond to a reduction in federal transfers, was entirely within their control.

It was a weak political defence and the Liberals lost seats in that election for cutting social programs.

Chrétien did not want to seem insensitive to a universal health care system that Liberals had often touted as one of Canada's defining characteristics. In fact, he intervened when the language in one federal budget gave the impression that the provisions of the Canada Health Act were negotiable. Sheila Copps said she took to the barricades to thwart the move:

> As deputy prime minister, I was given the privilege of reviewing the budget in advance. When I saw the reference to the Canada Health Act and the proposal to abolish it, I knew this was political dynamite. For a Liberal government to be doing this was a betrayal of our basic principles. I went to Martin with my concerns but he shrugged them off, saying it was too late because the budget had already gone to print. I immediately requested a meeting with the prime minister and showed him the fine print, voicing my outrage. He agreed with me, instructing the Department of Finance to take the offending words out of the budget. The Prime Minister knew that major policy shifts like an end to the Canada Health Act should not be slipped through as budget measures.[41]

In the early days of his third term, Chrétien established the Commission on the Future of Health Care in Canada, which was led by a former NDP premier of Saskatchewan, Roy Romanow. Chrétien and Romanow were good friends and had famously collaborated in 1981 on the agreement between the federal government and nine provinces to patriate the Canadian constitution with the Charter of Rights and Freedoms. Romanow also came from the province where universal health care was first established in Canada.

The commission's mandate was to recommend policies in support of the long-term sustainability of Canada's universally accessible, publicly funded health care system. In 2002, following 18 months of consultations with Canadians — including medical practitioners, academics, and other experts — the commission issued 47 recommendations that came with pleas for more money, greater coordination among governments, access to home care, prescription drug coverage, accessible electronic records, and targeted funds. In his award-winning 2012 book *Chronic Condition*, Jeffrey Simpson countered Romanow's conclusions and argued that Canada was already one of the world's biggest spenders on health care per capita. Our problem was not the investment, but mediocre results.

Although Chrétien did not have an opportunity to implement Romanow's key recommendations, Paul Martin signed a health accord with the provinces when he became prime minister. Martin labelled the deal a "fix for a generation." The "fix" was not structural or transformative, but simply locked in 6 per cent increases in federal transfer payments to provincial governments for 10 years. With inflation running below 2 per cent the deal was generous. While it was intended to enable the provinces to expand and improve health care, the provinces increased their spending over the period 1996 to 2010 by an average of only 3.3 per cent.[42] In other words, the federal transfers were a financial boon to the provinces.

There is no question that provinces took an initial hit from Chrétien's early budgets. But it was not a fatal blow. Indeed, most provinces could offset federal reductions by increasing their own taxes as provided for under the Canadian constitution (the only taxes provinces are prohibited from levying are indirect taxes such as duties). The notion that provinces were squeezed by federal cutbacks and forced to cut spending in the classrooms and hospital rooms because of a lack of federal money does not hold water. However, cuts to federal transfers gave provinces a useful foe and someone to blame when they initiated much-needed reforms to the delivery of health care.

During the Chrétien years, provincial revenues overall held steady relative to the size of the economy. This was largely owing to a strong economy and higher levels of employment, some of which is attributable to Chrétien's fiscal and monetary policies. A rising tide, as they say, raises all boats.

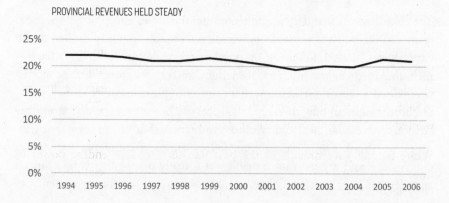

PROVINCIAL REVENUES HELD STEADY

The reality is that provincial finances did not deteriorate under Chrétien. In fact, the relative debt levels of the provinces declined while Chrétien was in office. Rather than resisting Chrétien, many provinces embraced and emulated the policies that were producing results, a phenomenon the Fraser Institute would later label the Chrétien Consensus.[43]

Taking consolidated federal and provincial into account, the overall fiscal position of Canadian governments improved at the same time that the federal government was cutting provincial transfers.

COMBINED FEDERAL & PROVINCIAL ACCOUNTS WERE RETURNED TO SURPLUS (BILLIONS)

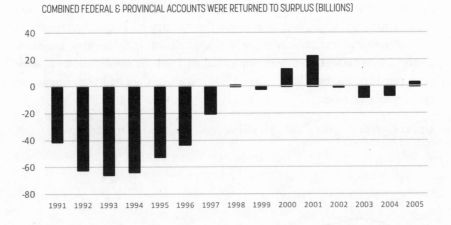

Advocates of a strong central government had long argued that Canada would suffer if there was not an integrated and robust system of federal transfer payments to hold the country together. Québec was thought to cling to Canada because federalism was, for the province, a profitable enterprise. So, what was the impact of the abrupt reduction in provincial transfers from the 1995 federal budget? The provinces derived revenue from other sources and even managed to reduce their debt loads. At the same time, they innovated on the design and delivery of social programs in ways that their citizens ultimately accepted. When Chrétien was asked if cuts in transfer payments had changed the nature of federalism, he replied yes, and for the better. "For many years the provinces said, 'Let us run these programs...' I said, 'Fine. Run them.'" The provinces wanted flexibility and Chrétien gave it to them.

While federal governments in the past had used their spending power to develop, implement, or impose programs in areas of provincial jurisdiction, Chrétien's government went in the opposite direction. He withdrew money

from the provinces and reduced federal clout. And he did so without com-
promising national unity. Eddie Goldenberg said that by being explicit about
the circumstances when federal spending power would be used, Chrétien ultimately legitimized federal incursions into provincial jurisdiction and strengthened the hand of the national government.

A KEY REASON WHY federal spending declined under Chrétien was a reduction
in interest costs. Beyond a general reduction in rates, federal interest costs fell
because financial markets perceived a lower risk to holding Government of
Canada treasury notes, and, as a result, the country no longer had to pay an
interest-rate premium. Canada's credit rating, according to Moody's, increased
by three notches between 1995 and 2002 to Triple-A stable. Lower interest
rates provided the best kind of spending cut since they had zero impact on
government services.

Under Chrétien, federal debt servicing was cut almost in half relative to GDP.

DEBT CHARGES SHRANK

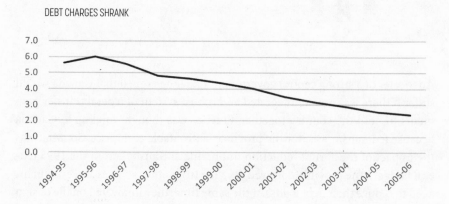

To put this in perspective, had the government's debt-to-GDP ratio in 2003–04
been the same as it was in 1993–94, the additional interest cost to the federal
treasury would have been $17.4 billion. The budgetary surplus in 2003–04 was
$9.1 billion, meaning that the savings on interest saved the government from
running a deficit.

After interest costs, the next largest swath of government spending is support payments. These entitlements include seniors' benefits, children's benefits, and employment insurance. The payments related to children did not change at all under Chrétien, while seniors' benefits, relative to the size of the economy, declined by 15 per cent. This was not due to direct cutbacks, but largely because the economy was growing at a faster clip than the general rate of inflation.

The major shift in payments to individuals was for employment insurance. This was halved under Chrétien in real terms with sufficient savings on its own to make the difference between surplus and deficit in most years after 1997. When Chrétien came into office, 14 of every 100 dollars of program spending was consumed by unemployment benefits. When Chrétien left office, these payments accounted for only 8.3 per cent of federal spending. Some savings came not from tighter eligibility rules, but as a result of more people working and fewer people collecting benefits.

Under Chrétien, the cost of running government departments and agencies dipped and then rose. Population growth and general inflation over this period would have caused the nominal costs of government to rise by about 12 per cent. But government spending fell by 9.4 per cent, a swing of 21.4 per cent in actual dollars.

The government cut spending on the bureaucracy by 6.6 per cent, or $2.2 billion. But not all federal departments were treated equally. The Canadian International Development Agency was cut by 26.3 per cent, Defence by 18.3 per cent, External Affairs by 9.7 per cent, Veterans Affairs by 2.5 per cent. Federal support for Crown corporations declined by $3.1 billion, a 45 per cent hit over just a four-year period. On the winning side of the ledger was Indian Affairs, which was not only kept intact but was given a 5.7-per-cent increase.

The department responsible for keeping tabs on federal spending, the Treasury Board, saw its portion of the public purse rise by 36.5 per cent over the turnaround period. It seems it takes money to save money. Similarly, the Privy Council Office, which serves the prime minister and functions as the head of the federal bureaucracy, saw its spending rise by 9.4 per cent. The House of Commons budget fell by a minuscule four-tenths of 1 per cent.

The CBC president, Tony Manera, resigned the day after the 1995 budget to protest a 27.3per cent cut in funding. Chrétien held firm, believing that if he made concessions in one area his broader package of cuts would have unravelled. By the time Chrétien left office, taxpayer support for the CBC was the same as it had been in 1993 in nominal dollars. Taking inflation and population growth into account, this worked out to a 30 per cent reduction.[44]

The cuts to the CBC budget were far short of the makeover that Martin had pitched to the minister responsible, Sheila Copps:

> I was taken aside by Paul Martin at a cabinet meeting and he said, 'If you want to raise money by privatizing the CBC, I have no problem with that. I will give you all the money — a billion dollars — and you can decide where to spend it in other cultural areas.' At the same time, he was promising Peter Mansbridge [host of CBC's *The National*] he would provide more money to the CBC. He must have been thinking I was really stupid. Why would anyone with political ambitions come out in favour of privatizing the CBC? I ended up creating a group in caucus 'Friends of the CBC.' I saw to it that the idea went no further while the CBC was under my protection as minister.

While the CBC privatization never made it to a cabinet submission, Copps also opposed Martin's budget commitment to defund Radio Canada International. Copps persuaded other cabinet colleagues and the wife of the prime minister to defend the service. "I spoke with Aline Chrétien, who suggested to her husband that this may not be a wise course of action. The prime minister was willing to weather the wrath of the minister of finance and he rejected the spending cut."

Aline Chrétien usually stayed behind the scenes on policy questions but was nonetheless an important advisor to her husband on sensitive issues. For example, she warned Chrétien not to go ahead with a plan to subsidize struggling Canadian professional hockey teams. Canadian teams were hurting financially, mostly because players were paid in US dollars and the Canadian buck was in the doldrums. Pressure to create a government subsidy was applied by Ottawa Senators owner Rod Bryden and NHL president Gary Bettman. Chrétien had a soft spot for Bryden, a well-known Liberal and a great salesman for his cause. Chrétien's chief of staff, Jean Pelletier, a former mayor of Québec City, was sympathetic because that city's team, the Nordiques, had moved to Colorado for financial reasons. And Lloyd Axworthy, a senior minister from Manitoba, had seen the Winnipeg Jets move to Phoenix.

Industry minister John Manley met with cities and provinces to work out a deal in which each contributed one-third to a comprehensive package. Three days after the government announced its financial lifeline for Canadian NHL teams on January 18, 2000, the proposal was scrapped. That was after Chrétien was told about the number of complaints that his constituency office received. To emphasize the point, his constituency assistant said she had never before received a complaint on a policy question. At the same time, some provinces, notably Ontario and Alberta, tried to distance themselves from the scheme.[45]

Manley said it was difficult to accept the blame since the initiative had received cabinet attention and had the support of the prime minister. Ottawa-Vanier MP Mauril Belanger, who opposed subsidizing the NHL, said Manley should be commended for having the courage to take a risk to help keep professional hockey in small-market Canadian towns.[46] But Manley said his future leadership ambitions suffered a massive blow.

> Bryden called after we announced the cancellation of the program saying my body language did not show I was behind the policy. He denounced me for never believing in it in the first place and for not selling it properly. This was easily my low point in cabinet. It was not something I thought or wanted to do. And it blew up. It had cabinet support; then everyone ran for cover.

The only sensible thing to do, said Manley, was to pull the program in its entirety. While the government was in a surplus position, Manley said the public didn't want to support giving money to rich hockey players. "I was going to the World Economic Forum later that week and I didn't want this playing out while I was in Switzerland of all places."

Chrétien would have done better to have followed Aline's advice in the first place rather than end up with egg on his face. But he had the good sense to reverse course as quickly as possible. This made the gaffe easier for the public to forget.

EVEN SO, BALANCING THE budget and achieving strong economic results did not deliver the sort of political benefit to Chrétien that might have been expected. Liberal candidates in the Atlantic provinces got a shellacking in the 1997 election, in large part because voters did not appreciate the government's reforms to employment insurance and other cutbacks. Of the 22 seats that Chrétien surrendered across the country in the 1997 election, 20 were in Atlantic Canada. It's not that Chrétien wasn't warned. After the 1995 budget, PEI cabinet minister Lawrence MacAulay told his wife not to make long-term plans to stay in Ottawa. It was close, but in 1997 MacAulay managed to hold his seat by 99 votes. In the face of predictable reprisals, Chrétien held firm.

In remaking government, Chrétien dispelled economic theories that suggested government restraint would dampen economic growth. Indeed, a smaller and less intrusive federal government helped to stimulate the economy. Investors became more confident and consumers became more optimistic. Structural changes meant that unemployment cheques were replaced by pay cheques. Lower interest rates and strong growth south of the border pushed the economy forward.

Chrétien said he didn't enjoy making the cuts, but for a man who took pleasure in being called Dr. No, he wasn't entirely uncomfortable either. What's clear is that Chrétien provided the decisive leadership that kept cabinet ministers in line while Martin delivered and defended the budgets that were instrumental to the fiscal turnaround. It was an effective and constructive partnership that produced enduring dividends for Canada.

BRAIN GAIN

When the second Liberal Red Book was rolled out for the 1997 election campaign, Chrétien was no longer talking about deficits. His pledge was that surpluses would be split evenly, with new programs getting one half and tax relief and debt reduction getting the other.[1]

Martin was not happy to have been put in what he called a "fiscal straitjacket." But he understood that after years of austerity it was good politics to offer Canadians a political platform with a fiscal dividend.[2] Still, Martin bristled at having a financial commitment imposed on him by Chrétien rather than one that he strictly controlled from his perch as finance minister.

In the budgets that followed the 1997 election, the Chrétien government invested in programs that spurred research and development activity, enhanced education and training programs, and made other investments that were designed to strengthen the Canadian economy and its competitiveness. In other words, Chrétien's priority was to lay the foundation for job growth and a productive economy. The priority was not on the social safety net.

In 1997, Chrétien's government established the Canada Foundation for Innovation to upgrade research facilities in universities, teaching hospitals, and non-profit centres. Although the investment was an incursion into provincial jurisdiction, no premier or university president refused the money on constitutional grounds. Chrétien's initial goal was to stop Canadian academic elites from moving to the US in what had become known as a brain drain, and perhaps entice a few to come back to Canada as part of a brain gain. Chrétien had been convinced that the investments would pay off by John Manley and his deputy minister, Kevin Lynch, and from university leaders, including Martha Piper (University of British Columbia), Robert Lacroix (Université de

Montréal), and Rob Pritchard (University of Toronto).

CFI began with an initial one-time fund of $800 million in 1998. Chrétien's enthusiasm for the program was evident from the fact that new funds flowed into CFI before much of the money they had been given had even been spent. In its first year of operations, CFI spent only $1.5 million of the $800 million grant. In year two, CFI disbursed only $27 million. By the time Chrétien left office, CFI had more than $3 billion in cash or investments on its balance sheet, all of which had been expensed on federal books to reduce the surpluses.[3] The auditor general objected to the practice of expensing money that was sitting in a bank account.[4] One advantage of not tying CFI to government accounting rules was that it gave CFI the flexibility to review grant submissions without pressure to disburse funds in any given year.

The Canadian Opportunity Strategy included a new Canada Education Savings Grant to help families save for their children's college and university education. Other education initiatives included the $2.5 billion Canada Millennium Scholarship Foundation to fund 100,000 scholarships over 10 years for underprivileged students. Initially, the proposal for the fund came out of the prime minister's office in September 1997, with an expected price tag of $1 billion. There was an internal debate about whether the fund would benefit those who displayed academic excellence or whether it should be for students of modest means. Martin had not initially been consulted about the foundation, which is surprising given the fiscal implications. But Martin eventually took over the file with the intent of becoming the nominal federal education minister, saying he didn't mind "getting his elbows up with the provinces" in the process.[5]

The idea for the Canada Research Chairs program was pitched to Chrétien by Robert Lacroix, the head of the Association of Universities and Colleges of Canada. In making his argument, Lacroix offered an anecdote from the Montreal Expos: "The Expos always have enough pitchers. Their problem is that they cannot retain their star pitchers like Pedro Martinez [who the Expos could not afford and ended up with the Boston Red Sox]." Eddie Goldenberg wrote that Lacroix had hit a grand slam home run with his pitch.[6] The government endowed 2,000 Canada Research Chairs across the country at a cost of $2.4 billion over 10 years.

The federal government had always supported research through the National Research Council, the Social Sciences and Humanities Research Council, the

Natural Sciences and Engineering Research Council, and the Canada Council for the Arts. But with the Canada Research Chairs, Chrétien took a risk by entering the provincial domain of education. David Zussman, an academic and Chrétien policy advisor, said that education to the prime minister was the great leveller in society. The key point, said Zussman, was that these programs were far more beneficial to society than programs of immediate consumption. While the incursion rankled some provinces, all were hungry for new money and accepted the use of federal spending power to this end.

The Canadian Institutes of Health Research was established after a scheduled 20 minute meeting turned into a full afternoon of brainstorming between Dr. Henry Friesen, president of the Medical Research Council of Canada, and Paul Martin. That and many helpful interventions by the prime minister's office led to the transformation and expansion of the Medical Research Council mandate to include funding for the social determinants of health along with a substantial increase in the organization's overall budget.[7] Related funding included the seed money to establish Genome Canada and permanent funding for the Network of Centres of Excellence.

The national affairs columnist for *The Globe and Mail*, Jeffrey Simpson, wrote that Chrétien's package of education and research initiatives would be among his most enduring and constructive legacies: "Behind all that petit gars de Shawinigan guff, Mr. Chrétien listened to some of the country's best minds and decided that Canada had a problem … and when the first biographies of him appear, barely a word will be written about these incredibly useful initiatives."[8] It was an ironic legacy, Simpson wrote, "for a prime minister not known for his cerebral interests." These programs, Simpson contended, better equipped Canada for competing in the world of knowledge.[9]

Simpson was countering a view that was widely held in the Parliamentary Press Gallery: that Chrétien was a do-nothing prime minister who was determined to hold power by making few mistakes and doing very little. But here was Chrétien transforming Canada's competitive position by making long-term investments in research and education where there was no immediate political payoff.

It was not just with direct government investments that Chrétien sought to reverse the brain drain. Targeted tax policy changes supported high-tech industries, entrepreneurship, and risk-taking. This included provisions that would allow investors to avoid capital gains tax by making new investments in qualifying small businesses. What Chrétien did not pursue were the policy prescriptions offered by conservative commentators: that you kept the bright minds in Canada through lower marginal income tax rates for those at the top of the heap.

EVEN PREDATING HIS EDUCATION initiatives, Chrétien sought to improve Canada's productivity by making investments in national infrastructure, notably roads, bridges, airports, and other national assets. In doing so he also established direct links with Canadian cities.

Municipalities are creatures of the provinces, so the federal government has no clear constitutional sway over how cities succeed or fail. But that hasn't stopped expansionist federal governments from using the spending power in the Constitution from stretching the four corners of the BNA Act to bypass provinces and establish a relationship with cities. Pierre Trudeau tried to dip his toe into municipal waters in 1971 when his Liberal government established the Ministry of State for Urban Affairs. But the provinces resisted the federal incursion and the ministry was disbanded in 1979.[10]

Chrétien came into office with a promise that Canadians would see construction cranes in the sky and that we would all be singing "Happy Days are Here Again." In practical terms, what he proposed was a public infrastructure program involving all three levels of government. The Canada Infrastructure Program was formally announced in January 1994, with provinces and cities eager to put up one dollar each to get another dollar from Ottawa. Even the Bloc Québécois, a party that would normally resist federal incursions, assigned a critic to make sure Québec got its fair share of the pie.[11]

But while Chrétien was in a giving mood to provinces and cities on infrastructure, he was also taking money away from provinces with cuts to transfer payments. The political advantage was obvious: Get credit for useful and visible community projects while taking little flak over what looked like an accounting manoeuvre on transfer payments. The annual decline in transfers in the 1995 and 1996 budgets of over $6 billion far exceeded the $2 billion one-time federal investment in infrastructure.

Once the federal government had surpluses on its hands, Chrétien took infrastructure programs to another level. This included funding the Infrastructure Canada Program and the Strategic Highway Infrastructure Program in 2000, and the Canadian Strategic Infrastructure Program and Border Infrastructure Program in 2001. The programs went over so well that they have been emulated by successive Conservative and Liberal governments alike.

AFTER THE BUDGET WAS balanced Chrétien had another target in mind. He wanted to help working families. His 1997 social policy reforms were innovative because they encouraged people to move off social assistance and into the workforce. It seems counter-intuitive, but myriad federal and provincial policies made it more profitable to stay on social assistance than to take a job. This barrier to joining the workforce became known as the welfare wall.

Chrétien's enriched Canada Child Tax Benefit (CCTB) included a working income supplement that was linked to provincial social programs. The reform was designed to improve the lot of some 1.4 million low-income Canadian families without taking anything away from those already on social assistance. When Chrétien introduced the CCTB in 1988 he said funding would rise if it did not take the country into deficit. Another benefit he introduced was to extend parental leave from 10 weeks to 35 weeks in 2000, and then to 52 weeks in 2003.

A decade after the CCTB was introduced the benefit levels had tripled. The CCCB was not only an attempt to burnish Chrétien's social legacy but also a way to handcuff his eventual successor with spending commitments. Chrétien got the credit for implementing policies that reduced child poverty while leaving less fiscal room for future prime ministers.[12] The net result of a better targeting of social policies was a meaningful decline in the poverty rates of families. Of course, Chrétien's most significant contribution to helping the poor were his policies that stimulated employment.

By putting the government on a sound fiscal footing, Chrétien ensured that social programs that helped those most at risk were less vulnerable to cuts. Had Chrétien not tamed the deficit and reduced the federal debt it is entirely possible that critical benefits could have ended up on the chopping block. While Chrétien made some employment insurance more difficult to access, he also delivered a stronger economy that benefited all regions of the country.

"We have done a lot for children," Chrétien said in 2002. "However, we still have a lot to do because we will never be satisfied."[13]

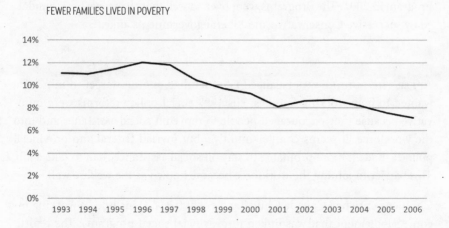

FEWER FAMILIES LIVED IN POVERTY

Chrétien and Martin did not just right-size government to what Canadians could afford, they transformed how federal tax dollars were spent in support of a more competitive and productive economy. They were both inclined to support basic research and scholarship. But even when they had fiscal room to invest, they continued to reduce the size of government.

TAX AVOIDANCE

Brian Tobin was a loyal member of Chrétien's Roman Guard, a group of Liberal MPs who sniffed out threats to his leadership. Chrétien listened carefully when, before the 1993 election, Tobin warned him that the Liberal caucus was restless and that a bold move was needed to bolster his grip on the party.

Tobin pushed Chrétien to come out against the GST: the much-maligned sales tax that the Mulroney government had implemented in 1991. As a former finance minister, Chrétien knew the previous tax on manufactured goods had been destructive and that there was no better alternative than the GST. Chrétien's key advisor Eddie Goldenberg also supported the GST.

The Manufacturers Sales Tax (MST) had made Canadian goods more expensive in international markets and gave a competitive advantage to importers over domestic manufacturers. The MST was not only an unreliable source of revenue but a cash cow for accountants and lawyers, who made a fortune concocting schemes to help clients avoid paying it. While many prime ministers before Mulroney were implored by economists to ditch the destructive tax, none had the political courage to do so.

Many Canadians mistakenly believed the GST was a completely new source of revenue for the federal government that was specifically intended to reduce the federal deficit. The GST was, in fact, designed to be initially revenue neutral.

Paul Martin was aligned with most Liberal MPs who wanted to make political hay out of the GST. Following a raucous caucus meeting, Chrétien said he was going to bend to the will of the majority and go against his own political instincts to oppose the tax. Goldenberg was furious and he told Chrétien that this was a decision he would come to regret. "Don't talk to me about when I am prime minister," he told Goldenberg. "I won't be prime minister if I lose the leadership of the party. Right now, my leadership is on the line. I can't afford to lose control of the caucus."[1] There was more than idle speculation that Chrétien might become the victim of a putsch.[2]

Opposing the GST was one thing, but when the legislation introducing the tax came before the Senate, Liberal members turned the Red Chamber into a circus, ringing cow bells while blowing kazoos. Only in Canada, Mulroney opined, could a 71-year-old man act so childishly and call himself a Senator.[3] Chrétien said the government was at fault for setting an implementation date for the GST before the legislation had passed the Senate, but his opposition was half-hearted.

Chrétien never precisely promised to abolish the GST. He proposed to replace the tax with a system that "generates the equivalent revenues, is fair to consumers and to small business, minimizes disruption to small business, and promotes federal-provincial fiscal corporation and harmonization." That was much more than what Liberal candidates wanted to say on the campaign trail so the pitch was shortened to "we will scrap the tax."

But Chrétien did not scrap the GST, and with good reasons. First, there were no viable alternatives in the federal realm that were either fairer or more efficient. Second, it would have taken cooperation from provincial governments to implement a harmonized tax. Few premiers wanted anything to do with the unpopular GST.

Critics likened Chrétien's abandonment of his GST promise to Pierre Trudeau's 1974 election promise not to institute wage and price controls. After the votes were cast that year Trudeau changed his mind. But Chrétien's about-face was different. The GST was not a proposal; the tax was in full force. The federal government had endured a painful and costly transition from the MST — a complicated tax with few registrants — to a relatively simple tax, but one that ensnared over one million businesses, charities, and not-for-profit organizations to serve as tax collectors. Businesses had already changed their accounting systems to charge the tax while still dealing with overlapping provincial sales tax systems.

Chrétien's government couldn't afford to give up the $15 billion in net annual GST revenue without adding substantially to the deficit, let alone reach his fiscal target. Martin, who co-authored the Red Book, called the GST good policy and bad politics. "The tax made eminent economic sense," wrote Martin. "The fundamental importance of the GST as a building block in the federal government's balance sheet is undeniable."[5] What Martin was saying was that while the Liberal party exploited the politics of the GST in the 1993 election, it knew the tax made good economic sense.

Rather than scrap the GST, Chrétien shifted his focus to integrating it with provincial sales taxes. Québec had largely completed sales tax integration while Mulroney was in office. But Chrétien could entice only three Atlantic provinces to join the system, and that was only after offering generous transitional payments plus promises to hire provincial revenue officers. The plan to harmonize the GST with provincial sales tax systems in Ontario and westward went nowhere. Chrétien believed his government went as far as it could and was prepared to let his efforts speak for themselves.

Martin thought the Liberal promise to scrap the tax — a promise he helped to craft — was so disingenuous that a public apology was warranted. Chrétien would have none of it, but he could not control Martin's need to beg for forgiveness. "It was an honest mistake," Martin confessed in the House of Commons. "It was a mistake in thinking we could bring in a completely different tax without undue economic distortion and within a reasonable time period."[6] Chrétien fumed and said to his caucus chair, Joe Fontana, "That fucking apology. That fucking Martin."[7]

Sheila Copps had told voters in the 1993 election campaign that if the tax was not nixed she would resign. It was a reckless promise to make, and one that few people believed she would keep. *Globe and Mail* columnist Jeffrey Simpson pledged that he would jump off the Parliament Buildings if Copps quit. Copps thought Martin's apology was designed to sideswipe the prime minister and "hang her out to dry." She added that within Liberal circles the GST stood for the "Get Sheila Tax." "He had no intention of fulfilling the Red Book promise to replace the GST," Copps said. "Martin often yelled at people in the Finance Department who dared to mention it as a source for their policy telling them 'Don't tell me what's in the Red Book. I wrote the goddamned thing. And I know it's a lot of crap.'" At one point, according to biographer John Gray, he told Finance officials, "Screw the Red Book."

Brian Tobin told Copps that if she resigned and ran again she would kill the issue, and that if she didn't resign her credibility would be shot. The prime minister tried to talk Copps out of resigning. Copps told Chrétien she would commission an overnight poll in her riding to find out what her constituents were thinking.

In the end, Copps followed through on her commitment and resigned, regaining the seat in a by-election a few months later. The real losers were the Canadian taxpayers who had to pick up the costs of the extra vote. Chrétien was displeased with Copps, but he still had his wife visit the riding during the by-election campaign.

While Chrétien had made Copps his deputy prime minister, he did not cut her much slack. He would tell people that because he was deaf in his right ear, he placed Sheila Copps in the seat at his left while in opposition, and then at the seat beside his right ear after the Liberals formed government.[8]

In the end, Chrétien could not have met his deficit reduction targets without the GST revenue. He made the right decision for Canada and kept the tax. The Progressive Conservative leader at the time, Jean Charest, later gave Chrétien his due: "He is the kind of politician who understood that good governments break bad campaign promises. He was able to do this well, without hurting himself."

The GST was certainly more stable and reliable than the former MST, but the popular notion that the GST was a cash cow that single-handedly brought the books into balance is a myth. The manufacturers' sales tax brought in

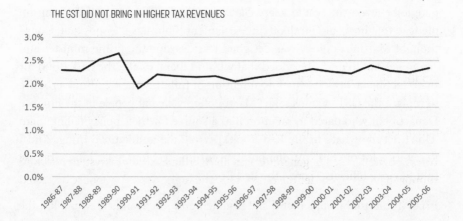

THE GST DID NOT BRING IN HIGHER TAX REVENUES

revenue equivalent to 2.6 per cent of GDP. During the Chrétien era, sales taxes never contributed more than 2.3 per cent of GDP as a relatively constant source of revenue.

CHRÉTIEN LIKED TO SAY that he delivered seven dollars in spending cuts for every dollar in new tax revenue. The ratio was closer to four to one but it was still good enough for Chrétien to say he kept his hands out of taxpayers' pockets.

One-time revenue was added by selling off Crown corporations. This included CN Rail and Cameco, a uranium company owned jointly by the Governments of Canada and Saskatchewan. More significant was the continuation of the sale of all but 18.7 per cent of the government's stake in Petro-Canada, which had been initiated by the Mulroney government. Beyond the sheer magnitude of the transaction was the symbolism. Petro-Canada was the brainchild of Pierre Trudeau and was established while Chrétien served in his cabinet. It had become a lightning rod for western alienation where its head office in Calgary was dubbed Red Square. If ever there was a break from past Liberal practices — and sins — the sale of Petro-Canada was it.

Chrétien's changes to the tax code amounted to no more than tinkering. This included a new approach to tobacco taxes. Sin taxes can usually be expected to forever be on the rise. But high tobacco taxes had stimulated a growth in smuggling. The government had evidence that Canadian tobacco companies were complicit in bringing untaxed cigarettes from the United States into Canada through Indigenous reserves on the Québec-New York border. The police said they were unable to stop the smuggling operations and public safety was at risk. A special cabinet committee recommended joint federal-provincial action to substantially lower cigarette taxes to a level at which smuggling operations could not make money.[9]

One early change in tax policy was to eliminate the $100,000 capital gains exemption that Mulroney's government had put in place to stimulate investment. Chrétien thought the tax break favoured the wealthy, a group he didn't mind alienating because he assumed they all voted Tory. Instead, the prime minister enhanced the capital gains exemption for small business and farming enterprises.

A less obvious revenue generator was an overhaul of the tax system for child support payments. Under the old system, the higher-earning spouse deducted payments made to the lower-income spouse. By eliminating the deduction, the government took in more taxes from the one spouse than it lost from the other.

As the government moved closer to a balanced budget, there was room for tax decreases, including the elimination of temporary surtaxes that had been imposed by Mulroney. After the government was in the black, the basic income tax exemption was increased, taking 400,000 Canadians off the income-tax rolls. Chrétien also scaled back the 3 per cent general surtax, which was eliminated for almost 13 million taxpayers.

The 2000 budget restored the full indexation of the personal income tax system, which meant that taxpayers would not find themselves in a higher tax bracket simply because of inflation. The middle-income tax rate was also lowered from 26 per cent to 23 per cent, and the 5 per cent deficit reduction surtax on middle-income Canadians with incomes up to about $85,000 was scheduled for elimination. Chrétien decreased the portion of capital gains subject to tax from 75 per cent to 66 per and then 50 per cent in 2000. Even corporate taxes came down over time, with the basic rate falling from 28 per cent to 21 per cent.

In Chrétien's early years, relative tax revenues rose. But after spending was brought under control and surpluses became the new normal, Canadians began to enjoy some tax relief. Looking at the big picture, Chrétien's tax take varied little from that of his predecessors.

OVERALL FEDERAL REVENUE WAS HELD STEADY

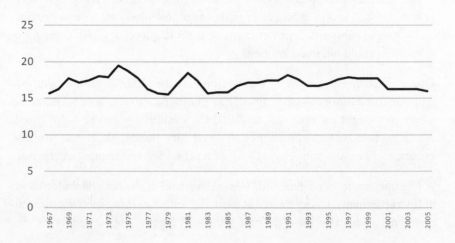

WHILE MOST TAXES UNDER Chrétien remained relatively stable, import duties declined — as would be expected under free trade within North America — as did revenue from energy. The larger gains for government revenue were in personal and corporate income tax, driven largely by an improving economy.

The biggest revenue loss was in employment insurance premiums paid by employees and employers. During Chrétien's tenure, EI premiums were cut in half as a per cent of GDP, although the account was always in surplus. EI spending declined because more people were working and because policy changes meant that fewer people were eligible to make claims. Revenues declined because contribution rates were reduced. This left more money in the hands of workers and their employers, delivering the same impact as a tax reduction. In the year the budget was first balanced, the annual surplus in the EI account was $7 billion. Without that surplus, Canada's 1997–98 accounts would have been in the red instead of the black.

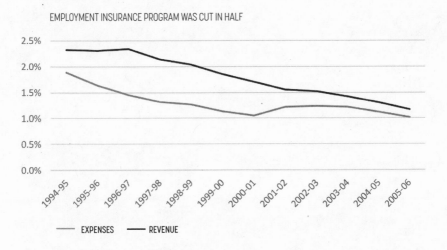

EMPLOYMENT INSURANCE PROGRAM WAS CUT IN HALF

CHRÉTIEN UNDERSTOOD THAT CANADIANS would not tolerate tax increases to balance the budget if they thought spending was out of control. Canadians were already stretched and were paying relatively more in taxes in 1993 than the average over the previous 30 years. Chrétien knew that making big changes to the tax system would do little to solve the nation's fiscal challenge. So, he did little to change the tax system. But when surpluses arrived he revealed that his instinct was to cut taxes. It was a choice that even conservatives across the country could appreciate.

PENSION ACCORD

Almost every Canadian felt some pain as the federal government worked its way from deficit to surplus. Whether it was reduced government services or a lower Canadian dollar, the cure for the hangover from the excesses of the 1970s and 1980s meant that taxpayers would have to pay more and get less. But what about public servants? As insiders, did they feel more of the burden of the pain more than everyone else?

Between 1993 and 1997, the cost of the federal payroll declined by 13.5 per cent, which saved a little less than $3 billion per year. This was a modest yet meaningful contribution to tackling the nation's $38 billion deficit. Payroll savings were not achieved by rolling back salaries but by shrinking the ranks of the public service. Because the workload remained the same, those who kept their jobs had to produce more.

Whether it was through innovation, attrition, or efficiency, the number of full-time and part-time federal public servants was chopped by close to 70,000 people during the deficit-slashing years, a 17 per cent reduction in their ranks, as the Canadian population rose by 7 per cent.

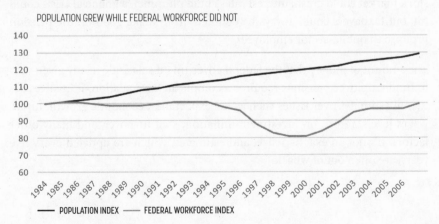

POPULATION GREW WHILE FEDERAL WORKFORCE DID NOT

— POPULATION INDEX —— FEDERAL WORKFORCE INDEX

So, the answer to the question is: Yes. The public service did their bit to help balance the budget. Chrétien captured these savings with minimal rancour, a feat he attributed to the respect he had demonstrated throughout his career for the work of public servants. He said government employees also understood that he was serious about balancing the books and was not one to make idle threats or back down in a negotiation.

While Chrétien right-sized government he also changed the demographics of the public service. The proportion of women in the public service rose from 47 to 53 per cent. The proportion of francophones increased from 20.7 to 24.9 per cent. For the first time in Canadian history, francophones had a stronger presence in the federal government than their overall demographic footprint.

On the whole, Chrétien enjoyed a productive and respectful relationship with public servants. But there was one government policy that so irritated public servants that they took their grievance all the way to the Supreme Court of Canada.[1] Chrétien and Martin had been scouring the books for every source of potential savings when they received some unexpected good news. While the government's books were bleeding red ink, the public service pension plan was in surplus.

Canadian public servants enjoy one of the most generous and secure pensions on the planet. Under their defined benefit plan, long-term employees could retire as early as age 55 with a pension that paid them two-thirds of the average of their best five years of earnings. The pensions were indexed to inflation, for life. Yet, despite the fiscal crisis in which private retirement accounts were tanking, the Chrétien government left the public servant cash-for-life bonanza virtually untouched. And the plan was virtually risk-free for recipients. The stock market could crash, interest rates could plummet, a financial crisis could hit, but taxpayers could always be counted on to make good on the pension promise to public-sector employees.

The amount of money that the federal government sets aside in any given year to fund employee pensions requires a complicated calculation. It involves actuarial estimates over issues such as life expectancy, economic growth, future wages levels, return on investment, inflation, staff turnover, and many other factors. It's not an exact science, and estimates, which are updated every five years, are often out of whack.

When the actuaries examined the public-sector pension account in the early 1990s, they concluded the plan was in surplus. Normally a surplus or deficit is modest and future contributions are adjusted over the coming five years. But the public service pension surplus was a doozy — some $30 billion.

The government could have treated retirees like lottery winners and handed out cheques. It could have declared a contribution holiday for employees and the government until the surplus had been wiped out, which is what the province of Ontario did from 1998 to 2002 when its pension fund was in surplus. Instead, the federal government scooped up the surplus and applied it to the deficit.

By 1996, half the surplus in the pension account had been reclaimed by the government. In addition, $800 million from the surplus was tapped to fund early-retirement incentives that helped to take 50,000 workers off the federal payroll. The unions representing public servants were outraged by what they called a theft and a betrayal.

To regularize the policy, the government passed Bill C-78 in 1999, which, among other things mandated that pension surpluses above 110 per cent of estimates be automatically returned to the government's accounts. What was ironic, the union argued, was that when this legislation was passed there was no surplus remaining to claw back.[2]

The public service unions fought the government's action all the way to the Supreme Court, where they lost in a unanimous ruling. The court contended that public servant pension contributions granted them a legal entitlement to a future benefit, but nothing more. That left it up to the government to decide how it would deal with shortfalls and surpluses.

As minority contributors into the pension fund, public servants had little to complain about. The surplus existed because the government had over-contributed in the past and it was simply recouping that amount. Not a dime was taken away from the pensions that public servants were promised. The Chrétien government made the right call, but it also got lucky. Had the $30 billion pension surplus been a pension shortfall, getting out of deficit would have been all that more difficult.

Chrétien's decisiveness, combined with an ability to move quickly on a policy change, worked to taxpayers' advantage. Before the unions knew what hit them, the money was scooped up and used to help the government reach its fiscal goals.

By the time Jean Chrétien became prime minister, the Canada Pension Plan (CPP) had become a ticking time bomb.

The CPP is designed to be a self-financing and segregated pension plan with matching contributions from employees and employers. It was initially designed to operate on a pay-as-you-go basis, meaning that the contributions from current workers fund payments to qualifying beneficiaries.

When the CPP was implemented, there were many more workers than recipients so the contribution rates were unsustainably low and the CPP's design did not consider basic demographic realities, such as the aging of our population and the slowing of population growth.

When the plan was launched, there were eight workers for every CPP beneficiary. In 1993, that fell to five to one and was projected to drop to three to one by about 2020. The math wasn't hard to figure out. The contributions from three workers were insufficient to sustain the promised pension benefits for one retiree. The actuarial calculations made in the early 1990s revealed that the CPP would run out of money in a generation's time. The CPP, in effect, was turning into a Ponzi scheme.

The unfunded liability in the CPP in the early 1990s was equal to the national debt. But because it was operated as a separate fund it did not figure into the government's deficit calculation or liabilities. It was "off the books" financing. And it was turning into a giant problem.

The government's actuaries calculated that for the CPP to be sustainable, premiums would have to rise from 5.5 per cent to 14 per cent of income. Even if the federal government was prepared to force that bitter pill on employee and employers — which they weren't — changes to CPP needed the approval of two-thirds of provinces representing two-thirds of the Canadian population to go ahead.

In 1997, governments decided to raise CPP premiums to 9.9 per cent of earnings, while protecting most, but not all, CPP benefits. The idea of increasing the retirement age was considered and rejected. The death benefit was decreased and the calculation of pension entitlements were revised to be less generous.[3] To offset the political noise of a CPP rate hike, the federal government lowered Employment Insurance premiums by about one-third.[4]

To avoid a massive increase in premiums, the government decided to allow CPP fund managers to make investments outside of government securities. Previously, the CPP fund could only be invested in bonds, treasury bills, and other low-risk fixed income securities. Thus, the CPP Investment Board was created.[5]

The reforms, which were led by Paul Martin, were sound. The 2013 actuarial report prepared by the Office of the Superintendent of Financial Institutions concluded that the CPP was financially sustainable over the long term without further increases in contribution rates.[6] While the CPP replaces only about 25 per cent of pre-retirement income, when combined with Old Age Security and other benefits, it's enough to keep most seniors above the poverty line.

Fixing the CPP accrued little political credit but much political risk. That explains why the United States has failed to reform its Social Security system, despite the evidence that the fund will be depleted by 2035. Chrétien and his provincial counterparts did what was necessary for the long-term survival of the CPP and the retirement incomes of Canadians.

Chrétien did not come into office thinking he would be dealing with the CPP and the public-sector pension plan. These were not issues he campaigned on, but he approached both with an open mind and the same methodology he brought to most problems: he fixed them permanently.

THE LOONIE

I t's not often that a Canadian politician is woken in the night to tend to a crisis. But it happened to Paul Martin on January 23, 1998.

The Bank of Montreal and the Royal Bank of Canada had just issued a press release announcing that they were going to merge. Martin was furious. He said the banks were trying to make an end-run around an orderly review of financial institution policy that was already in process. A preliminary report was scheduled to be released in a matter of months. Martin said the two banks were attempting to catch their competitors flat-footed.[1]

The government viewed the merger as a decrease in competition and an increase in economic risk to the country. At kitchen tables across the country, the worry was that there would be a decline in bank branches along with a loss of jobs. Chrétien did not think bigger was better. "You know, for me, even if I were 350 pounds, it will not make me a better prime minister."[2]

The *National Post* saw merit in the merger proposal, saying it would deliver lower-cost financial products to consumers and bolster the wages of bank employees. But in December 1998, the government announced that the bank mergers would not be allowed to proceed. The wisdom of that decision became apparent during the 2008 worldwide economic crisis when American banks, which had undergone a succession of mergers and deregulation, needed government bailouts to survive. Canadian banks, on the other hand, endured the global crisis with minimal outside help.

KEEPING A TIGHT REIN on the banks was an easy political decision to make. Far tougher for Chrétien was being in office for more than a decade and keeping inflation under control. During his time in the Trudeau cabinet — when

Canada had the worst inflation record among G7 nations — Chrétien witnessed how steeply rising prices wreaked havoc on the economy and savaged seniors' purchasing power. When the bank rate topped out at close to 20 per cent in 1981, the pain was felt by mortgage holders, consumers, and businesses alike. Ultimately it took a period of high interest rates and a recession to bring inflation down, but it was not an experience Chrétien wanted to repeat.

When Chrétien came into office, the inflation rate was just below 2 per cent and the 7-year term of the Governor of the Bank of Canada, John Crow, was set to expire. Chrétien thought the governor was doctrinaire and had gone overboard in the late 1980s with tight money policies that stifled job creation.[3] In November 1991, as opposition leader, Chrétien said the Mulroney government had the wrong mix of interest rates and dollar policies. Referring to Crow, Chrétien said, "Don't presume that anyone who works for me does not take instructions."[4] The chief economist for DRI-McGraw Hill, George Vasic, responded to Chrétien's utterings by saying Crow would tell Chrétien to take a hike before taking directions. Vasic warned there would be a run on the Canadian dollar if Crow was not retained.

In the 1993 election, Crow's tenure again came up for debate. When Chrétien was asked if he was worried about how financial markets might react to a rift between the government and the Bank of Canada governor, he replied, "I'm not here to represent financial institutions or unions. I'm here to represent ordinary Canadians."[5] Paul Martin was more sympathetic to John Crow and said the bank governor had to deal with the ineffective policies of the Progressive Conservative government and many provinces.

Chrétien also thought Crow was arrogant and was disrespectful of Parliamentarians. It disgusted Chrétien that Crow lobbied to be reappointed. He said that Gerald Bouey, a former governor that Chrétien knew, would never have done that. Chrétien gave his finance minister the choice of whether to renew Crow's contract. But he offered a warning if Martin chose to keep Crow: "I bet that, within two years, either you or he will have to go because he will have stifled the first signs of our coming out of the recession."[6]

Martin wanted Crow to be renewed, mostly because of the prevailing view in financial markets that this was the prudent course to follow.[7] *The Globe and Mail* was emphatic that Chrétien "must immediately and unreservedly reappoint John Crow to another term as governor of the Bank of Canada."[8]

THE SHAWINIGAN FOX   115

Martin wanted the Bank of Canada to work with an inflation target of between 1 and 3 per cent. Crow wanted zero to 2 per cent and would not budge. "My God," Martin wrote, "If we can't agree on something like this in which our objectives are similar and we have no crisis in front of us, what's going to happen when there is a crisis?[9]

The deputy minister of finance, David Dodge, was involved in the discussions with Crow. He said the breakdown was caused as much by personality as policy: "John [Crow] was not a very sympathetic person and he appears much crustier than he actually is. He was inherently rigid when Martin wanted a more supple approach."

In the end, Martin opted to replace Crow with Gordon Thiessen on February 4, 1994. Thiessen, previously deputy governor, was more amenable to Chrétien and Martin's way of thinking. Thiessen ended up having one of the easiest jobs in Ottawa. Because the government constrained the wages it paid its employees and got its spending under control, he had few inflationary pressures to deal with.

Thiessen also knew Chrétien would not become stressed from a decline in the value of the Canadian dollar. Indeed, when the loonie dropped in August 1998, Chrétien's reaction was to shrug, calling it a "reality of life" that was not causing inflation.[10] Business leader Tom d'Aquino warned that Chrétien should not seem indifferent, and argued that speculators would sense the lack of a backstop and would drive the dollar down farther. Author and historian Peter C. Newman marvelled at how Chrétien didn't care about the state of his country's currency. *National Post* columnist Diane Francis wrote that it was the equivalent of a corporate CEO talking down the value of his company. She suggested Chrétien be given a pink slip. None of this bothered Chrétien. He was content to accept the criticism and let the dollar slide to the level where a full economic recovery could be secured.

Inflation stayed below 3 per cent throughout Chrétien's decade in office and averaged close to the 2 per cent target that the Bank of Canada had set. In fact, the Canadian inflation rate was lower than the American rate in almost every year that Chrétien was prime minister.

INFLATION WAS KEPT UNDER CONTROL·

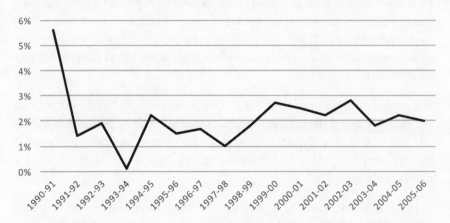

Lower inflation helped the governor of the Bank of Canada keep interest rates at historically low levels. A five-year mortgage taken out in 1990 could be renewed in 1995 with a 4 percentage point interest-rate drop. On a $200,000 mortgage, that saved a homeowner about $8,000 in interest payments per year. That's $8,000 after tax. Even at an average income tax rate, that was the equivalent of a $12,000 raise. Chrétien liked to say that the best tax cut Canadians ever received from his government was the reduction in interest rates.[11]

By the time Chrétien left office, the bank rate, which drives interest rate levels that consumers pay, was at historically low levels at around 3 per cent.

BANK RATE FELL TO HISTORICALLY LOW LEVELS

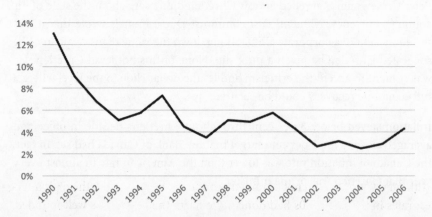

It had been decades since Canada enjoyed a combination of low interest rates, low inflation, and high economic growth. Allowing the Canadian dollar to float to its natural level of support was an essential ingredient in achieving this desirable mix of economic results. In the 1970s and 1980s, the Bank of Canada had reacted to a declining currency by raising interest rates. The worry was that a lower dollar would cause inflation and make consumer goods and business equipment more expensive to import, as well as making foreign trips more expensive. Same with fruits and vegetables for consumers, especially in winter months. A currency in decline would also have been a blow to our national psyche. When the Canadian dollar lost value in the early 1960s it was called the Diefendollar by the opponents of Prime Minister Diefenbaker.

Chrétien thought it made no sense to keep our dollar artificially high when our economic fundamentals were shaky. So, why fight economic reality with artificially high interest rates? With inflation in check, Chrétien saw a lower dollar as pro-employment because it made our exports less expensive on world markets.

From 1993 to 2002, the value of the Canadian dollar declined relative to the American buck from around 80 cents to below 65 cents. But by the time Chrétien left office and the economy had strengthened, the dollar was at about the same level as when he came into office.

LOONIE FELL, THEN ROSE, RELATIVE TO US DOLLAR

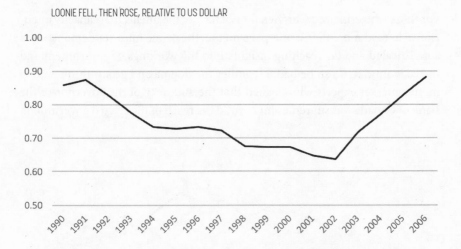

Although Chrétien was not a trained economist, his belief that the high interest rates in the late 1980s had done more harm than good was well-founded. When the government appointed a new governor in 1994, it wasn't met with much fuss, but that doesn't mean there was no shift in policy. John Crow, in his memoir, *Making Money: Finance, Politics and the Bank of Canada*, contends that the Chrétien government took control over monetary policy: "Decisions relating to inflation targets," wrote Crow, "are now effectively in the hands of the federal government, even if it chooses not to advertise the fact."[12] Crow was bitter that he had been asked to accept the government's view on an inflation target when he thought this decision should rest with the governor. While Crow had endorsed the aggressive inflation targets of the Mulroney government, he was not prepared to accept a weakening of the targets advocated by Chrétien and Martin. Crow said it was one thing for a governor to believe in a policy that the government accepts, but quite another if the governor pursues a policy because it's what the minister of finance wants.

In making his mark in monetary policy, Jean Chrétien had come a long way since his early meetings at the finance department with Mitchell Sharp when he conceded that, whatever was discussed, he "didn't understand a bloody thing." As prime minister, he quietly but profoundly changed the policy landscape so that the Bank of Canada became more responsive to the government's overall direction and strategy on economic management. By drawing on his experience as minister of finance, Chrétien used the appointment of Thiessen to achieve the result he sought.

For those who criticized Chrétien for not having the intellectual capacity or curiosity to read more than a one-page memo, the prime minister demonstrated sophisticated and far-reaching insights into the workings of government and the economy. To do so he had to counter the dogma and group-think among money market experts who posited that the authority of the governor of the Bank of Canada was supreme and beyond the reach of the elected government.

JOBS, JOBS, JOBS

In 2003, there were three million more people in the workforce in Canada than in 1993. During that period, the unemployment rate declined from 11.4 per cent to 7.2 per cent. Employment rose because of low interest rates, a low dollar, a smaller government, lower and more efficient taxes, free trade, infrastructure investments, and better skills development. While many of these outcomes can be credited to Chrétien economic policies, Canada was also lucky. The American consumer came out of an early 1990s recession with a vengeance. It was a happy circumstance that Chrétien did all he could to exploit.

JEAN CHRÉTIEN BELIEVED THAT every capable Canadian should put in an honest day's work. So, in 1996, he turned Canada's unemployment insurance system on its head. By changing its name to employment insurance, he signalled that its basic mandate was shifting from providing support to the unemployed to getting people back to work. He did this, in part, by making it harder to collect employment insurance and making the benefits less attractive to those who qualified.

Chrétien knew that tightening up the system would make his political life difficult. Had the economy been in better shape he might not have taken on the challenge of upsetting the status quo. But given the weak state of our national finances, there was no part of our economy that he was not prepared to touch.

The change in direction that Chrétien sought ran counter to the policies of the Liberal government he had served in the early 1970s. But Chrétien saw that after the rules were loosened to make unemployment insurance more generous and accessible, the number of claims in the years that followed almost doubled. Experts concluded that the reforms in the 1970s caused unemployment rates across Canada to rise, between two percentage points nationally and up to four percentage points in Atlantic Canada.[1]

In the late 1980s, unemployment benefits were scaled back by the Mulroney government, especially for those who quit their jobs or were fired for misconduct. But the program remained a huge drag on the Canadian economy. The system that had cost $500 million when Trudeau came to power, and $10 billion when Mulroney took over, had become a $19 billion behemoth when Chrétien became prime minister.

As much as Chrétien wanted to reduce the cost of unemployment insurance, an equally important objective was removing disincentives to work. Chrétien was informed that among households receiving social assistance, 45 per cent were employable. Of those, 40 per cent were chronic unemployment insurance claimants. This included seasonal workers, many of whom were employed for the minimum number weeks to qualify for year-round benefits. For many Canadians, claiming unemployment insurance had become a routine part of life and the foundation of their personal finances.

In a year-end interview with CTV News in 1993, Chrétien said that life for those on unemployment insurance was likely to change: "There's a lot of things that have to be done in society that are not done because we don't have the resources and, on the other side, a lot of people who would like to work and there is no work. So, can we not match the need with the availability of manpower?"[2] Chrétien offered the example of using the unemployed to clear out unwanted brush in a forest. The unions representing forest workers didn't like it, but better the unemployed be given something to do that provided a community benefit. This harkened back to public works programs that were implemented during the Great Depression of the 1930s.

In April 1994, Chrétien poured fuel on the fire when he said the country could no longer afford to keep people sitting at home quaffing an ale:[3] "We have to break that mentality in which people work long enough to qualify for social assistance then quit. It's better to have them at 50 per cent productivity than to be sitting at home drinking beer."[4] When asked to defend his comment — made at a black-tie dinner with newspaper executives — he said it was not the government that was complaining but the wives of the unemployed, who were upset about their husbands hanging around the house. The comment was obviously sexist and Chrétien half-heartedly apologized. He also noted that most of the mail he received was from wives who said his comments were bang on. But that didn't stop Reform Party MPs from calling Chrétien insulting and insensitive to "unfortunate Canadians."[5]

Chrétien's tightening of the employment insurance system was expected to save about $2.4 billion per year. Claimants also faced something completely new. Those who had high earnings and had collected employment insurance in the same year were subject to a claw-back of up to 100 per cent of benefits paid. The claw-back was most severe for those who had made frequent EI claims over the previous past five years (excluding maternity, parental, or sickness benefits).

The reforms were met with howls of protests from the Bloc Québécois (Canada's official opposition party at the time) and organized labour. Atlantic premiers, and even members of Chrétien's east-coast caucus, were similarly angered. The prime minister was burned in effigy and some government buildings were occupied in protest. Chrétien said he would always stand up for the little guy, the impoverished, and the disabled, but he had no sympathy for the lazy, who preferred collecting unemployment insurance cheques over putting in a hard day's work.

When a Saskatchewan woman with three university degrees confronted Chrétien at a town-hall meeting about her lack of job opportunities, he replied that some people were lucky and some were unlucky. If she couldn't find a job, Chrétien said, she should move.[6]

One analysis showed that while two-thirds of the unemployed got benefits in 1993, by 2000 those who qualified for payments, under the more restrictive criteria, represented only one-third of the unemployed.[7] But employment numbers went in the other direction. Under Chrétien, the unemployment rate fell by 4.4 points in Newfoundland, 5.3 points in PEI, 4.7 points in Nova Scotia, and 3.7 points in New Brunswick. While there were other factors at play, the areas that saw the greatest increase in unemployment over the 1970s when the insurance program was relaxed were the same areas that saw the greatest gains in employment when the program was tightened under Chrétien. Nationally, the unemployment rate under Chrétien fell by 3.4 percentage points.

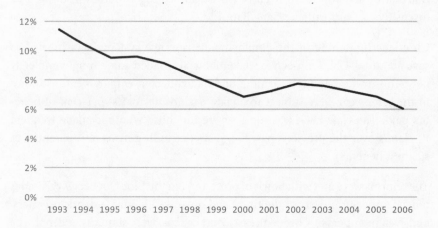

UNEMPLOYMENT RATE FELL STEADILY

Chrétien paid a price for these changes, even though the results were positive. He barely hung on to a majority government in 1997, losing 22 seats, mostly in Atlantic Canada. In Nova Scotia, he went from winning all 11 seats in 1993 to being shut out in 1997.

After being stung in the 1997 election, Chrétien eased some of the restrictions he had put in place on employment insurance. While seasonal workers rejoiced, the Canadian Chamber of Commerce labelled the about-face an "absolute farce."[8] The changes were opposed at the cabinet table by ministers Manley and Martin, but Chrétien prevailed.[9] As courageous as he was in tightening EI during a fiscal crisis, he demonstrated that his desire for political victory remained strong. In the 2000 election, he won 20 seats in Atlantic Canada, almost double what he had won in 1997.

CANADA'S MOST CONSERVATIVE PRIME MINISTER

Jean Chrétien was le petit gars, a populist, a scrapper, a Liberal. But he was also one of Canada's most conservative prime ministers.

David Zussman contends Chrétien was a situational prime minister who adapted his views to the conditions and challenges he faced in the moment. He was grounded by a deep set of values, said Zussman. "He was prepared to go in any direction to support these values."

It was not just on money matters that Chrétien had a conservative orientation. Biographer Lawrence Martin wrote that Chrétien was reluctant to act and only intervened in matters when circumstances compelled him to do so.[1] Columnist Paul Wells wrote that Chrétien was a traditionalist at heart.[2] In *The Globe and Mail*, Jeffrey Simpson wrote that Chrétien was a risk-adverse prime minister who never reached beyond the broad currents of public opinion.[3] Simpson wrote that Chrétien was not focused on new initiatives but on preventing bad things from happening:

> In this sense, Chrétien was the classic conservative, determined to avoid the worst outcomes, a cautious pragmatist aware of potential troubles. Chrétien was also an institutional conservative, having thrived with the existing system... He had little time for abstract arguments or theories or weeping structural reforms.[4]

Jean Charest saw Chrétien at work over many years — from the opposition benches in the House of Commons and also as premier of Québec. He said Chrétien's conservative values were a constant that came to him very early in his political career as a result of the influence of Mitchell Sharp: "He separated himself from Pierre Trudeau on that fact."

That was also the view from within Chrétien's cabinet. "Some commentators think Jean Chrétien is left of centre politically," wrote Brian Tobin. "But when it comes to fiscal matters he is very conservative. He knows that the clear majority of working families go through every day looking for ways to save money while stretching their budget from paycheque to paycheque."[5] Tobin added that Chrétien understood that before a dollar could be spent it had to be earned. He was not a big-spending bleeding heart, said Tobin.

The deputy minister of finance during Chrétien's early years in office, David Dodge, said Chrétien was an innately conservative man. "It was natural for him to be financially disciplined. It was a joy to work with him."

When he retired in 2003, *The Globe and Mail* called Chrétien a conservative in Liberal clothing: "His modus operandi was if it ain't broke, don't fix it, and if it was broke, what the hell, it might well fix itself. Inaction trumped action in his world view, unless inaction was impossible."[6]

Even after the books were balanced in 1997, Chrétien did not ramp up government spending. He remodelled, but did not expand basic social programs. Government payments to people fell from 5.7 per cent to 4.0 per cent of GDP while Chrétien was in office. *Toronto Star* columnist Thomas Walkom wrote in 2014 that Chrétien had decimated Canadian social programs. In many areas, he charged, Chrétien's Liberals, "gaily cherry-picked from the platforms of their right-wing opponents."[7] Chrétien paid down debt while keeping taxes low. He reduced the size of public service and applied the surplus in their pension fund to reduce the deficit. He even imposed large funding cuts to the CBC.

Some cabinet ministers, including David Collenette, thought Chrétien went too far on expenditure reductions: "A lot of people and communities were hurt, but the PM argued that the short-term pain would improve things in the long run." Of the many cuts Chrétien imposed, he regrets only one: the closure of the College Militaire Royal in St. Jean, Québec, which he later concluded ran counter to his national unity and bilingualism goals.

The investments Chrétien's government made after recording successive surpluses were not in social welfare but in infrastructure, as well as in basic research, and in higher education. These priorities, Chrétien believed, were building blocks for a robust Canadian economy. His core priorities were almost always economic in nature. Had Chrétien maintained the same level of program spending that he inherited from Brian Mulroney, the government would have spent an additional $53 billion in 2003, which would have represented about one-third of program spending.

When Chrétien heard complaints from people who couldn't find work in their hometowns he told them to move to where the jobs were. He scaled back unemployment benefits to encourage paid work.

Chrétien had compassion for the underdog and for those who struggled because of circumstances that were beyond their control. The working poor were the beneficiaries of many of Chrétien's reforms. But for the lazy, he had no sympathy. His small-town way of thinking meant that he did not tolerate those who felt entitled to live off the hard work of others.

Bob Rae's view was that Chrétien was generous without being naïve; that he understood the human condition well and what worked and what didn't. Chrétien understood that not every problem or grievance could be fixed by government and that people facing difficult circumstances and tough choices must move forward on their own.

One senior bureaucrat said that conservatism was part of Chrétien's DNA but that it was balanced with a desire to help the less fortunate:

> It's true that the 2000 budget provided one of the largest tax cuts in Canadian history. But Chrétien also believed in a positive role for government along with a deep commitment to fiscal responsibility. When finances improved, he undid the reforms that had been necessary in the mid-1990s that the government was forced to implement. But five years later he invested not just in people but in research and the core assets of the country. He made investments in healthcare and in 2000 through 2003 and began to rebuild social programs with the National Child Benefit, the most significant social investment since Medicare. He expanded employment insurance to include parental leave. He had an instinct to support children and the disabled.

It was only near the end of his time in office that Chrétien sought to burnish his progressive credentials. He restored some of the employment insurance restrictions that were imposed in his first mandate. He signed the Kyoto Accord that set targets for greenhouse gas emissions. And he led a campaign to eliminate land mines around the world.

But almost every economic policy that Chrétien championed while in office was designed to spur investment, create jobs, or strengthen the federal balance sheet. Lower government spending and balanced books increased the confidence of investors in the fundamentals of the Canadian economy. Lower corporate and personal taxes helped provide a climate that encouraged job creation. Reforms to employment insurance enhanced incentives to work. Support for basic research helped to keep our brightest minds at home. Funding for national and local infrastructure helped to bring our products to markets. In his heart, Chrétien believed in the well-worn conservative idiom that the best social program was a job. Under his leadership, the unemployment rate declined by one-third.

Chrétien, however, would prefer to be described as a classic liberal who was unafraid to use the power of government to improve the quality of life for ordinary Canadians. His associate deputy minister of finance, Scott Clark, recognized this when advising the government in advance of the 1995 budget: "You are still a Liberal but you have to be a small 'c' fiscal conservative to be a nice good liberal."[8]

"ARE YOU BETTER OFF than you were four years ago?" That's the question Ronald Reagan asked to great effect in a 1980 debate with President Jimmy Carter. Americans concluded they were not and elected Reagan as their 40th president.

So, were Canadians better off in 2003 than they were in 1993? Two McGill University professors, Tom Velk and Al Riggs, think not.[9] They point to the decline in the value of the dollar and a low Canadian growth rate per capita (when denominated in US dollars). But their analysis doesn't fully consider that letting the dollar slide to its natural level of support reflected the underlying economic reality that Canada faced in the early 1990s. The massive federal deficit and debt combined with low productivity and weak balance of payments is what drove down the Canadian buck. It would have been foolish to keep the dollar artificially high just to maintain purchasing power and possibly sustain the national ego. The cost of intervening in money markets to prop up the dollar would have been higher interest rates and lower exports, which would have hampered Canada's economic recovery.

Another factor to consider when assessing Canada's relative growth rate was the impact of taking massive government stimulus out of the economy. Reducing government program spending and downsizing and public-sector employment were all instrumental to getting the fiscal house in order. But there was a short-term price to pay in growth.

Consider how Canada's economic and fiscal position changed from 1993 to 2003, the time Chrétien was in office:

- Unemployment declined from 11.4 to 7.2 per cent.

- The gap between the Canadian and American unemployment rate narrowed.

- A $39 billion deficit was transformed into a $9.2 billion surplus.

- Government operations went from a $1.5 billion deficit to a $45 -billion surplus.

- Government spending as a per cent of GDP was reduced from 16.5 per cent to 12.5 per cent.

- The federal debt-to-GDP ratio was lowered by 40 per cent.

- The central bank rate declined from 4.4 to 3.0 per cent.

- The annual cost of interest to the federal government was cut by $4.3 billion.

- Canada's balance of trade surplus quadrupled, from $1 billion to $4 billion.

- Canadian exports doubled, from $16 billion to $33 billion.

- Per capita GDP rose from $27,200 to $35,540.

- The Toronto Stock Exchange index doubled from 4,000 to 8,000.

Virtually every standard-of-living measure improved under Chrétien. That includes Canadian living standards compared to the United States, which improved by two percentage points: from 82 to 84 per cent.[10] Canada's 3.5 per cent average growth rate was stronger than the 3.3 per cent rate in the United States. The inflation rate, which was largely unchanged under Chrétien, was lower on average than in the United States. And Canada substantially out-performed all developed nations on debt reduction. The data is difficult to dispute, although prime ministerial historian Michael Bliss wrote in 2002 that "the Chrétien years may go down in Canadian history as a time of squandered economic opportunities, years when we did not modernize, did not keep pace."[11] The reality was that under Chrétien the federal government became an economic and fiscal best practice for the world.

When countries struggled to recover from the 2008 global economic crisis, they came to Canada to study how we dug ourselves out of a debt spiral in the 1990s. Canada was also hit with hard times in 2008, but the fiscal strength that Chrétien had championed gave the government the capacity to steady the national economy in a time of stress. Canadian banks did not need a bail-out and housing prices remained firm, neither of which was the case in the United States.

While Martin delivered the budgets, it was Chrétien who kept his government and cabinet in line. David Dodge said that Chrétien needed no persuasion in making the tough calls or holding to a decision. A Liberal prime minister with conservative instincts was exactly what the country needed in 1993 and for the decade that followed. And that's exactly what Chrétien was.

THE WORLD

THE CLINTON YEARS

Though Chrétien had briefly served as Secretary of State for External Affairs under Prime Minister Turner in 1984, he was not what anyone would call a man of the world when he was sworn in as prime minister in 1993.

While many Canadian prime ministers have sought to burnish their personal image by rubbing shoulders with the globe's most powerful figures, Chrétien was not one to genuflect before those of affluence and influence, in Canada or elsewhere. He preferred to be popular in Moncton rather than Moscow; in Papineauville rather than Paris. His key ambition for Canada in matters of state was to be independent of the United States.

Chrétien thought that America was smug and uncaring, a country that hid behind its enormous wealth, its brashness, and its superiority to conceal poverty, inequality, and even racism. But he also saw European countries as too socialist, where governments were counted upon to solve all ills. Chrétien preferred the middle way that positioned Canada in between American individualism and European social democracies.[1]

Rather than use his pulpit to stake out bold policies in foreign affairs, Chrétien preferred the refuge of multilateralism, notably the United Nations. While campaigning in 1993, Chrétien promised that a Liberal government would support the international community in the revitalization of human rights. That may have sounded good to voters, but Chrétien never intended to take the lead in foreign policy. As long as Canada was deeply in debt, it would not be handing out cheques for development assistance or bragging at a NATO conference about increasing defence spending. Even so, he could not totally deflect himself from foreign affairs. Over his time in office he knew he would be obligated to attend international conferences, including the G7, G8, and G20, La Francophonie, APEC, the Commonwealth, and NATO.

Unlike Pierre Trudeau, who enjoyed grandstanding at international conferences, or Brian Mulroney, who forged close personal relationships at summits, Chrétien was content to play a secondary role when foreign leaders gathered. He was much more comfortable in his role as Canada's salesman-in-chief — leading delegations of provincial premiers and business leaders on missions around the world to sell Canadian goods and services — than taking bold positions as Canada's diplomat in chief.[2] Canada's contribution, thought Chrétien, was not in trying to solve the problems of the world but in being an exemplary country to its citizens.

CHRÉTIEN WAS DETERMINED TO land on middle ground in his relationship with American presidents. He would not take pot shots at the US simply to gain attention, but he didn't want it to look like he was in bed with the Americans either. Chrétien's instinct was to stand up to the Americans in public and be friendly with them in private. He understood the partnership would never be equal. He liked to say he never wanted to go fishing with the president of the United States because he didn't want to end up as the fish.

Over the previous 30 years, the relationship between Canadian prime ministers and American presidents had been all over the map. John Diefenbaker and John F. Kennedy despised one another. Pierre Trudeau got along with presidents Ford and Carter but struggled with Nixon and Reagan. Brian Mulroney sang *When Irish Eyes are Smiling* on stage with President Reagan and got George H.W. Bush to deliver on Canada's environmental concerns.

At a NATO meeting in Madrid in 1997, Chrétien was overheard to say, "I like to stand up to the Americans. It's popular. But you have to be very careful because they're our friends."[3] In his memoirs, Chrétien admitted that the powerful make for an easy target:

> When you're a mayor and you have a problem, you say it's the fault of the provincial government. When you're premier and you have a problem, you say it's the fault of the federal government. And since that the Federal government can't blame the Queen anymore, we blame the United States as much as we can, because it's the big shot.[4]

While creating the impression of distance between himself and President Clinton, the reality was that Chrétien was a great friend of the 42nd president. Because of their common interests in politics and sports, Clinton and Chrétien became close, even golfing buddies. Chrétien said that at summit meetings and on state visits he and Clinton would wallow in the tactics of election campaigns and vent their fury and frustration with the media. At one international conference, they escaped their security details and scampered over a stone wall. Even though Clinton was 15 years younger he could not match Chrétien's athleticism. But they could tease each other like brothers, with Chrétien prodding Clinton about his love of Big Macs.

Chrétien was close enough to Clinton to offer him brotherly advice on the Monica Lewinsky sex scandal: "Your private life is your own. You should just tell them all to go to hell. You're a good president, and the best thing you can do is keep doing a good job."[5] Privately, Chrétien would say that Clinton had a "zipper problem."

If Chrétien and Clinton were soulmates in the game of politics, their bond was hidden from view. Indeed, Chrétien argued he could do more for the United States by creating the illusion of distance. In one breath, Chrétien said he wanted Canada to be detached from America and in the other he offered to serve as a surrogate for the CIA.

> I have to tell you something. I don't want to get too close to you. Canada is your best friend, largest trading partner, and closest ally, but we are also an independent country. Keeping some distance will be good for the both of us. If we look as though we're the 51st state of the United States, there's nothing we can do for you internationally, just as the governor of a state can't do anything for you internationally. But if we look independent enough, we can do things for you that even the CIA cannot do.[6]

After Clinton's press secretary, Mike McCurry, issued glowing remarks about the friendship and close level of cooperation between the president and prime minister, he was asked to tone it down by Chrétien's communications director, Peter Donolo. "You're kidding me," said McCurry. "I have never had anyone ask me to downplay the connection before." It was not just that Chrétien wanted to assert Canada's independence from America, but he didn't like the politics of him getting too close to the big shots of the world.

Despite a campaign pledge to create distance between Canada and the United States, President Clinton was eventually featured on the back cover of Chrétien's memoirs. Clinton wrote that Chrétien knew as much about government as anyone he had ever seen and that they had a grand relationship: "He had enormous impact, not only because people liked him but because he is a genuinely good man. I doubt most Canadians know just how much Canada is admired as a result in the rest of the world." In Clinton's presidential memoirs he wrote that Chrétien was one of his best friends among world leaders, calling him an ally, confidant, and frequent golfing partner.[7]

During their seven overlapping years in office, Clinton and Chrétien faced few crises together and rarely called on one another for favours. Chrétien did persuade the American president to speak positively about the unity of Canada before the 1995 Québec referendum. And progress was made on "open skies" for air travel.

When Chrétien made a diplomatic gaffe and insulted America at the 1997 NATO meeting, he was happy to have a friend in the White House. At the summit, he told other world leaders that the American Congress operated by horse-trading: "You scratch my back, I'll scratch yours. You give me an airport and I'll give you a bridge. In Canada, we would be in jail for that." A nearby microphone broadcast his comments to the media room and it became a worldwide story.[8] Clinton told his good friend not to worry about it.

AMONG THE FEW SENSITIVE issues they faced together was the North America Free Trade Agreement. With NAFTA, both leaders needed to extricate themselves from campaign promises. Chrétien had campaigned against free trade in the 1993 election, as had Clinton in 1992, half-hearted promises since both leaders believed in free trade. In his memoirs, Chrétien pointed to a proposed North American free trade policy that he championed in 1971 as proof that he had always supported the idea.[9] His view was that Canada's true economic potential could be achieved only by opening itself to the world.[10] Free trade had been central to the beliefs of his political hero, Sir Wilfrid Laurier.

Coming from Shawinigan, Chrétien could see that much of what his community produced was destined for export. When Mulroney took the Canada-US Free Trade Agreement into the 1988 federal election, Chrétien did not disparage it on principle but said Mulroney had negotiated a bad deal for Canada. Chrétien understood the connection between trade and prosperity, which is why he invited free-traders to speak at Liberal policy workshops. In 1991, he told delegates at a Liberal-organized policy conference that protectionism was passé and that globalization was not right wing or left wing but simply a fact of life.

Building on the Free Trade Agreement with the United States, NAFTA was signed in December 1992 by the leaders of Canada, the United States, and Mexico. The Canadian government ratified the legislation without much fuss. But the deal had not yet been approved in the United States Congress and the newly elected Bill Clinton was looking to amend the deal with side agreements to cover labour and environmental standards.

In the 1993 Canadian election, Chrétien pledged to oppose NAFTA if the side agreements did not measure up. He said he would renegotiate both the Free Trade Agreement with the United States and NAFTA to obtain a subsidies code, an anti-dumping code, a more effective dispute resolution mechanism, and the same energy protection as Mexico.[11] The Liberal platform also referenced the need to protect Canada's fresh-water lakes and rivers from the Americans. Failing a successful renegotiation, Chrétien said the trade agreements would be abrogated, but only as a last resort.[12]

Chrétien's reservations about NAFTA got US presidential candidate Ross Perot very excited. "Mr. Chrétien, if you manage to block NAFTA from going through, I will erect a huge statue to you here in Texas," Perot declared. Perot was famous for saying that under NAFTA he could hear a giant sucking sound of jobs and investments going to Mexico. Chrétien sidestepped Perot. "Thank you very much, sir," he responded. "But, you know, there aren't many votes for me in Texas."[13] Chrétien later said that Perot should have offered to build a factory in Shawinigan.[14]

While Chrétien said the Tory-negotiated agreement left Canadian workers vulnerable, he warned voters in the 1993 election that the resolutely anti-trade policies of the NDP would grind the economy to a halt. He confronted one NAFTA opponent in the campaign by saying that Canada cannot build a wall at the border. If she didn't like trade, Chrétien said, she should vote for the NDP.

The day after the election, Clinton called Chrétien at his cottage to offer his congratulations. Chrétien took the call in his bedroom, calling in his grand-children to be part of the historic encounter. But Clinton got right down to business and raised their shared political problem on NAFTA.

Before Chrétien was sworn in as prime minister, he instructed Eddie Goldenberg, to speak with the American trade representative. Goldenberg wondered what he could accomplish in the absence of a cabinet and a minister of trade. Chrétien told him to make the best deal he could.[15] The speed with which Chrétien dismissed his campaign promise proves that it was never a serious commitment. Chrétien was not about to pull Canada out of a deal that would make the US a trading hub and Canada one of its spokes.

After Goldenberg set the parameters of a deal, Chrétien appointed Roy MacLaren, the most pro-free-trade MP he could find, to serve as his trade minister. Without breaking a sweat, the trade minister obtained a few flimsy side letters from the Americans on energy, culture, and water without the need to reopen the agreement.[16] A working group was established to seek review issues related to subsidies and dumping.[17]

Chrétien got what he wanted on two fronts. He attracted support from those who were concerned that Canada could not compete in a free trade zone with the low wages and loose environmental standards of Mexico. But he also sustained an agreement that he believed was in the best long-term interests of the country. He played his cards well.

Between 1993 and 2003, bilateral trade in goods and services between Canada and the United States doubled to almost $2 billion a day. According to Canada's ambassador to the United States, the number of controversial files involving trade declined by more than 90 per cent during the ten-year period, and less than 1 per cent of that trade was the subject of disputes.[18] The portion of Canada's GDP attributed to trade increased from 25 per cent to 43 per cent.[19] Trilateral trade within the North American region quadrupled between 1993 and 2014.[20]

The effects of NAFTA, combined with a lower dollar, made it easier for Canadian exporters to compete in foreign markets. Chrétien enhanced Canada's trading prospects by embracing the role of salesman-in-chief. He led numerous trade junkets around the world with provincial premiers and business leaders in tow. Liberal MP Mauril Belanger viewed the trade missions as not only good for business prospects but also for the unity of the country and an example of constructive federalism: "It provided an opportunity for leaders from different political parties to sit down in an airplane or hotel room far away from Canada to discuss or even iron out differences."

The premier of Newfoundland, Brian Tobin, observed that Chrétien and his nemesis, Lucien Bouchard, the sovereigntist premier of Québec, got along well on Team Canada trade missions: "They were more than polite; they were courteous and considerate of each other, and they joined with the other first ministers in sharing humorous war stories of life as a government leader."[21] Peter Donolo was pleasantly surprised when, on a Team Canada trade mission to India, Bouchard said that when travelling abroad Canada speaks with only one voice, that of the prime minister. The spouses and political staff of the premiers and the prime minister also got to know one another, which helped to create a sense of common purpose.

By supporting and implementing NAFTA, Chrétien earned the enmity of high-profile ultra-nationalists and anti-globalists like Maude Barlow. Barlow took to the streets and protested that there was not a sliver of difference between the Mulroney Tories and the Chrétien Liberals. Chrétien, according to Barlow, had become the political agent of big business interests and the neoliberal ideology that sustained them. A Globe and Mail editorial called Chrétien's conversion on NAFTA to be of Napoleonic proportions. But Chrétien suffered few political consequences for making the right call.

In his relationship with Bill Clinton, Chrétien got the best of both worlds. It did not appear to Canadians that he was taking direction from Clinton or polishing his shoes. But Chrétien's relationship with Clinton was as strong as any Canadian prime minister and American president before him. It would have astonished Canadian academics and foreign policy experts to hear Clinton speak so positively about Chrétien, a man they were convinced would flop on the world stage.

9/11

On the morning of September 11, 2001, Jean Chrétien was meeting with the Saskatchewan premier Lorne Calvert over breakfast at 24 Sussex Drive. David Collenette, the minister of Transportation, was delivering the keynote address at a conference of international airport executives in Montreal.[1]

Chrétien's meeting was interrupted after he was told by his executive assistant, Bruce Hartley, that a plane had crashed into the World Trade Center in New York. Initially, Chrétien assumed it was a minor incident and the conversation with Calvert continued. Collenette was at the podium delivering his prepared remarks when he sensed his usually attentive audience had become agitated. His assistant passed him a note: "Wind up your speech. There has been a tragedy." No one yet realized that the world was about to change.

Chrétien describes himself as calm in a crisis. He says he does not overreact and likes to solve problems quietly and methodically without turning them into drama. Like Franklin Roosevelt, whose wife Eleanor said he never lost his composure when Japan attacked Pearl Harbour, Chrétien didn't panic when the scale of the attacks on 9/11 became evident.[2] But he considered the situation serious enough to ask his wife to seek refuge at Harrington Lake, the prime minister's country retreat. She refused to leave his side.

The most pressing decision was what to do with the 224 planes that were over the Atlantic Ocean and destined for the United States. That issue landed in Collenette's lap. He said that it took air traffic controllers less than five minutes to determine which planes had sufficient fuel to return to their point of origin and which needed to land in North America. By then the United States had grounded all air traffic so any plane that entered American air space was at risk of being shot down. Short of ditching in the ocean, landing in Canada was the only option.

Collenette asked his deputy minister if he had the legal authority to decide where the planes should land: "We believe you do under the Aeronautics Act," she replied. It was not the definitive answer Collenette would have liked. There was no better place to get advice at that time so while Collenette was in his car driving back to Ottawa he issued the order allowing the planes to land in Canada.[3]

When Collenette made it to the Transport Canada Emergency Operations Centre, also known as Sit Cen, operation "Yellow Ribbon" was in full effect. Collenette said he focused on the facts at hand and avoided the images being shown on the television networks. Because of the risk that the planes being re-routed to Canada were controlled by terrorists, they were directed to less-populated areas. The town of Gander, Newfoundland, with a population of 10,000, received more than 12,000 air passengers.[4] Gander, and other locations in Atlantic Canada, had the double virtue of small populations, and, owing to the Second World War, runways that were long enough to handle large planes. Atlantic Canadians welcomed their visitors with open arms.

There were also 90 planes flying over the Pacific Ocean that were diverted to western Canadian airports. In total, some 33,000 travellers found themselves the beneficiaries of Canadian hospitality.

CHRÉTIEN DID NOT SPEAK with Collenette until 1:00 p.m. "You have made all the decisions," he told Collenette. "We don't need a cabinet meeting. Just carry on.'" Collenette had acted quickly and decisively. While it's surprising that he did not speak with Chrétien that morning, Collenette said that the prime minister was likely kept in the loop by his deputy minister speaking with the Clerk of the Privy Council.

But there was one decision that rose above Collenette to the prime minister. When a Korean Air liner failed to respond to the control tower in Anchorage, Alaska, it was put on the list of possible hijacked aircraft. Chrétien gave the American Air Force permission to pursue the plane over Canadian air space, and, if necessary, shoot down the aircraft after confirming the order with him beforehand.[5] Fortunately, communication was established before any missiles were fired. There is little doubt that if Chrétien had thought public safety was at risk, he would have given his permission to shoot down the plane.

Despite the crisis, Chrétien was not prepared to shut down Parliament Hill on September 11. That's even after the head of House of Commons security discovered an illegally parked car with a suspicious-looking package on the front seat. Chrétien wanted normalcy, not alarm, and rejected the recommendation to evacuate the parliamentary precinct.[6] He took a risk that others would have avoided.

Chrétien understood that symbolic support for America was just as important as deploying military resources. When he heard on the radio that Canadians were lining up to donate blood he went to a local clinic and gave them a pint of his own. Because he refused to allow his office to publicize the gesture, any inspirational benefits were lost. Chrétien spoke with Canada's ambassador to the United States, Michael Kergin, to find out how diplomatic staff in Washington D.C. were coping. While Chrétien sought to underplay the attack, he also told Kergin that the world would never be the same.

When Chrétien met Collenette in person that afternoon, he pressed his transport minister to open Canadian airspace for flying later that day. Collenette was surprised: "I don't think he understood the full logistical and security dimension of what was in play, which, I suppose, was understandable at the time." Before normalizing air traffic, Collenette wanted a better understanding of the risks. At a minimum, he first wanted to consult with his American counterpart. Chrétien's instincts were to go ahead with an event scheduled in Halifax for later that evening. He had initially misjudged the day and the moment, but eventually accepted the reality and the event was cancelled.

With the immediate crisis in hand, Chrétien turned his attention to a national ceremony that was being planned to honour those who lost their lives in the attack, including two dozen Canadians. Brian Tobin, the cabinet minister behind a massive unity rally in Montreal in the days before the 1995 Québec referendum, convinced Chrétien to hold an outdoor memorial service on Parliament Hill on Friday, September 14. When staff in the prime minister's office expressed concern about what would happen in the event of rain, Tobin replied, "People will bring umbrellas."

The event went ahead despite security concerns raised by the RCMP and local

Ottawa police. Chrétien said he did not want terrorists to dictate our conduct. He told the gathering of close to 100,000 people that Canada shared in the grief that Americans were feeling:

> There will be no silence from Canada. Our friendship has no limits. Generation after generation, we have travelled many difficult miles together side-by-side. We have lived through many dark times, always firm in our shared resolve to vanquish any threat to freedom and justice, and together with our allies, we will defy and defeat the threat that terrorism poses to all civilized nations. Even when we cry for our own dead, the message we send to our American friends is equally clear: do not lose courage. You're not alone in this. We are with you. The entire world is with you.[7]

A few days later, to remind Canadians that the target was terrorists and not Muslims, Chrétien visited a mosque in Ottawa.

PRESIDENT GEORGE W. BUSH called Chrétien on September 12 to express his appreciation for how Canada had welcomed air travellers. But when Bush addressed Congress on September 20, Canada did not make the long list of nations that had been singled out for praise. He thanked Egyptians, the people of El Salvador, and many other nations, but not Canada.

David Frum, a Canadian thinker and member of George W. Bush's speechwriting team, wrote that his stomach plunged when he read the first draft of the speech: "All references to Canada had been cut. The speech had been running long and somebody had reasoned that if we mentioned Canada, we'd have to praise all the other NATO countries by name, too, and many of them had been much quicker than Canada to offer aid and assistance."[8]

Frum was left to deal with the aftermath of the snub from his base in Washington D.C.:

> The omission stung and shamed Canadians with the power of a savage and unexpected slap, and the Canadians who felt the blow most keenly were America's best friends. I spent hours on the phone over the next week, taking calls from Canadians pleading for some explanation for the omission. Canada was not omitted to send some elliptical message.

Canada was omitted because it is easy to forget friends whose governments give you no cause to remember them.[9]

When Chrétien next met Bush at a private White House lunch on September 24, the president told him that no slight was intended by the omission.[10] Whether this was sincere or a conventional act of diplomacy is not clear, although Bush added that he felt there was no need to thank a brother.[11]

Chrétien was reluctant to go to Ground Zero, the World Trade Center site in New York City because he didn't want to have a photo-op over dead bodies. Nevertheless, two weeks after 9/11, Chrétien and other Canadian political leaders took a 15-minute tour of the site where 25 Canadians had been killed.

Unfortunately for Canada, American officials came to the hasty and incorrect conclusion that the terrorists who orchestrated the attacks on 9/11 had entered the United States from Canada. The implication was that an open Canadian border posed a threat to US security interests. Despite irrefutable evidence that the terrorists had never been to Canada, American officials, in some cases many years after the attack, never veered from that erroneous talking point.[12] Americans did not want to accept that the security failures were their own, including the fact that the terrorists learned their piloting skills in Florida. No red flags were raised when the trainees showed no interest in learning how to take off or land a plane. Had Chrétien's relationship with Bush been strong he might have been able to get the president to correct the record. But that never happened.

Chrétien demonstrated that he could handle himself when the world was in crisis. He remained calm and dispassionate, perhaps to a fault. But visits to America, a rally on Parliament Hill, speeches in the House of Commons, welcoming stranded airline passengers, even a pint of the prime minister's blood, were largely symbolic responses to the terrorist attacks. Our substantive response to 9/11 was yet to come. George W. Bush had been in office less than nine months when the world changed on 9/11. It was in managing the aftermath of this atrocity that the relationship between George W. Bush and Jean Chrétien would be defined.

THE EARLY BUSH YEARS

I t's not surprising that Jean Chrétien preferred the Democrat Bill Clinton to the Republican George W. Bush. Conventional wisdom tells us that a Liberal Canadian prime minister gets along best with a Democratic American president.

Unspoken preferences are one thing; public declarations are another. When Jean Chrétien told Bill Clinton that the Florida ballot counting that gave the win to George W. Bush over Al Gore was not legitimate, he wisely did so in private. But it was undiplomatic for Canada's ambassador to trumpet Al Gore's superior knowledge of Canadian-American issues in the middle of the 2000 American presidential election. "We know Vice-President Gore," said the Canadian ambassador. "He knows us. He's a friend of Canada."

The words were delivered during a speech in Ottawa, and they were true. Gore had spent eight years as vice president and had become well acquainted with Canada-US relations. Bush was the governor of Texas and, with good reason, knew more about Mexico than Canada. But diplomats are supposed to stay clear of the domestic politics of their host countries. The breach in protocol was made worse by the fact that the career diplomat in question was Raymond Chrétien, who happened to be the prime minister's nephew.

The prime minister liked to say that when his nephew called the White House his calls got answered because officials were told Chrétien was on the line.[1] But there was no advantage to Canada in what Raymond Chrétien said about Bush.

To add to the tension, Bush broke with tradition and made his first foreign trip after the election to Mexico rather than Canada. While the press called the move a snub, Chrétien said it mattered little. But it became one of many incidents that were catalogued by the media as proof that Canadian-American relations had taken a negative turn.

Chrétien had visited Washington the month after the president was sworn in and attended a 45-minute meeting in the Oval Office followed by a dinner with the president and his closest advisors. The leaders joked before the press about being cousins and going fishing together. When asked about Raymond Chrétien's remark, Bush said he was going to prove the Canadian ambassador wrong.[2]

Chrétien said he liked President Bush and that they had much in common. He said Bush was cordial, meticulous, and extremely polite and that they enjoyed talking about sports and politics.[3] Michael Kergin, Canada's ambassador to the US beginning in October 2000, thought the two leaders got along famously.

But for all the common interests and folksy charm, Chrétien and Bush were not friends. One telling sign is that during Chrétien's time in office Bush never made an official state visit to Canada and travelled north only to attend international summits. A Bush visit had been planned to Canada in May 2003, but was cancelled due to deteriorating relations. Near the end of Chrétien's term, his relations with the American president were nearly severed.

A RELATIVELY MODEST CANADA-US trade dispute arose in October 2000 after 72 PEI potatoes were discovered to carry the fungus Synchytrium endobioticum. Even though the fungus did not harm humans, the American government banned the importation of potatoes from PEI. In retaliation, if not good humour, Chrétien had PEI potatoes served to Bush at every meal when he visited Canada for the Summit of the Americas in Québec City in April 2001.[4]

A more costly and troublesome trade dispute arose after a single case of mad cow disease was detected on a farm in Alberta in May 2003. The Americans used the irritant to justify a ban on the importation of Canadian beef. Chrétien thought the ban was nothing more than an excuse for US producers to remove a competitor from the market so they could increase their prices and profits. The move devastated the Canadian beef industry and cost Canadian taxpayers billions of dollars in compensation. (While the taxpayers of Canada pitched in to help Alberta farmers, Chrétien was unimpressed that western Canadians gave his government so little credit for the support. Chrétien wondered, if the infected cows had come from the Maritimes, would "all those rich guys in Calgary" complain about him bailing out his friends in the East.)[5]

Had relations between Chrétien and Bush been stronger, the dispute over blemished PEI potatoes and a single mad cow might have been settled sooner and with fewer harmful effects to Canada. But Chrétien had little goodwill with Bush and the 43rd president was not about to go out of his way to do a favour for a Canadian prime minister who he thought was friendly to Democrats.

As a key architect of the Charter of Rights and Freedoms, Jean Chrétien was reluctant to pass legislation to limit individual rights. But a little more than a month after 9/11, his government introduced Bill C-36, the Anti-Terrorism Act. While the House of Commons justice committee met 19 times to evaluate the legislation, the bill was fast-tracked through Parliament, and came into force on December 11, just three months after 9/11.[6]

The bill made no reference to 9/11, but spoke of the need to counter acts of terrorism that constituted a substantial threat to both domestic and international peace and security. The object of the legislation was to suppress, investigate, and incapacitate terrorist activity. Before the Act was passed, the Criminal Code of Canada had not contained any reference to terrorist activity.

It did not pack the punch of the War Measures Act, the legislation passed mere days after the declaration of the First World War in 1914. But Bill C-36 nonetheless gave the police and national security agencies a stronger hand to both anticipate and defeat extremist groups, while toughening prison sentences for terrorists.

The conservative forces in the House of Commons did not put up much of a fight against the Anti-Terrorism Act. The fiercest critics came from within the Liberal party. "I don't know how many times I was told that I was just doing what George Bush wanted us to do," said Anne McLellan, the Public Security minister who navigated the bill through Parliament.

The key to bringing caucus members onside, she noted, was the support of Irwin Cotler, a Liberal MP who served on the House of Commons Justice Committee.

He was enormously helpful since he was viewed, and rightly so, by many in caucus, especially Québec caucus, as a global defender of civil

liberties and human rights. So, when Irwin said, 'Yes, we need this legislation because the primary responsibility of the national government in
ensuring the security of its citizens,' caucus members took notice. Irwin
Cotler helped us to make the case that our anti-terrorism legislation had
got the balance right.

After the bill was debated at committee, a sunset clause was added that required politicians to revisit and reaffirm some of the more intrusive elements
of the act every five years. This gave Chrétien a response to those who believed
he had moved too far and too fast. If there was evidence that his or any other
government had overreached with Bill C-36, it would have to defend itself,
typically at least once within its mandate.

There were two particularly controversial elements of Bill C-36. First, the
police were given the power to make preventive arrests and hold people suspected of planning a terrorist act without charge for up to 72 hours. Second,
judges were given the authority to compel a witness to testify in secret about
past associations and pending acts or face time in prison. With this provision, the government narrowed the definition of the constitutional right to
remain silent.

The bill also made it easier for the police to employ electronic surveillance
methods and to keep the findings of certain investigations secret. Further, it
made it a crime to fund terrorist groups, participate in or facilitate the activities of a terrorist group, or knowingly harbour a terrorist.

Chrétien thought he had struck the right balance between public safety and individual rights, believing that the new laws gave more weight to human rights
than most other countries. The legislation also had the advantage of demon-
strating to the Americans that we were serious about combatting terrorism.
In his memoirs, Chrétien boasted that while he was in office his government
never employed any of the more controversial elements of Bill C-36.[7]

The Conservatives were in power when the anti-terrorism bill came up for its
first renewal in 2007. As a minority government, the Tories could not overcome Liberal and NDP votes to annul the more intrusive provisions. It was not
until 2015 that a majority Conservative government passed Bill C-51, which
reinstated and even enhanced the anti-terrorism policing and investigative
powers that were in Chrétien's post-9/11 legislation. This time the Liberal caucus under the leadership of Justin Trudeau supported the bill.

WHILE CHRÉTIEN DID NOT want to appear either offside of public opinion or soft on terrorism after 9/11, it was evident that his heart was torn in this battle. On the first anniversary of 9/11, Chrétien told CBC news anchor Peter Mansbridge that the West was not doing all it could to address the problems that were festering in the developing world:

> You cannot exercise your powers to the point of humiliation for the others. That is what the Western world – not only the Americans, the Western world – has to realize. I do think that the Western world is getting too rich in relation to the poor world and necessarily will be looked upon as being arrogant and self-satisfied, greedy and with no limits. The eleventh of September is an occasion for me to realize it even more.[8]

Chrétien was roundly criticized for "blaming the victim." An editorial in the *Ottawa Citizen* pointed out to the prime minister that North America was attacked for what it represented: freedom of the individual, the equality of women, and rational inquiry.[9] Brian Mulroney said Chrétien was making the terrorists' arguments for them. "The root causes of terrorists are terrorists," said Mulroney. "We must hunt them down, bring them to justice, seize their assets and destroy their networks."[10] But Mulroney's predecessor, Joe Clark, who had reclaimed the leadership of the Progressive Conservative Party, came to Chrétien's defence: "I don't think there is any doubt that if you're sitting in the Third World [watching images of Western wealth] ... that can create a resentment that can lead to extremism."

The Americans were sufficiently unhappy with Chrétien's interview that the US defence secretary cancelled a meeting with Canada's defence minister.[11]

Whether intended as retaliation or not, Chrétien was concerned that Americans might cause harm to the Canadian economy by thickening their borders in the name of national security. Chrétien needed someone to manage the trade file who understood business and had the trust of American politicians on the security side. That person was John Manley, who had previously served Chrétien in the industry and foreign affairs portfolios.

Under Manley's leadership, a cabinet committee was established to oversee national security and the Canada-US border. Just three months after 9/11, the Smart Border Accord was signed by Manley and the US Homeland Security Secretary, Tom Ridge. The accord included a 30-point action plan, which included enhanced border security while facilitating the flow of people and goods. It also dealt with securing critical infrastructure and enabled the sharing of information between governments. Other key elements of the accord included common standards for biometrics, the use of permanent resident cards for all new immigrants arriving in Canada, and the Nexus system to expedite cross-border travel.

Despite the various measures applied by both governments to ensure the continued free flow of goods, there was compelling evidence of diminished trade between Canada and the United States after 9/11. Patrick Grady, a former official with the finance department, concluded in a paper for *Global Economics* that 9/11 ended a decade of strong growth in trade following the signing of 1989 Canada-US trade agreement.[12] Grady's analysis revealed that the portion of Canadian exports destined for the United States fell from 86.7 per cent in 2000 to 79.3 per cent in 2007. Excluding energy and forestry products, Grady's analysis suggested that Canadian exports of goods to the United States were 12.5 per cent lower than would otherwise have been expected.

It is impossible to know how trade would have been affected had Chrétien not given Manley the mandate to work with his American counterpart to facilitate the free flow of goods and services after 9/11. But there is no doubt that Chrétien understood the gravity of the situation and implemented the measures at his disposal on security to minimize the potential harm.

YES TO AFGHANISTAN

Following 9/11, Canada faced two major decisions on the deployment of troops in the war against terrorism and threats to international peace and security. The first decision was Canada's role in the invasion of Afghanistan in the months after 9/11. The second decision was whether to join the United States-led coalition that invaded Iraq in March 2003.

Canada joined the American-led campaign in Afghanistan — Operation Enduring Freedom — by committing a battle group of 800 soldiers and a contingent of special forces to Kandahar. Canada also provided C-130 air transport support that was based in the United Arab Emirates and ships that were operating in the Arabian Gulf. Canada was in this fight for over a decade, deploying more than 40,000 armed forces members in the largest Canadian military engagement since the Second World War.[1] A total of 158 Canadian soldiers and one diplomat were killed.

THE INTERNATIONAL SECURITY ASSISTANCE Force in Afghanistan was established through a December 2001 United Nations Security Council resolution. The mission had three objectives: conduct a war against the Taliban, train the Afghan National Security Forces, and assist in the rebuilding of Afghanistan institutions.

The Europeans wanted to exclude Canada from the mission because they thought it lacked the willingness to fight. Rick Hillier, who was chief of defence staff, wrote that the Europeans remembered our risk-averse approach in the Bosnian War, when Canada resisted pressure from US and the UK to initiate a bombing campaign. They had no faith, wrote Hillier, that Canada would pull its weight if things got tough.[2]

The higher ranks in the Canadian military also did not want to become part of ISAF (International Security Assistance Force), concluding it was a high-risk mission with no clear objectives or end in sight.[3] Hillier wrote that the Canadian military brass had little concept of what 9/11 had meant to the world:

> Even in the military, there was no appreciation that we had all witnessed one of those pivotal moments in world history. All senior officers, including many generals, said that … things had not changed fundamentally, that this was just a blip, just another attack.

This did not square with Hillier's view that 9/11 had changed everything. Hillier was not a "sausage general," a term used for those who had long stretches serving in the comforts of West Germany but lacked hard combat experience.[4] Though he had served at the base in Germany, Hillier also had experience commanding a division in Bosnia-Herzegovina.[5]

A Canadian battalion ultimately joined an American division in Kandahar. Hillier didn't believe the cabinet understood the mission, which was our first on-the-ground combat mission since the Korean War.[6/7] Former Chrétien defence minister John McCallum recalled the military telling him that ISAF was a treacherous mess, but he said he never understood how a security force in Kabul was more dangerous than a combat force in Kandahar.[8] The award-winning book *The Unexpected War: Canada in Kandahar* by Eugene Lang and Janice Gross Stein, chronicles how Canada ended up in Kandahar. The conclusion: it had a lot to do with the politics of Canadian-American relations.

Tragically, the first Canadian deaths in Afghanistan were caused by friendly fire. On April 18, 2002, an American pilot, without clearance, mistakenly dropped a 1,000-pound bomb on Canadian troops engaged in a night-time training exercise on a designated firing range. Four Canadian soldiers were killed and eight seriously wounded. President Bush called Chrétien to offer condolences on behalf of the American government. The deaths were a grim reminder to the Canadian public of the consequences of war and the dangers of the mission. A massive outpouring of grief included a nationally televised remembrance ceremony attended by the governor general and Prime Minister Chrétien.

The seriousness of the mission stood in sharp contrast to the publicized conduct of the defence minister, Art Eggleton. Eggleton became embroiled in a controversy when his former girlfriend was reported to be the beneficiary of a $36,500 untendered contract to write a paper about environmental illness and post-traumatic stress disorder among Canadian Forces personnel. Eggleton claimed that the funds were from his Parliamentary office budget so the usual procurement oversight was not required. The author of the report claimed her personal experience with mould was the source of her expertise in writing about environmental illness and chronic fatigue syndrome.[9]

The controversy came to light the month after the friendly-fire deaths. Chrétien's first reaction was to dump Eggleton from cabinet. Eggleton's former girlfriend said it would break her heart if her former beau lost his seat at the table. Chrétien seemed unconcerned with her feelings.[10] "Perhaps after almost nine years, people got a bit too comfortable," Chrétien observed when announcing Eggleton's dismissal in May 2002.[11] (Eggleton stayed on as a Liberal MP, but was appointed to the Senate in 2004 by Paul Martin.)

John McCallum, a former chief economist for the Royal Bank of Canada, was appointed to the defence portfolio. When asked at his swearing-in ceremony if he had any military experience: "Well, I served as a cadet for two years when I was in high school." That suited Chrétien, who preferred ministers to be outsiders to their departments and not captive to them.

McCallum's initial priorities were the procurement of new equipment and a larger military budget.[12] But his department had a more pressing issue. They needed to respond to a diplomatic note from the United States asking Canada to renew and revise its troop presence in Afghanistan. Canada's chief of the defence staff, Ray Henault, also sought permission to accept an invitation from the American military to attend a planning meeting in Florida on potential operations in Iraq. That decision was elevated to Chrétien, who refused.[13]

The hawkish and prickly American defence secretary, Donald Rumsfeld, had turned his attention away from Afghanistan and towards war in Iraq. He wanted Canada to fill a breach and lead an ISAF mission in Kabul, Afghanistan so that more American troops could be liberated to depose Saddam Hussein in Iraq.[14/15] Rumsfeld had more faith in the Canadian military than he did European troops. "The problem is, there aren't enough of you," he told Hillier. "We'd like to have double, triple or quadruple [the number of Canadians] around."[16]

Beyond the geopolitical dimensions of Canadian involvement in Iraq, Chrétien was worried that if he mismanaged the issue, Paul Martin might convince a significant number of Liberal MPs to rebel against his leadership.[17] Martin had been equivocal about Canada's involvement in the war so it was not clear what side of the issue he would come down on.[18] Better, thought Chrétien, to take Iraq off the table by consuming Canadian military capacity with a renewed commitment to Afghanistan. No one would accuse Canada of shirking its international peace and security responsibilities if we had boots on the ground where the Taliban was lurking. Chrétien knew this would satisfy the Americans while Paul Martin would lose a potential wedge issue.

When McCallum went to Chrétien in January 2003 to get his permission for a new Canadian mission in Afghanistan, the meeting lasted less than 15 minutes. McCallum remarked how easy it was to get an approval from Chrétien. "Yes," Chrétien responded, "but don't come around here too often."[19]

The military brass only learned of the decision to send 2,000 troops to Kabul when McCallum announced it in the House of Commons. As Hillier dryly noted:

> Surprise is a well-established principle of war, but we soldiers like to surprise the enemy, and in this case we were surprised by our minister... The driving force behind the decision was clearly not our readiness or ability to carry out the mission, but the political cover needed to allow Canada to say no to the United States when asked to participate in operation Enduring Freedom.[20]

Canada committed to taking over in Kabul in August 2003. Chrétien concluded this was a "very good deal for Canada." By that he meant it was a safer mission for Canadian troops than what they might face on the ground in Iraq.

ON APRIL 23, 2003, the UN Security Council authorized the expansion of the ISAF mission from the areas around Kabul to all of Afghanistan. Hillier worried that Canadian troops did not have the proper support in place to function properly in Kabul:

> One equipment challenge reared its head immediately; we had not resolved the shortage of desert kit and we still had green camouflage uniforms as opposed to the lighter coloured desert pattern camouflage

... The shortage of available fabric made it simply impossible to get Canadian desert pattern uniforms for soldiers in time for this mission ... [and] the majority of our equipment was passed its expiry date.[21]

The green uniforms looked like, and were nicknamed, "relish." Troops had to be flown into Afghanistan on borrowed aircraft and Canada needed American ground transport to reach their bases.[22]

The other challenge that worried Hillier was that his troops were exhausted:

> We did not have nearly enough soldiers, and the ones that we did have were fatigued from the Bosnian experience, the constant rotations in and out of the former Yugoslavia and the great sense that nothing was quite a change for the better. We had "ghost" units — battalions or regiments that were supposed to have 750 or 800 people on strength but which instead could muster maybe 450 soldiers, and out of that 20 per cent or more would be unavailable for deployment for one reason or another.[23]

Chrétien's longer-term plan was for the military to extract the 2,000 troops from Kabul by the fall of 2004 and replace them with 200 troops as part of a provincial reconstruction team. The mission was succeeding just as Paul Martin became prime minister in December 2003.

As the ISAF mission in Kabul came to an end there was much debate within the Canadian government about exactly where the 200 to 300 members of the provincial reconstruction teams would be. Canada's ambassador to Afghanistan, future Conservative cabinet minister Chris Alexander, recommended Kandahar.[24] There were safer locations, but they had already been claimed by other countries that were quicker to choose where to deploy their troops. Chrétien later suggested that indecision within the Martin government resulted in Canadian troops being sent to the killing fields around Kandahar.[25]

Chrétien was more reluctant than most to go to war, but he was clearly not a pacifist. In 2015, Chrétien wrote in *The Globe and Mail* that peaceful dialogue does not always work, that war was sometimes unavoidable.[26] The mission in Afghanistan was Canada's key contribution to what the US described as a worldwide war against terror. Canada demonstrated that it retained a worthy military force and that it was prepared to fight for a just cause.

Of the 158 brave Canadian soldiers who lost their lives in Afghanistan, only six fell during Chrétien's watch. But the casualties did not alter his view that force was needed to achieve peace and security.

NO TO IRAQ

Six weeks after Jean Chrétien was elected Liberal leader in June 1990, Saddam Hussein invaded Kuwait. At first, Chrétien said Canada would have to join its allies in the fight, provided the war was sanctioned by the United Nations or NATO.[1] In mid-September, he was critical of Brian Mulroney for not recalling Parliament to debate Canada's role in the conflict.[2] In November, he told the Liberal party youth wing that he wanted to be friends with the United States, "but I don't want to be looked upon as someone who just says, 'Yes, yes, yes, yes' when the big boss calls." He accused Canada's foreign affairs minister, Joe Clark, of trying to look like "Rambo" with his tough talk.[3]

In January 1991, Chrétien declared that if there was to be a war, the 2,000 Canadian military deployed in the Persian Gulf region should return home: "We strongly, strongly reject the use of force now." He said war would be dangerous and it would not solve the problem.[4] But his position was not unanimously supported in the Liberal caucus.

John Turner, Chrétien's predecessor, applauded the decision of the Mulroney government from his seat in the House of Commons. Chrétien appeared to be losing control of his caucus and was labelled an appeaser to a brutal dictator. A week later, Chrétien had a change of heart, saying that because the war was inevitable, it was his duty to support our troops. To get Saddam Hussein out of Kuwait "you have to crush him," Chrétien told reporters.[5]

As PRIME MINISTER, CHRÉTIEN was, for the most part, a reliable and consistent supporter of US-led military incursions around the world. And it didn't matter whether the actions were sanctioned by the United Nations or not. Allan Rock said that the lack of a resolution did not stop the prime minister from supporting Canada's involvement in the 1998–99 war in Kosovo:

> Kosovo was not sanctioned by the Security Council because of the Russian veto. [Nonetheless], Canada took full part. It was possible in that circumstance, however, to use a clause in the NATO charter as a basis for intervention. But you will find serious arguments from international lawyers about whether that clause justifies the use to which it was put. But it was a basis with which to intervene. Kosovo was legitimate. Whether it was legal is a different matter. We thought that it was.

Defending his government's support for the Kosovo campaign Chrétien said that Canada's participation was "the most recent example of how our foreign-policy is dictated not only by our interests but our values. Our values as Canadians. Our basic human values."[6] Chrétien did not lust for war and he did not seek credit for Canada's involvement in Kosovo. He rejected numerous speech drafts that spoke of the glory and valour of our troops.

When Bill Clinton signed the Iraq Liberation Act of 1998 calling for regime change, Chrétien told Winnipeg schoolchildren, "If you don't want to pay the price of maintaining peace, you will have a lot of war." Speaking later in the House of Commons, Chrétien took direct aim at Saddam Hussein:

> If there is one thing Canadians cannot abide that is any flaunting of the clearly expressed wish of the United Nations Security Council. And if there is one question on which the Security Council has spoken out clearly, it is the threat that Saddam Hussein represents to his neighbours, and the entire world, with his weapons of mass destruction – his nuclear, chemical and biological weapons. We have proof that they were producing and are still producing them, and we want to terminate this production.[7]

By this he meant that Canada was prepared to go to war against Iraq at that time, arguing that a military strike against Iraq was justified to secure compliance with Security Council resolution 687 and all other Security Council resolutions concerning Iraq. Chrétien invoked the policy that Brian Mulroney had followed in 1991 when he made UN approval a necessary precondition to Canadian involvement in Kuwait against Iraq in 1991.[8]

THE CLERK OF THE PRIVY Council sent Chrétien a briefing note on August 14, 2002, warning that war in Iraq was inevitable, but with untold consequences:

> U.S. action against Iraq to implement regime change is a question of when, not if, using the justification that the Iraqi government is a sponsor of terrorism and a developer of weapons of mass destruction ... The integrity of Iraq and regional stability will be severely threatened if Saddam Hussein is ousted, particularly if Israel is drawn into the conflict .... (and with the) enormous challenge of rebuilding a post-Saddam Iraq (the Iraqi opposition remains divided and no clear future leadership has been publicly identified).[9]

Chrétien knew that a war in Iraq was inevitable with or without Canada. But he did not believe the case for war had been made. And he did not believe that a consensus for war could be achieved at the United Nations. At the 2002 World Summit on Sustainable Development in Johannesburg, South Africa, Chrétien sparred with British Prime Minister Tony Blair about the pending war: "Okay Tony. If we're getting into the business of replacing leaders we don't like, who's next?"

Chrétien thought that Canada should not be in the business of removing dictators, especially in a turbulent part of the world. Allan Rock recalled the prime minister asking that if it was about regime change then who gets to pick the regime that needs to change. "Maybe my name is on a list somewhere," Chrétien told Rock. "I want to see the list."

Chrétien pointed out to Blair that there were terrible dictators all over the world — such as Robert Mugabe of Zimbabwe — but Iraq got noticed because it had oil. "I want to be with you guys," he said, "but I can't go without a United Nations resolution." Blair accepted his advice and brought up the need for a UN resolution when he met President Bush at Camp David the following weekend. After that meeting, the president said he would give the United Nations another try.[10]

On September 9, 2002, Chrétien and Bush met to announce improved border security at the Ambassador Bridge between Detroit and Windsor. Chrétien told Bush that Canada would join the war if it was sanctioned by the United Nations: "If you get a resolution, George, don't be worried, I'll be with you. But I have to tell you, I've been reading all my briefings about the WMD and I'm not convinced. I think the evidence is very shaky." More than shaky, Chrétien said. There wasn't enough evidence to persuade a Shawinigan municipal court judge. This was the sort of common-sense test Chrétien was inclined to impose.

Bush offered to send his intelligence experts to Ottawa to brief Chrétien. The prime minister declined, saying Canadians wanted their government to be independent on such matters.[11] Besides, Canadian officials close to the prime minister believed that the CIA evidence that Bush relied upon was biased. Chrétien was told that the foreign policy experts from the US State Department had been crowded out by White House and Defence Department officials. While Chrétien refused an American-led briefing, the military and the defence minister, Bill Graham, did not. But Graham thought the prime minister was keeping his options open, especially when he told his caucus on October 2, 2002, that Canada would go to Iraq if the United Nations was convinced that war was justified.

ON NOVEMBER 8, 2002, UNSC Resolution 1441 gave Iraq one final opportunity to disarm or face "serious consequences." Saddam Hussein relented on November 13 and agreed to allow weapons inspections to resume under a team led by Hans Blix.

There were strong advocates for and against the Iraq war within Chrétien's government. The more business-friendly ministers supported the war out of a desire to oust Saddam Hussein and maintain good relations with the US. Those who were opposed came from the more progressive wing of the Liberal caucus. According to senior federal bureaucrats, the three key departments — Defence, Foreign Affairs, and Finance — operated under the assumption that Canada would send troops to fight in Iraq.

Some caucus members and business leaders worried that Canada would suffer economic reprisals for staying out of the war. Chrétien called this position nonsense: "Give me a list of all the goods and services that the Americans are buying from us just because they love us." No one could convince Chrétien that American business leaders were influenced by emotion.[12]

The sentiment within the prime minister's inner circle opposed lining up with George W. Bush. At a NATO summit in Prague, Chrétien's communications director, Françoise Ducros, told Chris Hall of CBC News that Bush was a moron. While Hall made no mention of the observation in his own reporting, Bob Fife of the *National Post* overheard the remark and reported the story.[13] Fife didn't attribute the quote to Ducros, but it didn't take long for the culprit to be identified. Chrétien wrote in his memoirs that he was ready and willing to defend Ducros, in part because she was coaxed into making the comment. He said it was not a mortal offence, but because she was planning to return to a job in the federal civil service he accepted her resignation.[14]

Another Bush insult came from Liberal MP Carolyn Parrish. She was overheard saying, "Damn Americans, I hate those bastards." Bill Graham remarked to the US ambassador to Canada, Paul Cellucci, that just as the American president can't control every crazy statement made by a Republican congressman, so Chrétien can't be held to account for Canadian wackos. A more significant diplomatic transgression came from a Chrétien cabinet minister. Herb Dhaliwal said that Bush had let America and the world down by "not being a statesman."[15] Chrétien told Dhaliwal he was wrong but did not insist on his minister making a public apology. This incident led to the cancellation of a planned lunch between the prime minister and Cellucci.[16]

Chrétien did himself no favours with Bush when, in May 2003, while speaking with reporters in the back of an airplane on the way to Greece for a Canada-European Union summit, he talked about the dangers of the US budget deficit, even reminiscing about his friend Bill Clinton. The Bush administration had reached its breaking point with Chrétien, culminating in a telephone call from National Security Advisor Condoleezza Rice from aboard Air Force One to her Canadian counterpart, Claude Laverdure. Rice declared that the relationship between Bush and Chrétien was "irreparably broken."

CHRÉTIEN INSISTED THAT THE justification for war with Iraq was lacking. Speaking to the Chicago Council on Foreign Relations on February 13, 2003, Chrétien said that while Canada supported the defeat of state-sponsored terrorism and taking weapons away from dangerous dictators, war must always be the last resort because of the human suffering it produces and the inevitable unforeseen consequences. And any war, he argued, should be first authorized by the United Nations. Rather undiplomatically, he turned his guns on his American hosts. "Great strength is not always perceived by others as benign. Not everyone around the world is prepared to take the word of the United

States on faith."[17] In other words, the United States and its president were not to be trusted. Harsh and brave words, especially when spoken on American soil. A senior bureaucrat who worked on the speech believed honesty is what America should expect from a friend: "It was a responsible way to act. And doing it in public and without fear gave it a weight it would otherwise not have had."

While UN authority was Chrétien's threshold for participation, he had also said previously that the UN should not be in the business of declaring war. In the lead-up to the 1991 war in Kuwait he had asked, "What is the fundamental principle of the United Nations? It is the peaceful resolution of disputes, not the initiation of wars."[18]

When pressed by reporters about the kind of evidence he needed to believe that Iraq possessed weapons of mass destruction, Chrétien responded: "I don't know. A proof is a proof. What kind of a proof? It's a proof. A proof is a proof, and when you have a good proof, it's because it's proven." The quote saturated the airwaves and became the subject of ridicule. The *National Post* wrote that when the proof came it would be too late for action, and by not pre-emptively striking, the US and its allies would assume intolerable risks, including the prospect of Hussein acquiring nuclear weapons.[19]

Many international observers believed that Saddam's use of chemical weapons on the Kurdish people in 1988 constituted an act of genocide. But Saddam had not used chemical weapons in the following 15 years. That gave Chrétien some comfort that another act of genocide was unlikely.

Even though Canada's two-year term on the United Nations Security Council had expired in December 2000, Chrétien thought he could play middleman between the United States and the United Kingdom on one side, and France, Germany, Russia, and China, on the other.[20] Chrétien told his foreign affairs minister, Bill Graham, that there were times when it was better not to be on the Security Council.[21]

Eugene Lang, who served as an advisor to defence ministers John McCallum and Bill Graham, believes that Chrétien would have pushed for a Canadian presence in Iraq had he thought that genocide was taking place:

> Saddam Hussein was a tyrant and a dictator. But there were many other countries who oppressed their population and we did not intervene mil-

itarily. Had this been genocide in Iraq I am convinced that the Liberal government would have been on the ground, even at the pointy end of the stick.

But far from working the halls of the UN to build the case for war, Chrétien did the opposite, persuading other countries to follow Canada's lead in not joining the "coalition of the willing," as Bush called it. Mexican president Vicente Fox and Chilean president Ricardo Lagos told Chrétien they wouldn't join the Americans if Canada did not take part.[22] In effect, Chrétien was the leader of the coalition of the unwilling.

But there were more important opponents to the war that Chrétien could count on. Even if a United Nations resolution passed in plenary it would still need to pass the Security Council where any one of Russia, France, and China could exercise their veto.[23] Because a veto was inevitable, Chrétien knew that it was almost certain that the United Nations would never sanction war in Iraq, and his offers to mediate an agreement were, at best, gratuitous.

Predictably, the Conservative opposition supported the American position. On January 29, 2003, Stephen Harper made the case for war in the House of Commons:

> This party will not take its position based on public opinion polls. We will not take a stand based on focus groups. We will not take a stand based on phone-in shows … or other vagaries of public opinion. We will take our position the way real leaders and great nations make decisions at such moments in history … In my judgment, Canada will eventually join with the allied coalition if war on Iraq comes to pass.

At the same time that Canada was being pushed to make a decision to send troops into Iraq, there was also pressure to maintain or enhance our presence in Afghanistan. It was a challenge and an opportunity. Bill Graham, Chrétien's minister of foreign affairs, took the view that staying in Afghanistan "gave us cover for not going to Iraq."[24] The politics of the situation was not lost at National Defence headquarters. "Everyone in uniform," noted Rick Hillier, "recognized the intense desire of Prime Minister Jean Chrétien's government to stay out of the [Iraq] invasion force; that the American actions in Iraq were politically charged; and that how we dealt with this might affect our long-term relationship with the United States."[25]

On March 17, 2003, the British Foreign Office pressed the Canadian government on whether it would provide military, political, and humanitarian support for the invasion of Iraq. British officials gave a deadline of noon that day. Chrétien delivered his answer not in a diplomatic communiqué but in the House of Commons. Moments before rising in the House he read the official statement to the ministers of foreign affairs and defence in the prime minister's office. While they were asked for their views on wording, Chrétien said that his decision on the matter was final.

Given the enormous pressure both within Canada and from our allies, senior cabinet minister Anne McLellan said that Chrétien's instincts were needed most at that moment:

> There was something visceral about [Chrétien's] decision. His gut told him that this was not the way to go for Canada: there was too much confusion, too much uncertainty around the existence of weapons of mass destruction, that people were acting too hastily without knowing what the consequences would be. He did what he thought was right for Canada and its citizens. He would never have acted out of fear, even if that meant irritating the United States.

The Americans were not warned that the announcement was coming, something the foreign affairs minister thought was a mistake. After Chrétien spoke in the House of Commons, the US ambassador to Canada was given the news he didn't want to hear. But he was also told that Canada would say good things about the president and bad things about Saddam Hussein. Condoleezza Rice told her staff in the White House that the rhetoric coming out of Canada would be on a low boil, "enough to satisfy Canadian public opinion without being belligerent or provocative."[26]

Derek Burney, Canada's ambassador the United States from 1989 to 1993, thought Chrétien made the right decision but that his tactics fell short of the mark: "Announcing it in the House of Commons to wild cheers was, in my view, pretty shabby treatment of an ally that protected our national security." Burney recalled that when Mulroney decided not to get involved in the US Strategic Defence Initiative he phoned Reagan privately, in advance: "He did not want to score cheap political points to show that he could stand up to the U.S."

Bush's chief of staff, Andrew Card, told Chrétien that the White House always thought Canada had been making political noise but would "do the right thing" in the end. But he did not accuse Chrétien of double-crossing the United States:

> You told us right from the beginning what you intended to do, and it was our mistake that we did not take you seriously. We assumed that, at the last moment, a practical guy … would decide to come along. That was our fault. We should have believed you. Others may have double-crossed us, but not you.[25]

The nickname that staff in the west wing of the White House gave Chrétien was "Dino." That was short for dinosaur, stemming from their view that Chrétien had yet to clue in to how the world had changed since 9/11.[28]

But what bothered the Bush administration most was how Canada used its influence to keep other nations to stay out of the war, notably Mexico.

In his public statement, Chrétien claimed he had worked hard to forge a compromise at the Security Council. "Unfortunately," Chrétien declared, "we were not successful. If military action proceeds without a new resolution of the Security Council, Canada will not participate."[29] To take some sting out of the decision, the government stated that Canadian ships would remain in the Gulf region and would continue their mission against terrorism.[30]

Brian Tobin said Chrétien made a gutsy call because it ran contrary to expectations. It was proof, Tobin said, that Chrétien could not be intimidated. Not by the prime minister of the United Kingdom and not by the president of the United States.

STEPHEN HARPER, ALONG WITH his foreign affairs critic Stockwell Day, took the unusual step of writing to the *Wall Street Journal* to share their disgust with Chrétien's decision:

> For the first time in history, the Canadian government has not stood beside its key British and American allies in their time of need. The Canadian Alliance — the official opposition in parliament — supports the American and British position because we share their concerns, their worries about the future if Iraq is left unattended to, and their

fundamental vision of civilization and human values. Disarming Iraq is necessary for the long-term security of the world, and for the collective interests of our key historic allies and therefore manifestly in the national interest of Canada. Make no mistake, as our allies work to end the reign of Saddam and the brutality and aggression that are the foundations of his regime, Canada's largest opposition party, the Canadian Alliance will not be neutral. In our hearts and minds, we will be with our allies and friends. And Canadians will be overwhelmingly with us.[31]

Harper and Day also spoke of resentment in Western Canada, suggesting that Chrétien's decision was intended to appease Québec public opinion. Alberta politician Ted Morton described it this way: "As the Iraqi war reminded us, Canadian foreign policy is set by public opinion in Québec, which has meant abandoning our historical allies."[32]

WHEN OPPOSITION POLITICIANS POINTED out that 100 Canadian troops on exchange with American forces were in the Iraq war zone, Chrétien was unperturbed. In addition to the troops, Canada left three ships in place in the region, which exceeded the contribution for all but three countries that were part of the US coalition. When pressed by defence department legal advisors about the rules of engagement, Chrétien provided a non-answer: "We are not parties to the conflict, and the ships are staying where they are." Bill Graham thought the generals leaked information to the press in the hopes that it would force the government to clarify its position.[31] Chrétien thought that removing our embedded forces would have been an unnecessary slap in the face to our closest ally. It was also a way to participate without endorsing US policy. Canada's defence minister was happy to have something positive to say to the American ambassador.[34]

While Bush said little about Canada's decision, he was unhappy. By agreement, a Bush state visit to Canada was cancelled. Chrétien said he was relieved not to have Bush exposed to anti-war protests on the streets of Ottawa or in the House of Commons.[35]

There was no substantive diplomatic retaliation against Canada for not joining the American-led coalition, although Canada was excluded from the "Five Eyes" community for a short period. (Five Eyes is an intelligence-gathering alliance made up of Canada, Australia, New Zealand, the United Kingdom, and the United States.) This was the equivalent of a two-minute minor penalty in hockey. There were no direct trade sanctions against Canada. Chrétien reminded Bush that buying oil from its most trusted supplier would always be in American interests and that many American baseball players would still play with Canadian-made baseball bats.

A poll of Canadian business leaders showed that 57 per cent had feared economic harm from the decision not to participate in the Iraq war. The head of the Canadian Council of Chief Executives, Tom d'Aquino, warned that "millions of micro-transactions going across the border" would be made more difficult for Canada. *Globe and Mail* columnist John Ibbitson wrote that Canada would pay a price for not going along with George W. Bush. But none of these fears were realized.

BRIAN MULRONEY, WHO ADVOCATED for Canadian participation in the Iraq war, predicted that our relations with the American government would improve, but only when Chrétien was replaced by Paul Martin.[36]

It's not idle speculation to say that another prime minister might have made a different call. Almost certainly, Stephen Harper would have sent Canadian troops to Iraq. Eddie Goldenberg said Canada should be grateful that Martin was not in the top job in 2003 because it's likely he also would have sent the military to the front lines in Iraq.

Jack Layton, the leader of the NDP, noted that Martin spoke volumes with his silence when the Iraq war was being debated. John Manley thought Martin's view on Iraq "was based on what way the wind was blowing." Sheila Copps, then Chrétien's minister of Canadian Heritage, said that Martin had been working very hard to get Chrétien to join the Americans in the war: "There's no doubt in my mind that if Paul Martin had been the leader, we would have gone to Iraq with the United States." Peter Donolo takes a similar view: "Martin was a huge believer in conventional wisdom and elite opinion. He had a Tony Blair-like ideology. And he was cagey with what he was saying in the media."

While campaigning to replace Chrétien as Liberal leader, Martin said he would conduct bilateral relations with the United States on a more sophisticated basis: "Our goal must be to keep our two nations open to each other."

In what the *New York Times* suggested was a reference to the Iraq war, Martin added, "The absence of consensus in the U.N. should not condemn us to inaction. Multilateralism, after all, is a means not an end ... Let's not forget that September 11 was a watershed for Canada too."[37] Martin told biographer John Gray that he didn't think Canada could protect itself from international terrorism by ignoring the fact that it was part of North America. "So I think it's going to require greater cooperation with the Americans in terms of defence."[38]

Martin was worried about more than the damage to Canada-US relations. He told Larry Summers that he would not attend a session on Canada–US relations because it would "present another opportunity for the media to jump on the differences in his and Chrétien's positions."[39]

When Martin formed his cabinet, he picked David Pratt as defence minister. Pratt had been an outspoken advocate for the Iraq war while chairing the House of Commons defence committee.[40] On the day after he was sworn in as prime minister, Martin visited National Defence headquarters, a place Chrétien oddly avoided in his ten years in office. Martin told the officers, "No nation can isolate itself from the perils and the trials and the tribulations that the world goes through."[41]

George W. Bush had placed a moratorium on countries that did not participate in the war, preventing them from bidding on $18.6 billion in budgeted reconstruction contracts in Iraq. The ban was lifted the month after Paul Martin became prime minister. After having breakfast with Bush, Martin chose to highlight the difference he was making, saying, "It actually does show that working together you can arrive at a reasonable solution."[42]

IN HIS MEMOIRS, CHRÉTIEN wrote that he was mystified by Bush's decision to go to war. "If it was to establish democracy, that's a long shot." Worse, he argued, the Iraq war had proven that "with enough persistence, sacrifice, and resolve, the world's greatest superpower can be taken on and possibly beaten."

Chrétien said his decision was one of the most important moments in Canadian history. "It proved to the world and us that we are a proud and independent nation," he wrote, "that Canadians had held firm to our values as a keeper of the peace through multilateral institutions no matter how great the threats and uncertainties we faced."[43]

It's difficult to imagine that Chrétien had better information about the existence of weapons of mass destruction in Iraq than the US president or the British prime minister. The difference was that Chrétien interpreted what he saw more objectively. And his instincts were to challenge rather than to simply accept what he was told. The American government had concluded that its case against Saddam Hussein was a slam dunk. But they were biased towards war and Chrétien was not.

- What did Chrétien know that other world leaders did not? Why was he intent on keeping Canada out of the war?

- Was it his instinct that Canadians did not want to be a satellite of the United States?

- Did he want Canada to use its forces primarily for peace-making, as was his instinct in other conflicts?

- Did his insight into global affairs tell him that the geopolitical risks of destabilizing a perilous part of the globe would place the region in uncharted and dangerous waters?

- Did he believe Saddam Hussein would never use weapons of mass destruction even if he had them?

- Did he believe it was hypocritical to take out Saddam Hussein but leave in place other brutal dictators who were not sitting on oil reserves?

- Was he following the public opinion polls and was he concerned that if Canada went to Iraq the prospects of a federalist Liberal victory in the upcoming Québec election would have been affected?

- Did he believe that war was the last resort?

The answer to each of these questions is yes. Having made the decision, Chrétien was less interested in proving that he was right than in ensuring Canada did not suffer for refusing to join the American-led coalition. That's why he did not admonish Bush and Blair or tell them they had it wrong. He didn't throw stones or stand on the high moral ground. His cover was the shield of the United Nations.

It would be simplistic to say Chrétien downloaded control of Canadian foreign policy to the United Nations. He did not follow the will of the UN as much as he used the international body as armour against criticism and possible retaliation from the American and British governments. Tying Canada's policy to a UN resolution was another way of telling the Americans that they had not made the case for war. If there was definitive proof that Saddam Hussein posed an imminent threat to his neighbours because he held a stockpile of weapons of mass destruction then the UN might have sanctioned war. But better for Canadian economic interests to stand behind the concept of multilateralism than to question the truthfulness of the American president.

In retirement, Chrétien said that he frequently meets people on the street or at airports who tell him how grateful they are to him for keeping Canada out of the Iraq war. Chrétien likes to remind them that it wasn't an easy call and that he was opposed at the time by newspaper columnists, business leaders, and even members of his own caucus.

Canada didn't win any favours from the United States and the United Kingdom for its decision, but the damage was minimal. Chrétien barely rated a mention in George Bush's book Decision Points, which provided extensive coverage of the reasons for launching a war in Iraq. Chrétien told a partisan audience in 2015 that it was normal to have disagreements among friends and that George W. Bush was never forceful with him about Iraq. "It was Tony Blair who had that job," said Chrétien, "Tony was to look after the colony."

At times, Chrétien referred to the British prime minister as "Tory" Blair because his policy choices ran counter to those of his Labour Party predecessors. Blair did not speak with Chrétien for over a year after Canada refused to fight alongside the United Kingdom. Blair also said nothing about Canada's decision to stay out of Iraq in his autobiography, but did write that Chrétien was a wily and experienced old bird who was a strong force at international meetings and who made good sense by being "firm and dependable without being pushy." He called Chrétien a good guy and a tough political operator, "not to be underestimated."[44]

To say today that the choice was easy or clear is to deny the voices who condemned Chrétien at the time. And it was not just his political opponents. A critical Globe and Mail editorial said he used pretzel-like logic to make the wrong choice on Iraq.[45] The editorialists at the Sudbury Star wrote that

Chrétien "aligned us with self-serving European and Asian nations more in-terested in their financial interests in Iraq than saving that country's people from torture, murder, rape and oppression."[46] The *Ottawa Citizen* wrote that Chrétien's refusal to support the US-led coalition because it lacked a specific UN sanction "effectively surrendered Canada's sovereignty to such stalwarts of democracy as China and Russia. We pretend to be America's allies so long they protect us militarily and we benefit economically, but we don't want to associ-ate ourselves with them when their foreign policy offends our sensitivities."[47] *The Windsor Star* concluded that Chrétien played dumb and used the UN as an excuse not to do what is right. "What an embarrassment," the paper wrote.[48] To say the editorials were ten-to-one against Chrétien is to exaggerate the one. Columnist Don Martin said the Parliamentary Press Gallery fully expected Chrétien would follow Bush on Iraq.[49]

Conrad Black suggests that Chrétien was not relying on highly tuned instincts on world affairs when he kept Canada on the sidelines. Deposing Saddam was the right call, said Black, but only because the US tried to turn Iraq into a de-mocracy, something no one predicted:

> They should have got rid of the top 50 people, installed a new strong-man, and said that if he annoyed the West again, he would suffer the same fate as Saddam. That's what I thought we were going to do and I was talking to senior figures in the U.S. administration and British government every week. The wheels came off when Rumsfeld and Bremer disbanded 400,000 military and police, told them they were unemployed but allowed to keep their weapons and ordnance. It was insane but unforeseeable by Chrétien or anyone else. I think he was just self-consciously obsessed with not being too friendly with the U.S.

History will continue to judge the merits of the Iraq decision. But there can be no dispute that in rejecting one of the most important requests of any American president, Chrétien demonstrated the absolute sovereignty and in-dependence of the Canadian government. Peter Donolo wrote that this deci-sion established the Chrétien Doctrine. In effect, he countered elite opinion that the Free Trade Agreement with the United States had compelled Canada to align its foreign and defence policies with the US.[50] "Every subsequent prime minister," Donolo wrote, "can rely on that doctrine with the confidence that Canada could take a path that was independent of the economic giant to our south without fear of reprisal."

Chrétien kept Canada out of a complicated, bloody, costly, and protracted war in Iraq that, 15 years later, has few defenders. He followed his instincts, confounded the experts, and saved Canadian lives. He put Canada on the right side of history, which is the ultimate test of any prime minister. Meanwhile, Canada's relationship with the United States has not only survived but remained strong. This from a man we were told would embarrass Canada on the world stage.

TURBOT WAR

Elected to the House of Commons at the age of 25, Brian Tobin was a founding member of the Rat Pack, a group of four Liberal MPs tasked with getting under Brian Mulroney's skin during question period. Tobin made a name for himself as a smart, fearless, and feisty MP from Newfoundland with a gift of delivering one-liners and clever putdowns. He was every bit Chrétien's match as a political scrapper.

Tobin had the unenviable task of serving as Chrétien's fisheries minister in 1993 when there were few fish to be caught in Atlantic Canada. Since the cod stocks had been depleted by decades of overfishing, Tobin's job was not so much to manage the fishery but to deliver government funds to support the families of out-of-work fishermen. Tobin's Tory predecessor, John Crosbie, also a Newfoundlander, had placed a moratorium on cod fishing in 1992 that put 35,000 people on the unemployment lines. It was supposed to last two years, but everyone in the fishery knew it would endure much longer. For Tobin, the moratorium was personal: "I have witnessed no political moment more agonizing than watching John Crosbie announce the closure of the fishery, in a hotel conference room, while fisherman pounded at the door, demanding to be let in. That day, the cod fishery was no more."[1]

The next species headed for the endangered list was turbot. International fishing convention gave Canada control of its fishery for 200 nautical miles (349 kilometres) from our shores. But the Grand Banks of Newfoundland, where turbot could still be found, extended a little beyond the 200-mile limit.

While few Canadian fishermen disrespected Canadian and international fishing moratoria and quotas, Spanish trawlers were filling their boats. In response, through the passage of the Coastal Fisheries Protection Act, Tobin claimed the authority to protect straddling fish stocks beyond Canada's 200-mile limit. The European Union said our legislation was illegal. They countered that disputes should be settled by international agreements reached through organizations such as the Northwest Atlantic Fishing Organization.

Tobin sought fishing restrictions from NAFO that were similar to what Canada had imposed on itself. The European Union assumed it had the votes to control NAFO rulings and could set whatever quotas and allocations it saw fit. But Tobin persuaded Norway, Japan, Russia, Iceland, and Cuba to endorse the Canadian position. This was enough for Canada's proposal to curtail quotas to pass. But NAFO was disinclined to enforce the new regulations.

Tobin said he was prepared to use all measures available to stop the "scoundrels and thieves" from overfishing. He told Newfoundland fishermen the moratorium would not last a day longer than necessary. Yet, whenever Tobin sought to use the powers in the more expansive legislation Canada had passed, Canadian officials resisted, preferring a softer and more diplomatic approach.

Tobin asked the prime minister how much authority he had to resolve the conflict. "As much as you take and as much as you want," responded Chrétien. "So we understand each other, if you do a bad job I will find another minister." Tobin knew his neck was on the line. "The truth is," said Tobin, "most ministers will stay away if a course of action is dangerous or risky. Or they will pick up the phone and get directions from the centre. There is nothing wrong with that. But a few people in government will go beyond the boundaries of what is safe and cautious."

On Tobin's orders, Canadian fisheries inspectors began intercepting boats that were violating our laws regardless of the vessel's point of origin. Tobin pointed out that the pirates were not the fishermen, but the men wearing blue suits sitting in corporate boardrooms and ordering captains and crews to break international law in the name of short-term profits.[2]

After one American ship was seized and escorted into St. John's Harbour, Jim Blanchard, the American ambassador, protested to Tobin, demanding that the vessel and her crew be released immediately. "Or what, Jim?" Tobin asked. Blanchard had no response.[3] Everyone was operating in uncharted waters. To add insult to injury it was not unusual for some Spanish vessels to seek permission to enter St. John's Harbour to refuel and permit seasick crews to recover.[4]

The inspectors soon discovered that many vessels had two sets of books, one that showed a fish haul that was within Canadian and international law and another that recorded the fish that were stored below deck. The first log might indicate that 30 per cent of the catch was turbot but inspectors discovered it was actually 90 per cent.

The real question was what Canada would do if NAFO orders and Canadian laws were not respected. Tobin was prepared to use all of Canada's military assets to win his battle. The defence minister, David Collenette, supported the goals but he wrote to Tobin that the military needed proper authority and rules of engagement before any mission could be accepted:

> The Office of the Judge Advocate has consistently expressed its grave concerns about the legality under international law of using force, including disabling force, outside Canada's 200-nautical-mile exclusive fishing zone...[Without proper authority and approval]...the Judge Advocate General will not be able to, nor will he certify the legality of the rules of engagement.[5]

For a time, Collenette refused to return Tobin's phone calls. With emotions running high, senior staff in the Prime Minister's Office understood why the defence department wanted to slow things down. But not Tobin. He said he never had a more sobering day than the one he spent reviewing the rules of engagement, drawn up in secret, and given to our naval officers: "We were literally assessing firepower and discussing potential casualty risks."[6]

Gordon Smith, the deputy minister of foreign affairs and a former ambassador to the European Union, wondered why Canada would be so aggressive and upset over some "smelly little fish that nobody else seemed to care a damn about."[7] Tobin knew he was swimming upstream. When the prime minister's foreign policy advisor, Jim Bartleman, urged caution, Tobin exploded: "It's gutless people like you who have sold out our fishermen year after year, in the interest of giving no offense to countries of the European Union." But Bartleman was not being insensitive. "I know how you feel," he told Tobin. "I'm a member of Canada's First Nations Community, so I know about being forgotten in the face of powerful interests."[8]

The Reform Party and its fisheries critic, John Cummins, said Tobin had taken leave of his senses and was out of his depth. "Tobin is not dealing with a couple of flagless rust buckets this time and nobody wants him going out there and arresting European Union vessels," Cummins said.[9] Tobin understood he was not following convention: "To have a department of fisheries lead that kind of initiative in the context of all the levers of government, was, to say the least, unusual."

The editorial writers at *The Globe and Mail* thought Chrétien and Tobin were in waters that were way over their heads. Under the headline "More Fish Foolishness," the *Globe* wrote of the government's jingoism, bombast, rudeness, and contempt for international law.[10] Following the cancellation of a meeting between Chrétien and the EU trade commissioner, the *Globe* suggested some fence-mending was in order: "Admiral Tobin continues to let his tongue flap like a turbot in a net." Rather than playing to a few irate fisherman, the *Globe* suggested that Chrétien focus on retaining Canada's image as a moderate law-abiding nation.

The issue came to a head in March 1995 when Tobin was told that a Spanish trawler, the *Estai*, was scooping up fish just outside the 200-mile limit. The Canadian Coast Guard along with an armed naval contingent were given instructions to board the fishing vessel and seize its nets. Five Spanish trawlers intervened to shield the *Estai* from the Canadian armada.

The confrontation with the Estai was a test of Canada's resolve. Canadian patrol vessels were armed, but so too was a nearby Spanish naval ship. Tobin turned to Max Short for advice. Short was a gruff, plain-spoken departmental official from Newfoundland and a former fisherman. He was 5 feet 3 inches, but stood tall.

> Tobin: Max, that damn Estai has been running for hours now and she won't stop. What do you suppose the Spanish fishermen aboard her are saying right now?
>
> Short: Ah. They're feeling proud, minister. Proud of themselves, and proud of their fleet. They're making fools of us.
>
> Tobin: What are the Canadian fisherman going to feel if we don't stop the Estai?
>
> Short: Minister, it will haul the guts and soul right out of them if we don't stop that boat. We should chase her all the way to goddamn Ireland if we've got to."

"Gentlemen," Tobin said to the undersecretary of foreign affairs and the prime minister's foreign policy adviser, "I'm ready to sign the order to have our vessel fire across its bow and make her stop. Will you sign it with me?"[11] The first order was to fire across the bow of the Estai. If that didn't work the *Estai*'s propellers were to be the next target. The orders were signed.

The *Estai*'s captain surrendered after the first shot was fired and the crew was charged with violating the Canadian moratorium. After the seizure, Spain forced Canadians to apply for a visa before entering their country. The Spanish tourism industry protested and the measure was overturned within a month.

The Reform Party critic called the seizure a public relations exercise: "It's absolutely disgusting, outrageous."[12] But when the *Estai* was towed into St. John's Harbour it was greeted with cheers from residents.

Spanish leaders and key figures in the European Union accused Canada of committing an act of piracy in international waters. The Canadian embassy in Madrid was pelted with eggs and rocks by protesters from the fishing ports of Galicia. Spain elevated the conflict by sending ten trawlers to the Grand Banks, accompanied by a military escort. Officials from the European Union protested and asked that the International Court of Justice settle the dispute. Tobin wanted the matter to be decided in the court of public opinion.

The *Estai* was found to have kept two log books. Canadian officials also discovered a false bulkhead where tons of processed turbot were packaged and hidden. By international standards, 80 per cent of the turbot was less than the minimum size. Not only were the net openings too small, but there was an inner lining to the net allowing only fish that were three inches or less to escape. Officials also discovered that the catch included 25 tons of American plaice, a protected species.

The international community was still not convinced. Tobin had the illegal nets, but he needed a way to generate news coverage. The opportunity came with a scheduled speech he was to give at the United Nations in New York. Also speaking at the meeting was Emma Bonino, the European Union Commissioner of Fisheries.

Tobin had the net from the *Estai* trucked from St. John's to New York City under the guard of fisheries enforcement inspectors and the RCMP.[13] Foreign Affairs Canada was uneasy about the use of the prop and warned the prime minister that trouble was brewing. Chrétien called Tobin to ask if what he was hearing was true, telling Tobin that some people in government had warned him that "we would look nuts" by the accepted standards of international diplomacy. "It's your neck," Chrétien said. "If it works I will take the credit. If it doesn't I will get a new minister of fisheries." But there was no question that Chrétien was up for the fight.

In his formal remarks, Tobin made no mention that he had brought the nets with him to New York. Then Bonino took the bait and stepped up to the mic:

> Where is the net? Who has seen this net? I have not seen the net. Nobody has seen the net. Only the Canadians have seen this net. I would not be surprised if they don't find heroin, cocaine, I don't know what's next.

Bonino called Canada a nation of pirates and a danger to sailors on the high seas. When Tobin was pressed by reporters to respond to Bonino's challenge he had the opening he sought: "Do you want to see the net for yourselves?"

Tobin escorted the international media to two chartered buses that were parked in front of the United Nations. From there they went to a barge on the Hudson River where the illegal nets were hoisted under the guard of the RCMP: "I speak for those who have no voice," said Tobin, "the fish." He continued:

> We're down to the last, lonely, unloved, unattractive little turbot clinging to its fingernails on the Grand Banks of Newfoundland saying … someone reach out and save me in this eleventh hour as I am about to go down to extinction.[14]

The Estai was released from Canadian custody after posting a $500,000 bond. But Spanish fishing vessels continued to return to the Grand Banks under the protection of a patrol boat.

Tobin wrote of an incident in which a Canadian fisheries patrol vessel was alleged to have nearly sideswiped a Spanish trawler in the dead of night. When pressed by the Spanish ambassador for an explanation, Tobin cast doubt on the captain's version of events, claiming that the seamanship of the Canadian Navy should not be questioned. To allegations that he encouraged the encounter, Tobin slyly wrote in his memoirs that he had "no comment."[15] Canada responded to ongoing Spanish incursions with three fisheries department patrol boats, two coast guard ships, a supply vessel, and two military frigates.

While Tobin was on a war footing, officials from foreign affairs, the Prime Minister's Office, and the Privy Council Office wanted to take the file back from Fisheries and Oceans. Tobin said that if he had ever received instructions from the prime minister to back off, he would have resigned.[16] But the prime minister never blinked. Chrétien issued rules of engagement to Canadian forces to fire on the Spanish ships if they exposed their guns.

Chrétien called the Spanish prime minister and told him to get his naval vessels out of the Grand Banks and what would happen if they didn't. A less combative prime minister and minister of fisheries might have sent a diplomatic note of protest over the dispute.

The fact that Canada and Spain were NATO partners made the conflict even more uncomfortable for member states. How could members of the same military alliance be at war with one another? David Collenette was in a difficult position. He believed Canada was justified in protecting the fishery and that Tobin had been effective in making Canada look virtuous and the Spaniards dishonorable. He defended the decision not to back down in the face of international pressure. He believed that the US and the UK took our side "only because they realized the prime minister was not going to turn the other cheek."

The Spaniards backed down. So did the European Union. Canada won the Turbot War, largely because Tobin and Chrétien were not afraid of a scrap when it came to protecting the fishery. Chrétien was certainly not trying to impress the bureaucrats at Foreign Affairs or foreign ambassadors. But he did impress Max Short and all Newfoundland fishermen.

LIBERAL TRADITIONS

Civilians in former war-torn countries are killed each year by detonating land mines. While the mines may be an effective defensive weapon against tanks or invading armies, they can't distinguish between an armoured personnel carrier and children playing in a field.

The president of the Red Cross, Cornelio Sommaruga, met with Chrétien in May, 1994 and asked Canada to lead a campaign to ban land mines from the planet. Chrétien thought Canada was the right country for the mission given the reputation he believed we had built for peacekeeping. Initially, the Canadian military opposed the ban because they saw anti-personnel land mines as a legitimate defensive weapon and had always used them responsibly. But they fell into line when cabinet made it a priority.[1] Chrétien became the international champion for an agreement while his foreign affairs minister, Lloyd Axworthy, provided the ground game that made the treaty a reality.

A United Nations treaty requires the signatures of at least 40 countries to become international law. Signatories were asked to commit to never use antipersonnel landmines, destroy whatever stock they had in their possession, clear all existing minefields, and assist the victims of landmines.

Princess Diana was a passionate advocate for a ban on land mines. Tragically, she died barely two weeks before the land mines treaty was drafted. But her personal commitment to the issue was a significant factor in bringing the British government on board.

Ultimately, more than 160 countries signed the Convention on the Prohibition of the Use, Stockpiling, Production and Transfer of Anti-Personnel Mines and on their Destruction. The convention is also known by another name: the Ottawa Treaty. That the treaty was signed in Canada's capital was a nod to the leadership that Chrétien and Canada provided.

But what is also significant about the treaty is the countries that refused to ratify it. That group includes the United States, Russia, China, India, and Pakistan. In the end, the countries that did not use land mines were eager to sign, and those who used them for defensive or offensive purposes were not.[2]

While the US was not on board, Chrétien said it was a close call: "I spent all night on the phone with Clinton talking about it. He said he wanted to sign it, but his chief of staff didn't."[3] Clinton told Chrétien that some of his generals would resign if he signed the treaty. Russian leader Boris Yeltsin said he would sign, but only if the Americans were on board.

As the policeman of the world, the American military did not want to renounce a weapon that might keep its troops from harm. The US was not about to abandon its ally, South Korea, by committing to remove the best deterrence to a North Korean threat. Land mines have been deployed in the demilitarized zone between North and South Korea and in some places are the only physical barrier that prevents a North Korean army from marching across the border. Even President Barack Obama, a Nobel Peace Prize winner, upheld this position. His spokesperson noted that if the US signed the treaty it would not be able to meet its national defence needs or security commitments.[4] One former US diplomat put it this way: "Lloyd Axworthy had every right to express his views and criticisms of our policy; but we exercised our right not to listen."[5]

That did not limit Chrétien's enthusiasm for the treaty, nor cause him to underestimate its importance: "On December 3, 1997, 122 governments did put their signatures on the Ottawa Treaty in front of a joyous crowd of 2,500 people from around the world. For me, it will always be one of the greatest achievements in Canada's diplomatic history."[6] That is, to say the least, an exaggeration. While Canada invested $100 million to implement the treaty, its net enduring benefits are difficult to measure. The net number of landmines in use did not decline following the passage of the treaty.

Axworthy and Chrétien were nominated for a Nobel Peace Prize for their efforts. The Nobel jury determined that the initiative was worthy, but gave its 1997 award to an American, Jody Williams, who served as the co-ordinator of the International Campaign to Ban Landmines. Chrétien said he was happy that the award was given to a cause that was initiated by his government in 1994.

CHRÉTIEN CITES HIS ROLE in the creation of the International Criminal Court as one of his key international accomplishments. The Court holds to account perpetrators of genocide and crimes against humanity when nations within that jurisdiction are unable or unwilling to do so. By 2016, the court had indicted 39 tyrants, including Muammar Gaddafi of Libya. Although the court appears noble in intent and virtuous on its surface, it has not been endorsed by the United States, China, and Israel.

Much of the background work to establish the court was carried out in the early 1990s by various UN members, following the creation of ad hoc tribunals that responded to atrocities in the former Yugoslav and Rwanda. A series of foundational meetings for the international court culminated in a conference in Rome in June 1998. A month later the treaty was adopted by a vote of 120 to 7. The 60 formal country ratifications came thereafter, including from Canada in December 1998.

Chrétien and his foreign affairs minister Lloyd Axworthy claimed that Canada took a lead role in creating the court through lobbying, hosting formal meetings, and by providing the financial support that enabled poor countries to participate in negotiations. More significantly, it was a Canadian diplomat, Philippe Kirsch, later to become a judge and then president of the court, who chaired the pivotal conference in Rome.

While Chrétien took a leadership role in creating the court, he failed to bring George W. Bush onside. The US president told Chrétien that he would never defer to an international court or condone placing an American citizen outside its own legal system. Chrétien argued that the international court had no jurisdiction over a country with a good legal system. Bush was not convinced and said he would never sign.

After the Kuala Lumpur War Crimes Tribunal found George W. Bush and Tony Blair guilty for their leadership in the Iraq War, human rights activists took the case to the International Criminal Court. The court concluded in 2006 that the decision to go to war in Iraq fell outside its jurisdiction.[7]

CHRÉTIEN HAD NO GREAT ambition to change the world. And he felt no guilt when Canada did business with communist or repressive regimes. "I'm not allowed to tell the premier of Saskatchewan or Québec what to do. Am I supposed to tell the premier of China what to do?"[8]

He made friends with Vladimir Putin, naively believing the Russian strong-man when he said he worked as a spy in the KGB simply because he needed a job after graduating from university.[9] Chrétien did not view Putin as a com-munist, nor did he think that he was ethically compromised. He and Putin became friends and even made plans to go on a ski vacation together in the Caucasus. They also talked about getting together at the Canadian-Russian Arctic border.[10] Of course, there was a time when George W. Bush also looked at Vladimir Putin as a man he could do business with. But Bush became wise to Putin's intent and his methods and the relationship soured. Chrétien's in-stinct to give Putin the benefit of the doubt was surprising, especially after many of Putin's opponents ended up dying in unusual circumstances.[11]

Chrétien was initially impressed by Fidel Castro, calling him one of the most extraordinary personalities of the twentieth century. Even Aline Chrétien found Castro to be a charmer. In December 1994, Chrétien lobbied unsuc-cessfully to get Cuba invited to the summit of the Americas in Miami. The gathering included 34 countries in North, Central, and South America with Cuba the only excluded country. Chrétien was proud of the fact that his pres-ence at the summit provoked a protest on Miami streets by Cuban exiles who were opposed to Castro.[12] In the process, he befriended the leaders of many Caribbean nations, some of whom called Chrétien the Godfather.

While Chrétien did business with ugly regimes he discretely endeavoured to expose human rights abuses. When he visited Cuba in 1998 he raised the plight of four political prisoners. He also asked that Cuba sign the UN's Covenant on Economic, Social and Cultural Rights. That would have been quite a leap for a country that still featured billboards on the streets that read "Socialism or death!"[13]

Castro admonished Chrétien for intervening in Cuba's domestic political is-sues. The dictator asked him if French president Charles de Gaulle had pro-vided an example of "constructive engagement" when in 1967 he proclaimed "Vive le Québec libre" in support of Québec's independence from Canada.[14]

It was an uncomfortable moment for Chrétien when his visit to Cuba was ex-ploited by Castro to trumpet his disdain for the United States. At the airport arrival ceremony, Castro condemned America for killing people through hun-ger and sickness. "That is genocide," Castro bellowed. "That's turning a nation into a ghetto and applying to it a new version of the Holocaust. It's like using biological, chemical or nuclear weapons."[15] Castro added that US officials who imposed a trade embargo on Cuba should be brought before international tribunals and prosecuted as war criminals.

After 13 Cuban athletes defected to Canada during the 1999 Pan-American Games in Winnipeg, Castro declared that Canada was joining the United States as the second enemy in the north. But the resentment did not last long. At Pierre Trudeau's funeral in 2000, Castro gave Chrétien some domestic political advice: "If I were you, I would call an election." Chrétien did, shortly thereafter.[16]

Although Chrétien was prepared to nudge repressive regimes towards greater respect for human rights, he tried to avoid doing so in a way that would put the jobs of Canadian workers at risk. Chrétien saw high-minded diplomatic gestures as pointless. He was a cheerleader for trade and investment, even if it meant making friends with Cuba, Russia, China, or Saudi Arabia.

CHRÉTIEN SAID THAT PRIME ministers often travel abroad when they are in trouble at home. Better, he thought, to fix what's wrong on the home front. For the most part, Chrétien was wary of making grand diplomatic gestures and he rarely made waves on the international stage. His view was that Canada should lead by example rather than lecture others about where they fell short.

Nonetheless, in April 2000 Chrétien went against his instincts and took a 12-day trip to Israel, Egypt, Jordan, Lebanon, Syria, and Saudi Arabia. It was the first time a Canadian prime minister had ventured to the Middle East. Officials advised Chrétien not to make the trip, but if he did go, they recommended he be careful with his language and certainly not make any jokes, advice he ignored. The reviews of the trip said it was a disaster.

On the plane to the Middle East, reporters asked Chrétien why he was considering supporting a unilateral declaration of independence by the Palestinian Authority yet would not give Québec the same right.[17] Chrétien later held a news conference with Palestinian Liberation Organization leader Yasser Arafat and publicly declared that Canada might support such a declaration: "I believe, personally, it is better to keep it as a pressure point for the negotiations and that is the position of Canada." The Israelis said this view would jeopardize the peace process. Chrétien's communications director told reporters that whatever the prime minister said, that was not what he meant.

When Chrétien met Israeli Prime Minister Ehud Barak in West Jerusalem, he was criticized for not also visiting Arab East Jerusalem. The PLO called it an insult to the peace process. A flummoxed Chrétien responded, "I don't know if I am in West, South, North or East Jerusalem right now. I came here to meet with the Israeli prime minister and here I am."[18]

Next, he endorsed Israel's claim to the Sea of Galilee, or Lake Tiberias, another point of contention in achieving peace. He explained himself this way: "Apparently, there was a border that was occupied a long time ago and there was war and so on. For a Canadian, we have 30 million lakes so we don't see it in the same perspective but I can understand the need for Israel to keep the only lake they got." It was a substantive point given that Lake Tiberias provides 40 per cent of Israel's fresh water.

The next day Chrétien offered to accept as many as 15,000 Palestinian refugees to Canada. The PLO was offended: Palestinians wanted a homeland, not an exit strategy.

Liberal MP John Bryden was dumbfounded by the criticism and smelled a conspiracy. "I believe the prime minister's visit and the remarks he made were a setup," he wrote in a *National Post* op-ed. "He was working from a prepared script on behalf of the parties to the peace process." Bryden continued, "If Canada floats these bargaining positions — as Mr. Chrétien did — then they are put on the table without giving offence to the rival governments."[19] But that's not what happened.

The Windsor Star pointed out that of the 65 people who accompanied Chrétien on the trip there were only two foreign policy advisors: "The PM did not acquit himself well on his Middle East junket," stated the editorial, "and [Chrétien's] limited abilities as a world statesman were evident. It was yet another sign that it's time for the prime minister to move aside."[20]

Chrétien thought he was treated unfairly:

> The Middle East trip in 2000 was one time when the news being broadcast back home seemed to have nothing to do with the events on the ground... Canadians got the impression that the tour was nothing but a series of gaffes from beginning to end. It was as though the reporters had decided collectively, or had been ordered by their editors, to bring their obsession with petty scandals and succession squabbles of Ottawa on the journey.[21]

More likely, he should have exercised more discretion in his remarks, or never should have taken the trip in the first place. He was out of his element. Norman Webster, a former editor-in-chief for *The Globe and Mail* and *Montreal Gazette*, wrote that what Chrétien said in the Middle East was not untruthful or erroneous, but is was hazardous. "The bottom line is that Chrétien has been a diplomatic disaster," Webster wrote. "He seems to think he can say anything he wants, anywhere, without taking account of the context and without consequences. It isn't what he's been saying that's stupid; it's the fact that he's been saying it."[22]

The trip reinforced the image that foreign policy elites had of Chrétien: that he did not have the knowledge and nuance needed to lead on the world stage.

CANADA DOES NOT HAVE the seventh-largest country by population, nor is it the seventh-largest economy. Yet Canada has a privileged seat at the G7 table where social and economic issues are discussed with countries that have significantly more wealth and population. The original G6 included the governments of the United States, Great Britain, France, West Germany, Italy, and Japan. But the United States and Japan wanted to dial down the European influence and insisted that Canada be invited to join in 1976. Chrétien favoured adding Russia to the G7 and used Canada's influence as host to the 1995 meeting in Halifax to extend an invitation to Moscow to participate. An inebriated Russian president Boris Yeltsin made his presence known at the meeting when he tried to climb on a stage with Russian acrobats.[23] For a brief period, the G7 became the G8, until Russia's membership was revoked in 2014 following its annexation of Crimea.

When Paul Martin was finance minister, he thought the G7 club was not sufficiently inclusive or consultative of emerging economies. He thought it unfair that G7 countries could lecture other countries on their economic management from a lofty height. "We needed to engage them in a process in which we would work together for mutual benefit," Martin wrote, "if we were to deal with today's financial crises and to prevent tomorrow's."[24] Thus the G20 was born. Martin became its first chairman.

From a world order point of view, the G20 made perfect sense. What was the logic of having an economic forum that did not include China, Australia,

South Africa, Turkey, Russia, Brazil, and other powerful nations?

While Martin was a big supporter of the G20, Chrétien was not. He saw the larger group as a watering down of the influence Canada enjoyed as a G7 member.

Chrétien thought so little of Canada's role in creating the G20 that it's not mentioned as an accomplishment in his memoirs. The G20 did not impress George W. Bush either. He told Canada's foreign affairs minister, Bill Graham, that he didn't want to go to another of those "damn meetings" where some far-off leader would read him a lecture.[25] But to Martin's credit, the G20 has endured and remains a fixture in the schedule of world leaders.

WHILE INVESTMENTS IN THE military and international development were curtailed in Chrétien's early years, once the government was in surplus the urge to spend kicked in. Both Chrétien and Martin were keen on giving a break to some of the poorest and most heavily indebted countries around the world with loan forgiveness.

Martin had one advantage on the international stage that Chrétien could not match. He had become friends with Bono, the frontman for the popular rock band U2. The relationship began at the IMF World Bank meetings in 2000 in Prague, when Martin was told Bono wanted to meet him. Martin asked, "Who is Bono?"

Martin's staff was giddy with excitement and set up the meeting: "We discussed my decision to take a forward position on debt relief," said Martin, "which was obviously the root of his enthusiasm. But, surprising as it may sound, we connected because he is also a policy wonk."[26] Bono said he was impressed that Martin was more than just a money man: "He actually had a vision about [debt relief]. I was grateful to him for ... sticking his neck out and getting into trouble with all the rest of the big shots here."[27]

Chrétien was not impressed by rock stars. Three former Canadian prime ministers, including Chrétien, joined Stephen Harper at the 2013 funeral of Nelson Mandela, to whom Chrétien had presented an honorary Canadian citizenship. Bono was there as well. He asked Arthur Milnes, a PMO staffer, if he could meet with members of the illustrious Canadian group, but Harper declined. As Bono left the reception, Chrétien was heard to say, "There goes the head of state of the heads of state."

Paul Martin did not win any friends in the United States when he issued a press release calling on rich nations to immediately grant a moratorium on debt-service payments to developing countries. "What in God's name have you done?" asked US Treasury Secretary Larry Summers in full view of others at the G7 summit. Summers was annoyed that Martin had gone beyond what had been agreed at the negotiating table: "I can't believe Martin did that. It was the stupidest thing I ever heard of."[28] Summers' view was that the focus should be on enduring development results and not a wave of the debt-forgiveness wand. It did not help that Summers was given no warning of Martin's pitch.

Chrétien and Martin were not always on the same page on such matters. At a March 2002 international conference on development financing in Monterrey, Mexico, Chrétien committed to doubling Canada overseas development assistance with at least half of the money earmarked for Africa.[29] Martin, who was sitting beside Chrétien when the commitment was made, was unhappy that the prime minister had made a financial pledge without his agreement.

WHEN CHRÉTIEN BECAME PRIME minister, he sought no attention for Canada or himself on the world stage. Unlike Brian Mulroney and Pierre Trudeau, Chrétien did not have much of a foreign policy agenda. He did not revere superpowers or genuflect before international celebrities. His disdain for snobbery and elitism meant that other world leaders could not make him feel inferior.

While travelling the world and attending international summits, Chrétien was more concerned about how he was perceived in Canada than what the New York Times said about him. That left Canada in good stead, especially when he kept Canada out the Iraq war, a conflict that the leading American editorialists supported.

Mauril Belanger, a Liberal MP who served under Chrétien, said the enduring legacy of the prime minister was providing a voice of modesty and reason on the world stage. Over time, Bélanger said, world leaders turned to Chrétien for advice at summits around the globe, where he had become a source of wise counsel. It wasn't because he knew the details of every issue and conflict in world affairs, said Belanger, but because of his personable approach, his humour, his instinct, and his judgment. And he spoke to leaders from all states, big and small, with respect.

DECADE OF DARKNESS

A decade of darkness. That's how General Rick Hillier described what the Canadian military endured during the 1990s.[1] It's not unusual for a retired military officer to venture into the domain of public policy and civic discourse, but when Hillier offered this blunt assessment in 2007 he was chief of the defence staff, serving the Conservative government of Stephen Harper. He had been promoted to the military's top job in 2005 by a Liberal prime minister, Paul Martin.

Hillier didn't much care that he upset Liberal MPs who had previously served in the Chrétien or Martin cabinets. Hillier said our fighting forces had made themselves an easy target when Canada needed to dig itself out of a financial hole in the 1990s. There was no clear vision then for the role of the Canadian Forces, he said, adding that the military leadership was weak and the deplorable conduct of a few front-line officers had undermined public confidence.[2]

Chrétien understood that he might not have been popular at defence headquarters, but that was never his objective. He knew the Canadian public preferred defence cuts to closing hospitals or reducing spending on seniors. And since defence accounted for about one-quarter of all departmental spending, even the defence minister, David Collenette, accepted the budget math. Chrétien wrote in his memoirs that he believed the military understood and accepted the fiscal and political realities he faced and that the minister of defence and the chief of the defence staff were not bitter about the cuts or reallocations.[3]

But even without a fiscal crisis, Chrétien was disinclined to make defence spending a priority. He said that no amount of money would satisfy the military hawks and that the country should expect a peace dividend following the end of the Cold War.[4]

A KEY PLANK OF the 1993 Liberal Red Book was the cancellation of the Tory plan to spend $6 billion to acquire EH101 helicopters. More than just a money-saving move, ditching the high-profile purchase was a vote-getter. The generals did not put up much of a fight. Their priority was to retain their base budget for troops, for operations, and for ongoing capital spending.

But if the prime minister was intent on gutting the military he made an odd choice for his first minister of defence. When David Collenette was asked to take the job, he looked at Chrétien with incredulity:

> [The prime minister] did not ask me what my personal inclination was on defence policy. I think that was a mistake because I was quite different from him and other senior ministers. I was born in central London the year after the War ended and our neighbourhood had been heavily bombed. We lost seven of our family around the corner one night in the Blitz. Kids grew up in my school without fathers. It was utter deprivation for many. I was conditioned in my early years by the War and its aftermath so I did not share some of the more pacifist views than others did around the cabinet table. It was one thing to cut expenditures and deal with all the superfluous facilities that should have been axed many years ago but were sustained for political reasons. It was a bigger issue as to whether you believed in the combat capability of the Canadian military, which I did.

Collenette impressed the generals when he fought the anti-military sentiment in the prime minister's office, a task he described as exhilarating. But the war Collenette was fighting was a battle his predecessors had been losing over the previous 30 years.

There was a time in the 1960s when a force contingent of 100,000 was drawn as a red line by our military leaders. By the time Chrétien became prime minister the military was closer to 90,000. Chrétien brought that number down to 60,000. Even when the budget was balanced the number of troops did not increase.

REGULAR-FORCE MILITARY WAS SLASHED

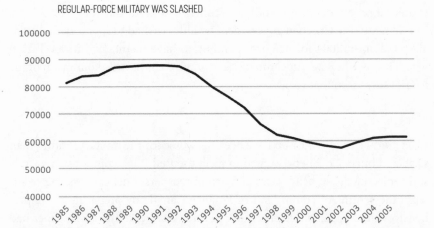

In 1960, there were 67 soldiers for every 1,000 Canadians. There were 44 in 1970, 33 in 1980, 32 in 1990, and 19 in 2000. In one generation, our fighting forces had been cut, effectively, by two-thirds. Over the 1990s, the cut was 40 per cent.

The accepted NATO target for defence spending is 2 per cent of GDP. Canada has not met this commitment since 1971. In 1995, Canada was tied with Spain and ahead of Luxembourg on defence spending as 1 per cent of GDP, but behind 15 other nations.[5] European NATO countries were spending twice as much on defence relative to GDP, while the United States spent three times our relative investment. If there was a peace dividend to be reaped from the end of the Cold War, Canada was taking more than its fair share. The Americans cut defence spending in the 1990s, but the gap with Canada grew ever wider.

NATIONAL DEFENCE COSTS WERE CUT BY ONE-THIRD UNDER CHRETIEN

Under Chrétien, defence spending declined by one-third, from 1.5 to 1 per cent of GDP. The Chrétien government would have had to spend an additional $6 billion in 2004 for defence spending to have maintained its level from where it was when he came into office, enough to have wiped out much of the federal surplus in that year.

COLLENETTE SAID IT COULD have been far worse for the military. Rather than slash and burn, Collenette wanted to meet the Red Book commitments while still replacing aging helicopters and armoured personnel carriers. He countered the sentiment coming out of Finance Canada by preparing a comprehensive white paper on defence policy and investment. The white paper had gone through regular channels but was leaked to the media before its scheduled release date. The suspicion was that the leak came out of Finance Canada to put the brakes on new spending. That's when Collenette got the ear of the prime minister.

> Mr. Chrétien had never been minister of national defence so he tended to follow my advice more so than he did with some other ministers in portfolios which he himself had headed in the Trudeau years. When push came to shove, I got the support I needed from the prime minister not to cut our budget as much as Finance was urging in 1995.

Collenette said the prime minister was not anti-military and had no difficulty understanding the significance of D-Day when the 50th anniversary celebrations were held. At the formal event that marked the occasion, Chrétien proudly read the names of four Shawinigan soldiers who had served with his brother and died in the war.

Chrétien understood the military wanted the most modern weaponry, although he said dire predictions of catastrophic equipment failure were never realized. Hillier disagreed and said that sending vehicles designed only for training into combat zones, "was as close to criminal in the eyes of our soldiers as one can get."[6]

Over time, Hillier saw that Canada was forced to rely on the use of civilian contractors to do work normally assigned to the uniformed troops. He said these contractors were often untrained, unarmed, and only nominally subject to military discipline.[7] Fortunately, because deployments under Chrétien were closer to peacekeeping, the enemies Canadian troops encountered were often poorly equipped. But not always. Collenette heard bullets overhead while travelling with deputy minister Bob Fowler in an armoured personnel carrier in Bosnia in 1993. "I'm glad we're in a bloody APC with helmets on," Collenette said to Fowler. Fowler laughed. "Minister, these things are too thin-skinned and won't do us a damn bit of good if we take a direct hit."

After multiple rounds of spending cuts, the military brass was loath to offer up ideas when Chrétien asked what else they could do without. That's when the generals gratuitously put two of their military colleges on a list, including the only college in Québec. When given the option to shutter the College Militaire Royal, in St. Jean, Québec, Chrétien barely paused and said, "Close it!"[7] It was one of the few important decisions Chrétien regretted, largely because of its symbolic significance for national unity and its impact on the ability of our armed forces to operate in both official languages.

IT WAS DIFFICULT FOR THE military to withstand the political pressure for spending cuts when Canada's fighting forces were shooting themselves in the foot. A pivotal event was the humanitarian mission in Somalia in 1993 that ended with the brutal torture and death of a Somali teenager, Shidane Arone, at the hands of two members of Canadian Airborne Regiment. The military made matters worse by attempting to cover up the killing, which led to a public inquiry being called. A grisly picture of Canadian soldiers posing with the bloodied and beaten Arone horrified the public. One of the accused soldiers attempted suicide and suffered permanent brain damage, making him unfit to stand trial. Private Kyle Brown was sentenced to five years in prison for his part in the horrible crime. Videos of hazing rituals within the Airborne Regiment provided further evidence that all was not right with the military culture.

Since the inquiry dealt with an incident that had not occurred under his watch, Chrétien thought he was on safe political ground. Launching the inquiry was included in the 1993 Liberal platform so it would have been difficult to set the idea aside. Collenette said public inquiries were very unpredictable and could even be dangerous, "But we had campaigned on it so it became party policy."

As it turned out, the cause and origin of bad news didn't matter. The government of the day still wore the scandal. The public seemed not to distinguish between acts that occurred under the previous Progressive Conservative government with decisions that were made under the Chrétien government. One senior official observed that all that Canadians remembered was the incident itself. Collenette said that the government-appointed commissioners went on "fishing expeditions" and ultimately lost focus. The inquiry was shut down just before the 1997 election. The Chrétien government said it wanted to move on from the incident, largely because of reports that it was killing morale in the military. Despite predictions to the contrary, terminating the inquiry was a non-issue in the election campaign, in large part because the government had nothing to hide.

Hillier believed the focus on a few bad apples in a rogue unit misrepresented the reality of the Canadian military.[9] The Chrétien government saw it differently and disbanded the Canadian Airborne Regiment in 1995.[10] While the public accepted the decision the military was shell-shocked. Hillier wrote that the government read the public opinion tea leaves and realized that it had a free hand to "cut us savagely" without fear of reprisal.[11]

Hillier was galled that even as it imposed severe spending cuts, the Chrétien government was dispatching an increasing number of Canadian soldiers to hot spots around the world. Hiller recounted that our troops were sent into areas without maps or local intelligence and without proper equipment and training.

Morale in the military was low to begin with. But the Somalia Affair, in addition to numerous overseas missions, including Somalia, Yugoslavia, Kosovo, Haiti, Rwanda, the Congo, Ethiopia, and Eritrea, brought Canadian troops to a breaking point. Poor equipment and low pay did not help. The ability to fight also took a hit after human rights legislation was used to remove fitness requirements for everyone in uniform.

The government's enthusiasm for peacekeeping missions inspired Saturday Night magazine to feature an article titled "Nobel Fever." The suggestion was that Chrétien and foreign affairs minister Lloyd Axworthy were lusting for praise from the United Nations and were willing to use Canada's fighting personnel to the point of exhaustion.[12]

Fate intervened to give Canadian troops two important opportunities to win popular support at home. The 1997 Red River flood in Manitoba came first. The civilian emergency management systems in place to respond to the natural disaster were haphazard and disorganized. The armed forces came to the flood zone with an integrated communications system and ample supplies of essential food and water. The military's mission-oriented command and control structure was exactly what was needed in that time of crisis. Canadian soldiers proudly and professionally performed their duties beyond all expectations.

The 1998 Ice Storm that paralyzed much of eastern Ontario and western Québec also helped to change the way citizens looked at their army. Once again, the capabilities and eagerness of the men and women in uniform were on full display. It was not only a relief effort, but a significant contribution to national unity and a demonstration to Québecers that their national government was there to help.

Public opinion towards the armed forces began to turn.[13] A 2002 Compas poll showed that 72 per cent of those surveyed wanted the defence budget increased.[14] An Environics poll revealed that three-quarters of those surveyed supported additional investment in personnel and equipment so the Canadian Forces could do their jobs. This was not the sentiment Chrétien had faced during the 1993 election.

On top of the humanitarian work, after 9/11 soldiers were making sacrifices in fighting the Taliban and Al-Qaeda. The conversion of public opinion was evident when groups of soldiers returned from their tours in Afghanistan. At first, they didn't know what to make of the crowds that had gathered to greet them in Edmonton. From their military bases, they could see residents lining the highway and side streets for kilometres on end holding signs filled with messages of admiration and affection. Hillier wrote that this display was not something that had been seen since the Second World War. "My god, what is this?" the troops wondered.[15]

CHRÉTIEN'S LEGACY ON NATIONAL defence is encapsulated in Hillier's description of a decade of darkness. But the darkness that descended on the military was not based on the prime minister's worldview, ideology, or inherent bias. It was about extracting Canada from a fiscal pit.

The fiscal darkness that fell on the military also fell across most government departments, although defence and industry were hit harder than most. As government finances improved, some of the cuts were reversed. That included an $800 million increase in permanent funding for the military in the 2003 budget, which was every penny that the military had asked for. Initially, Chrétien told his finance minister to scale back on the number because "you never give a minister everything he asks for." But Chrétien relented when he was convinced the funding request was not padded. Chrétien was not anti-military and generally chose strong ministers of defence to protect their realm. Ultimately, he did what most Canadians had asked of him.

The Canadian military learned over the 1990s that the willingness of a government, whether Liberal or Conservative, to invest in defence arises not from demonstrated need but from the support the military enjoys from the public at large. The members of the military ultimately repaired their relationship with Canadians with their heroic behaviour at home and abroad. Nonetheless, Chrétien can rightly be criticized for following the vagaries of public opinion that resulted in a weakening of our national defence.

A CIVIL SOCIETY

MISFIRE

Jean Chrétien was a street fighter at heart, but he was never comfortable with guns.

Despite representing a rural riding where hunters are in abundance, Chrétien did not understand why people wanted to keep firearms in their homes and near their children. Chrétien reluctantly went on hunts from time to time, but never owned a gun. "I'm afraid of them," Chrétien wrote, "and [I] don't really find much sport in killing birds or animals."[1] It was a position that most Liberals and many city dwellers found appealing.

Compared with the US, Canada has always viewed gun ownership as a privilege rather than a right. Starting at Confederation, you could not carry a handgun in Canada unless you had a good reason. A registry for handguns was established in 1934. Automatic firearms were put into the same category as handguns in 1951. After 1977, anyone wanting to buy a gun was required to obtain a Firearms Acquisition Certificate. In 1991, a waiting period on the purchase of guns was imposed, as well as formal training on gun safety. And policies and programs were regularly updated to help keep guns out of the hands of people who might be dangerous or unstable.

With the urbanization of Canada, Chrétien thought he was on safe ground taking gun control to another level. What Chrétien had in his sights was the registration of all guns, including shotguns and rifles, which Canadians used primarily for hunting. He knew this would cost him votes in rural Canada, but he calculated that there were a lot more votes to be won in cities than on farms.

It's not clear when Chrétien decided to toughen Canada's gun laws but the change in policy was not in the 1993 Liberal platform. The Red Book made only a minor reference to banning the importation of restricted firearms into Canada, while also prohibiting anyone convicted of an indictable drug-related offence, a stalking offence, or any violent offence from owning or possessing a gun. Hunters and long guns were not mentioned.

Chrétien's ultimate action on gun control was inspired by the slaughter of 14 women at Montreal's École Polytechnique in 1989. Another key incident was the shooting in Toronto in early 1994 of a 23-year-old woman, a bystander who was killed during a robbery.

Justice Minister Allan Rock was given responsibility for coming up with the government's response to gun violence.[2] Rock was said to have preferred a more incremental approach that tackled the root causes of gun crime. But Chrétien intervened at the 1994 summer Liberal party convention and insisted that tougher gun control laws should be passed. His view was endorsed by party members.

The year after the Toronto incident, and on the sixth anniversary of the École Polytechnique massacre, the Chrétien government passed Bill C-68, a law that banned short-barrelled and small-calibre handguns. In addition, all long guns, including shotguns and rifles, were to be registered in a centralized system by 2003, and the sale of ammunition was to be restricted to licensed gun owners.

Chrétien did not see the registration of long guns as much of a burden. The logic was that if Canadians didn't feel their basic freedoms were violated when required to register their cats and dogs, they could hardly object to registering their guns. But getting two million law-abiding gun owners to register their firearms and follow new regulations on safe gun storage was much harder to achieve than passing a law in Parliament. Chrétien said he would not yield to the gun lobby, a position that *The Windsor Star* predicted would garner him nationwide support.[3]

The front-end business case for the registry pegged the costs at $119 million, which were to be offset by $117 million in fees. In other words, this was designed to be an almost revenue-neutral proposition. But the registry quickly turned into a financial sinkhole. The background checks to license gun owners became more intensive than anticipated, certainly more so than for pet owners. When gun owners protested, the Chrétien government responded with an expensive and largely futile marketing campaign. Facing stiff resistance, registration fees were dropped. Seeing no revenue and soaring costs, the auditor general calculated taxpayers would be hit with a $1 billion charge over ten years.[4]

Gun control had never been a particularly partisan issue in Canada. But it didn't take long for opposition MPs to call the registry a denial of civil liberties and an affront to the taxpayer. The stronger argument was that the registry would fail to meet its stated goal of crime reduction. Rock responded that in ten years, we would look back at the registration of all firearms and wonder what the fuss was about.

The enacting legislation was fast-tracked through the House of Commons, but that didn't prevent nine Liberal and eight NDP MPs from voting against the bill. Progressive Conservative MP Peter MacKay said he would disobey the law, although he later relented. Chrétien punished the recalcitrant Liberal MPs by removing them from their Parliamentary committees.

The Government of Alberta threatened to launch a constitutional challenge to the national registry, arguing that it was an invasion of provincial jurisdiction and a violation of Charter and Aboriginal rights. A survey of Albertans, however, showed that most supported the legislation.[5]

The task of implementing the registry was given to the Department of Justice, which had no experience in running such a program. To win over police forces, the department agreed to almost every tweak that they asked for. That increased the complexity of the system. And it was hard to explain to people from rural Canada who had been life-long gun owners why they had to complete a 12-page form.

It was not an easy file for Rock's successor at Justice to manage. In fact, Alberta MP Anne McLellan said she would have preferred a different assignment at the time: "It was not just the gun registry but youth justice, young offenders, victims' rights and generally the sense that Liberals were soft on crime."

McLellan saw that the implementation of the registry was not just a societal shift but a massive information technology project. She noted that there are few large-scale information projects of the kind in Canada, or elsewhere, that have been delivered on time and on budget. There were no off-the-shelf solutions and everything had to be customized to meet the legislated requirements.

What made the technology program so complex were the policy choices that were made soon after the gun registry was conceived. The registry had become a wish list for everyone involved in the justice system, and implementation issues were largely ignored. Allan Rock testified before Parliamentary committees that the problem was not the registry itself, which he argued came in well within the budget:

> The big spending was in the background checks for licensing. That grew like topsy over time. The reason it ran up to the level that the Auditor General referenced was because of the demands and requests from police forces for the inclusion of other background variables and factors that were not contemplated when the registry was conceived.

Rock was regularly briefed by his officials at day-long retreats where he was told the implementation plan was well in hand. But the reality was otherwise. "If I could reach back in time to change something," Rock said, "it would be asking the tough questions about what these scope changes meant to the cost and complexity of the program."

By 2004, McLellan believed the gun registry was running more or less the way the government had hoped and with costs under control. After the country had made the upfront investment to bring the program online, she lamented the fact that the subsequent Conservative government dismantled the registry in 2011.

The political calculation on the registry was easy to get wrong. Chrétien would have seen the polls indicating cross-country support for the registry because people believed it would make communities safer. But the enthusiasm behind this support was modest at best. On the other hand, opponents of the registry were livid at the government and were determined to punish the Liberals for messing with their lives. For Chrétien, the upside was negligible and the downside was significant.

Allan Rock noted that the month that the Tory bill went through to dismantle the registry, public support for the program was at 72 per cent in the polls. "But the 28 per cent who were opposed were prepared to man the barricades."

Politics aside, was the system worth the money? The argument made by long-gun owners was that there was no evidence that those with criminal intent would heed the law. But many police chiefs across the country believed that the information contained in the registry was useful in helping to protect civilians and police officers. For example, an officer called to a home for domestic violence might take a different approach knowing that there was a gun on the premises. Data compiled by the Canadian Association of Chiefs of Police showed that the registry was used 10,000 times a day, an indication on its own that the system had some value.[6]

Chrétien also thought the registry was doing its job. In his memoirs, he cited data that showed that between 1991 and 2002, close to 500 fewer Canadians per year were killed by firearms and that homicides by rifles and shotguns declined by 64 per cent. He noted that more than 9,000 people were either refused licenses or had a license revoked, suggesting the registry kept guns out of the hands of potentially dangerous people.[7] However, the link between the registry and this data was never confirmed.

To Chrétien, the issue of gun control was not just about public safety, but Canadian values. While at Michigan State University to receive an honorary doctorate of laws in May 1999, Chrétien said the National Rifle Association was one export that Canadians would never buy. "We have one of the toughest gun controls laws in the world. And Canadians want to keep it that way," he said. "Charlton Heston (an actor and prominent gun advocate) should know that when it comes to his gospel on guns, Canada is not the promised land."[8]

Since 1991, the overall crime rate in Canada has declined dramatically, but experts don't agree on why. Statistics Canada cites a variety of factors, including "an aging population, changing policing practices and strategies, the rise of technology, shifts in unemployment, variations in alcohol consumption, evolving neighbourhood characteristics, or changing attitudes towards illegal and risky behaviour."[9]

The downward trend in gun crimes has continued even after the registry was abolished in 2011, evidence that critics say proves the registry did not cause the decline.[10] Other countries that did not create long-gun registries experienced similar downward trends over this period.[11]

There were other issues at stake. Sheila Fraser, Canada's auditor general, wanted to know why Parliament was not informed that the program was seriously over-budget. She did not question the government's prerogative to implement the registry or even to spend more than was forecast. "What's really inexcusable," she charged, "is that Parliament was in the dark. I question why the department continued to watch the costs escalate without informing Parliament and without considering alternatives."[12] The auditor general did what she could to focus the country on the roll-out of the program but Allan Rock thought she had crossed a line:

> I always believed that Sheila Fraser went out of her way to produce an attention-getting report. To get the headline she wanted she needed the billion-dollar figure, and to get that number she calculated the cost for the entire firearms program over a ten-year period.

Whatever the cost, on this issue the government denied MPs the opportunity to discharge one of their most important duties: to provide oversight on the public purse. Even advocates of the registry had a hard time defending the costs, which gained the moniker "boondoggle" in Parliament and in most press reports.[13]

The Conservative Party made great gains in rural Canada in every election after the Chrétien-Martin years by promising to repeal the gun registry, something they delivered with their majority government in 2011. While Justin Trudeau voted against Harper's measure, when running to be the leader of the Liberal party in 2012 he cited the gun registry as a failed and divisive policy and said that there were better ways of keeping Canadians safe.[14] The 2015 Liberal platform emphatically noted, "We will not create a new national long-gun registry to replace the one that has been dismantled."

Allan Rock believes that the Conservative campaign against the registry was not evidence-based but ideological. "It was religious, it was connected to their philosophy, and it was connected to people who don't like the government asking questions about them. The registry got a bum rap."

The gun registry was a scandal because of what it cost, the unnecessary burden it imposed on gun owners and the absence of demonstrable benefits. From a policy perspective, the registry was ill-supported and its implementation was fundamentally mismanaged.

Chrétien may have been correct that most Canadians thought the registry was a good idea in principle, but he was blind to the fervent opposition in rural Canada. The protests across the country by gun owners were heard loud and clear by MPs in all parties. When members of the Liberal caucus voted against the legislation, that should have signalled to Chrétien he was entering dangerous territory. The political cost to Chrétien appeared on election day in 1997 and 2000, when the Liberals lost seats in rural ridings. That price might have been worth paying if the registry made the country safer.

Certainly, the gun registry could have been better managed. It might have endured and gained wider acceptance if the program had been simplified and the costs had been lower. The question often asked, but never definitively answered, is: what good might have been done had the money spent on the gun registry been invested elsewhere? Would Canadians have been safer if that money had gone into policing, community outreach, infiltration of gangs and organized crimes, or education on the safe use of firearms? The conclusion of gun owners, and ultimately rural voters in general, was that Chrétien's registry had missed its target.

KYOTO BOUND

There are two distinct periods to consider when assessing Jean Chrétien's record on the environment. The first is the early years of his administration, when a short-term fiscal crisis and anemic economic growth were the government's priorities. The second is the period after the country's fiscal health had been restored and the prime minister was intent on leaving a progressive legacy.

On environmental leadership, Chrétien had a tough act to follow. It might be assumed that a pro-business conservative would have a poor record on environmental issues, but Brian Mulroney was celebrated for his eco-friendly accomplishments. In 2006, a panel of experts chose Mulroney as Canada's greenest prime minister.[1]

Mulroney's view was that progress on the economy and the environment went together. That's why, even in the face of a massive deficit, he increased the federal budget for environmental initiatives. Jean Charest, his environment minister from April 1991 to June 1993, said that when Mulroney met with presidents Reagan and Bush he made action on acid rain one of his top bilateral priorities. This led to the signing of an acid rain treaty, one of Mulroney's seminal accomplishments.

There were reasons for activists believed that Chrétien would build on Mulroney's legacy. Not only did he have people in his cabinet, like Paul Martin, who saw the environment as a pressing priority, but Chrétien had distinguished himself in Pierre Trudeau's cabinet, where, as the minister for Indian and Northern Affairs, he established ten national parks.[2] In the previous 100 years, only 18 parks had been designated. Chrétien's moves included Canada's first national park in Québec. Successive Québec governments had resisted federal intrusion, but Chrétien was determined to establish a federal park in his home riding in the St. Maurice Valley. Officials in his department thought the area Chrétien had in mind was swamp land until they were taken on a guided tour. Chrétien ultimately mounted a grassroots campaign to pressure the Québec government to allow La Mauricie National Park to become a reality.[3]

Chrétien's environmental credentials were also burnished when he halted a controversial project to build a pipeline through the Mackenzie River Valley in 1974. Chrétien appointed Justice Thomas Berger to lead an inquiry into the project's environmental and social impacts. Berger's report ultimately quashed the pipeline.

IN 1992, THE MULRONEY government set an ambitious target for reducing carbon dioxide emissions. Not to be outdone, the 1993 Liberal Red Book took the targets to an even higher level: a cut in greenhouse gas emissions by 20 per cent from 1988 levels by the year 2005. The Red Book also included a promise to work more collaboratively with the provinces and to appoint an environmental auditor general.

To signal where the environment stood among his priorities, Jean Chrétien chose as his first environment minister his deputy prime minister. But Sheila Copps, a take-no-prisoners politician, struggled in the portfolio. Less than a year into the job, she acknowledged that the government was falling short of the mark. "Oh God. Am I convinced [we will meet our GHG targets]? No. I'm not convinced. But I also think that we have to keep pushing."[4] By pushing, she meant moving the forces of opposition from within her own government.

Elizabeth May, who was executive director of the Sierra Club of Canada during the Chrétien years, said that there was nothing wrong with the Liberal goal on greenhouse gasses (GHGs). The problem was that the words were not backed up by deeds. When a federal-provincial task force explored ways to reduce emissions early in Chrétien's first mandate, May said the prime minister's office took a carbon tax off the table. "They couldn't even talk about it," said May. "Mulroney was committed to his target but Chrétien sabotaged his campaign promise almost immediately. Mulroney gave leadership from the top down. Chrétien pretended to understand climate change, but he didn't." Despite his past actions as a minister and his bold campaign commitments, Chrétien was criticized by environmentalists for over-promising and under-delivering.

When government spending was slashed in the 1995 budget, the environment department suffered more than most with a 48 per cent hit.[5] A weak economy also meant the government was disinclined to impose new regulations or environmental standards on business. While the minister of finance was known to be a staunch supporter of environmental causes, he felt he could not cut hard in some areas and leave the environment envelope untouched.

A frustrated Copps began to lash out about inaction on climate change, as well as the weaknesses in the federal environmental-assessment process. She even criticized a government bill that would allow cabinet ministers to negotiate agreements without the oversight and approval of the environment minister. She was also upset with a provision that delegated certain authorities on the environment to the provinces.[6]

According to May, the fossil-fuel lobbyists wanted Copps removed as environment minister. But May acknowledged that getting rid of Copps would have mattered little since fiscal restraint and short-term economic growth were the government's priorities.

When pressed to decide between Canadian jobs and a potential threat to the environment, the Chrétien government came down on the side of jobs. One example was the government approval of Atomic Energy of Canada's sale of CANDU nuclear reactors to China with what May called the biggest external loan in Canadian history:

> In making the sale they bypassed the Canadian Environment Assessment Act. The Sierra Club of Canada took them to court, personally suing (trade minister) Art Eggleton and Paul Martin in the process. AECL claimed the EA was done in China (in Chinese) and that it could never be made public because of censorship. And they insisted the Chinese EA be submitted in evidence to the federal court, but kept secret. We won the case in the lower court and lost on appeal. Costs were assessed against us and we reluctantly accepted AECL's offer that the case be dropped without payment of their costs. It was heartbreaking not to be able to take the case to the Supreme Court.

The environmental lobby was also upset that Chrétien abandoned his 1993 election promise to appoint an environmental auditor general, or EAG. This independent office was intended to report directly to Parliament. One of its proposed duties was to investigate citizen complaints where there was reason to believe that the government's environmental policies or laws had been ignored or violated. The proposed office was also to report annually on federal environmental programs and spending. Whether it was due to the cost of the office, or the realization that the EAG would become a high-profile critic of the government, the prime minister chose not to fulfill this campaign promise. What was provided instead, said May, was a small contingent of staff buried within the auditor general's office and without much of a budget.

BEFORE THE 1993 CAMPAIGN the Liberals had not won a seat in Alberta in the previous six elections. Fresh in the minds of voters coming into that campaign was the imposition of the National Energy Program in the early 1980s under the Liberal government of Pierre Trudeau. Although rising unemployment and falling house prices ravaged Alberta in the aftermath of the NEP, Chrétien thought the criticism was unfair. He said the Trudeau government played a key role in the development of the oil sands that brought jobs and prosperity to Alberta for a generation. Chrétien believed that oil sands projects were good for the economy and for national unity. He was proud of his role in cobbling together critical early investments in the oil sands by the governments of Canada, Alberta, and Ontario in the 1970s.

In the 1993 election, the Liberal candidate in Edmonton Northwest, Anne McLellan, was declared the winner by a single vote, although a recount boosted her margin of victory to 12. Chrétien wanted to hold the seat and gave McLellan the energy portfolio to show westerners that he had their backs. Elizabeth May contends that Chrétien placed his support for McLellan and the goal of winning more seats in Alberta ahead of responsible stewardship of Canada's natural resources.

May was sickened by the billions of dollars Chrétien put into oil sands development. She said that Canada already had one of the friendliest regimes in the world for oil exploration and that Chrétien and Alberta premier Ralph Klein lowered the bar even further:

> When oil was at $30 per barrel the industry needed serious support to make money out of bitumen. Ralph Klein dropped the royalty rate for oil

sands bitumen, which was only payable after capital costs had been recovered. Then Chrétien gave accelerated capital cost allowances that gave oil companies huge write-offs they could use against the profitable segments of their operations. It was all about seats in Alberta and what the Chrétien government thought would provide short-term economic growth.

McLellan said it was a difficult ask of the finance minister to forgo revenue in the short term to realize a medium to long-term gain economic gain that was expected from oil sands investment:

> At the time, we were cutting 50,000 public servants from the payroll and the budget for my department, Natural Resources Canada, was cut in half. I was convinced that the changes requested (by the Oils Sands Task Force) were the right thing to do, so I and my officials went to Paul Martin and the Department of Finance and made the argument that oil sands investment would create high-paying private sector jobs and increased corporate taxes, not just in Alberta but across the country.

To gain public support for the policy change, McLellan challenged the industry — in particular Syncrude president Eric Newell — to travel across the country to chambers of commerce and boards of trade to talk about why oil was not just an Alberta resource but a national resource. McLellan believes the government's investment paid off:

> Because of where the oil sands are today, people forget that in the early 1990s it was not clear that the resource would be developed on a major scale. The basic technology around extraction was proven but the economics were uncertain. Major capital investments were needed to get to the scale where the oil sands were viable. We didn't need to wait long to see the benefits of the capital investments realized. Both the federal and provincial treasuries have gained from the policy changes in terms of royalties, corporate income tax, and the personal income tax that came from the thousands of jobs that were created, not only in Alberta but across the country. We got where we needed to be to liberate tens of billions of dollars of capital Investment. It was a great example of two levels of government and industry working together. We took a risk and it paid off.

As it turned out, of the four seats the Liberals won in Alberta in 1993, only two were held in 1997. But even maintaining these two seats was important to Chrétien because it meant he was changing the view in western Canada that the Liberal party was its enemy. The last time Liberals had won a majority of Alberta seats in a federal election was 1908.

May was outraged that McLellan did not concede a negative environmental impact from the oil sands. But McLellan said the government did its homework and acted rationally and responsibly: "We were respectful (of environmental concerns) and we met the arguments of others."

As THE GOVERNMENT SHIFTED its attention away from fiscal and economic challenges, it gave a higher priority to the country's environmental health. Not only did the government pass the Species at Risk Act, but as Chrétien's time in office was coming to an end he latched on to the Kyoto Protocol as a legacy game-changer.

The Kyoto Protocol was an international treaty that required Canada to reduce GHG emissions to 6 per cent below 1990 levels. The agreement would only come into force in February 2005, which meant that Chrétien could ratify the treaty without having the burden of implementation.

Despite early promises to work closely with provinces on environmental issues, there was little national consultation by the Chrétien government on Kyoto. Jean Charest, the Liberal premier of Québec when Kyoto was signed, said Chrétien was flying by the seat of his pants. Having served as Mulroney's environment minister, Charest knew how difficult the targets would be to reach without broad public, industry, and government support in place.[7]

When Chrétien brought the Kyoto Protocol to cabinet for discussion there was no plan in place to demonstrate that Canada could meet its targets. Another key concern was that the American government had decided not to sign the treaty. This risked placing Canadian industry at a competitive disadvantage. Chrétien countered President Bush's efforts to kill the Kyoto Accord by deploying his deputy prime minister, Herb Gray, to keep negotiations alive at a special conference in The Hague in 2001. Predictably this failed, but for his efforts, the Sierra Club of Canada conferred on Gray the John Fraser Award for Environment Achievement, its highest honour.[8]

The Liberal caucus urged Chrétien to sign the accord; two-thirds signed a petition to that end. This was a peculiar way for caucus to communicate with its party leader. Coming at a time when future leader Paul Martin's supporters were trying to pressure Chrétien into retiring, Chrétien's team thought the bizarre move had less to do with Kyoto and more as a way of undermining the prime minister's leadership.

On September 2, 2002, Chrétien announced that Canada would ratify the Kyoto Protocol, becoming the 98th country to do so.[9] The announcement was made at the United Nations World Summit on Sustainable Development in Johannesburg, South Africa. Chrétien pointed to extreme weather events around the world and the scientific evidence of climate change as justification for Canada's decision.

The Canadian Alliance Party and the government of Alberta were firmly opposed. Alberta contemplated a constitutional challenge because natural resources were within provincial jurisdiction. Alberta's environment minister, Lorne Taylor, charged that Chrétien's goals were political and personal. "I think it's about leaving an international legacy and I think it was inappropriate. Nobody has any idea of the impact," Taylor said. "I think we need to understand clearly the implications for Canadians."[10]

Although Chrétien did not need Parliamentary approval to sign the accord, it was good politics to put Kyoto to a vote. This flushed out his opponents to go on the public record, including recalcitrant Liberal MPs. Chrétien limited the debate in the House of Commons to only eight days, but that did not deter the Bloc Québécois and the NDP from supporting the government.

Anne McLellan understood that the Kyoto protocol was political dynamite in her home province:

I was in my office in Edmonton, at Canada Place, on a Friday afternoon and I got the call from the PMO giving me a heads up that the prime minister was on a flight to South Africa to sign the Kyoto Accord. Well, that was not my best Friday afternoon. It was a difficult time. I told Eddie Goldenberg that depending on how this played out I could not support Kyoto if it made it impossible for the industry to have a future. I was worried about the uncertainty around the implementation of the accord, which could have bled investment to other jurisdictions.

If McLellan could not find her way to support the signing of the accord she would have to leave the cabinet. She went to work to soften what she saw as a potential economic blow. She worked closely with, among others, the Canadian Association of Petroleum Producers to ensure the industry did not overreact.

The prime minister was not opposed to the resource sector and he did not want Alberta to build a firewall around itself in response, as Stephen Harper and others had once suggested. He was determined that, whatever the economic impacts, Kyoto would not be another National Energy Program that had decimated the economy of Western Canada in the early 1980s.

Allan Rock, who was then the minister of industry, was similarly motivated. He met with the energy sector and told them that the absence of a plan meant that there was ample room to address their concerns. But he admired Chrétien's leadership and political courage: "There are some similarities to what John Kennedy did when he challenged America to send a man to the moon and return him safely to earth. He didn't have a plan but the mission was accomplished."

When Canada signed Kyoto, a national poll by EKOS revealed that 62 per cent of Canadians were on the government's side, although in oil-rich Alberta support was only 40 per cent.[11] The survey also showed that an overwhelming majority of Canadians were prepared to accept a lower standard of living if it meant progress was made on climate change. Only about one-third were worried that Kyoto might have a negative impact on jobs.

Chrétien's environment minister, David Anderson, acknowledged that ratification was based more on the prime minister's vision than a sense of confidence the government could meet its commitment. "He gets the right gut feeling. And he's got the antenna, which very few people have, the political antenna," Anderson said. "His critics fail to realize it is one of the signs of his genius that he doesn't want to know too much about certain things."[12]

Allan Rock said Kyoto could have been studied to death but that "sometimes in public life you have to decide." Chrétien ignored his critics who wanted a blueprint rather than a vision: "I thought it was important first to establish an obtainable target and then to figure out how to meet it step by step, year by year."[13]

Paul Martin was concerned about a lack of engagement with the provinces. He wrote that pitting Ottawa against the provinces had "no place in the great national challenge that lies ahead of us." Jean Charest said that when he was at the Rio Earth Summit he brought the provinces to the table along with industry: "When Chrétien signed Kyoto he was on his own."

Martin proposed that a parliamentary committee be charged with cross-country consultations to develop an implementation plan that would be acceptable to the provinces. Martin thought Canadians needed to understand that Kyoto meant personal lifestyle changes. He also wanted to use the government's $1.5 billion profit from its sale of Petro-Canada to develop low-carbon energy solutions, such as from wind and solar.

A few months after Kyoto was signed, but before it was passed in the House of Commons, Martin argued for a delay. "Canadians are entitled to know the benefits and the costs. I believe that it is very important, much more preferable, if we can achieve national consensus on the implementation plan."[14] Martin called Chrétien's approach policymaking by photo-op. Fearing the politics of the issue, Martin ultimately endorsed Kyoto. But within Liberal circles and among environmental activist circles he continued to express reservations. "We were able to calm Paul down," observed Elizabeth May. "We convinced him that we could reach the targets with a plan developed after he became prime minister."

Herb Dhaliwal, Chrétien's minister of natural resources when Kyoto was signed, called Martin a flip-flopper. "At one time, he said he wanted to delay ratification. Now he thinks it's very important to move very quickly so that we can get ahead with our technology. He keeps changing his position on a regular basis. I wonder what he'll say tomorrow."[15]

It's interesting that Martin was recalcitrant about committing to a goal without a plan because that's what the government did with its fiscal policy. By his own admission, he didn't think the government's fiscal goal would be achieved, let alone exceeded, when it was set in the 1993 election campaign. But it was the target that disciplined and energized the system. Setting out a vision is precisely what leaders are supposed to do.

A senior government official who was involved in the Kyoto decision said Chrétien wanted to be on the right side of history. Without that leadership, he said, the worthy goal of saving the planet might never be achieved.

The Sierra Club of Canada gave Chrétien an award for ratifying Kyoto. But according to Elizabeth May, this was not because they thought he was an environmental hero. It was to give the prime minister ammunition in dealing with the opposition in the House of Commons, and from Ralph Klein and the Bush administration. Still, she criticized Chrétien's "joke" of an implementation plan.[16]

PAUL MARTIN WAS PRIME minister when Canada hosted the United Nations Climate Change Conference in November 2005. Like Chrétien before him, he was unable to put a credible Kyoto implementation plan on the table. When the Liberal leadership was up for grabs in 2006, Michael Ignatieff, a candidate who had recently returned to Canada from teaching at Harvard University, chastised the Martin government and its environment minister Stéphane Dion for failing to reduce GHG emissions. "We didn't get it done," became a Conservative tag line against Dion after he became Liberal leader in 2006.

Rather than worry about a plan, Stephen Harper's Conservative government rescinded Canada's Kyoto commitment in 2006, the only signatory country to do so. The Conservative government argued that because the United States and China were not signatories, the protocol would never work. This avoided penalties as high as $14 billion that could have been imposed on Canada for failing to achieve Kyoto targets.

The Liberal party made no mention of Kyoto in their 2015 election platform, but pledged to fulfill a G20 commitment to phase out subsidies for the fossil fuel industry. Justin Trudeau also committed to ending the cycle of setting arbitrary targets. Along with his minister for the environment and climate change minister, Trudeau proclaimed that "Canada is back" at the Paris COP Conference in December 2015 where the United Nations framework on climate change was addressed.

CHRÉTIEN SAID HE WAS PROUD of his government's record on the environment. His view was that the science of climate change was not well known when he became prime minister in the early 1990s, and that supporting oil sands development for economic gain was not done at the expense of the environment. When the research on climate change became more conclusive and government finances had stabilized, Chrétien signed Kyoto. He did so while facing significant opposition, including from his likely successor, Paul Martin, and some of his western MPs and cabinet ministers.

A decade after he left office, the economic impact of climate change and the implementation of the Kyoto Protocol have not been felt and cannot be calculated. Rather than bind his successors to a commitment or a plan, Chrétien simply set out a vision and direction. Chrétien cites Kyoto as a key element of his legacy, but subsequent events tell us that his actions, so far, are less consequential.

IMMIGRATION

The 1993 Red Book boasted that the Liberal party was the natural home for new Canadians. Indeed, for most first- and second-generation immigrants, it was a succession of Liberal governments that welcomed them to Canada. It helped their case that since Sir John A. Macdonald, for every day the Tories held power the Liberals had two.

Few political analysts doubted the pro-immigration bona fides of the Liberal party or the symbiotic relationship it enjoyed with ethnic communities. Many immigrant communities equated the freedom and equality of opportunity that attracted them to Canada with liberalism and the Liberal party. The Charter of Rights and Freedoms, which was especially prized by recent immigrants for its protection of minority rights, came into being under Pierre Trudeau.

The Red Book made a few commitments on immigration, pledging to balance humanitarian and economic considerations while accepting a fair share of refugees. The Liberal target for immigration, at 1 per cent of the population each year, was largely unchanged from the previous Progressive Conservative government.

The only hint at a Liberal policy shift in 1993 was its prioritizing of family-class applicants. This message was designed to win votes in immigrant communities and appeal specifically to those who wanted to bring their relatives to Canada. With the total number of immigrants staying constant, more relatives meant that skilled workers would be moved down the priority list.

Another vote-getter was the Liberal promise to undo Mulroney's decision to attach the immigration department to a broader portfolio that included prisons, police, and parole. "For me," said Chrétien, "it's giving the ministry of immigration an image that it should not have. Immigration is what made Canada and the immigrants of this land feel that they are good citizens."[1]

WHILE CHRÉTIEN PROMISED TO prioritize family-class immigrants, he did precisely the opposite. In late 1995 the immigration minister, Sergio Marchi, announced that the proportion of economic immigrants would increase from 43 per cent to 53 per cent.[2] At a time of economic stress, Chrétien thought it was better to let a 25-year-old skilled electrician into the country than his 70-year-old grandfather. Of the more than two million immigrants who landed in Canada during Chrétien's time in office, more than 60 per cent were university or college educated, or held a trade school certificate.

Under Mulroney, there was an equal number of family class and economic immigrants. But under Chrétien it was almost two to one in favour of the economic class.

Another shift was to prioritize those with English and French language skills. This was thought to lower settlement costs and accelerate integration into the

IMMIGRATION WAS LINKED TO ECONOMIC GROWTH, NOT FAMILY REUNIFICATION

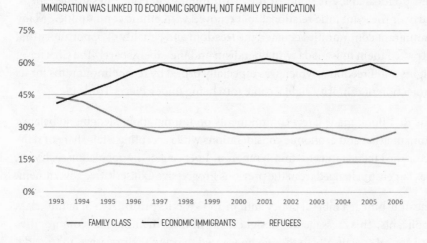

workforce. The temporary foreign worker program was enhanced because it helped Canadian businesses remain competitive. The last thing Chrétien wanted was a straight line from the immigration line to the welfare roll. That's why one of his first changes in immigration policy was to grant work permits to refugee claimants.[3] Another change was to require sponsoring relatives to pick up the tab if a refugee ended up on welfare.

While the Liberal line was that they did not take a law-and-order approach to immigration, the reality was that the government applied additional resources to deport those who had no status in Canada, especially criminals. A toll-free "snitch line" was even considered as a tactic to track down illegal immigrants.[4]

Chrétien's policy shift on immigration was biased in favour of economic growth, but the approach tugged at his conscience. Was it fair, he wondered, for Canada to pick the best-of-the-best from less-developed nations? Should a poor country that raised and trained a medical professional not expect some benefit from their investment? Despite his apprehensions, Chrétien was pulled in the direction of short-term economic growth and at the least possible cost to the federal treasury. That included the government looking to recover its administrative costs through a $975 landing fee, which was assessed on all immigrants, including refugees. Canada was the only country to apply a fee to refugees, although this measure was abolished in 2000.

THE OVERALL IMMIGRATION RATE under Chrétien was just below three-quarters of 1 per cent of the population. This was well below the government's 1 per cent target that was implied in the Red Book and less on average than what had been achieved under Brian Mulroney.[5]

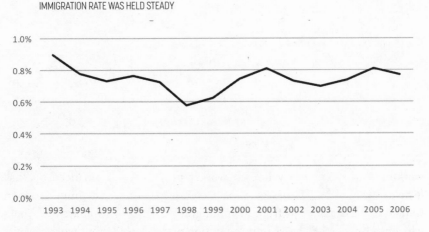

IMMIGRATION RATE WAS HELD STEADY

Chrétien was pro-immigration, but not just for economic reasons. The data revealed that immigrants who landed in Québec were overwhelmingly federalist. That case could not have been made any stronger than when Premier Jacques Parizeau blamed the loss of the 1995 Québec referendum on money

and the ethnic vote. While Parizeau was widely condemned for the xenopho-
bic undertone of his comment, Chrétien's immigration minister said much the
same thing when he told a reporter that new Canadians were a strong contingent of the No vote.[6]

Other than as a force for national unity, Chrétien used immigration to support his government's economic goals. His intent was not to remake society as
much as it was to make the country prosperous.

INDIGENOUS AFFAIRS

Three weeks before the 1968 federal election, a voter asked Jean Chrétien about his government's policies towards the "Indians" of Canada. "Do you want a frank answer? I don't know a damn thing about it."[1]

Two weeks after the election, Pierre Trudeau appointed Chrétien as his minister of Indian and Northern Affairs, the seventh person to hold the portfolio in seven years. Chrétien resisted the posting, sensing it was a graveyard for ministers. But Trudeau turned Chrétien's ignorance to advantage: "Nobody will be able to say that you have any preconceived views of the problem."[2]

While the challenges facing Chrétien in 1968 were evident, the solutions were not. Indigenous peoples in Canada have long been the victims of discrimination, abuse, and oppression. They have protested the loss of unceded territory, the abrogation of treaties, disrespect of their cultural heritage, and general exploitation under the Indian Act. Poverty has been rampant.

Pierre Trudeau had long advocated for equality and individual rights and he opposed special rights for any individual or group, including Indigenous Canadians. He said it was inconceivable that one segment of society would have a treaty with another. He called the Indian Act a policy of apartheid and wanted it repealed. He also wanted to do away with land claims and make Indigenous peoples the responsibility of provinces.[3]

Chrétien consulted Indigenous leaders on Trudeau's ideas and found no consensus. Nonetheless, he pursued Trudeau's vision and attempted to enact the most sweeping reform of the Indian Act since Confederation. It did not go well. He learned that Indigenous peoples did not identify as individuals, but as tribes and nations. He learned that their fear of assimilation and losing their

identity was stronger than the sense of discrimination they perceived. Their outrage forced the Trudeau government to scrap the government's proposed reforms.[4]

Chrétien realized that he did not understand the communities he was expected
to serve. He initiated a more respectful and inclusive dialogue or, as he put it,
he listened while Indigenous leaders gave him hell. Having been pilloried for
being out of touch, even heartless, Chrétien learned from his mistakes. Being a
populist meant not sticking your neck out on policies that may be sound intel-
lectually but may irritate the community you are expected to serve. Chrétien
was on safer ground when he fought for increased funding to Indigenous organizations, appointed a land claims commissioner, and increased the number
of Indigenous people working in his department.

His zeal and frenetic pace caught up with him in 1973 when he was diag-
nosed with exhaustion, indigestion, and a possible heart attack. He spoke with
Trudeau about his future and was offered an appointment to the judiciary.
For a man who desired and needed action, Chrétien knew he would never be
happy on the bench. When Indigenous leaders heard rumours that Chrétien
would be shuffled out of his portfolio, Trudeau was bombarded with telegrams
urging him to keep their minister in place. Indigenous peoples had embraced
Chrétien after he embraced them, including adopting an Indigenous child,
Michel.

After six-and-a-half years as minister of Indian Affairs, Chrétien had not lost
his sense of humour or his penchant for being politically incorrect: "I'm quite
happy. I still have my scalp."[5]

EXPECTATIONS IN INDIGENOUS COMMUNITIES were high when Chrétien
became prime minister. Their way of life on reserves and elsewhere had
changed little over the years. They were plagued with poor housing, unsafe
drinking water, high unemployment, poverty, a lack of educational opportunities, and health services that were below national standards. Red Book
campaign promises included the gradual winding down of the Department
of Indian Affairs and a laundry list of other ideas including the creation of a
National Aboriginal Development Bank, Aboriginal control over housing, an
Aboriginal Head Start program for preschool children, the incorporation of
Aboriginal healing methods into healthcare delivery, and an alternative justice

system for Aboriginal peoples. The commitment that had the biggest fiscal risk was a promise to create an independent commission to speed up and facilitate the resolution of land claims.

With Chrétien's ministerial experience and his personal commitment to improving Indigenous relations, the newly-elected Liberal government was poised for a possible breakthrough.

Then, in May 1995, a draft government report on Aboriginal self-government was leaked to the press. The report proposed that indigenous communities would be given a range of powers that would normally be associated with municipalities and provinces.[6] Indigenous leaders took exception to the government negotiating "behind closed doors" and for formulating secret plans and documents. They also objected to being categorized as municipalities when they saw their identity as nations. It was not a good start.

Chrétien had advocated for an increase in spending on Indian Affairs, which was opposed by his finance minister. To the prime minister's astonishment, Paul Martin argued that because many Indigenous Canadians lived in Third-World conditions, that federal spending in this realm should be counted as the equivalent of foreign aid. While this would have enabled Canada to claim it was closer to its target for official development assistance, the symbolism of labelling the government's support as the equivalent of charity would have been offensive to most Canadians and to Indigenous communities.[7] Chrétien saw nothing but political havoc in Martin's suggestion and it was dropped.

The most significant decision that Chrétien made respecting the Indian Affairs department was to leave its budget untouched while other government departments saw their funding slashed, in some cases by close to 50 per cent.

In November 1996, Chrétien received the report of the Royal Commission on Aboriginal Peoples. The commission, which was struck by Brian Mulroney in 1991 and cost more than $50 million, heard from close to 2,000 people and organizations and examined over 200 research studies. Its report, called A Blueprint for Change, came with a staggering 440 recommendations.

Chrétien responded with an action plan titled *Gathering Strength*. Among the plan's more powerful directives was a $350-million Community Healing Fund in response to the residential schools tragedy in which young children were removed from their parents and sent to strict and abusive boarding schools run by various Christian churches. Chrétien's government also apologized for the actions of past Liberal and Conservative governments.

Progress on settling land claims was hard to detect. An industry of professionals enjoyed a healthy living off the tedious negotiations. Chrétien had once asked one obstinate lawyer, "Are you for the Crees, the trees, or the fees?"[8] Chrétien put a new treaty process in place in Saskatchewan and reached agreements with Yukon First Nations. Following extensive land claims negotiations and a plebiscite, Chrétien built on the work of Brian Mulroney and established the territory of Nunavut, giving Indigenous communities greater control of their circumstances within their territory.

Nearing the end of his time in office, Chrétien was troubled that his government had fallen short of its goals to improve the lives of Indigenous Canadians. Out of frustration, he established a committee of ministers to develop a cross-cutting government-wide approach and plan. Eddie Goldenberg said the committee was good at producing lengthy papers but was too large and it went nowhere. Ministers acknowledged there was a significant problem, but Goldenberg was perplexed that they all thought their departments were doing well.

PAUL MARTIN HAD THE advantage of a large surplus at his disposal when he reached an agreement with Indigenous leaders and the provinces (excluding Québec) in Kelowna, BC. The accord promised a $5 billion investment over five years, but it was ratified the day before his government was defeated in the House of Commons. That made it something of a blank cheque that others would have to honour.

When Stephen Harper became prime minister, he endorsed the Kelowna targets on education, health, housing, and economic development, but with a much-reduced level of financial support. In June 2006, Martin introduced a private member's bill to force the implementation of the Kelowna Accord on the minority Conservative government. Since private members' bills cannot include an expenditure of public funds, the legislation was deemed unconstitutional. During Harper's tenure, progress on Indigenous issues was lacking, and many affected communities organized themselves to help defeat his government in the 2015 election.

IT'S DIFFICULT TO ARGUE that there has been a minister or a prime minister who was more personally attentive to the plight of Indigenous Canadians than Jean Chrétien. He was hampered in his early years as prime minister due to a lack of fiscal flexibility, but even then, he prioritized Indigenous investments. Other leaders might have gone in a different direction.

In May 2016, close to 50 years after he became minister of Indian and Northern Affairs, Chrétien was asked what the government could do to alleviate the dire conditions and a rash of suicide attempts at the Attawapiskat First Nations community in northern Ontario:

> There's always tragedies of that nature that occur, and the government has to do its best to cure it, but it's not easy. It's an extremely difficult situation … The problem is isolation, and it is difficult to have economic activities in some of these areas. When I quit politics in '86 for a few years, I kept working with the Natives. I went to northern Manitoba, and it is extremely difficult to have a life there. But they are traditional. They want to be close to the land. They are nostalgic about the past when they were going hunting and fishing, and it takes time … It's desirable to stay if they want to stay but it's not always possible. So you cannot have a statement that is generic. It's extremely difficult. It's one case at a time. It's difficult culturally for them all the time.

Chrétien was accused of promoting a policy of assimilation. Perhaps feeling the inadequacy of his answer, Chrétien excused himself from reporters, saying, "I have nothing to do with politics anymore." But that didn't mean Chrétien had stopped caring about Indigenous people, or that he had given up hope. Having been the longest-serving minister of Indian and Northern Affairs he knew that the problems were so engrained, and the relationships with government so dysfunctional, that breakthroughs were unrealistic and progress would come only in small steps. And repairing the damage could not be solved with money alone.

Chrétien was not satisfied with the progress he had made when he relinquished power in 2003. Nonetheless, his approach to problem-solving of making practical and tangible progress, rather than making sweeping and visionary statements, delivered some results. The income of Indigenous Canadians remained substantially below the national average but the gap had narrowed considerably across all related categories. Progress was also seen in the Community

Well-Being Index, which combines data on incomes, housing, education, and employment.[9] Indigenous graduation rates went to record levels. That circumstances were better for Indigenous Canadians when he left office than when he arrived was as much as any prime minister could boast.

SAME-SEX MARRIAGE

Pierre Trudeau famously said, "The state has no place in the bedrooms of the nation." As prime minister, he changed the laws to remove homosexual acts from the Criminal Code. His next move on individual rights came in 1982 with the patriation of the Canadian constitution and the adoption of the Charter of Rights and Freedoms. But the Charter was silent on the rights of gays and lesbians. Trudeau had determined that the matter was too controversial, so he declined to include discrimination on the basis of sexual orientation. That left the fate of gays and lesbians, in that moment, in the hands of elected officials, who were otherwise slow to make changes to the status quo.

Section 15 of the Constitution bans discrimination before the law, and in particular discrimination based on mental or physical disability, race, national or ethnic origin, colour, religion, sex, or age. Citizens who felt that their natural human rights were denied had the option to seek redress with a constitutional challenge in the courts. The words "in particular" suggested that the list was not exhaustive and that discrimination on a basis that is analogous to those listed could be considered. In other words, the court can "read in" rights where it feels it's appropriate. This approach is consistent with what is known as the "living tree" doctrine under which constitutional interpretation adapts to the times. In fact, it is not unusual for the Supreme Court to overturn one of its own rulings because of how society has evolved.

This "living tree" approach has been criticized by those who believe that the courts are usurping the role of elected legislators. But advocates of the principle point to the reluctance of Parliament to address sensitive societal issues. Indeed, governments have often sought guidance from the Supreme Court when they have lacked the political courage to act on their own.

In the 1998 case of Delwin Vriend, who had been dismissed from his position as a lab coordinator at King's College because of his sexual orientation, the Supreme Court ruled that the exclusion of homosexuals from protection against discrimination in Alberta violated the equality provisions of the Charter.

In 1999, the Supreme Court of Canada ruled that same-sex couples were entitled to enjoy most of the same financial and legal benefits as married couples, although it did not confer the right to marriage. In response, Chrétien clarified the federal position in February 2000 with the passage of Bill C-23, the Modernization of Benefits and Obligations Act, to align Canadian laws with the court ruling. To counter criticism, a clause was inserted in the bill that defined marriage as the lawful union of one man and one woman to the exclusion of all others. Chrétien deflected the more progressive members in his caucus by saying some would have to put water in their wine to get the bill passed.[1]

Soon a succession of provincial courts ruled that it was discriminatory not to allow a same-sex couple to marry. In July 2002, an Ontario court gave the federal government two years to extend marriage rights to same-sex couples. The Ontario Court of Appeal upheld the lower court ruling in June 2003. Chrétien was in a cabinet meeting when he was notified of the ruling. His first reaction was to launch an appeal. That's when John Manley intervened and said, "Before we appeal maybe we should read it." The Chrétien government, on the recommendation of the House of Commons Standing Committee on Justice, declined to challenge the ruling.

The federal government's change of heart on same-sex marriage was difficult for Chrétien to accept. But he was loath to challenge the Charter or the courts on issues related to human rights:

> Believe me, for someone of my generation, born and brought up in the Catholic, rural Québec of my youth, this is a very difficult issue. I have learned over 40 years in public life that society evolves, and that the concept of human rights evolves more quickly than some of us, and sometimes even in ways that makes him feel uncomfortable. But at the end of the day, we have to live up to our responsibilities.[2]

Chrétien resisted calls from the opposition and some within his own caucus for the law to recognize civil unions between gays and lesbians so that the term "marriage" could be reserved for a relationship between a man and a woman. He also rejected a proposal to have the issue determined through a national referendum:

> To have a referendum to decide the fate of a minority, it's a problem. It's why we have constitutions to protect the minorities. It's why you have the Charter of Rights. So, if it is always the majority vote by referendum, who will defend the minorities?[3]

Within a week of the Ontario Court of Appeal ruling, Chrétien committed his government to introducing legislation to recognize same-sex marriage. He said his government would also affirm the right of religious organizations to solemnize only those marriages that were consistent with their teachings. Sensing a division in Liberal ranks — and to cater to his political base — Stephen Harper, then leader of the Canadian Alliance Party, placed a resolution before the House of Commons in September 2003 to affirm that the word "marriage" could not be used by gays and lesbians. He trapped some Liberals with the motion, which was narrowly rejected by a vote of 137–132. Harper pledged to take the issue to voters in the federal election that was expected in 2004.[4]

For political cover, Chrétien had his same-sex marriage bill referred to the Supreme Court before submitting it to the House of Commons. The court provided limited guidance, saying only that the federal government had the jurisdiction to act. But the court suggested that full equality meant that gays and lesbians should be able to marry. The Supreme Court ruling was handed down days before Chrétien retired from office, so it was up to Paul Martin to follow through.

Initially, Martin said same-sex marriage was an issue he was "wrestling with."[5] During the 2003 leadership campaign, Martin declared he was in favour of gay marriage, but he added he was open to alternatives and debate. The editorial writers at the Montreal Gazette suggested that if you're for same-sex marriage then Martin is your man. But if you are opposed, Martin is still your man. "He appears immune to the criticism that he is vague and indecisive. But there is a real risk that in government he will have trouble making unavoidable hard choices."[6]

Martin's government introduced governing legislation in 2005. The motion passed on a free vote, with MPs allowed by their parties to vote with their conscience rather than along party lines. There were members of all parties who voted against the bill, including most Conservative MPs. In 2005, Canada was one of only four countries to have legislation on same-sex marriage. It would be another ten years before the US Supreme Court ruled on the issue.

Stephen Harper committed his party to holding another free vote on same-sex marriage after the 2006 election, even though many members of his minority government caucus saw only trouble in revisiting the issue. Nonetheless, Harper asked MPs to vote on marriage as the union only between a man and a woman, but it was defeated by a vote of 175 to 123. Harper said he would not reopen the question again in the future. In the 2015 election, there was not a single reference to same-sex marriage in any of the parties' platforms. The issue had been settled, not just in Canada but in much of the rest of the world. The Chrétien government had come to its determination earlier than most. While Martin took the issue to its definitive conclusion, it was Chrétien who stuck his neck out on same-sex marriage.

Chrétien had to reconcile his small-town and traditional views with a modern and inclusive outlook on human rights. Having played an instrumental role in the Charter of Rights and Freedoms, it was inevitable that Chrétien would come down on the side of expanding individual liberties. For this, and other social reforms launched by Chrétien, *The Economist* magazine referred to Canada as being "rather cool." In a cover story published in September 2003, it wrote that "this social liberalism points to an increasingly self-confident country."[7]

Chrétien's management of the same-sex marriage question, and his personal conversion from opponent to champion provided a rare instance of both columnists and editorial writers singing the prime minister's praises.

A POLITICAL LIFE

SHAWINIGATE

When the police used pepper spray on protesters at the 1997 Asia-Pacific Economic Cooperation summit in Vancouver, the media and opposition politicians labelled the incident Peppergate. In the echelon of scandals using the suffix "gate," it hardly rated as a major event.

The APEC summit was about lowering trade barriers, creating jobs, reducing poverty, and increasing educational opportunities. To protestors, it was about a system that produced an unjust distribution of wealth.

As chair of the summit, Chrétien was focused on running the meeting and delivering a joint communiqué by the established deadline. The police were responsible for calming the crowds and protecting the security of world leaders and their advisors. Some of the more aggressive protestors were pepper-sprayed by the RCMP. Whether the tactics were appropriate or not, the media wanted to know if Chrétien had supported the measures. When asked, he said he didn't have a clue what the media were talking about, then light-heartedly added that pepper is something he puts on his plate.

It's not clear whether Chrétien was being flippant or had difficulty understanding the question because of his hearing impediment. But he could not understand why the remark became so controversial. It may have appeared to be insensitive, but he did not see his remarks as "the massacre of the innocents."

Protestors alleged the prime minister had sacrificed their rights of peaceful protest so he could make Canada look good in the eyes of foreign leaders. The event became a public spectacle, in part because thought leaders such as *Globe and Mail* editor-in-chief William Thorsell attacked Chrétien for being cruel. Thorsell suggested Chrétien was a deeply troubled man with personal insecurities that clouded his judgment:

> At what risk did Mr. Chrétien place the country because of his suspicious fear of those who might be smarter than him, or who had bested him in some earlier confrontation ... It becomes a paranoiac world in which the cardboard signs of students standing for the rule of law and freedom of speech against the universally acknowledged transgressions of foreign leaders turn into dangerous weapons ... Pepper spray is better than a baseball bat or water cannon at controlling students.[1]

In response to media attention and public criticism, the RCMP Complaints Commission launched an inquiry into police conduct. More than 150 witnesses were heard over 160 days of hearings. The 453-page report highlighted mistakes made by the RCMP. Chrétien was cleared of the accusation that he had interfered in the security operation or had a hand in the decision to use pepper spray, but there was evidence that an aide in the prime minister's office pressured police to calm the scene.

Chrétien was upset that a $12 million inquiry was held in the first place. It was a high price, he said, for a television soap opera.[2] Inquiries, he thought, made lawyers rich and damaged the reputations of police and public servants. Gossip and innuendo prevailed, he said, because the standard rules of evidence don't apply.[3] Had it been up to him, the inquiry would never have taken place.

SHAWINIGATE WAS A MUCH larger political scandal, involving a golf course, a small inn, a Crown corporation, the newspaper industry, the Supreme Court, the RCMP, and a prime minister. What Shawinigate didn't involve was large sums of money.

In his memoirs, Chrétien deemed the affair trivial and not worth recounting except for the attention it received in the media. There was no official finding of guilt on Chrétien's part and no one from his political entourage lost his or her job.

As Chrétien tells it, the saga began in 1988, when he was out of politics and, along with some partners, purchased the Grand Mère Golf Club. He said he was motivated by his love of the game and from the pleasure of owning a golf course that was once the bastion of the Shawinigan big shots.

The new golf course owners were then approached by Consolidated Bathurst about leasing the Auberge Grand Mère, a run-down hotel adjacent to the golf course, for an annual rent of one dollar. Chrétien's group invested about $200,000 to spruce up the property. In April 1993, while leader of the opposition, Chrétien and his partners transferred the lease on the Auberge Grand Mère to a local businessman, Yvon Duhaime. Chrétien claims that the $200,000 selling price was paid in full, giving him a clean break from the Auberge.

In November of that year, just as Chrétien was being sworn in as prime minister, the Chrétien family holding company sold its interest in the Grand Mère golf course to Jonas Prince, a Toronto real estate developer. The terms included an interest-free loan. While Chrétien had no residual interest in the golf course, he retained the risk associated with the loan to Prince. It has never been explained why a Toronto real estate tycoon would want to make a minor investment in a golf course in Shawinigan. Did Prince take a sudden interest in Québec golf courses? Or was he doing a favour for a newly elected prime minister? A Conservative politician who dug deep into the matter concluded that the reason Prince bought Chrétien's interest in the Grand Mère Golf Club will likely go with him to his grave. It was only when Prince sold the golf course to a third party in 1999 that the loan to Chrétien's company was paid off.[4]

In September 1996, prior to Prince discharging his debt, Yvon Duhaime had sought a $1.4 million government loan from the Business Development Bank of Canada to spruce up the Auberge he had taken over from Chrétien's group. The loan application was rejected on its merits by bank officials. But in August 1997, the BDC granted Duhaime a smaller loan of $615,000.

The BDC is a Crown corporation whose board of directors and president are appointed by the federal government. In the fall of 2000, it was revealed that Chrétien had called the president of the BDC, François Beaudoin, on two occasions to inquire about the status of the loan application. Chrétien said that he had made these calls in 1997 in his capacity as the MP for Saint-Maurice, and not as prime minister.

Beaudoin said he felt pressured by Chrétien because the prime minister controlled his appointment as president of the bank. Chrétien wanted the loan approved to keep the Auberge in business because it meant more jobs for the community he represented. It could be argued that it would be unfair to the prime minister's constituents if they were denied assistance from their elected MP just because he was the head of government. Chrétien claimed he applied no undue pressure and simply presented the virtues of the loan application to his community.

David Zussman contends that there is a serious policy issue at stake that has never been studied: "What is the role of the PM who is also an MP when it comes to his own riding? Landing in some awkward places will always be a problem in our Parliamentary system."

Chrétien had been through this sort of conflict before when he served in Pierre Trudeau's cabinet. A commercial dispute before the courts affected jobs in Shawinigan. The judge took more time to decide the case than Chrétien thought was necessary, so he gave him a call. Chrétien said he did not ask the judge to rule one way or the other but just to make his decision so that the community could move forward. Prime Minister Trudeau admonished Chrétien for interfering with the court. But Chrétien refused to apologize and said he would not abandon the unemployed in his riding. John Rae, a former executive assistant to Chrétien, wrote that the sophisticates from Toronto and Montreal might wonder why he would extend himself to his constituents to get grants and loans for special projects, exposing himself to criticism in the process. Chrétien told him, "If I don't who will? *The Globe and Mail* and the *National Post* don't vote for me and they don't care about Shawinigan."

Industry Minister John Manley, who had the BDC in his portfolio, said he didn't trust Beaudoin and found him to be obsequious. He also questioned Beaudoin's ethics and was concerned he had used his delegated authority to enhance his BDC pension. Manley thought Beaudoin tried to increase his odds of being reappointed to another term by hiring Jean Carle as a BDC vice president. Carle, who had no experience in the banking sector, had most recently been a staffer in the prime minister's office. In fact, there were media reports that Carle was an unofficial member of the Chrétien family. Manley did not want to renew Beaudoin's appointment, at least not for a five-year term. But when the appointments list came before cabinet, the prime minister's appointments secretary had Beaudoin down for a full five years on the prime minister's recommendation.

In August 1999, the BDC called in the $615,000 Auberge loan. Beaudoin said the decision led to him being forced out of office although, officially, he resigned. In December, the BDC annulled the severance agreement it had reached with Beaudoin. The case landed in court. After spending $4.3 defending its position, the government lost the case and Beaudoin's payments were restored. Chrétien later told Manley that he should have listened to him when he recommended that Beaudoin not be renewed.

As far as Chrétien was concerned, Shawinigate was the perfect Canadian scandal: "No sex, no violence." He noted that he even lost a bit of money on the transaction.[5]

But Chrétien was denounced in the press and by opposition politicians. He thought that Progressive Conservative leader Joe Clark was reckless with his accusations and abused his parliamentary immunity so that he could not be sued for defamation of character. Clark's main contention was that Chrétien continued to have a financial interest in the golf course because of the money he was owed by Jonas Prince. If the Auberge did well, Clark argued, then so would the golf course and Chrétien's prospects for getting the loan repaid would increase. By helping Duhaime, Clark alleged, Chrétien was helping himself.

Clark, who had a confidential source on the ground in Shawinigan, spent much of his allotted time in Parliament pursuing the scandal.[6] Clark demanded an RCMP investigation and a public inquiry. Chrétien thought he deserved better from Clark, who had once approached him about appointing his brother to the bench.[7] When the RCMP concluded that there were no grounds to proceed with an investigation, Chrétien triumphantly remarked, "Somebody said to me that he started out as Joe Who. Now he's Joe McCarthy."[8] Chrétien enacted some revenge by ensuring that when Clark visited Washington he was denied an invitation to the White House to meet President George W. Bush.[9]

Chrétien and the Liberals bristled at the criticism. When Progressive Conservative house leader Peter MacKay approached his Liberal counterpart, Don Boudria, about the possibility of obtaining a larger budget for parliamentary staff, MacKay was told that the money might flow if his party laid off on Shawinigate.

It was difficult for the public to follow the complexities of the case, but that did not stop the media from digging into the story. The *National Post* led the charge and dedicated significant investigative resources to it. Chrétien called it a witch hunt. In a Post editorial on March 27, 1999, Chrétien was alleged to have profited personally from advocating to government agencies. The prime minister believed that Conrad Black, the founder of the *National Post*, was behind the editorial. Chrétien said Black had a thirst for influence, conservative ideology, and profit.[10]

In a letter to the Post published on April 10, 1999, Chrétien accused the newspaper of conducting a smear campaign against him by he deliberately omitting relevant information and being highly selective in its use of other details in its reporting. The prime minister admitted that mistakes were made but he didn't feel that an independent inquiry, as opposition MPs were calling for, was justified.

Chrétien's friend Izzy Asper, whose company owned the *National Post*, took the scandal to another level in 2000. Asper had been leader of the Manitoba Liberal party when Chrétien served in Trudeau's cabinet, so the two men were well acquainted. Izzy's son, David, came to the Chrétien's defence in an editorial. He wrote that the *National Post* had succumbed to "mischievous, unfair scandal-mongering as opposed to things that really count." The editorial appeared under the headline "To Chrétien's Accuser: Put Up or Shut Up." The editor of the *National Post* countered that it would have been a dereliction of duty to have ignored the story in an editorial headlined "We Put Up – Now Why Don't You Shut Up?"

The *Ottawa Citizen*, another publication under Asper's ownership, had assigned a senior writer to dig into Shawinigate. In a stinging report, the *Citizen* revealed that Chrétien's financial interests had not been placed in a blind trust when he said they were:

> Only one word — lying — describes this behaviour, and that's what Mr. Chrétien has done in these situations. From his failure to reveal an unpaid debt of more than $300,000 owed to him when he became prime minister in 1993, through his repeatedly contradictory statements about whether that debt was in a blind trust (it wasn't), right up to his refusal to admit (until media reports proved otherwise) that he personally lobbied the president of the Federal Business Development Bank (whom he appoints) to give a loan to the auberge, Mr. Chrétien's actions and words have inflamed, not calmed, the controversy.[11]

When the reporter and the editorial desk suggested a headline for the 4,000-word story that included the word "lie," *Citizen* publisher Russell Mills proposed "double standard" as a less inflammatory term. The double standard was about Chrétien keeping his job while one of his ministers had recently been fired and another demoted for ethical lapses.

Soon after the story appeared, Mills was fired by David Asper. Asper said that a clear line existed between the editorial pages and news coverage, which the publisher had breached. He also refuted charges that the firing came at the behest of Chrétien: "No politician has any ability to influence how we run our business. We simply have certain principles which we believe in and stand up for. And even if we have to take some public flak for them, we're willing to do so."[12] The principle Asper referenced was "balanced coverage." Asper also said that he had not been given notice of the story that alleged Chrétien duplicity. Ironically, the weekend before being dumped Mills had been recognized by Carleton University for his exemplary contribution to journalism in Canada. In the months that followed, Mills was awarded the Nieman Fellowship, which included a residency at Harvard University.[13]

Globe and Mail columnist Jeffrey Simpson came to Mills's defence by rebuking the "lickspittle" Aspers. Simpson wrote that with Chrétien in power, the dangers of media manipulation was magnified because of his vengeful and paranoid nature.[14]

To BOLSTER HIS CLAIM that he had acted properly throughout this ordeal, Chrétien asked his ethics counsellor to render judgment on the matter. Chrétien had created the office following a series of scandals involving Mulroney cabinet ministers.

The 1993 Liberal platform had included a promise to appoint an independent ethics commissioner to govern the conduct of public officials and lobbyists. The commissioner was expected to guard and reinforce the rules by which ministers, MPs, senators, political staff, and public servants managed their personal interests and dealt with those outside of government. While few disagreed with Chrétien's intent, Mitchell Sharp, who had become an advisor to the prime minister for a dollar per year, warned that an independent office would be complicated and expensive.[15] Since the government was intent on reducing spending and simplifying government, Chrétien heeded Sharp's advice. Rather than an independent commissioner, Chrétien opted for an ethics counsellor, who would not give rulings but would offer advice to office holders and the prime minister.[16]

No longer was it the duty of every office to examine their conscience with a mind to upholding the highest ethical standards. As long as the ethics counsellor gave a thumbs up — even by the slimmest of margins — then a cabinet minister, even the prime minister, was in the clear.

Howard Wilson, Chrétien's ethics counsellor, had a reputation for issuing rulings that were government-friendly. One exception concerned Lawrence MacAulay, a cabinet minister from PEI. Wilson advised that in 2002 MacAuley was in a conflict by lobbying for funding for a police training centre where his brother was president. Chrétien reluctantly accepted MacAulay's resignation, but objected to the ruling. "Do you want us to be eunuchs in our jobs," Chrétien asked?[17] MacAulay returned to cabinet in 2015 as Justin Trudeau's minister of agriculture.

If Shawinigate was only about the non-disclosure of a loan on Chrétien's part, it could easily have been forgiven. Indeed, after the prime minister's ethics counsellor reviewed all aspects of the file, he exonerated Chrétien, noting that no financial gain was involved. But this conclusion comes with an asterisk: the ethics counsellor reported directly to the prime minister, not Parliament. Had an independent ethics commissioner come to the same conclusion, the credibility of the finding would have put Chrétien on more solid ground.

Brian Tobin, who became responsible for the BDC portfolio after Manley, said he looked at Shawinigate from all angles and concluded that the prime minister may have been guilty, but only of bad politics: "I have no doubt that he wishes he had never made the call, just as I have no doubt that he harbored no expectations of a personal gain from it.[18]

For the public, Shawinigate was a complicated and convoluted affair. It involved small amounts of money and lacked a smoking gun. But Chrétien was riled when opposition members and the media accused him of dishonesty.

We have yet to reconcile the inevitable conflict that exists for prime ministers and cabinet ministers who serve as both decision makers for the country and as advocates for their local constituents. There is a line that should not be crossed but there is no consensus on precisely where that line should be. Chrétien was strongly biased towards the betterment of his constituents, a stance that aligned with his political self-interest. Even after leaving politics he supported tourism and business development opportunities in the hometown he once represented.

The affair consumed much more political oxygen than was necessary. In the end, Shawinigate was small potatoes. But it was a bigger scandal that it needed to be because of how Chrétien reacted to his integrity coming under attack. It was a rare lapse in political judgment for a man who made few missteps when it came to his personal conduct.

A BILLION-DOLLAR BOONDOGGLE?

P ut a billion-dollar program on the table to deliver grants to businesses and community groups and good luck trying to keep political fingers out of the pot. Bureaucrats are seriously outmatched when politicians get involved in how grant money gets distributed. Even taxpayers expect their MPs to deliver goodies to their home riding.

The names for federal grant programs are often elegant and high-minded: Transitional Jobs Fund (TJF), Canada Jobs Fund, Youth Internship Canada, Social Development Partnerships, and Sectoral Partnerships. But few of these programs escape other labels: pork barrel and political slush fund. That doesn't mean the programs are illegal, but you would have to be naive to believe politics is removed from the equation.

Under the Chrétien government, the TJF had the objective of creating permanent jobs in regions with unemployment rates above 12 per cent. But that criteria, as it turned out, was not universally applied. Data showed that grants were handed out to ridings held by Liberal cabinet ministers, where the unemployment rate was well below that threshold.[1] In 1999, following complaints by opposition MPs, auditor general Denis Desautels agreed to examine the $330 million TJF program.

The minister responsible for the program, Pierre Pettigrew, was replaced in August 1999 by Jane Stewart. While Stewart told reporters that she was investigating the TJF, she tried to pre-emptively squelch rumours that a portion of the fund was set aside for ministerial discretion, even though HRDC officials in Atlantic Canada complained in writing about the practice.[2]

As questionable files began to emerge in the press, and access-to-information requests rolled into the department, Stewart tried to get ahead of the story. On

January 19, 2000, she admitted that not all was well with the program. She was not the minister at the helm when the grants were handed out, she said, but she was going to get to the bottom of it.

Stewart exposed the results of a routine audit that found evidence of misman-agement in 459 projects worth $234 million. Project submissions were found to lack appropriate rationale, monitoring was lax, efficacy was in short supply. Fifteen per cent of active files did not even contain an application form. While the entire program covered 17,000 projects with total grants exceeding $1 bil-lion, a forensic investigation was initiated for 37 projects worth $33 million.

"There was no way I could sweep this under the carpet," Stewart declared.[3] When the opposition suggested her resignation was in order, Stewart was de-fiant: "No way. Quitters quit. This isn't the time to quit. I've got a tiger by the tail and I'm going to bring this one to ground."[4] Given the potential magnitude of the brewing scandal, it didn't take long for the opposition to give it a name: The Billion-Dollar Boondoggle.

The union representing HRDC workers was not going to let its members take the blame. When it was revealed there was back-dating to make it appear that proper approvals were obtained for some files, the union responded that this was done following political direction. The prime minister's office suggested it was a case of sloppy bookkeeping.

Opposition parties alleged political interference in the program. Chrétien countered with a question: If politics was involved, why did more than half of the job-creation grants go to opposition ridings? But that statistic didn't explain why Stewart's riding received $30 million in job grants over three years despite not qualifying for the program because of a 6.5 per cent unemploy-ment rate.

When Stewart struggled to explain the origins of the scandal in a media scrum, Chrétien jumped in and bailed her out of a tough spot. "The minister and the department are doing the right thing," he said.[5] But it was evident to the press that Stewart had lost the prime minister's confidence to handle the file and she never fully recovered her standing in cabinet or with the press.

While Stewart claimed the grants were divorced from political influence, Chrétien was known to step in when the welfare of his riding was concerned.

In the 1993 election, he reminded voters of the benefits of having a local MP who is also the prime minister: "When a dossier for Saint-Maurice lands on a cabinet minister's desk … need I say more?"[6]

The arbitrary nature of how grants were approved caused irritation even within Liberal ranks. MP Roger Galloway was angry that a $1 million grant for a call centre in his riding was rejected while a minister from a nearby riding found success. "My objection," asserted Galloway, "is that this is using other people's money in favour of one municipality over another, with no apparent reason for doing so."[7]

The temperature on the scandal rose further when the RCMP took an interest. The Mounties initiated 19 separate investigations, three of which involved Chrétien's riding. One of those investigations involved a grant of close to $1 million to hoteliers, including the Auberge that Chrétien and his partners had sold in 1993. The program explicitly prohibited grants for restaurants and bars. An HRDC official noted in a 1997 email that the grants in question were approved because Chrétien had already announced them in public. They thought it would be bad form to contradict the prime minister.[8]

Placeteco Inc., a plastics company in Chrétien's Shawinigan riding, was insolvent, yet it received a $1.2 million TJF grant. The owner of the company, Claude Gauthier, boasted of the support he had received from the prime minister's office. Public servants were instructed to do "everything that is legally possible" to process the request.[9] Six months after receiving the grant, the company went bankrupt.

Chrétien defended the program and its goals by saying the problems that had been revealed were administrative and not political in nature. "The accounting has not been done according to the best standards, and we are looking into that," he said. "All of these programs are good programs. It is for job-creation, it's youth job-creation, it's literacy programs and so on." The only blame Chrétien would accept was that his 1995 cutbacks in the civil service, which included 5,000 jobs at HRDC, may have left the department understaffed. He also suggested that the decentralization of the program to regional HRDC offices may have caused a problem.[10]

But Chrétien could not escape the perception that the program was politically tainted. This was bolstered by the fact that in the run-up to the 1997 election,

74 of the 172 TJF grants went to Québec ridings where the Liberals faced close races against the Bloc Québécois.

THE AUDITOR GENERAL'S REPORT on the program confirmed the results of the internal audit. The report concluded the program was plagued by serious mismanagement, sloppy paperwork, poor internal controls, and a lack of due process. While the auditor general did not explicitly single out individual politicians, he asserted that accountability mechanisms were deficient, in part because individual MPs and ministers were given a role in approving projects. He said bureaucrats had two masters: their department and elected officials, both of whom were hard to ignore. The AG recommended that MPs should be limited to an advisory role in the review of grant applications. But even this would not eliminate the possibility of political interference.[11]

The AG also gave the government a convenient out by noting that the problems his office discovered were not unique to the Chrétien government. Finally, he gave Minister Stewart credit for being open about the problems and for taking the initiative to fix the mess.

The prime minister responded by wondering why opposition members objected to programs that helped the disabled, Aboriginal people, illiterate Canadians, and unemployed youth. Chrétien also reminded the opposition that the AG did not find a single case of malfeasance by public servants or politicians. In fact, he sympathized with public servants who were eager to provide a fast service, which may have inadvertently short-circuited the appropriate spending controls.

Scandals of this sort did no damage to Chrétien in his St. Maurice riding. In the 1997 election, his Bloc Québécois opponent said Chrétien had done some good things for the riding and that the subsidies were helpful. Chrétien's opponent said that if he was elected the money would continue to flow into the riding. Chrétien responded by saying that the key to getting federal money was to elect government members and not Bloc MPs who were condemned to perpetual opposition.[12] It was another way of confirming that political influence remained a fact of life, which ran counter to his assertion that the problems were sloppy bookkeeping and weak bureaucratic controls.

Liberal organizer Pierre Corbeil pursued Québec companies that had received

TJF grants for contributions to the Liberal party of Canada. Evidence was presented in court that showed that Corbeil was paid $165,000 in commissions from the sponsorship program to keep quiet and not implicate the Liberal party.[13] Corbeil pled guilty to charges of influence peddling and was sentenced to two years of probation and a fine.

Two other criminal convictions, for fraud and theft, were handed down in relation to the scandal. Paul Lemire and Mario Pépin had served on the board of directors of the Shawinigan-based Canadian Institute of Tourism and Electronic Commerce, which had received a $2.5 million grant that was not fully used for the purpose intended. Both were sentenced to two years less a day. Lemire, who pleaded guilty, was fined $10,000, while Pépin, who was convicted after a trial, was ordered to pay a fine of $400. Both fines were significantly lower than the money they defrauded from taxpayers. The press noted that Lemire had accompanied Chrétien on a Team Canada trade mission to Asia in 1996 and that he had served as a mediator between Chrétien and former Québec premier Lucien Bouchard.[14]

It was not surprising that a few people from Shawinigan sought to trade off their supposed relationship with Chrétien for personal gain. But just because they said they were friends with Chrétien didn't mean that it was true. Chrétien would casually say that everyone from Shawinigan was his friend. He wondered what he was supposed to say: that he didn't like a constituent he barely knew?

In the end, Chrétien thought the HRDC scandal was political theatre. No politician or bureaucrat was sanctioned. The amount of money that HRDC could not account for was minuscule in the grand scheme of things. And those from outside the government who abused the public purse were convicted and punished.

Chrétien said he was entitled to expect that public servants would follow the spirit and letter of the law. If they were being pressured by a political master to do something that they considered questionable, they had a duty, Chrétien said, to bring the issue to their deputy minister. If the deputy could not resolve a conflict, the matter should be escalated to the Clerk of the Privy Council.

No system can be totally free of political interference. As infrastructure minister, Allan Rock had to determine how a $3 billion grant program was allocated. He built a process that involved meetings with the provinces and mayors to determine collective priorities. He also met with regional political ministers and members of the Liberal caucus to get as many views as possible. "It's a rational system," Rock said. But he also acknowledged there was a political element: "I did not want to do anything that harmed our electoral prospects, which I took into account."

According to Arthur Kroeger, a highly respected former civil servant who served as a deputy minister for 17 years before retiring from government in 1992, the problem HRDC files accounted for 3 per cent of the grants that were distributed. The billion-dollar figure reported in the media was an extrapolation from an auditor general's report on what were called "problem files." Kroeger added that "error-free government is bureaucratic government."[15] While it's shocking to hear that grants were handed out without a formal application on file, it turned out that in some cases this meant that applications took different forms, such as a series of letters that confirmed terms and conditions.

The primary problem with the Transitional Jobs Fund was not fraud but political influence exercised over which ridings and which companies were given grants. The payoff to the government was dishing out money to ridings held by influential cabinet ministers and to ridings where a Liberal incumbent was vulnerable to defeat. It's disheartening that no Canadian government has been immune to such temptation. For example, following the 1995 G7 summit in Halifax, the community was given a $13 million fund for community projects. The Conservatives topped that gift with a $50 million fund to say thanks to Huntsville when that region hosted the G8 in 2010. Much of the public's attention was drawn to the construction of a gazebo at a cost of $100,000. Some of the infrastructure projects were given to communities that were 100 kilometres away from the G8 site. After receiving complaints from a Liberal MP, the RCMP launched an investigation into the G8 community fund and concluded that no crime had been committed. But the auditor general had plenty to say, noting that applications for grants lacked a paper trail and that rules were broken from beginning to end. NDP MP Pat Martin called the fund "hog-troughing" of the highest order. "It seems like a legacy to the minister. You did everything but build a statue to (Conservative MP) Tony Clement in the riding." Despite the revelation, the Harper government went from a minority to a majority in the 2011 election.

HRDC funds were not supposed to be a gift, or a way of saying thank you, or a vote-buying slush fund. The funds were expected to help regions facing high levels of unemployment and some disadvantaged Canadians. By and large, this is how the program was managed, but it was nonetheless tainted by political influence. But the questionable grants were a small portion of the overall program. Chrétien could have used his power to reform and improve the system to better serve Canadians. But it was not a billion-dollar boondoggle and the scandal qualifies more as a footnote to Chrétien's legacy and not a major chapter.

SPONSORSHIP

Jean Chrétien thought federalists in Québec were timid. Because they were worried about offending the nationalist sentiments of their home province, they declined to express their pride in Canada or display its symbols.[1] He lamented that there were no more Canadian flags on post offices or in immigration courts in Québec. He was frustrated that Ottawa doled out money to Québec without requiring public recognition.

Chrétien wanted to raise the federal profile in Québec and give Canada the credit he thought it deserved. This was the genesis of the sponsorship program. Unfortunately, rather than promote national unity, as was its intent, the sponsorship program harmed the fabric of the nation and undermined confidence in the ethics and competence of the federal government. The recklessness with which the program was run, and abused, was an embarrassment to Canada. It also served to reinforce a notion held by many Canadians that Québec was the most corrupt province in the country.

DURING THE REFERENDUM CAMPAIGN, and especially in its final few days, Chrétien made promises to help persuade Québecers to put their trust in Canada. In the aftermath, Chrétien established an ad hoc committee of ministers, known as the Unity Committee, to make good on those promises.

Acting on the 1996 Unity Committee report, Chrétien approved a $50 million annual investment to boost the profile of the federal government across Canada, but mostly in Québec. The money came from a fund that was earmarked for unforeseen emergencies and other contingencies. Following the close call in the referendum, Chrétien thought national unity qualified as an emergency.

Despite the intent, the money was spent in peculiar ways that had little to do with that emergency. Sponsorship dollars were dumped into such inconsequential events as car and bicycle races, music festivals, tennis tournaments, youth exchanges, and tourist attractions.[2] Over the years, Chrétien's government channelled about $332 million into the sponsorship program to help prop up close to 2,000 events. About $150 million went to communications agencies for production fees and commissions.

The actual flow of funds and operational oversight was the responsibility of the minister of Public Works and Government Services Canada (PWGSC), Alfonso Gagliano. An accountant by training, Gagliano cut his political teeth as a trustee for an east-end Montreal school board before being elected to Parliament in 1984, one of the few Liberals from Québec to hold back the Progressive Conservative sweep.

After winning re-election in 1988 and 1993, Gagliano was brought into cabinet in 1996 as minister of labour before being promoted to the PWGSC portfolio in 1997. He was also the political minister for Québec, meaning that he was never far removed from fundraising for the Liberal party. That also made him a magnet for those seeking political appointments as well as contractors and professionals hoping to do work for the federal government.

Eddie Goldenberg said it was a mistake to have a political minister also serve as the government's principal purchaser of services.[3] The temptation to use the power of the treasury to enhance the political prospects of the party in power was not a new phenomenon, but is best avoided.

On the bureaucratic side, responsibility for the sponsorship program ultimately rested with Ranald Quail, the deputy minister of PWGSC. He delegated operational authority to Charles Guité, an experienced public servant. But as it turned out, Guité was more political warrior than faithful government bureaucrat. Guité declared he was battling to save his country. "When you're at war," he said, "you drop the book and the rules and you don't give your plan to the opposition."

The sponsorship program may have had a clear goal — to keep Québec in Canada — but it did not have clear terms and conditions that would have limited the ability of rogue bureaucrats and politicians from doing whatever they wanted. A senior official in the privy council office said the rules were so loose that it was a program "you could drive a truck through."

Another key player in the sponsorship program was the prime minister's chief of staff, Jean Pelletier. While Pelletier had no authority to control or direct the fund, his ongoing presence in the administration of a government program was unusual, to say the least.[4] Indeed, for a prime minister's chief of staff to meet regularly with a mid-level bureaucrat from a line department, like Guité, was unprecedented. A former senior bureaucrat observed that when a call goes out from the PMO, everything inside a department stops. "The first thing a bureaucrat does is stand to attention. The second thing they do is to say yes to whatever question is asked. PMO staff need to appreciate the weight their office carries."

Guité was operating above his pay grade by meeting with the prime minister's chief of staff. The person who was missing in action at those meetings was the top bureaucrat at PWGSC. Chrétien contended that if Ranald Quail felt pressured or discomforted by the operation of the sponsorship program, he should have told the Clerk of the Privy Council.

Chrétien wrote that he never received a single memo or phone call about problems with the sponsorship program. "As long as I was assured that the money was being used to advance the cause of national unity and nothing else," he wrote, "I obviously didn't have any time or any reason to go through the program's hundreds of contracts myself."[5] Chrétien defended the program as a tool that helped to preserve Canadian unity.[6] But did it? There is no evidence that sponsorship dollars had any positive impact on national unity.

Chrétien contends that what tarnished the program was a small number of unscrupulous individuals who broke the rules and dishonoured themselves for personal gain. But it was much more than that. The Liberal party itself was directly implicated in wrongdoing.

The sponsorship program ran from 1996 to 2004, which largely overlapped Gagliano's time at PWGSC. There had been rumours circulating in Ottawa that the sponsorship program was tainted, particularly after a *Globe and Mail* access-to-information request revealed that the government paid $550,000 to an advertising firm, Groupaction, for a report that no one at Public Works could locate. The company said it had delivered three copies of the report but did not keep a copy for itself, which, if it's to be believed, takes sloppiness to unprecedented levels. Guité said he recalled seeing the report.

When Don Boudria succeeded Gagliano in 2002, he was told about the access-to-information request:

> I gave them a week to locate it or I would tell the media myself that the department could not produce the document. I walked into a cabinet meeting and the prime minister asked me, 'What are you going to do about that report?' I said I was thinking about calling in the auditor general. He agreed and added if the report did not show up I should call the police. He was a man who feared a non-answer more than the answer.

Auditor general Sheila Fraser heightened the seriousness of the brewing scandal by calling in the RCMP to investigate senior public servants who, in her words, "broke just about every rule in the book."[7] Her work began in 2002 with the review of three contracts totalling $1.6 million that had been awarded to Groupaction. Fraser's findings were so troubling that the scope of her work was urgently expanded to cover all sponsorship activities, including federal Crown corporations.

The government had to assume the public took everything the auditor general said as unimpeachable. In a poll on the HRDC scandal conducted in 2000, more than 70 per cent of those surveyed said they believed the auditor general, compared with only 26 per cent who believed federal cabinet ministers.

Unlike the HRDC scandal, for which the initial allegations were proven to be grossly exaggerated, the sponsorship scandal escalated and implicated bureaucrats, politicians, political aides and private sector beneficiaries. It was revealed that ad firms that were friendly to the Liberal party were awarded contracts for which little or no work was done. Groupaction and its affiliates had donated $70,000 to the Liberal party over the previous five years and its principals had been active in their political campaigns.[8] Additionally, some of the funds that were paid to ad firms were then funnelled back to the Liberal party to pay its political organizers.

The auditor general's report on the entirety of the sponsorship program was tabled on February 10, 2004. "Our findings are disturbing," Sheila Fraser told a Parliamentary committee. "The non-compliance with contracting rules extended beyond PWGSC and into five major Crown corporations and agencies."[9] Fraser concluded there was widespread mismanagement, payment of commissions for intergovernmental transactions, and payments where there was little evidence of value. Perhaps worst of all, the auditor general concluded, was that the government had deliberately kept Parliamentarians in the dark. It may not have reached the level of a cover-up, but Fraser concluded that Parliament was misinformed about the program's objectives, and how it was run. This included bypassing the Parliamentary appropriation process.

The auditor general discovered that not only were guidelines blatantly disregarded but in many instances, there were no guidelines whatsoever. The Sponsorship Program, she concluded, was operated on an ad hoc basis with weak controls and next to no oversight by PWGSC's central services. The usual segregation of duties was abandoned, which allowed Charles Guité to approve projects and invoices for payment. Usually, fraud requires the collusion of multiple parties, which is difficult to establish and sustain. But when one person controls a process from beginning to end, the likelihood of fraud is substantially increased.

PAUL MARTIN WAS PRIME MINISTER when the AG report on the sponsorship scandal was released. He claimed to know nothing about the program, which he said was managed out of Chrétien's office. He accepted no responsibility as minister of finance, nor did he apologize on behalf of the Liberal party of Canada. To many, this did not pass the credibility test. "You cannot take credit for being a financial genius," said Eddie Goldenberg, "and then say you were in the bathroom when the sponsorship program took place. It happened on his watch."

To demonstrate that he was taking the matter seriously, Martin referred the matter to a Royal Commission, formally known as the Commission of Inquiry into the Sponsorship Program and Advertising Activities. It soon became known as the Gomery Commission.

The commission consumed the public's attention, with riveting testimony from the major players involved, including Chrétien and Martin. Justice John Gomery's final report found:

- clear evidence of political involvement in the administration of the sponsorship program,

- insufficient oversight at the senior levels of the public service,

- a veil of secrecy and an absence of transparency in the contracting process,

- reluctance by virtually all public servants to go against the will of a manager who was circumventing established policies and who had access to senior political officials,

- gross overcharging by communication agencies and their subcontractors,

- use of the program for purposes other than national unity,

- a complex web of financial transactions involving kickbacks to a political party,

- agencies with individuals on their payroll who were working on Liberal party matters,

- a refusal by ministers, senior officials in the prime minister's office, and public servants to acknowledge their responsibility for the problems of mismanagement that occurred.

Gomery noted that the deputy minister of PWGSC, Ranald Quail, abdicated his responsibility to control, direct, and oversee the actions of officials in his department. "The duty of Mr. Quail," concluded Gomery, "was to better inform himself of the situation and to call Mr. Guité to account for his deficient administration." But it was not just deficient administration; it was fraud.

Gomery concluded that Chrétien's chief of staff, Jean Pelletier, and Chrétien himself must have known that a program of discretionary spending would be open to error and abuse. Pelletier was seen to be overpowering government officials:[10]

> By choosing to give direction to Mr. Guité personally, Mr. Pelletier bypassed the normal methods of administration of government programs and effectively eliminated the oversight that would have been provided by Mr. Quail and his department. The notion that Mr. Pelletier and Mr. Gagliano could provide political input without strongly influencing the decision-making process is nonsense and ignores the obvious reality that the expression of an opinion to a subordinate official by the Prime Minister's Chief of Staff or the Minister amounts to an order.

Mr. Pelletier's actions in meeting with Mr. Guité in the absence of Mr. Quail or his representative constituted political encroachment into the administrative domain.

Gomery did not judge Chrétien's conduct as harshly as Pelletier's:

> Since Mr. Chrétien chose to run the Program from his own office, and to have his own exempt staff take charge of its direction, he is accountable for the defective manner in which the Sponsorship Program and initiatives were implemented

A high-level top public servant said that however inappropriate were the meetings between Pelletier and Guité, no one can constrain senior people in the public service from doing their jobs: "These jobs are all done under tough circumstances and public servants are never liberated from doing their duty. It's nonsense to suggest they get a pass because someone met with the PMO. In this case the public service did not perform to the level it should have."

Gomery noted that there was no evidence suggesting that Chrétien or Pelletier were aware that a fraud had been perpetuated. Eddie Goldenberg, who was at Pelletier's side throughout his time in the PMO, said that he was an imposing figure, but that he would not do anything that was wrong: "He would have said to Guité you have 10 contracts going here and there. Don't you think that breakdown should be different? He might have made some suggestions but he didn't say break the law."

Gomery singled out Gagliano for his direct dealings with Guité and his questionable role in selecting projects. The commissioner let other ministers off the hook, concluding they were left out of the loop by a small cadre of political aides and officials who were directing the program. Martin was exonerated for his conduct since he was not involved in the supervision of spending directed by the PMO or PWGSC.

However, the Liberal Party of Canada was not given a pass. Gomery concluded that in accepting cash from advertising executives to pay its staff and expenses, the Liberal party ought to have known it was in violation of the Canada Elections Act. Martin promised that some of the funds that had been redirected into Liberal party coffers would be repaid to taxpayers.

Martin suspended the presidents of Crown corporations that were associated with the sponsorship scandal, including executives at the Business Development Bank, VIA Rail, and Canada Post. These Crowns all had former politicians or political aides in senior positions, although none were implicated in wrongdoing. There were other government entities involved in sponsorship activity, including the RCMP and the Old Port of Montreal, but the government did nothing visible to them in terms of sanctions.

Charles Guité was convicted on 5 counts of fraud and sentenced to 42 months in prison. Jean Brault, the head of one of the advertising agencies involved, pleaded guilty to five counts of fraud and was sentenced to 30 months in prison. Jacques Corriveau, a Liberal organizer whose company billed $9 million for sponsorship-related contracts, was charged with fraud, forgery, and laundering the proceeds of crime. Corriveau was convicted by a jury on November 1, 2016, on three fraud-related charges, sentenced to four years in prison, and ordered to pay a $1.4 million fine.

Another Liberal-friendly advertising executive, Jean Lafleur, pleaded guilty to 28 counts of fraud, sentenced to 42 months in prison, and ordered to repay $1.6 million to the government. Where it could, the government went to civil court to recover misappropriated funds.

CHRÉTIEN AND PELLETIER BELIEVED that Gomery was biased against them, not just because of the conclusions he reached but because of his conduct during the commission's hearings. For example, when Gomery was interviewed by the media while the commission was in session — an unwise decision on his part because he had not heard all the evidence — he described Chrétien's use of golf balls emblazoned with the prime ministerial logo as "small-town cheap." Later, when giving testimony, Chrétien paraded several golf balls he had received from world leaders before the commission, including from his friend Bill Clinton. He also referenced golf balls that he had been given by the legal firm where Gomery's daughter worked. It was a demonstration he had rehearsed with his wife the night before his appearance, although he had not alerted his legal counsel, David Scott, of his plan.

Even before Gomery's injudicious media interview, he riled Chrétien by appointing Bernard Roy as the commission's chief counsel. Roy had been principal secretary to former Progressive Conservative prime minister Brian Mulroney. There was enduring tension between the former prime ministers because of a letter written by the justice department during Chrétien's time in office. The letter sent to Swiss authorities inquired about possible illegalities on Mulroney's part related to the acquisition of Airbus planes. Early in 2005, Chrétien petitioned to have Gomery removed, which was denied.

Chrétien thought the bureaucrats who ran the sponsorship program should have been traced back to the Mulroney administration. Guité and the businessmen who exploited the program were not, Chrétien asserted, Liberal figures. In fact, the agencies who booked sponsorship ads were selected based on experience that was gained while Mulroney was in power.

When Gomery's report was released, Chrétien said the wrong person was given credibility. Why, Chrétien wondered, would Gomery take the word of Guité, someone who lined his pockets with taxpayer money, over Pelletier, a man who had dedicated his life to the service of his city, his province, and his country? Chrétien and Pelletier sought to have Gomery's conclusions set aside on the basis of a "reasonable apprehension of bias." The federal court agreed and Gomery was criticized for his predilection for media attention and for having publicly expressed himself before all the evidence was heard. Judge Max Teitelbaum wrote that Gomery's public comments indicated that not only did he prejudge issues, but also that he was not impartial. In a separate judgment, the government of Canada was ordered to pay $200,000 each to Chrétien and Pelletier to cover their court costs.

CHRÉTIEN COULD NOT UNDERSTAND why Martin called a public inquiry instead of simply allowing the RCMP to do its work and prosecute the guilty parties. This would have saved the taxpayers $60 million and might have lengthened Martin's time as prime minister.

The Conservatives were intent on linking Martin to the scandal to bolster their electoral prospects. The gist of their argument was that either Martin didn't know what was going on, in which case he was incompetent as finance minister, or he did know and was covering up the truth. Indeed, when Martin lost the 2006 election, most observers concluded the sponsorship scandal was an important factor.

Like Chrétien, PCO officials also advised against calling a public inquiry. Not only did the inquiry do much to tarnish the reputation of the public service — much of it deserved — the legacy of Gomery's recommendations was to create a generation of public servants that were rules-based and process-driven. "There is little room for innovation and risk-taking because of Gomery," said Wayne Wouters, a future Clerk of the Privy Council. Wouters said the report slowed down government because oversight became oppressive.

Rather than claim innocence and trumpet the scandal to make Chrétien look bad, Martin would have done better politically to accept responsibility for his government's role in the fraud and his lack of oversight as minister of finance. Goldenberg thought only political stupidity could explain the calling of the Gomery inquiry.

While Chrétien's name will be forever linked to the sponsorship scandal, there is nothing in the public record that suggests he did anything legally wrong. At most he is politically accountable for having approved the use of federal funds for a program that was ineffective at best and damaging to the country at worst. Putting $50 million into a program to engage in battle with the separatists was entirely consistent with his scrapper mentality, but letting the program operate without clear guidelines or measures to evaluate its effectiveness was an error, born out of what could be called post-referendum stress disorder, an affliction that clouded his usually reliable political instincts.

What upsets Chrétien most about the sponsorship scandal is that it ran counter to its purpose. What was supposed to be an investment in Canadian unity became a focal point of division. Rather than counter Québec government propaganda that supported the separatist cause, it became one of the sovereignists' weapons. Chrétien should have known that Québecers were never going to embrace Canada simply because the Canadian flag was seen at car races and fishing derbies. In short, it was a poorly conceived program and bad public policy. Some say it would not have damaged Canadian unity to the extent it did had Martin not called a public inquiry. McGill University historian Desmond Morton said Gomery deserves a statue in Québec City for aiding the sovereignty movement.[11]

The sponsorship scandal is more than a footnote in the history books. It ranks with the Pacific scandal under Macdonald and the Beauharnois Scandal under Mackenzie King as one of the most significant in Canadian history.

FRIENDS AND RELATIONS

Jean Chrétien believed that an effective prime minister cannot afford to have friends. They may ask for favours. They may be difficult to fire or demote if they are not doing a good job. But he did have relationships that helped him navigate the challenges of leading Canada.

He had not focused much on girls before he met Aline Chaîné. But he thought she was the prettiest girl in Shawinigan. Aline was 15 and Jean 17 when their romance blossomed. Smart and ambitious, Aline was first in her class at secretarial college. She had a powerful influence over her beau, turning him from a brawler and a rebel into a serious and responsible student. Jean's mother saw Aline as a guardian angel and a source of salvation for her wayward son.

Chrétien admitted that falling for Aline changed his life:

> I realized at that time that I wanted to marry Aline eventually, and I had to behave to be able to find a good job and have a home and all that. I became obsessed … that I had to succeed in order to become a lawyer, to become a politician, to have a family, and so on. That made me think about serious things. The fun was over at that time, you know. Real life had hit me.[1]

While Jean was away at law school and Aline remained in Shawinigan, they remained faithful to each other. His classmates found this so unusual that they nicknamed him Jean Fidele. Aline and Jean were married on September 10, 1957. He was 23 and she was 21. The wedding was a modest affair so as not to impose a burden on the parents of the bride. It was held on a Monday morning so Jean could work a double shift on the weekend at the mill. Jean insisted the couple not be married by the local pastor, who was a Conservative, noting that the bishop for their community said heaven was Conservative blue and hell was Liberal red.[2] The couple's honeymoon was a quick three-day outing to Lake George, New York.

Aline helped her husband with personnel decisions and was a sounding board on what ordinary Canadians were thinking. "She is a person who will tell me exactly what she expects and what she believes and that doesn't give me any problems. It is very useful," said Chrétien.[3]

Aline enjoyed playing piano and had a classic sense of style that served as a counterweight to her husband's unsophisticated persona. When her husband was being sworn in a prime minister, she asked one of Chrétien's trusted advisors, David Zussman, if she looked like the wife of a prime minister. "No Madame Chrétien," Zussman replied. "You look like a prime minister."[4]

Chrétien went home most days to have lunch with his wife. It was not only a chance for him to get away from the clamour on Parliament Hill, but also allowed him to check in with his most loyal and candid advisor.

IT WAS A LONG WAY from being a small-town political scrapper from Québec to having a semi-regular audience with Queen Elizabeth. Chrétien was not only friendly with the Queen but had the inner confidence to candidly share his thoughts with her. When the Queen asked Chrétien if she should apologize for Britain's mistreatment of Maori villages under the colonial regime in New Zealand, he was blunt. "If you do that in New Zealand, I will have to ask you to do the same thing in Canada. But I warn you, we have more than 600 First Nations bands so you'll be on your knees for quite some time."[5]

The Queen would remember well an incident when a Québec radio host, Pierre Brassard, impersonated Chrétien and broadcast his 17 minute fraudulent conversation with her on air. In the conversation, the Queen agrees to a request to deliver a message in the aftermath of the Québec 1995 referendum. "I didn't think he sounded quite like yourself," the Queen later told the real Chrétien. "But I thought, given all that duress you were under, you might have been drunk."[6] It's admirable that Chrétien included this self-deprecating anecdote in his memoirs, and it's noteworthy that the Queen had such friendly relations with her Canadian prime minister.

The Queen found Chrétien to be a charmer, but not particularly articulate. She told Conrad Black that she found him difficult to understand in either of Canada's official languages. Black also noted that when Chrétien appeared on television in France, he was given subtitles.

Québec-based columnist Lysiane Gagnon predicted in 1993 that Québecers would not embrace Chrétien because of his substandard French.[7] She added that he spoke French just as he speaks English. Norman Webster of the *Montreal Gazette* wrote that Chrétien's French may be rough, and his English rougher, "but no one ever said he doesn't communicate."[8] When Chrétien insulted separatist leaders from Québec by saying they wanted their own country so they could drive around in a limousine with, "des flags sur le hood," the language snobs in Québec cringed. But everyone understood the sentiment.

But the Queen didn't much care how Chrétien spoke. In July 2009, she conferred the Order of Merit on Chrétien in recognition of his exceptionally meritorious service to the Crown. The Order is an exclusive club, comprising only 24 living members at any time. This rarefied company includes the Queen's husband and son. Only three other Canadians have been awarded the honour: William Lyon Mackenzie King, Dr. Wilder Penfield, and Lester B. Pearson.

WHEN BRIAN MULRONEY ANNOUNCED that he was stepping down as prime minister in February 1993, Jean Chrétien, then his opponent in the House of Commons, offered quiet respect: "The prime minister and I may have had over the years the same dream, to wage the good fight."[9]

They had once been friendly and Mulroney admired Chrétien's political skills. When the Parti Québecois won the 1976 provincial election and Robert Bourassa resigned as Liberal party leader, Chrétien was pressured to leave Ottawa and take up the federalist cause in Québec. "Jean," said Brian Mulroney, "you have no choice. You have to be in the race." A prominent Québec lawyer at the time, Mulroney had just lost his bid to lead the federal Progressive Conservative party to Joe Clark.[10]

After the Tories were humbled in the 1993 election, Chrétien said little about Mulroney. It was not in his interest to weaken a Tory party that was at war with the Reform Party for the conservative vote. Better, thought Chrétien, to make that war last as long as possible.

About two years after Mulroney left office, a German magazine revealed that $11 million US had been paid in 1988 to lobby Air Canada to purchase 34 Airbus Industrie A320 jets.[11] The person said to have been on the receiving end of much of this money was Karl-Heinz Schreiber, a Canadian lobbyist of German origins. Schreiber was also known to have worked with Frank Moores, a former Newfoundland premier and political confidante of Brian Mulroney. Moores had been appointed to the board of Air Canada by the Mulroney government, but resigned in 1985 amid rumours that he had lobbied for Airbus.

The CBC television program *The Fifth Estate* was working the Canadian angle to the story, including a possible link between lobbying dollars and Canadian politicians. The RCMP revealed that they had opened a file on Airbus when the sale was made to Air Canada in 1988, but were no longer investigating the case when the German magazine reported on Schreiber's lobbying efforts.

The Fifth Estate's investigative account alleged that a $40 million kickback from Airbus went into two numbered Swiss bank accounts. One of the accounts, it was reported, was connected to a lobbyist close to Mulroney, and another to "a high-ranking Canadian politician" whose code name was "Devon." Mulroney had once lived on Devon Street, which sent conspiracy theorists into high gear. A cover-up was alleged, but the RCMP said that just because Airbus Industries paid a commission to a lobbyist did not mean a criminal act had been committed.

The Airbus contract caught the attention of Stevie Cameron. She was the author of a 1994 bestseller on Mulroney that was provocatively titled *On the Take*. Cameron updated her book to include material on the Airbus affair and she was later identified as an RCMP informant.

Kimberly Prost, a senior counsel at Justice Canada, sent a letter to Swiss authorities that claimed the RCMP had "reliable information that Mr. Schreiber was given commissions in order to pay Mr. Mulroney and Mr. Moores to ensure that Airbus Industrie obtained a major contract with Air Canada." These commissions were alleged to have been deposited in a Swiss bank account.

Mulroney said he had nothing to do with Air Canada's decision to buy Airbus and that he had not received a cent from Airbus or anyone else in relation to Airbus. He wanted the letter withdrawn and instructed his lawyers to meet Justice Canada officials to answer their questions. Justice Canada would only commit to keeping the letter confidential.

It was only after the letter was leaked and published in the *National Post* on November 18, 1995, that Mulroney launched a lawsuit claiming $50 million in damages for the government's "false and reckless allegations" that had the effect, he alleged, of damaging his reputation, hurting his family, but also besmirching and distorting the good name of Canada.[12]

Derek Burney, an experienced bureaucrat who became Mulroney's chief of staff, said that a senior official would not have sent the letter to Swiss authorities making allegations about a former Canadian prime minister without having cleared the letter with the responsible minister. Allan Rock confirmed that Herb Gray, the solicitor general, knew about the letter before it was sent. Rock said that based on the information in the hands of the government at the time that the letter ought not to have been sent with the wording that it contained.

Chrétien was in Osaka, Japan when he was informed by Peter Donolo that news of the letter was about to break. He called Eddie Goldenberg to find out what was behind the story. Without making any inquiries of the RCMP, they concluded that the national police service would not pursue a former prime minister unless they had a good reason to so. Goldenberg commented as much to Jocelyne Bourgon, the highest ranking public servant: "Trust me, Eddie," Bourgon said. "They know what they are doing." Goldenberg resisted pressure from friends he had in common with Mulroney to kill the investigation. "Do you really think," he asked rhetorically, "that it's a good idea for the PMO to get involved with an RCMP investigation?"

Chrétien said he had nothing to do with the letter that was sent to the Swiss and that he felt sorry for Mulroney. "He had suffered enough humiliation when his great party had been reduced to two seats in the wake of his retirement. As far as I was concerned, he didn't need to be hit with anything else."[13]

The government had no intention of settling Mulroney's lawsuit until it was revealed that the RCMP was the likely source of the leak and that an RCMP inspector had told Stevie Cameron about the letter. In January 1997, Mulroney was given a payment of $2.1 million for his legal and other costs. Chrétien said he was relieved to put the matter to rest and that the proper thing to do was to accept the word of a former prime minister.[14] The settlement included a statement that there was no evidence of political involvement in the case. To his credit, Chrétien phoned Mulroney after the settlement was reached, but Mulroney refused to take the call.[15]

While Mulroney claimed victory, government officials made the point that the $2.1 million settlement was not for damages and that the RCMP was free to continue its investigation. In other words, there was no immunity. The government simply admitted that the language used in their letter was sloppy. Prost was not disciplined for her conduct, or for the fact that she cost the taxpayers $2.1 million.

Mulroney received total vindication from the RCMP on the matter six years after the settlement was reached. But this was not the last time that Mulroney and Schreiber were given front-page treatment. In 2006, long after Chrétien had resigned, the CBC reported that Schreiber had in fact given Mulroney $300,000 in cash (Mulroney said it was $225,000). Mulroney said the payment was for advisory services. Schreiber stoked the controversy by trivializing the work that Mulroney said he performed for the fee.

At one point, Schreiber said he gave the money to Mulroney as a simple act of kindness and that it was not connected to Airbus. But his story kept changing. The Mulroney-Schreiber affair eventually landed on Prime Minister Harper's desk, which led to a public inquiry being called on November 8, 2007. The terms of reference for the inquiry were written by David Johnston, a future governor general of Canada.

Schreiber said he had much to reveal. But he would not cooperate, he warned, if he was extradited to Germany where he faced criminal charges. Liberal members in the House of Commons called for Schreiber's extradition to be delayed, which only fueled his desire to use the inquiry as his ticket to remain in Canada, rather than possibly land in a German prison.

Schreiber's testimony revealed little, although he confirmed the money had nothing to do with anything Mulroney did while he was prime minister. This conclusion was affirmed by Gomery, although he wrote that the payments Mulroney accepted from Schreiber in private life were inappropriate. It cost federal taxpayers $16 million to reach a conclusion that was obvious to all concerned.

Allan Rock said that the government would not have paid Mulroney $2.1 million to settle the lawsuit had it been known that Schreiber made cash payments to the former prime minister. But he also said the government was still wrong to have sent the letter to Swiss authorities in the first place.

Chrétien said he was mystified why Mulroney took cash payments from Schreiber. He was also mystified why Harper would call a public inquiry into the conduct of a former leader of his party. Chrétien could have told Harper that public inquiries are expensive, divisive, inflammatory, and rarely serve the public interest.

CHRÉTIEN WAS NOT ONE to court the establishment, at least not openly. So, it would surprise many Canadians to know that he enjoyed, with one notable dispute, a friendly relationship with business and media titan Conrad Black.

When Chrétien was a cabinet minister in the 1970s and 1980s, he often met with Black at his posh Toronto office. As prime minister, Chrétien invited Black to 24 Sussex Drive to talk politics and foreign affairs. They also met the odd time in London, England. Their discussions of world views were illuminating to Chrétien and intended by Black to benefit the Canadian cause. Black had enjoyed similarly good relations with Pierre Trudeau, John Turner, and Brian Mulroney, as well as with many world leaders. President George W. Bush once asked Chrétien if he knew Black: "I really like the guy," said Bush.[16]

It didn't bother Chrétien that Black's Canadian newspaper of record, the *National Post*, was unabashedly conservative. But Chrétien took exception when the paper questioned his integrity over the Shawinigate scandal. Black, who by then had been living in the United Kingdom for a decade, never thought the episode was a matter of great consequence and was surprised that Chrétien was bothered by the routine journalistic inquisition. But the deed did not go unnoticed or unpunished.

As proprietor of the London-based *Daily Telegraph*, it was a precedent that Black be summoned to serve in the British House of Lords. As the appointment made its way through the vetting process in 2001 a UK official raised a possible red flag. Could a peerage be granted to a citizen of Canada? It was determined through the offices of the chief of protocol for Canada and the British High Commissioner in Ottawa that Black could accept the peerage provided he was a dual citizen and did not make use of the title while in Canada. British prime minister Tony Blair called Black and offered to serve as sponsors for the citizenship application, along with his home secretary, Jack Straw. The forms were processed within a day.

The Globe and Mail revealed that an appointment was soon to be announced and outlined some of the thorny issues that had already been resolved behind the scenes.[17] But the pending appointment did not sit well with the Canadian prime minister. Chrétien used the Nickle Resolution as his tool. Passed by the Canadian Parliament in 1919, the non-binding resolution was a request to King George V not to confer titles on Canadians who were resident in Canada. Roy Thomson gave up his Canadian citizenship to become Lord Thomson of Fleet because he couldn't become a dual citizen. That was before the Canadian law was updated in 1977 to allow for dual citizenship. Chrétien's objections notwithstanding, Blair was told by his officials that the appointment was on solid legal ground except that it was unacceptable to place the Queen in the awkward position of receiving conflicting advice from two Commonwealth prime ministers. Black attempted to test Chrétien's legal authority to block the appointment, but no Canadian court was prepared to accept jurisdiction.

What was clear from multiple media reports was that Chrétien's obstinacy had nothing to do with the Nickle Resolution and everything to do with extracting political payback for the rough ride he had received from Black's Canadian newspapers over the Shawinigate scandal. The Reform Party's deputy leader, Deborah Grey, called Chrétien the small-minded guy from Shawinigan. "You can't believe this man would behave this way: 'If you bug me, you offend me, you dig into my business dealing, you will pay a price.'"[18] Chrétien's staff admitted that the prime minister took some pleasure in showing that the powerful and wealthy did not always get want they wanted from government.

Black renounced his Canadian citizenship as a condition for taking his seat in the House of Lords, saying that he would take it back "when this nonsense was over." Following a dispute over his business dealings in the United States, Black served 37 months in a US prison for convictions that were subsequently vacated by the United States Supreme Court. In his memoirs, Chrétien gloated that Black had made a bad deal: "Becoming Lord Black of Crossharbour was more important than remaining a Canadian citizen. It wasn't a choice I would have made myself."[19] But after Black resumed residency in Canada in 2012, Chrétien said that Lord Black would be welcomed in Shawinigan.

MOST CANADIANS THINK OF Chrétien as a protégé of Pierre Trudeau. But Sir Wilfrid Laurier was firmly at the top of Chrétien's list of inspirational leaders. As prime minister, Chrétien used Laurier's desk and had an oil painting of Laurier in his office.[20] He admired Laurier's penchant for compromise and his rejection of extreme views. Laurier, Chrétien noted, understood that a nation as diverse and far-flung as Canada could not survive polarization. He was also struck by Laurier's populist instincts and his essential optimism.[21/22] Laurier, Chrétien said, remained a guiding light and a constant presence over his 40 years in public life.[23] Chrétien also liked what the election of Laurier said about Canada: that the country could choose a French Canadian prime minister when only 30 per cent of the seats in the House of Commons were from Québec.

Lester B. Pearson was another inspiring figure to Chrétien. It was Pearson who gave him the aspiration and confidence that he could become Canada's first francophone minister of finance. When asked about being appointed a minister by Pearson on April 4, 1967, Chrétien light-heartedly noted it was not because of his brilliance. Chrétien recalled how he had been recruited to pitch in a friendly baseball game that pitted MPs against journalists. Chrétien said that Pearson was so impressed with his grit and desire to win that he put him in cabinet.[24]

Chrétien was initially wary of Pierre Trudeau. He told Lester Pearson he wasn't sure a man like Trudeau, whom he viewed as a provocateur and an intellectual millionaire, could get elected in Québec.[25] At first, Chrétien kept his personal distance from Trudeau. He sized up Trudeau to be something of a loner: "He's an extremely private person, apparently self-sufficient, like a monk in some ways." But Trudeau put Chrétien at the top of his list when handing out his most difficult assignments. Trudeau sent Chrétien to Finance when the economy was in rough shape, to Justice for the referendum campaign and as the government's constitutional fixer, and to the energy portfolio to quell western resentment over the National Energy Program.

When party apparatchiks dismissed Chrétien's bid for the Liberal leadership in 1984 because of a pattern of alternating between English and French leaders, Trudeau came to Chrétien's defence. He told his caucus that leadership was a question of ability and not a candidate's first language.[26]

It was Trudeau's intellect and vision that Chrétien most admired. Other than on Meech Lake and the Charlottetown constitutional accords, Trudeau did nothing to undermine Chrétien while he was Liberal leader. Even during the 1995 referendum and debates over the Clarity Act, Trudeau shared his opinions only when speaking privately with Chrétien.

To Chrétien, Trudeau was a great prime minister and the driving force behind the Charter of Rights and Freedoms. So when Trudeau died in 2000, Chrétien wanted to give the former prime minister the highest honour possible. The problem with his first idea of naming Canada's highest peak after Trudeau was that it had already been named for Sir William Edmond Logan, a Canadian geologist and founder of the Geological Survey of Canada. Facing stiff opposition, Chrétien let Logan remain on his perch, but it was one of the few decisions he came to regret in his career.[27]

Chrétien ultimately settled on four commemorations. First, a mountain in British Columbia's Premier Range was renamed Mount Pierre Elliott Trudeau. Second, the Trudeau Foundation was established and endowed with $125 million of taxpayer money. It remains the only such foundation in the name of a Canadian prime minister.

Like the tallest peak, the third honour was problematic. The proposed $151 million judicial building located on the grounds next to the Supreme Court of Canada was to be named for Trudeau. When Chrétien made his announcement, he was accompanied by Justin Trudeau, then 30 years of age and a student at McGill University. Justin remarked at the time that he wasn't ready to enter politics. "I'm not going anywhere near politics, we know that, not for a good stretch."[28] But Paul Martin squashed the Trudeau tribute and the building when he became prime minister. Martin said he wanted to save the money to invest in health care rather than on low-priority items.[29] It's unlikely the cancellation was for financial reasons since the government was in surplus at the time. It's more likely that Martin wanted to undermine Chrétien while also distancing himself from Pierre Trudeau.

The fourth honour was renaming Montréal's principal airport Pierre Elliott Trudeau International Airport. It was an ironic choice because Trudeau did everything in his power to close the Dorval facility by investing heavily in the opening of Mirabel Airport. Trudeau's government had expropriated huge tracts of farmland for Mirabel, which at the time had the largest footprint of any airport in the world. Originally expected to cost $425 million, Mirabel's final bill came in close to $1.5 billion (about $6 billion in 2017 dollars). When the airport opened in October 1975, Trudeau boasted that it would be so magnificent that "Torontonians will be down here on their knees."[30] Eventually, Mirabel could only find use as a cargo facility.[31]

Chrétien described Trudeau as a man of brilliance, action, grace, style, wit, complexity, courage, and someone who inspired young Canadians to engage in acts of citizenship. While he had left an indelible mark on his eventual successor, it would be wrong to call Trudeau Chrétien's mentor or confidante. Their relationship was professional. Chrétien faithfully executed his duties and did what Trudeau asked of him. But it was evident during his time in cabinet that he thought Trudeau's fiscal policies lacked rectitude and his approach to the provinces was too restrictive. While prime minister, Chrétien sustained Trudeau's policies that he believed in, but didn't hesitate to change course where he thought Trudeau had missed the mark.

CHRÉTIEN WAS 33 WHEN he was named to the cabinet in April 1967. He was the youngest cabinet minister so far that century. Claude Ryan, editor of the widely-circulated and influential Québec newspaper *Le Devoir*, thought there was a future in politics for a man with populist instincts like Chrétien, but his praise was qualified:

> Jean Chrétien is in a different class. He has neither the advanced education nor the prestigious background of his two new colleagues (Trudeau and Turner) without being what one calls a man of influence, without always being sufficiently nuanced in some of his affirmations, he possesses a practical strength and hunger for action, which make him a logical candidate for the cabinet. A balanced cabinet should include a good balance between intellectuals and specialists on the one hand and practical men on the other. Mr. Chrétien is a good practical type, Mr. Trudeau a purebred intellectual, and Mr. Turner finds himself somewhere between the two.[32]

Chrétien did nothing to counter Ryan's opinion. He believed that being perceived as someone who grew up on the wrong side of the tracks was an advantage. When speaking to English audiences Chrétien would say "I'm a goddamn pea-souper and I am proud of it." He even called himself a "frog" before an English audience. A fellow cabinet minister, Jean-Luc Pépin, called Chrétien's remarks, "massively demeaning."

But Chrétien was prepared for the ridicule. In his first autobiography, Chrétien wrote:

I have always had to pay a political price among the intellectuals of Québec for using slang, emotion, and jokes in my speeches, but the St. Maurice Valley was a region of populist politicians famous for their colourful style … Since I had to fight populists I learned from them, and even tried to outdo them. That has often shocked and annoyed the intellectuals who exaggerate my humble beginnings or conclude I am uneducated.[33]

Chrétien liked doing battle with the elites whom he thought were overrated as a political force. In his prime ministerial memoirs, he wrote that intellectuals have less influence in Québec than they think. He said he had been in government long enough not to be impressed by editorials and abstract theories. But Allan Rock, a senior cabinet minister under Chrétien, said that the prime minister was as sophisticated and intelligent as anyone around the cabinet table or in the bureaucracy:

He retreated to his study in the evening to listen to classical music, on which he is extremely knowledgeable. He is capable of the most nuanced conversation about a remarkable diversity of subjects. He has wide tastes in art and wine, although food does not interest him as much. He is a highly-sophisticated man of the world with an active and powerful intellect. Those who think he is a country bumpkin make a serious mistake. It's a mistake that he actively encourages and against which he has profited enormously in the course of his political career.

It irritated the intellectuals around the cabinet table when they were corrected by Chrétien. As a cabinet minister, Chrétien pointed out an error about a constitutional matter made by the Clerk of the Privy Council, Michael Pitfield. Pitfield sought revenge by trying to demean Chrétien. He asked him if the point he was making came from the writings of Alexander Hamilton or Thomas Jefferson. "Tell me, Michael," Chrétien responded, "what baseball teams do these guys play for?" Chrétien said he had never heard Trudeau laugh so hard. It was the sort of comment that caused many people to admire Chrétien and others to be infuriated by him.

Chrétien simply did not respond well to snobs. He and his law school mates made a prank phone call to one of their more pompous professors. Imitating the voice of a federal cabinet minister, the mischief-makers informed the professor he was to be summoned to the Senate. The would-be appointee was told to keep the news strictly confidential, but Chrétien and his gang knew it would be too difficult for the professor to withhold the secret. A reporter was tipped off and a phone call to the professor led to a lengthy interview. The news was featured in a Québec City newspaper the following day, only to be retracted when the joke was revealed.[34]

Among his cabinet ministers, the only person Chrétien claimed personal affection for was Stéphane Dion. He was pals with Bill Clinton, but that was not a relationship Chrétien wanted to advertise. He enjoyed his political staff, but only enough to exchange some banter around the office. In 1992, while travelling to Washington DC with his communications director, Peter Donolo, he told journalist Anthony Wilson Smith that Peter was a wonderful guy and he does great work, "but he is not my friend." At Donolo's retirement dinner in 1999, Chrétien ended his toast by saying, "Peter, now I can call you my friend."

WHETHER IT'S THE GOVERNOR General or a member of the board of a port authority, the prime minister is held accountable for the behaviour of everyone the government appoints.

For some positions, such as judicial appointments, a formal process is in place for recruitment and vetting. This constrains a prime minister from appointing a friend or partisan to the Supreme Court. But for many positions, the key qualification is that a nominee embraces the political party in power, supports the aims of the government, or knows someone in a position of power.

Chrétien was not naive about the motivation of office-seekers. He told his ministers that people who want an appointment will pretend they are your best friend, but after you give them what they want they will rarely be grateful. He said one applicant "kissed the floor from the front door of the Parliament buildings to my office to get that appointment," but once in the office said he was only there because of his superior qualifications. Chrétien understood that there were not enough appointments to keep all political partisans happy, but that it remained a useful tool to reward faithful service or a convenient way to create openings in Parliament for rising stars.

Goldenberg wrote that some of Chrétien's appointments were excessively partisan and that, despite his pledge to the contrary, he occasionally got himself in trouble for stubbornly insisting on rewarding certain political friends for past support.[35] He also thought Chrétien was a soft touch when it came to hard luck cases. "I concluded that [some seeking appointments] had been such nuisances that instead of sending them packing, as he should have, Chrétien felt sorry for them and made the mistake by giving them what they wanted, just to get them out of his hair."[36] One such appointment was George Radwanski. A gifted journalist, Radwanski wrote a flattering biography of Pierre Trudeau in 1978 and served as a Chrétien speechwriter before he was appointed as Canada's privacy commissioner. There was no criticism of the appointment by opposition parliamentarians, but what they didn't know was that just before the appointment Radwanski had declared bankruptcy to avoid having to pay a $540,000 tax bill to Revenue Canada.

Radwanski's disregard for his fellow taxpayers didn't end there. As head of the Privacy Commission, he dinged the public purse for close to $500,000 in extravagant travel and hospitality expenses. The ensuing scandal cost him his job; he resigned in 2003 after serving only half of his seven-year term. MPs voted unanimously to find him in contempt of Parliament. Radwanski was charged with fraud and breach of trust, but he was acquitted on all counts in 2009.

But not all of those rescued by Chrétien came back to haunt him. Jim Munson, who had a strong temper, and a mercurial career as a journalist, found himself without a job in 2001. Chrétien brought him into his office as communications director in August 2002. In December 2003, in Chrétien's final days in office, Munson was appointed to the Senate. Unlike many other senators, Munson was a solid contributor in the Red Chamber.

Over its history, the Senate has been a safe landing pad for political bagmen and party organizers. Chrétien made 75 appointments to the Senate, which amounts to almost three-quarters of all seats in the chamber. Some of the appointments were former Liberal premiers or provincial party leaders, including Catherine Callbeck of PEI and Sharon Carstairs of Manitoba. Some were old political warhorses, such as Eugene Whalen and Jean-Robert Gauthier.

Chrétien also had a habit of appointing those who were close to the mandatory 75-year age limit. This offered the advantage of increasing the overall number of appointments and the pool of the grateful but did not necessarily enhance the effectiveness of the Senate since short-term senators had little opportunity to develop legislative expertise.

Of the 75 Senate appointments, only a handful reflected badly on Chrétien. Mac Harb, a Chrétien loyalist and a 15-year MP for Ottawa Centre, was charged with fraud and breach of trust related to the claims he made for housing and other expenses. The charges were later dropped. Raymond Lavigne was appointed to the senate in 2002 to open up a House of Commons seat for Liza Frulla, a former Québec provincial cabinet minister. Lavigne was convicted of fraud and breach of trust related to his Senate expenses in 2011 and was sentenced to six months in prison and six months of house arrest.

Chrétien also used the appointment process to reinforce notions of inclusion, equity, and addressing past wrongs. Just as Diefenbaker appointed the first woman to cabinet and the first aboriginal member of the Senate, Chrétien elevated Beverly McLaughlin, a Mulroney appointee, to be the first female Chief Justice of the Supreme Court. Chrétien made six Supreme Court appointments, representing two-thirds of the court's composition. Two of the six were women. None of the six has been proven to be controversial.

Other notable appointments included Adrienne Clarkson as Canada's second female Governor General. While there were questions at first about her ability to connect with ordinary Canadians, she proved herself to be one of the military's most fervent supporters and developed a common touch that drew the affection of most Canadians.

Overall, the number of controversial appointments made by Chrétien were minor and he used his powers to put people in high places to good effect.

WHILE BRIAN MULRONEY HAD a strained relationship with Canadians, he commanded almost universal respect and loyalty among the Progressive Conservative MPs who served under him over his nine years in office. Even opposition MPs recalled moments when Mulroney's personal grace and decency made a difference to them in moments of stress. Chrétien, on the other hand, had a strong connection with ordinary Canadians, but he did not receive a warm embrace from many of the MPs who served by his side.

While there were certainly some cabinet loyalists who sang Chrétien's prais-es, few made the case that their "boss" was among the greats. *The Montreal Gazette* wrote that in Chrétien's final months in office, all he had around him were "personal cronies," and that the bonds of loyalty from ministers, MPs, and senior mandarins had worn thin.[37] Chrétien's unwillingness to befriend those who served with him was a factor. A more significant issue was the bruising civil war with Paul Martin.

In his retirement, Chrétien did not assemble his old gang very often to rem-inisce. There was a rare celebration held in Toronto to mark Chrétien's 80th birthday and his 50 years of public service, which 700 people attended. The proceeds from the event went to La Maison de la francophonie de Toronto. It was an all-party affair with Jean Charest, former leader of the Progressive Conservative Party, serving as the host. Prime Minister Harper, who could not attend because of foreign travel, sent a warm video greeting. Paul Martin, who had a prior engagement, sent no greetings, although he and another former Liberal leader, John Turner, lent their names to the organization of the event.[38] Ed Lumley, a long-serving minister under Pierre Trudeau, said it sent a strong signal that the past was past. The show of unity, Lumley added, was designed to help the new Liberal leader, Justin Trudeau. "The fact is, we all want to do our best for Mr. Trudeau. He doesn't need to inherit the problems of the past. So, the onus, I think, is on all of us to put aside whatever differences we have."[39]

While the speakers highlighted Chrétien's long and faithful service to the coun-try he loved, only former NDP premier of Saskatchewan Roy Romanow dared to say that history will record "that he was one of the best prime ministers that this great country has ever had."[40] But if Chrétien was given the choice between the love and respect of ordinary Canadians versus that of Liberal power bro-kers, the choice would have been easy. For Chrétien, the country always came first. It was no accident that he ended every speech he gave with the words, "Vive le Canada."

RISKY BUSINESS

In Canada, we worry far less about the safety and security of our elected leaders than in most countries. An RCMP security detail protects the prime minister, but with far less fame and regard than that afforded to the American Secret Service.

Chrétien had no concerns or anxiety about his safety. He rejected a newly commissioned and more modern airplane for prime ministerial travel so that he would not appear extravagant or presidential. No one would fault Chrétien for using a plane that had been bought and paid for by the previous government, but he rejected the upgrade on political grounds. He may have had second thoughts, however, after an attempted flight from Sweden to Canada in 2001 aboard one of the government's Challenger aircraft had to be aborted. The plane's decompression system malfunctioned at 27,000 feet and cabin pressure was lost. The jet plunged thousands of feet in mere seconds. Chrétien and his executive assistant, Bruce Hartley, donned emergency oxygen masks as the jet limped back to Sweden. Chrétien ended up hitching a ride back to Canada on a Canadian Forces Airbus.[1]

But the prime minister had more trouble on the ground than in the air. Not more than a week after the 1995 Québec referendum, Chrétien had to make a trip to Israel to attend the funeral of its president, Yitzhak Rabin, who had been assassinated by an Orthodox Jew. While preparing for the trip the prime minister turned to Eddie Goldenberg and said, "You know, with all the emotion provoked in Québec by the referendum, I could be next after Rabin."[2]

The night before his Israel trip, Chrétien had trouble dozing off so his wife gave him a sleeping pill. While he slept, Aline heard a commotion outside the door of their bedroom at 24 Sussex Drive. She got out of bed and came face to face with an intruder, who was putting on a pair of gloves. He held a long knife in his right hand. "Who are you?" Aline demanded. The intruder would later tell the police he did not want to harm the wife of the prime minister. "I just wanted to cut her husband's throat."

Aline ran back into the bedroom and shut the door. She was shaking as she woke up her husband, alerting him to an intruder in the house. "Come on," Chrétien replied. "Aline, you had a bad dream. There can't be a stranger in the house. We're surrounded by security." She pressed the panic button on her bedside table to alert the RCMP at the security booth that immediate help was required. "Come right away," Aline implored the RCMP.

Aline told her husband that the intruder looked like Forrest Gump, the oddball movie character who frequently found himself at turning points in American history. Then Chrétien saw a shadow. He reached for the closest weapon at hand: a heavy Inuit sculpture of a loon that he grabbed by the neck. In that moment, he reverted to his role as the street fighter from Shawinigan.

Chrétien was ready to defend himself and his wife until the RCMP arrived. When they finally did show up, the circus continued. The officers didn't have a key. It took 20 minutes from the time they received the panic call until they had the assailant in hand. The intruder had been spotted by security cameras, but the two officers in the booth thought it was a third constable doing his rounds. It turned out that officer was not on patrol, but was playing cards with one of the governor general's security detail.

Just before boarding his flight to Israel, Chrétien told an RCMP officer that he could just as well be wearing his red serge uniform "carrying my coffin."[3] The would-be assassin, André Dallaire, was a well-educated, under-employed, and mentally unstable man. He was distressed by the referendum result and wanted to kill the prime minister. Dallaire was charged with attempted murder, but was found not guilty by reason of mental illness. The Chrétiens were displeased that their assailant, who received a conditional discharge less than a year after the assassination attempt, was assigned to live at a group home not far from 24 Sussex Drive.[4]

The RCMP downplayed the incident and attempted to deflect the criticism they rightly deserved. Commissioner Phil Murray eventually conceded his force was at fault: "We expect immediate response. We did not get immediate response."[5] An RCMP investigation concluded that Chrétien's security detail comprised low-ranking and poorly-trained Mounties who were ill-equipped. Even the floor plans of the stately residence were outdated. Four junior Mounties were suspended and three senior officers transferred.[6] But the real problem was the naiveté of the RCMP and its complacency in protecting the prime minister. The commissioner was caught unprepared and admitted that the RCMP just didn't think security threats to political leaders happened in Canada.[7]

The Chrétiens received little compassion for what they had endured. There are not many people in Canada who would be expected to show up for work the morning after having been awoken in the middle of the night by a deranged would-be killer outside their bedroom door. That the prime minister travelled halfway around the world that morning to attend the funeral for someone who did not escape an assassin's bullet only magnifies the ordeal. Months later, Aline asked Eddie Goldenberg if he thought her husband would be killed because he was prime minister.

Other world leaders have reacted less than insouciantly after an assassination attempt. In the aftermath of the shooting of President Ronald Reagan in 1981, just 60 days after inauguration day, his wife Nancy was so shaken that she resorted to consulting an astrologist to determine the days her husband would be safe to travel and otherwise appear in public. Reagan's chief of staff lamented the fact that the itinerary of the leader of the free world was determined by the alignment of the stars.

Had Aline Chrétien not alerted her husband to the intruder, had Chrétien not been at the ready to confront the assassin with an improvised weapon in hand, had the RCMP not eventually arrived to subdue the mentally unstable assassin, Canada might look like a different country today. It was not long before Chrétien felt the need once again to protect himself from what he considered to be a threat.

NATIONAL FLAG DAY IN Canada commemorates the replacement of the Canadian Red Ensign with the Red Maple Leaf in 1965. The adoption of the new flag was contentious, with Liberal Prime minister Lester B. Pearson battling it out with his nemesis John Diefenbaker. While Diefenbaker opposed the flag's design and wanted the matter decided in a national referendum, the dispute was resolved in the House of Commons, where the new flag was approved by a vote of 163–78. But this was not before tempers flared on Parliament Hill. Progressive Conservative MP Bob Coates and Liberal MP George McIlraith got in a shouting match in a crowded elevator on the flag's first day. Chrétien jumped into the fracas and grabbed Coates by the lapels of his suit jacket and pushed him up against a wall.[8] What his party saw that day was that Chrétien was a team player, and an enforcer to boot. It was not a new role for Chrétien. At the age of 27 he got into a heated argument with a fellow lawyer who had insinuated that Chrétien was a success only because his big brother helped him out. Chrétien responded with a barrage of punches. Had charges been laid, his legal and political career might have been stopped in its tracks.[9]

Chrétien wanted to pay tribute to both the flag and the Liberal prime minister who made it a reality. He declared February 15, 1996, to be Canada's National Flag Day. It was not a national holiday so the commemoration at a ceremony in Hull, Québec drew little public interest.

With Parliament Hill as the backdrop, a large group of school children was present to celebrate the occasion. Chrétien was happy to meet and greet the children and others who had gathered to pay tribute to Canada and its history. But other forces were also present at the event. While Chrétien attempted to speak at the podium, a gang of protestors hurled insults and droned the prime minister out with air horns. They claimed to be protesting changes to the unemployment insurance system. They also made disparaging remarks about the Canadian flag only months after the unity of Canada had been tested in the Québec referendum.

The prime minister was distressed that a national celebration had turned into an ugly spectacle. He cut his remarks short to mingle with the crowd. But the protestors held their ground and tried to block Chrétien's path. In the blink of an eye, he grabbed one protestor by the throat and threw him to the ground. Then he grabbed a bullhorn from another protestor. The RCMP eventually intervened and escorted the prime minister out of the melee while subduing those involved in the ruckus. Afterwards, the RCMP defended their conduct be saying proper protocol was followed and that Chrétien was never in any danger during this "minor altercation."

"It had only been three months since someone had tried to assassinate me," wrote Chrétien, "so my reaction was instinctive and probably angrier than it would have been otherwise." It happened so fast that Deputy Prime Minister Sheila Copps, thinking the protestor had slipped on the ice, asked if he was all right.

It was instinctive for Chrétien to meet force with force. When he was teased in his youth because of a birth defect that left him deaf in his right ear and distorted his mouth he always went on the offence. Backing down from confrontation was not in his character. It didn't help that he was usually the smallest kid in his class, an attribute that earned him the nickname Ti-Jean, a short form of Petit Jean. When he was 14 years old, to bolster his ability to stand up to bullies Chrétien sought the advice of a trusted physician to help him grow. The doctor was his older brother, a gynecologist. Dr. Chrétien handed his kid brother some vitamins.[10] Chrétien wanted to be ready for any fight that came his way.

Initially, the media reaction to the Flag Day chokehold was that the prime minister had lost his composure, which Chrétien understood. "The television clips and newspaper photographs looked damaging, not least because the sunglasses I had been wearing at the time made me look like a mobster." The editors at the Montreal Gazette wrote that Chrétien was out of line and what he did was disgraceful. "The prime minister has to be above the fray. He has to show more dignified behaviour than that."[11]

When Aline Chrétien first heard the story, she wondered if her husband would have to resign. But Don Newman, senior parliamentary editor for CBC Television and the host of the daily show *Politics*, said the incident merely confirmed what people already thought of Chrétien: that he was a scrapper at heart.

The RCMP guards called Chrétien's manoeuvre "the Shawinigan handshake," a moniker that stuck to Chrétien as a term of affection. When Chrétien's team was told that the protestor's dental bridge was damaged, Peter Donolo told his boss not to worry because there was a government infrastructure program for bridges that could handle the expense.

The next morning, Chrétien called feisty Newfoundland premier Brian Tobin to ask what he thought of the incident. "I think you are in deep shit," said

Tobin. "Everyone in Newfoundland thinks you should have kicked that guy in the balls rather than grab him by the throat."

It wasn't just the Canadian public that was on Chrétien's side. Foreign leaders cheered him on. More fun was had when Chrétien donated the sunglasses he used that day to the youth wing of the Liberal party to be put up for auction. After a criminal complaint was filed against the prime minister for common assault, the Québec justice minister intervened to block the proceedings. The street fighter had won another battle. In retirement, Chrétien happily retells the story and laughs that a "pugnaciously strong ale" is marketed in Québec under the name Shawinigan Handshake.

While the RCMP may have tightened up security after the confrontation on Flag Day and the assassination attempt at 24 Sussex Drive, at at least one more event the prime minister's security detail let him down. While in Prince Edward Island in August 2000, Chrétien was hit in the face with a cream pie. It seems local officers were unfamiliar with Chrétien's habits and desire to mingle with the crowd. Nor were they alert enough to notice someone in the crowd wearing a winter overcoat on a hot summer day. While incarcerated, the protestor's cell mates roughed him up. "Apparently," Chrétien remarked with some glee, "they were fans of mine."

WINNING

Jean Chrétien was blunt about how he measured his success: "To be frank, politics is about wanting power, getting it, exercising it, and keeping it." To Chrétien, politics was a sport with winners and losers. Jousting with his adversaries in the House of Commons, he said, was a highlight of his day.[1]

He liked cornering his opponents, exploiting their weaknesses, and celebrating when he knocked them out. His record in the ring was 12–0. That covers 11 general elections and one by-election.

As THE 1970S WOUND down, Chrétien knew that Trudeau would not stay in power much longer. He told a deputy minister at that time that it was John Turner's turn but that he was hoping to hang in there long enough to be prime minister.[2]

But Chrétien hoped not to have to wait. He was a natural candidate to succeed Trudeau when he retired in 1984 given his national popularity, experience in all key cabinet positions, an extensive political network, and ambition.

Nevertheless, there were obstacles he could not overcome. The pesky Liberal tradition of alternating between French and English leaders did not work in his favour. While the convention may have benefited Trudeau in 1968 when he succeeded Pearson, it offended Trudeau's sense of fairness in 1984. Trudeau admonished those in the Liberal caucus who thought Chrétien should be dismissed because of his mother tongue: "If alternation is everything, then I don't belong here as prime minister. I thought I was selected because I was good, not because I was French."[3]

Chrétien's more challenging obstacle was John Turner. In 1975, Turner resigned as Trudeau's finance minister over a clash of personality and policy. Turner went to Bay Street for almost a decade but remained the front runner to replace Trudeau. Chrétien didn't like Turner and thought he was overrated as a politician. Chrétien was also annoyed that Turner had sent a newsletter to his corporate clients that was critical of the Liberal government. Chrétien thought it bad form for a former finance minister to be cashing in by lambasting a sitting finance minister from his own party. Chrétien's prediction that Turner would flop went unheeded.

Liberals didn't think that a Trudeau protégé like Chrétien would succeed in 1984. They were worried about winning seats in Québec after the patriation of the Constitution in 1981 over the objections of the government of Québec. The Liberal party hierarchy wanted change.

Even Chrétien's friends in cabinet lined up with Turner. André Ouellet was a senior Québec cabinet minister who had been good friends with Chrétien. Their wives were also close. Ouellet controlled much of the party machinery in Québec so his support was critical to winning the leadership. Ouellet told Chrétien not to worry "I will be with you." Then he changed his mind. Marc Lalonde, another Québec heavyweight and Trudeau loyalist, said it wasn't the time for another francophone leader.

But Chrétien could hardly expect his francophone friends in cabinet to work for him just because of language. In 1968 he had supported the unilingual Mitchell Sharp for Liberal leader rather than his fellow Québecer, Pierre Trudeau. And it's not that Sharp had much in common with Chrétien's populist approach to politics. Despite being pressured to support Trudeau by cabinet heavyweights, Chrétien could not be dislodged from Sharp until he withdrew from the race.

It wasn't just ministers from Québec who abandoned Chrétien in 1984. Chrétien's parliamentary secretary, Ed Lumley, a man who Chrétien had taken under his wing, lined up with Turner. When Lumley told Chrétien that he wouldn't work hard for Turner, Chrétien was angry: "For Christ sakes. If you want to support the guy, work hard for him. Don't double-cross him like you double-crossed me."

There was also an element of snobbery within Liberal ranks. Those who had served under Trudeau did not see the folksy and street-smart Chrétien as leadership material. They thought he lacked eloquence in English and French, something Chrétien thought was a strength. "There is a big, big gap between the intellectuals and the people. The intellectuals live in an unreal world, and I'm very happy they don't consider me as one of their friends."[4]

It was tough enough not having the support of his cabinet colleagues, but Chrétien also had to deal with 1,000 super-delegates who were accredited to the leadership convention. These were automatic delegates who were entitled to vote by virtue of the senior positions they held within the party or as provincial and federal elected representatives. The super-delegates were also the people at the front of the line for patronage posts and who would benefit by being close to the leader. Had Chrétien won his fair share of these delegates he might have had a fighting chance.[5]

Turner was denied a first ballot victory, falling just short with 46 per cent support compared with 31 per cent for Chrétien. Even though three of the four candidates who dropped out after the first ballot endorsed Chrétien, he still came up short. Turner took it on the second ballot with 54 per cent support.

After Turner was declared the winner, Liberal party president Iona Campagnola conceded that Chrétien was second in the ballot but "first in our hearts." In effect, she foretold the challenge Turner would have in uniting the party after the convention. He made this more difficult by making Marc Lalonde and André Ouellet co-leads of the party in Québec along with Chrétien.

Progressive Conservative leader Brian Mulroney called Chrétien to say how much happier he was to face Turner in the 1984 election, especially in Québec.[6] Chrétien responded by saying Turner was just like the hockey player who looked good in the draft but underperformed when he was on the ice.

Turner, who thought he had momentum, ignored Chrétien's advice not to call a snap election after the leadership convention.[7] Whatever momentum existed was crushed in the television debate when Turner was eviscerated by Mulroney. One campaign calamity after another followed for Turner. The Liberals went from winning 147 seats in 1980 to only 40 in 1984 and from 74 of 75 Québec's seats in 1980 to just 17 seats in 1984. Brian Mulroney's win gave him the largest number of federal seats for any party in Canadian history.

MANY LIBERALS OPENLY ACKNOWLEDGED that they had made a mistake in choosing Turner, a fact the Progressive Conservative government exploited. When Chrétien rose to ask a question in the House of Commons, the Tories opposite would shout "Leader! Leader!" Turner belittled Chrétien, causing the reserved Aline Chrétien to tell a CBC reporter that her husband didn't have to "take that shit."[8] Chrétien toughed it out in the Liberal caucus until February 1986.

Turner and Chrétien were so different it was difficult for Liberals to draw comparisons. David Collenette, one of the few ministers to have served in the cabinets of Turner and Chrétien, said that when Turner came back in 1984 he was out of touch and looser in his language and behaviour than he thought a leader should be. Turner wanted to dump Collenette from cabinet because he wanted fresh faces. But Collenette was its youngest member. Turner changed his mind and Collenette stayed.

Sheila Copps, who was an MP under Turner and who went on to become Chrétien's deputy prime minister, remarked that the two men had dramatically different styles:

> Chrétien loves the political intrigue and backroom machinations of politics. John Turner did not want to get his hands dirty. When Turner faced an internal revolt, he seemed caught by surprise and had no strategy to fight back. He assumed loyalty. Chrétien assumed nothing. He wanted to continually prove himself while Turner may have felt he was entitled to win. Jean Chrétien was a better counter puncher.

Brian Tobin, who also served under both leaders, had supported Turner in 1984 because he believed in the Liberal practice of alternating. But he said that Turner did not have Chrétien's surefootedness: "Chrétien was a mountain goat who could navigate the cliffs and made it look effortless. For Turner, ragged cliffs were unfamiliar territory."

Tobin learned from Chrétien that votes were not just won at election time. In early 1985, Chrétien visited Tobin in Newfoundland, where they got bogged down during a heavy snowfall that had shut down the highway. "You know what?" Chrétien said to Tobin. "All these people on this side and on the other side, they're voters. They're stuck here and we're stuck here, so let's go out and meet them." The surprises on the faces of the drivers who rolled down their windows to say hello to Chrétien told Tobin all he needed to know about the power of retail politics.[9]

CHRÉTIEN SAID HIS RESIGNATION as an MP in 1986 had nothing to do with John Turner's leadership. But few believed him, especially after he mused that he would not rule out a return to Parliament: "I am leaving politics because I now intend to do something else, and I have no plans for a comeback. But you never tell the fountain you will never drink its water again."[10]

While still a Liberal MP, Chrétien wrote his first memoirs in 1985, entitled *Straight from the Heart*. The book sold a remarkable 300,000 copies and re- mains among the most widely-read Canadian political autobiographies of all time.[11] Anna Porter, the book's publisher, had asked Chrétien on three occa- sions to write the book and he said no to each request. After she put a cheque in front of him, he said yes. More than a critical and commercial success, it reminded Canadians that Chrétien was a leader in waiting. But Turner was de- termined to win back hearts and minds in his party and fight another election.

Away from Parliament, the populist small-town Québec politician went blue chip and accepted positions at a prestigious law office, an investment capital firm in Toronto, and the boards of several major Canadian companies. But he was never far from Liberal politics. A few months after Chrétien resigned, and just before a Liberal convention where John Turner's leadership was to be tested, a Gallup poll was leaked to the press that showed a Liberal party under Jean Chrétien would hold a 19 point lead over the Progressive Conservatives. Of those surveyed, 42 per cent preferred Chrétien as leader to only 19 per cent for Turner.[12] The source of the poll was never revealed but it was an or- chestrated leak arriving at the doors of several media outlets at the same time. John Turner remarked that the timing of the leak was curious: "I don't rule anything out."

While Chrétien professed neutrality in the leadership review vote, when he ar- rived at the convention, the forces in favour of and opposed to Turner clashed and the police were called in. Turner ended up with the support of 75 per cent of the delegates, many of whom were "instant Liberals," plucked from various communities and interests for the sole purpose of sustaining Turner's leadership. David Collenette, who was then national director of the Liberal party, did not see Chrétien as agnostic in the leadership review: "The way that Chrétien was treated by Turner after the 1984 leadership contest engendered certain predictable feelings, which made it difficult for him leading up to the 1986 leadership review."

In the early days of the 1988 federal election, John Turner struggled. A few high-ranking Liberals predicted that Turner would take the party to its worst showing ever and rumours circulated about a plan to dump Turner mid-campaign and put Chrétien in his place. It was a preposterous suggestion on many levels, the least of which is that it violated the Liberal party constitution. But the musings revealed the weak hand Turner held among party faithful and the voters at large. Liberal strategist Richard Mahoney said the attempted coup was arrogance on parade: "They thought because we were the natural governing party that we could get away with that shit."

Turner found his purpose and voice in the 1988 free-trade election and more than doubled Liberal seats from 40 to 83. But a Progressive Conservative majority government remained and Turner announced his resignation in May 1989.

IT WAS CHRÉTIEN'S TURN to be the heir apparent. When the leadership votes were counted, Chrétien was first in Liberal hearts and first on the ballot. With 57 per cent of the votes, Chrétien more than doubled the tally of his rival, Paul Martin, who had 25 per cent support.

But the victory was not universally celebrated by the intellectuals in his home province. Alain Dubuc of *La Presse* could not understand why English Canada and its media were so enamoured of Chrétien. In the *Toronto Star* he wrote an open letter to English Canada:

> We often feel that there is an Uncle Tom quality in your relationship with Chrétien. You seem to be touched by this modest but grateful French-Canadian ... [but] that doesn't wash here. We are not swept along by his basic drive or his pride in having succeeded in this Anglo-Saxon world that is Canada, a little like a first-generation immigrant grateful for being able to go to the top of his country of adoption ... In short, he is an anachronism...Ask yourself if this guy can lead the eighth power of the world, if you want him to represent you around the globe. We think not.

Jean Pelletier, Chrétien's long-time friend and future chief of staff, wasn't worried about the critiques, calling Chrétien's folksiness his inherent strength. Chrétien relished the opportunity to admonish Dubuc:

> Let's recognize this for what it is: outright, if thinly veiled, snobbery. I'm sure pundits in other countries have, at one time or another, said the same things about Harry Truman, or John Major, or Helmut Kohl, or Lech Walesa, or Boris Yeltsin. No, I didn't go to finishing school. No, I wasn't raised in a cosmopolitan city like Montréal or Toronto. But I guess I'm a little naïve. I always thought that substance was more important than form ... That competence, ideas and conviction counted for more than expensive suits and pretty words.[13]

To GAIN ENTRY TO the House of Commons after winning the leadership, Chrétien ran in a by-election in New Brunswick rather than his home province. When asked why he was abandoning Québec, Chrétien said the point of the by-election was to win and that's what he intended to do. In the post-Meech Lake period, Chrétien knew he was not in a position of strength in Québec.

As opposition leader, Chrétien was ineffective and displayed an uncharacteristic lack of confidence. He waffled on many issues, including the introduction of the GST, free trade with the United States, and how to address a Mohawk blockade of a golf course in Oka, Québec. At one point, he refused to answer a question because he said it required the expertise of a lawyer. A bemused press corps reminded Chrétien that he was a lawyer.

His most awkward moment involved Canada's role in the war in Kuwait. Chrétien said that military action in the Middle East was dangerous for the long-term security of the region and for the United Nations. Despite Iraq's overthrow of the Kuwait government, Chrétien said Canadian forces should remain in the region only to enforce an embargo and sanctions, "but if there is war our troops should be called back." When John Turner, who continued to hold his seat in the House of Commons, sided with Mulroney on Kuwait, Chrétien moved his predecessor to a smaller office on Parliament Hill.

Mulroney mocked Chrétien by saying when the shooting starts, he runs. When Chrétien visited George H.W. Bush in February 1992, Mulroney ridiculed the trip, saying the opposition leader wanted to meet the enemy. But it didn't distress Chrétien that he was not perceived to be best buddies with Bush. While he wanted "the money shot" of a picture of him in the Oval Office to demonstrate that he belonged on the world stage, he told Bush, "We are friends of America … but friendship is friendship and business is business."[14]

Jean Charest, who had been a key member of the Mulroney government, saw virtue in Chrétien's awkwardness on the opposition benches:

> He was not effective as leader of the opposition. He did not like the job. It was only later on that I understood that if a leader of the opposition likes his job, and he's good at it, and he applies for that job, the Canadian electorate will give him that job. The most important thing for Chrétien was to win the next election. His focus was to prepare his party for the campaign from a policy perspective and organizational perspective.

Chrétien's closest advisors thought he needed to reclaim his persona as a man of the people. But there were limits. When offered the line by his communications director, Peter Donolo, that "Mulroney acts in time of economic distress only when [the high fashion store] Holt Renfrew goes bankrupt" Chrétien said he couldn't say it. "Why not," asked Donolo. Chrétien opened his suit jacket to reveal a Holt Renfrew label.[15]

Under Turner, the Liberal party did little to move away from its traditional policies. Chrétien realized the party needed a makeover. They had lost two elections and were carrying an array of policy positions that had been discredited. These included an attachment to the big spending and big deficit ways of the 1970s and 1980, the National Energy Program that poisoned the well for Liberals in western Canada, and opposition to free trade.

But a shift in policy required intellectual heft. There is a tradition in Canada of political parties holding non-sanctioned conferences to reinvent themselves. The Tories held such a conference in 1942 in Port Hope, Ontario to discuss Canada's war and post-war problems. It was an invitation-only roundtable on Canadian policy designed to make the Tory party a relevant and a winnable political coalition. The point of the conference agenda was to urge Conservatives to think "progressively," particularly in social policy.

Under Pearson, the Liberals held a thinkers' conference after they were trounced by Diefenbaker in 1958. The Study Conference on National Problems was convened in 1960 at Queen's University in Kingston, Ontario. The conference was organized by a future Chrétien mentor, Mitchell Sharp, and included speakers such as Walter Gordon, who argued against foreign direct investment and for Canadian ownership of assets and businesses.

In November 1991, Chrétien sought to bring liberal thinking up to date at a conference in Aylmer, Québec. Traditional Liberal policies of economic nationalism and protectionism were substituted with pitches for free trade and globalization. Chrétien called the shift not right-wing or left-wing, but a move to more realism. David Zussman said the importance of the conference cannot be overestimated: "It was critical to bringing him up-to-speed. A common theme was that you had to get your fiscal house in order before you can deal with other issues you may want to work on."

Chrétien also tended to the organization and election preparedness of his party, which included obtaining the power for the leader to appoint a limited number of candidates. This avoided special-interest or single-issue candidates from getting on the ballot while enabling Chrétien to recruit star candidates and to help him to increase the number of women running under the Liberal banner.[16] The bottom line was that Chrétien could appoint candidates that he knew would help him win government and reject candidates that would give him trouble.

PRIME MINISTER KIM CAMPBELL, who became Canada's first female prime minister in June, 1993, was thought to be whip-smart and a breath of fresh air. Over the summer of 1993, her approval rating eclipsed Chrétien's by a margin of two to one. Chrétien concluded that Campbell was overrated and that the emergence of two regional political forces, the Bloc Québécois and the Reform Party in Western Canada, spelled trouble for the governing party.

But Liberal MPs and candidates were getting anxious about Campbell. And not without reason. In the month before the election a national poll revealed that 40 per cent of respondents thought that Campbell would make the best prime minister while only 23 per cent sided with Chrétien.[17] In Québec, it was 42 per cent for Campbell and 8 per cent for Chrétien. Québec's leading newspaper, La Presse, carried a column that predicted Chrétien would lose his home riding.[18] In a broader poll of Québecers on politicians they trusted most, Chrétien came in last with only 2 per cent support.[19]

Chrétien thought Liberals who displayed weakness got what they deserved:

> There are always nervous Nellies in any organization. If they cry they will be seen as cry-babies, and people don't vote for cry-babies. They vote for people who have confidence in themselves. If there are a few nervous Nellies, I would like to have the names so that I could put some backbone in their back ... In politics you don't panic.[20]

Peter Donolo, Chrétien's communications adviser, said some MPs were angry about the comments and blamed him. He thought they were simply running scared: "Some turned into chocolate soldiers, melting when the heat was turned up. But they lacked courage and were acting like losers."

The Progressive Conservative brain trust thought Chrétien was yesterday's man. This included Jean Charest, who was then the deputy prime minister in the Campbell government:

> After I lost the leadership race I spoke with a few columnists about how Chrétien was not well liked across the country and that we were going to outperform him in the campaign. Their response was, and I never forget this, 'Do you really think this guy who has all his experience is all of a sudden going to be a bad campaigner?'

It was advice Charest unwisely ignored. Like Charest, Brian Mulroney had predicted Chrétien's populism and charm would cause Liberal fortunes to rise, but not for long. He wrote that Chrétien s intellectual insolence, vanity, and habitual Liberal arrogance would catch up with him.[21]

Chrétien's team knew they needed to show that their leader had energy and spunk. In the days before the official launch of the 1993 election, the Liberal campaign chair, John Rae, talked Chrétien into allowing a Canadian Press photographer watch him waterski. It was a gamble, Chrétien acknowledged. If he fell that would be the picture they would use. He was thinking of the photograph that was plastered across the front pages of newspapers during the 1974 election campaign showing Progressive Conservative leader Robert Stanfield fumbling a football. No one in the press was interested in the photos of Stanfield throwing one of his many perfect spirals. Chrétien enjoyed a better fate as the water skiing photo showed him smiling with the sun shining from behind and, as Chrétien noted, "the perfect arc of water in my wake."[22]

On the eve of the election call, Conservatives held a six-point lead in the polls among decided voters. Few people aid thought Brian Mulroney had bequeathed a winning hand to his successor, but it was far from a sure loss.

As Chrétien predicted, Campbell stumbled, and at the worst possible time. Moments after the election contest was announced, she told reporters waiting outside Rideau Hall that Canadians might have to wait until the turn of the century before meaningful progress would be made on unemployment. Politicians are supposed to inspire hope, not deliver grim doses of reality. The media jumped all over the gaffe, an early indication that the press was intent on giving the prime minister a rough ride.

In the first few weeks of the campaign, the Tories were running neck and neck with the Liberals when Campbell made one of the most astonishing statements ever uttered by a national leader stumping for votes. When pressed by reporters about a so-called hidden agenda on social programs, the prime minister initially said, "The first budget of the new government will be in February of 1994, and Parliament will come back this fall. I think there is ample opportunity to engage Canadians in a serious dialogue and to work with provinces to find the best way to deliver those services." This response struck reporters as odd. Did she not think that the best time for dialogue with Canadians on these issues was during an election campaign? No, Campbell said: "I think that's the worst possible time to have that kind of dialogue … the issues are much too complex to try and generate some kind of a blueprint in the forty-seven days that's available in an election campaign … This is not the time … to get involved in a debate on very, very serious issues."

By contrast, the Liberals released a slick and comprehensive policy platform called the Red Book. It was an unconventional approach. Leaders had traditionally dribbled out election promises over the course of a campaign. It helped Chrétien that the Tories initially had no platform and no policies, and no Blue Book of their own. When they tried to create a platform document in response it was thin gruel and fell flat.

The Red Book was a brilliant campaign tactic that struck a middle ground on the key issues. There was a promise to expand affordable child care spaces, but only if a Liberal government first hit their deficit targets. Chrétien promised to replace rather than scrap the GST, with the proviso that this necessitated a deal with the provinces. The Liberal campaign was not entirely high-minded. At one point the Liberal war room dispatched a young Liberal wearing a chicken suit to confront Campbell at an Ottawa campaign speech to make the point that she would not defend her decision to cancel a proposed helicopter purchase.[23]

Chrétien said campaigning was easy. All he had to do was get up in the morning and read about another Tory misstep. Near the end of the campaign, the Tories ran a television ad that ridiculed Chrétien's leadership and mocked his facial paralysis that had also left him deaf in his right ear.[24] "It's true," Chrétien said, "that I have a physical defect, God gave it to me. When I was a kid people were laughing at me. But I accepted that God gave me other qualities and I'm grateful." It was a line Chrétien had waiting all his political life to deliver.

Chrétien captured 60 per cent of the seats with 41 per cent of the vote. The Liberal majority in the House of Commons was accentuated by a split in the vote on the right between the Reform and Progressive Conservative parties. The results were also skewed by the sudden rise of the Bloc Québécois. The separatist party from Québec now became Canada's official opposition in the House of Commons.

Despite the win, the Liberal party continued to struggle in Western Canada, winning only 15 of the 72 seats west of the Manitoba border. They also won only 25 per cent of Québec seats, but that included Chrétien's home riding of Saint-Maurice. They came out on top in all but one seat in Atlantic Canada and took 98 of 99 seats in Ontario.

While the Reform Party bested the Tories by 2.5 percentage points in the popular vote, on the seat count the score was 52 to 2. The last thing Chrétien wanted was a merger of these two warring political cousins. He even helped the Progressive Conservatives along in their search for a new leader by appointing Kim Campbell to be the government's consul general in Los Angeles.[25] It may have been a magnanimous gesture, or it may have been a brilliant political strategy to give Jean Charest a jumpstart in rebuilding his party.

Despite exceeding expectations, historians and political commentators were slow to give Chrétien credit for the win. Michael Bliss wrote that any reasonably competent Liberal leader would have won the 1993 election.[26] Of course,

Bliss had never thought much of Chrétien; once referring to him as Pierre Trudeau's "lightweight errand boy."[27] It's true that Trudeau put Chrétien in charge of the 1980 Québec referendum and the constitutional negotiations that followed. Chrétien was a loyal soldier to Trudeau and his best connection to ordinary Canadians, but he was not an errand boy.

TYPICALLY, AFTER A BRIEF honeymoon, a government loses popularity over time because of mistakes and the need to make national decisions that cause distress in certain communities. But over Chrétien's first term as prime minister the Liberal party consistently hovered at between 40 and 50 per cent support in the polls while the Reform and PC parties each languished at between 10 and 15 per cent. Even combined, the Tory and Reform vote did not pose a threat to Chrétien's re-election.

Chrétien knew that Reform couldn't build on its populist base in Western Canada and also attract more moderate conservative voters in Ontario and Atlantic Canada. Chrétien was dumbfounded that the Reform Party did not move heaven and earth to broaden their base and make a full-court press to take over the Progressive Conservative party immediately after the 1993 election:

> The Tories were down and out, with virtually nothing left but their history, so it would've been easy for Reform to take control from the inside by the buying of memberships riding by riding, electing the local executives, nominating the convention delegates and party delegates, and making sure that whoever became the next Tory leader was a friend ready and willing to merge with Reform.[28]

But Manning did not have the strategic smarts or wherewithal to implement a plan that would have shaken Chrétien's hold on power. That gave Jean Charest and the Progressive Conservative Party the time to rebuild and become a credible political force in time for the 1997 election, just as Chrétien had hoped.

Chrétien was not impressed by Manning and the diversionary politics he brought to the House of Commons. Rather than champion issues Canadians really cared about, Chrétien wrote, Manning pursued "half-baked ideas" about direct democracy and Senate reform.[29] Chrétien also viewed Manning as too much of a preacher's son with a holier-than-thou persona who lectured others about moral standards. Chrétien also thought Manning was a hypocrite when he used money from donated by Reform Party members to buy suits and a car.[30]

MANNING READIED HIMSELF FOR the 1997 campaign by undergoing a personal makeover. He had laser surgery on his eyes, shed his nerdy glasses, got his teeth capped, his hair coiffed, a colour chart done, his wardrobe updated, and a voice coach added to the Reform team. Both reporters and political opponents ridiculed the makeover, remarking that while Manning came to Ottawa to change government, it was Manning who underwent the change.

Just as Chrétien was about to launch his re-election campaign, the banks of the Red River in southern Manitoba overflowed. With Winnipeg at risk of a catastrophic flood, Chrétien went to Manitoba in the hopes that he could neutralize the disaster as an election issue. He later acknowledged it looked cold-hearted and calculating when he dropped a symbolic bag of sand on a hastily constructed dam.[31] He could have waited. It was only 43 months since the last election, when the traditional term of a government is at least 48 months. But his 20-point lead in the polls, plus the fear of an economic downturn, persuaded him that the timing was right. With hindsight, Chrétien said he regretted not postponing the election for at least a month to allow Manitoba time to recover from the flood.

The last time a majority government lasted less than 43 months was 1911 when Sir Wilfrid Laurier sought a mandate to implement free trade with the United States. It was an election he lost. But a Liberal victory in 1997 was never in doubt. The only question was which of the Reform and PC parties would win the battle of survival. As the campaign progressed, the Tories had reached 25 per cent in the polls compared with just 18 per cent for the Reform Party. That's when Reform tapped into the anger and resentment that many western Canadians felt about the special treatment they believed had been reserved for Québecers. It wasn't just a policy-based objection over regional subsidies or equalization payments.

Reform produced a television ad that said Canada was fed up with Québec politicians running the country. An array of black and white mug shots of Québec politicians, including Chrétien and Charest, was shown with red slashes stamped across their faces as if they were equivalent to a hazardous and banned substance. Unlike the ad that the Tories used in 1993 to ridicule Chrétien's facial paralysis, the Reform Party ad took on a whole cadre of people.

The Liberals did not run an inspiring campaign and Chrétien did not have as much fun as he had in 1993. A copy of the Liberal platform was stolen from a print shop and faxed to Reform Party headquarters before Liberal candidates had seen the document. Red Book II was also uninspiring and was titled *Sharing our Future Together*, which Jean Charest pointed out spelled SOFT.

The Tories were picking up steam and even Liberals admitted that Charest had won the French debate. But so what, they asked. "Who is going to be his Minister of Finance?" Charest had no one on his team who could step up to that portfolio. Then Chrétien told the French CBC that if there was another referendum he would not accept the outcome if the vote was 50 per cent plus one. "With that," said Charest, "he repolarized the vote in Québec between the federal Liberals and the Bloc Québécois, which squeezed me out. Until that moment, I had momentum and was positioned to pick up 30 to 40 seats in Québec." Charest said that Chrétien turned the election into a shadow referendum where federalists sided with the Liberals and separatists with the Bloc Québécois. Charest was left in no-man's land and ended up with only five seats in Québec.

Despite earning only 38.5 per cent of the popular vote, Chrétien was returned as prime minister with a majority government. With a strong showing from the NDP and the Tories, as well as the modest pick-up by Reform, Chrétien's Liberals were reduced to 155 seats in a 301-seat legislature. There were no Liberal members from Nova Scotia, one member from Saskatchewan, two from Alberta, and six from British Columbia. Winning 101 of 103 constituencies in Ontario helped Chrétien overcome his weak spots.

With strength in Atlantic Canada, the Tory seat count rose from 2 to 20. The Reform party won zero seats east of the Manitoba border but picked up eight seats in Western Canada to become the official Opposition in the House of Commons. In other words, the anti-Québec politician campaign worked.

Despite losing 22 seats, Chrétien won his second consecutive majority. He knew he had paid a price for balancing the books and for the tighter conditions he imposed on unemployment insurance. Chrétien thought that by choosing Halifax to host the G7 conference in 1995, voters would have given him some credit, but he went from winning all 11 seats in Nova Scotia in 1993 to zero in 1997. It was not just Atlantic Canada where Chrétien was under threat. He still won his own seat, but in the 11 times he ran in Saint-Maurice he never came closer to defeat than in 1997.

THE 2000 ELECTION WAS unexpected for three reasons. First, it took place a little more than three years after the 1997 campaign. Second, there was no compelling reason to go to the polls. Third, Chrétien had promised himself and his wife that he would only run in two elections as leader.

So why a third campaign? Chrétien had said he didn't want to push his luck, citing the desire for change as one of the most enduring and powerful forces in politics. "Get out while you can," he often said, "Don't get greedy." But his decision to run in his third election was selfish. He wanted to thwart Paul Martin from becoming prime minister.

Stockwell Day, who beat Preston Manning to become the Canadian Alliance leader in July 2000, was Chrétien's serious challenger. He was youthful, energetic, and did not have the political baggage that Preston Manning carried from having split the conservative movement in two while Brian Mulroney was prime minister. Joe Clark had come out of retirement to lead the PC party. Chrétien's worry was that Conservatives would abandon Clark and unite behind Day. But the media found Day an easy target for ridicule. The day after his by-election victory to enter the House of Commons, Day arrived at a press conference on the shores of Okanagan Lake dressed in a wetsuit and riding on a jet ski. The media ridiculed the stunt. But they didn't comment negatively when Chrétien, 66, proved his vitality by taking a white-water rafting adventure with a photographer in tow.

The press later hounded Day when he mixed religion and politics by refusing to work on Sundays. The mockery went further when CBC humorist Rick Mercer said he would use the Alliance Party policy on voter-initiated referenda to ask the country to change Stockwell's name to Doris. The ensuing petition gathered 370,000 names, which exceeded the 350,000 required to trigger a vote under Canadian Alliance policy.[611]

There were many reasons not to call an election. Chrétien's advisors reminded him of a recent Ontario provincial campaign when a popular Ontario premier,

David Peterson, was defeated after going to the polls well before the end of his mandate. The federal Liberal caucus was similarly worried. Just before the election was called, about 30 Liberal MPs spoke up against the idea at their weekly caucus meeting.

To shore up his support in Atlantic Canada, Chrétien relaxed some of the rules on employment insurance that had cost him votes in 1997. His industry minister, John Manley, wasn't happy about backtracking: "After the 97 election, and before the new cabinet was formed, the old ministers were at the table. Doug Young [from New Brunswick] said, 'Don't roll things back. Some of us have paid the ultimate price for this.'" Eddie Goldenberg said that it was more than just a political calculation and that Chrétien was influenced by people in Atlantic Canada who were struggling to make the transition to full-time work.

So as not to appear opportunistic, Chrétien needed an excuse to call the election. While Day was still getting accustomed to Parliament Hill, he challenged Chrétien to call an election. "I almost crossed the floor to kiss him," said Chrétien. "He could hardly blame me for calling one after three-and-a-half years when he himself had demanded it."[32] Chrétien deferred the election call because of the death of Pierre Trudeau on September 28. But a month after the funeral, and a massive outpouring of emotion for Trudeau, Chrétien visited the governor general, on October 22, and asked for a vote to be held on November 27.

The Liberals went into the campaign with 48 per cent support compared with the Alliance at 21 per cent, the Bloc and NDP at 10 per cent each, and the Tories pulling up the rear with 8 per cent. Rarely had the Tory numbers been so low, which gave the Canadian Alliance its best shot at burying their political cousins. Tory leader Joe Clark bravely chose to run in Calgary, an area where the Reform Party had its deepest roots. A defeat for Clark would have ended his leadership and likely his party along with it. His brightest moment of the campaign came in the debates when he accused Chrétien of taking the country into an election just to keep Paul Martin from the top job.

The desire for change helped the Canadian Alliance move to within striking distance of the Liberal party in the polls. That's when the Liberal campaign went into attack mode over Day's socially conservative views, which were popular in Alberta and Saskatchewan, but political deadweight in the rest of the country.

Warren Kinsella, a Liberal war room operative, had the clever idea of ridicul-
ing Day's beliefs that the world was 6,000 years old and that Adam and Eve
were real people who walked the earth with dinosaurs. On CTV's Canada AM,
Kinsella said that Day should be told that *The Flintstones* was not a documen-
tary. Kinsella amplified his point by holding up a stuffed animal, Barney, the
dinosaur from a children's television program. The Liberal campaign hierarchy was unhappy with Kinsella for doing the stunt without permission. But
Chrétien thought it was brilliant. He asked Kinsella to tell him exactly what
happened. After hearing a first-hand account, Chrétien asked Kinsella, "Okay,
now tell me one more time."[33]

The Liberals took 172 seats, a gain of 17 from the 1997 campaign. The Canadian
Alliance maintained official opposition status with 66 seats, a gain of 6. The
NDP seat total plummeted from 21 to 13 seats, enough to stay alive at the
margins. Joe Clark managed to win his Calgary riding in a province where the
Alliance won 23 of 26 seats. Had Clark lost, the Tories would have been below
12 seats, the threshold for official party status. There was evidence that the
Liberal party put the word out to its supporters to vote for Clark to help keep
the family feud among conservatives alive.

While Brian Mulroney said Chrétien won three majorities without having to
break a sweat because of divisions within conservative ranks, what is often
overlooked was how Chrétien kept the left-leaning New Democratic Party to
an average popular vote of less than 9 per cent over three campaigns. In the
two elections before 1993, the NDP won an average of close to 20 per cent of
the vote. In the two elections after Chrétien left, the party won 16.5 per cent
support. That suggests that Chrétien took votes from the right and the left, in
part by making the point that if he didn't win the country would be run by
Preston Manning and the Reform Party.

Winning three majorities put Chrétien in the same league as Sir John A.
Macdonald, Sir Wilfrid Laurier, and William Lyon Mackenzie King.

OVER HIS THREE ELECTIONS as Liberal leader, Chrétien dominated Ontario,
taking 97.7 per cent of its available seats. He also won 51 per cent of the popular vote in Ontario, which suggests that even without conservative vote-split-
ting he would have dominated the province. Other than a stumble in 1997, he

was an overwhelming winner in Atlantic Canada. He did little to reverse the Liberal wasteland in the West although Chrétien won 10 per cent of the available seats in Alberta over three elections. Before Chrétien, the Liberal party had not won a seat in Alberta since 1968.

For a native of Québec, his record in his home province was less impressive, taking just 36 per cent of its seats. But he saved his best result for last, winning almost half of Québec's seats in 2000. Chrétien took pleasure in this result since it came just eight months after the passage of the Clarity Act.[34] Nothing made him happier than beating Québec separatists. A close second was up-staging Paul Martin. Chrétien's 36 seats from Québec in 2000 compares well with the 21 seats Martin won in 2004 and the 13 in 2006.

DESPITE AN UNBLEMISHED ELECTORAL record, Chrétien wanted to change how campaigns were fought. In his final year in office he sought to strengthen the democratic process by taking big money out of politics.

The first major set of modern political finance reforms had been introduced in 1974. Under the Election Expenses Act, political parties faced new restrictions on how they could raise and spend money, including the requirement to disclose the names of political donors. Public subsidies in the form of tax credits encouraged individual contributions. Regulations were put in place in 1983 to control third-party spending during election periods. But these reforms did not limit the amount that an individual, union, or corporation could donate. And the act said nothing about the financing of leadership campaigns.

In exchange for strict limits on corporate and union donations, Chrétien brought in a per-vote subsidy that gave political parties $1.75 every year for each vote received in the last election. What's odd about Chrétien's reforms is that every party stood to benefit except the Liberals. By then, the Conservatives had developed an impressive fundraising apparatus built around individual contributors. The Green Party of Canada and the NDP also had strong support from individual donors who shared their party's ideological leanings. The Bloc Québécois had an abysmal record at fundraising, so the subsidy was found money and ultimately represented about 90 per cent of its annual revenue. It was only the Liberal party that had disproportionately relied on the corporate donations that were squelched under Chrétien's rules.

When the political finance law was introduced in 2003, the president of the Liberal party, Stephen LeDrew, called it "dumber than a bag of hammers." Martin supporters called it perplexing and a move designed to hobble the Liberal party, or more particularly Chrétien's successor.[35] Martin, however, was grateful that the new rules were not in place in time for the 2003 Liberal contest. The donors who gave millions to his leadership campaign, including while he was finance minister, have never been disclosed.

Chrétien said that if Martin challenged him on his per-vote subsidy law, he would call a snap election. The bill to implement election financing reforms was not introduced in the House of Commons by a minister but by the prime minister himself, a first for Chrétien.[36]

The per-vote subsidy program could be criticized for giving the highest-subsidy payments to incumbents. But that's not why the Harper Conservatives phased out Chrétien's reforms beginning in 2011. Harper claimed that taxpayers should not be funding political parties. But it was widely acknowledged that he also wanted to weaken his political opponents.

It can't be said that Chrétien was trying to gain an advantage for his party by introducing the per-vote program. His intentions were noble, but in this case, his reforms didn't stick.

FIVE DAYS BEFORE PAUL MARTIN became prime minister on December 12, 2003, Canada's chief electoral officer accepted the registration of the new Conservative Party of Canada, formed by the amalgamation of the Progressive Conservative Party and the Canadian Alliance Party. In March 2004 Stephen Harper became the Conservative leader. But not all Tories were impressed. Joe Clark, a two-time former leader of the Progressive Conservative Party, refused to support Harper or the newly united party.

Despite the merger, polls revealed that Martin had maintained the strong lead in the polls that he had inherited from Chrétien. A week after Martin took office the Liberals enjoyed 43 per cent support nationally, with the Conservatives far behind at 17.5 per cent.[37] That didn't stop Martin from distancing himself from Chrétien. "We are going to have to change the way things work in Ottawa," Martin said at his swearing-in ceremony. "We have to restore Canadians' trust that their government is listening to them."

On May 23, 2004, Martin walked to Rideau Hall to request that the governor general call an election for June 28. Martin went into the campaign talking about new federal spending and investments in infrastructure and child care. Harper pitched tax cuts. Martin had every reason to be confident. Despite new revelations about Liberal spending abuses, an EKOS poll gave the Liberals a healthy lead, with 38 per cent support compared with 30 per cent for the Conservatives, and 18 per cent for the NDP. The Bloc Québécois carried 45 per cent support in Québec compared with 30 per cent for the Liberals. The election was Martin's to win or lose.

The Conservatives were strongest in rural constituencies where the opposition to Chrétien's long-gun registry was strongest. There was some harshness to the Conservative campaign, which was launched under the slogan "Demand Better." Stephen Harper could not shake the perception that he had a hidden agenda to implement socially conservative policies on abortion and same-sex marriage. There was also a fear that under Harper social programs were at risk and a two-tiered health system was on its way. Harper was also criticized for supporting the Iraq war and for telling Atlantic Canadians that they suffered from a culture of defeatism.

The big unknown was the extent to which the public would punish the Liberal government for the sponsorship scandal. Martin's attempts to deny responsibility for the misuse of taxpayer dollars made him appear weak.

With a little more than a week before Election Day, the polls had tightened. That's when Martin went negative, asking Canadians if they wanted to live in a country where a woman did not have the right to control her body. The Tories handed Martin a gift when one of its MPs suggested the Charter of Rights would not constrain Conservative ideology. This not only scared Red Tories, but frightened many NDP supporters into voting Liberal to deny Harper a victory.

Martin squeaked out a minority government in an election with the second-lowest voter turnout in Canadian history. It was far from the juggernaut that had been predicted when he took over from Chrétien. Martin lost 21 per cent of Liberal seats and 4 per cent of the popular vote. Harper had failed to fully unite the right, taking only 30 per cent of the vote when the combined Alliance-PC vote in the 2000 election was 38 per cent.

Martin did all that he could in 2004 to convince voters that he was not Jean Chrétien. Chrétien contends the plunge in Liberal votes was proof that the voters agreed with him. Liberals began to think that they may have underestimated Chrétien and overestimated Martin.

John Rae, who managed five of Chrétien's national campaigns, was asked to explain how he felt to have amassed such victories under le petit gars de Shawinigan. He replied with the same words Ron Turcotte used when he was asked about how he won the Triple Crown of horse racing: "It was simple. I rode Secretariat."

THE RIVALRY

MUTINY

Only once in Canadian history has an elected prime minister effectively been overthrown. And it didn't happen because of corruption, incompetence, or even unpopularity. It didn't matter that Jean Chrétien was a senior statesman leading a majority government and with a record of accomplishment. Paul Martin orchestrated a takeover of the Liberal party and launched a civil war within its caucus because he was worried that Jean Chrétien would thwart his prime ministerial ambitions.

Martin's lust for power initially backfired, his impatience only lengthening Chrétien's time as prime minister. When Martin was finally given the keys to 24 Sussex Drive, his enduring aversion to Chrétien also contributed to his undoing as prime minister. When Martin should have been using his energy to counter a united conservative movement, he extended the civil war within Liberal ranks, which weakened his party and led to its defeat in the 2006 election.

MARTIN CLAIMS THAT IN THE late 1980s he did not know Chrétien well but he thought he was "a nice guy."[1] Chrétien wrote that he had fished and golfed with Martin a few times and that they had traded political war stories. A common connection was business magnate Paul Desmarais. Martin had worked for Power Corporation, a Desmarais-led conglomerate. Desmarais's son, André, was married to Chrétien's daughter, France.

Martin was not deeply involved in the 1984 Liberal leadership race won by John Turner; his company provided some buses to the Chrétien campaign, so there were no early indications of a rivalry. Martin also moderated the leadership debates.

Tension between Martin and Chrétien was not evident until they faced one another in the battle to succeed John Turner in 1990. When that campaign started, Chrétien said he didn't pay much attention to Martin because he didn't see him as a serious threat.[2] Martin assumed the contest would be nasty after having observed what he called the "trench warfare" that occurred between the Chrétien and Turner forces for the entire time Turner was the leader.

Martin was a determined and well-resourced candidate. At the core of his campaign was a group of Liberal activists who were upset with how Chrétien had undermined Turner.[3] While Martin had friends in the Liberal caucus, he had nothing close to the network of supporters that Chrétien had built after 30 years of relationship-building in the Liberal party in virtually every riding in the country.

During the leadership campaign, Chrétien and Martin differed on only one substantive issue: the Meech Lake Accord. The divide over Meech Lake came to head at a leadership debate in Montréal when Martin supporters, who had been bussed in from Ontario, screamed that Chrétien was a traitor to Québec. Eddie Goldenberg said this made Chrétien "white with anger." Being called a turncoat to his native province was not something Chrétien would forgive or forget.[4]

In debate, Martin lambasted Chrétien over Meech Lake. "Jean, for the love of God, you want to be prime minister of Canada but you give no indication where you're going. You have not understood Quebec and you are gambling dangerously with the survival of Canada."[5]

At the leadership convention, Martin further admonished Chrétien as being out of touch, saying, "I don't think Jean understands modern Québec. I think he doesn't understand that modern Québec will not be pushed around."[6] It was clear during the campaign that Martin had little respect for what Chrétien had accomplished or his approach to governance. Martin told *Maclean's* magazine that Chrétien had no agenda for Canada other than to muddle through the issues. It was that sort of thinking and "fiddling around," Martin charged, that led to massive deficits when Chrétien was in cabinet.[7]

After Chrétien won — and Meech Lake died — some high-profile Martin supporters donned black armbands at the convention, saying they could not serve in the same party as Chrétien.[8] Yet Chrétien had won the contest on the first ballot by a margin of more than two to one over Martin. It was fair game for Martin to build his credentials for the next time the leadership opened up and to use the campaign as an opportunity to express his ideas. But Martin went further than that. Biographer John Gray concluded that Martin pursued a scorched-earth policy without apparent regard for the fate of the new leader or the party.[9] Even Martin admitted that the poisonous atmosphere that had been created during the campaign would be difficult to overcome. "How is all this going to work?" he wondered.[10]

Bob Rae observed that personal relationships are never improved by intra-party competition and that it takes a lot of hard work to re-establish a personal relationship in the aftermath of a leadership competition. And Chrétien was not one to easily forgive a slight. Rae recalled that he had refused an offer from Chrétien to serve as his executive assistant in 1971. Twenty-two years later, on the day after Chrétien was sworn in as prime minister, Chrétien chastised Rae, who was then premier of Ontario, for not having accepted the offer. Chrétien was mostly having fun in the moment. But Rae's view was that it was a good idea not to have any memory for slights.

Martin and Chrétien never reconciled after the 1990 contest. The conversations between them remained awkward, and the exchanges, limited as they were, lacked authenticity. The rivalry endured.

Martin's team, according to Bob Rae, was difficult to deal with and displayed a devotion so intense that it clouded their judgment. They fought to win every battle and skirmish without thinking about where they stood in the war. Within the Liberal party you could be a Chrétien supporter or a Martin supporter, said Rae, but not both. When Rae ran for the Liberal leadership in 2006 he found himself in no-man's land: "I agreed with Paul on Meech Lake and with Chrétien on the Clarity Act. As time went on I saw that the division was completely dysfunctional to the government and the party."

The obvious step for Martin after losing the leadership campaign in 1990 was to apologize and make amends with Chrétien so that all Liberal guns could be pointed at Brian Mulroney and the Progressive Conservative government. But a few months after the leadership convention, Martin refused to introduce Chrétien at the annual Liberal party fundraising event in Montréal. The civil war had not ended. It had just begun.

IN HER BOOK *TEAM of Rivals*, Doris Kearns Goodwin tells the compelling story of how Abraham Lincoln embraced his adversaries to form the strongest and most inclusive government possible during the darkest period in American history. Of Salmon Chase, who contested the Republican nomination in 1856 and 1860, Lincoln said he was a great secretary of the treasury but he had one problem: presidential fever. Like Chase, Martin had prime ministerial fever.

Like Lincoln, Chrétien's instincts were to embrace his key rivals. Lincoln and Chrétien can't be compared based on the challenges they faced, but there were similarities: both were lawyers from small towns, both were underestimated by their contemporaries, and both were great storytellers who used humour to great effect. Neither felt any need to boast to establish his superiority.

After winning the leadership, Chrétien asked Martin to take on the highest-profile position on his front bench. But Martin rejected becoming the Liberal finance critic, preferring to be the opposition critic for the environment. It was a peculiar request. He explained it to Eddie Goldenberg this way:

> No one would expect me to be minister of the environment. On the other hand, if I am the finance critic in opposition, everyone will expect me to become minister of finance after the election. If for any reason I am not appointed, it will appear that I have been downgraded, and I don't want to risk any potential future humiliation.[11]

He need not have worried, since after winning the 1993 election Chrétien asked Martin to be his finance minister. But Martin refused the offer. Martin said he wanted to be the minister of industry and international trade. Chrétien was stunned. "I know you want to take over from me someday. But if we don't solve the deficit, there will be nothing left to take over. It's the biggest problem we have." Still, Martin refused to go to finance. It was reported that Martin was taking advice from his mother, who worried that holding the government's purse strings was a graveyard portfolio for the politically ambitious.[12/13]

Chrétien then offered the finance job to John Manley. When Manley met Chrétien the Saturday after the election he was hoping for a junior portfolio in cabinet. He swallowed hard when he was told it was finance. They spent an hour talking about the deficit and whether John Crow should be reappointed as the governor of the Bank of Canada. "It was clear from the beginning that he was a total hawk about the deficit," said Manley.

After hearing that Martin was headed to industry, the deputy minister of finance, David Dodge, got involved. "Look," he told Martin, "this is where the power is. Regardless of how it worked in your father's day, this is where the key decisions are made." It was only on second thought that Martin shifted his strategy. Perhaps, his advisers thought, finance was a better path to becoming prime minister.

The government had not been sworn in yet and Martin had already changed his mind on a critical decision. Dodge welcomed Martin to the department by offering his congratulations on becoming the CFO of the Government of Canada. "CFO?" replied a stunned Martin, "I wouldn't hire myself to be CFO of any of my companies."

Chrétien told Martin that success at finance would pave the way to the prime minister's office. It was magnanimous for Chrétien to acknowledge Martin's ambitions in this way given the insults his rival had levelled against him during the 1990 Liberal leadership campaign. Martin strategist Richard Mahoney said Chrétien was a genius for making his rival the second most powerful person in government, and for rarely, if ever, second-guessing him. "It was an impressive jujitsu move from a very practical politician and leader."

Martin spoke with Manley about the last-minute swap in portfolios but did not admit that it was his own indecisiveness that was at the heart of the game of musical chairs. In fact, he used the occasion to diminish Manley:

> You got the job I wanted. I really wanted industry. It's a great job. Industry is what the Red Book was all about. But the buzz on Bay Street when they tested your name was that nobody knew you so I have to do finance even though I don't want to.

Manley said it was the first time that he realized he and Martin not only had a different view of the world but the facts as well.

THE ONLY SERIOUS POLICY disagreement between Chrétien and Martin came in 1995 and was over a proposed cut to seniors' benefits. Chrétien thought the cut wasn't needed for the government to meet its deficit target of 3 per cent of

GDP. Martin felt that he needed to scale back a social program for his budget to have political credibility. The coming years showed that Chrétien was right about both the numbers and the politics.

After 1995, Martin's adherence to fiscal discipline was epitomized by his remark that the government would meet its targets "come *Hell or High Water*." In the same vein, Prime Minister Chrétien supported Martin come *Hell or High Water*. But the popular credit for the fiscal turnaround was given mostly to Martin. This, according to Peter Donolo, followed a concerted effort by Martin supporters to make the accomplishment a solo story rather than a team effort.

Despite Martin being touted as the government's financial genius, the reality was that Chrétien consistently had a better handle on the numbers than his finance minister did. Sheila Copps said that Martin's commitment to fighting the deficit was a national legend, but added, "What people didn't know was that every expenditure had been reviewed by a whole team starting with the prime minister and including every minister in the government."

As much slack as Chrétien gave Martin, the prime minister's office was present in every key economic and financial decision. It was not unusual for Goldenberg to speak with Martin several times a day. This helped to define the latitude that Martin had on strategic initiatives without having to worry about blocks from the prime minister.

Jean Charest said that a finance minister could do little on his own: "I don't accept for a moment that Chrétien was just some bystander taking notes. The real test of the government's resolve to balance the books was not the finance minister acting as the chief financial officer, but the prime minister backing him up and keeping a lid on demands from cabinet ministers."

FROM HIS PERCH AS finance minister, Martin exercised influence if not control over a wide range of government policies. As an example, the theme for Martin's 1998 budget was not economics but education. The finance minister made the program choices on policies for early childhood learning, student debt, education savings programs, scholarships, and health research. Martin himself was surprised at what he could accomplish from the finance department:

It is only in retrospect that it seems strange to me that initiative[s] of this kind should have been led by [the] federal department of finance. The truth is that within a couple of years of the 1993 election, we pretty much got accustomed to dominating most policy debates [with the exception of Québec].[15]

When Mitchell Sharp was sitting in the House of Commons gallery for one of Martin's budget speeches, he leaned over to ask Eddie Goldenberg a question: "I realize Martin is minister of finance. Is he also minister of health, and minister of industry, and what other portfolios does he have which might be evident in the rest of the budget?"[16] None of this was a surprise to Goldenberg, who, as the prime minister's representative, was intimately involved in every decision that Martin made.

While tensions were evident throughout Martin's time in cabinet, the consensus is that the relationship served the country well until March 2000. "They had a job to do and were on the same team," said David Dodge. "As a deputy minister of finance what more could you ask for? Their offices dominated the government's big picture thinking and neither could have succeeded without the other."

When Chrétien let Martin play in other portfolios, it made for bad blood around the cabinet table. For the 1998 budget, Martin told Health Minister Allan Rock that he could not have the funding he sought for the health programs he was proposing. At a dinner with senior officials Martin said to a frustrated Rock, "Oh go to hell" and "Screw you."[17] But the money was, in fact, available and Martin simply wanted to deny a leadership rival a potential win. Eddie Goldenberg concluded that Martin would only compromise as long as it was seen to be his decision and not forced upon him by a colleague.[18]

The chemistry between Chrétien and Martin was bad, and they mostly spoke through Eddie Goldenberg.[19] "The lines of communication were not direct," said John Manley, "but they were there." Manley once heard Chrétien complain that Goldenberg spent more time with Martin than he did with him. Before anyone in cabinet took an issue to Chrétien they knew the iron rule: "First check it with Eddie."[20] Historian Michael Bliss wrote that Goldenberg had more influence on Chrétien than any political assistant to a prime minister in Canadian history.[21]

Eventually, Martin's grip on government policy became so tight that it caused distress in the Prime Minister's Office. Once the books were balanced, Chrétien wanted to open up the spending taps in the areas of arts, culture, and foreign aid. Chrétien's senior advisors told Martin to increase the budget, a request he resisted.[22]

AFTER THE 1997 ELECTION, Martin claims that his staff urged him to start preparing for a leadership run. With Chrétien having won two majority governments, Martin felt justified in being open with Liberal party members about his desire to serve as leader.

Chrétien did not say publicly that he would retire at the end of his second term because he said he did not want to become a lame-duck leader. Despite Chrétien's desire that leadership aspirants keep their ambitions in check, Martin established a trust fund in 1999 for his leadership campaign under the title "Project 2000."

Chrétien assumed his position within the Liberal party was untouchable. But the uncertainty about his intentions to seek a third term caused some caucus members who were loyal to Martin to get nervous.[23] Chrétien sometimes joked about his longevity by pointing out that his political hero, Sir Wilfrid Laurier, won four elections; and that he was still younger than Ronald Reagan at the outset of his presidency. Backbench MPs who wanted Martin to take over so they would get a shot at a cabinet post were getting impatient. It was a non-issue to Chrétien, who had no intention of running for a third term. He had made a pact with Aline to serve only two terms and there was nothing on the horizon that would enable him to change her mind.[24]

On March 10, 2000, 27 months into Chrétien's second mandate, and on the eve of the biennial Liberal party conference, about 25 Liberal MPs and key Martin organizers held a secret meeting at the Regal Constellation Hotel near the Toronto airport. The point of the meeting was to get Paul Martin into the leader's chair at the earliest possible opportunity.

Martin had a strong following among Liberal MPs, a fact he attributed to Chrétien having lost the confidence of his caucus. "Unlike Brian Mulroney," Martin wrote, "who held his fractious party together for so long in part by a meticulous attention to the individual needs and personalities of his caucus,

Jean Chrétien did little to cultivate the ordinary MP."[25] But Bill Graham, who served under Chrétien as the chair of the House of Commons foreign affairs committee and then foreign affairs minister, had an entirely different take on the prime minister's attentiveness to individual MPs:

> He understood the perils of isolation at the top. He appreciated the need to keep even the lowliest backbencher satisfied and in the loop. He felt that every member, including opposition members, deserved his respect. As a result, he made a point of saying that his door was always open to any MP who wanted to speak to him. It might take a few days or even a few weeks to get an appointment, but he kept his word ... Another channel that Chrétien kept open was to invite individual MPs to have lunch with him at 24 Sussex on a rotation basis. He seldom included his ministers, because he saw them more regularly; rather, he treated these occasions as an opportunity to relax with his backbenchers and to get to know them better.[26]

Graham wrote that Paul Martin went to extraordinary measures to gain the support and loyalty of Liberal MPs. In Graham's case, this included a four-hour dinner with two bottles of wine at a chic restaurant across the river from Parliament Hill.[27] Martin's assistant, Ruth Thorkelson, alerted Martin when he should send to notes of congratulations on the births of children and grand-children of MPs or offer condolences when appropriate. After Carolyn Bennett was involved in a dust-up with Chrétien in caucus over party financing, Martin pulled her aside and invited her to dinner.[28]

Graham thought the Martin cabal was populated by those desperate to get into cabinet before they were all past their best-before dates.[29] He wrote that this behaviour was unseemly and that Chrétien deserved to make his own decision about when to step down.

Graham worried about the damage that was being done within the Liberal party from an open revolt. When the national director of the Liberal party asked Graham what it would take to make his riding association more neutral, Graham responded that it was too late and that the Martin forces were entrenched. He also observed that wresting control of the party to hasten the prime minister's retirement was counterproductive to Martin's ambitions.[30]

Brian Tobin could see that Martin had more than an upper hand in a future leadership contest. "It was a closed shop. We could not even get membership forms. If you were not a member of the Martin union, you could not sell a membership." Tobin thought Chrétien had let his guard down:

> There was no pushback against Martin for so long that at one point Jean Chrétien woke up and realized that Paul had established a government within a government, a caucus within a caucus, a bureaucracy within a bureaucracy. All this was done while he was a sitting and popular prime minister. By the time he woke up that reality had gone on for too long and it had gone too far. His instincts were telling him there was a problem but his advisors were telling him to relax.

Chrétien thought Martin was in a solid position to ultimately take over and that he didn't need to go behind his back to stir up a revolt. He thought Martin was ungrateful: "Hadn't I convinced him to become minister of finance and to accept the deficit-cutting strategy that he had adopted as his own as soon as it turned out to be a success, and bolstered his reputation by supporting him through thick and thin, all the time aware of the games he was playing to try to undercut my authority? I was hurt by his betrayal."[31]

The meeting at the Regal Constellation was Chrétien's decisive wake-up call.

Martin and his supporters were eager to send Chrétien packing from 24 Sussex Drive. But Martin claims that he hoped the hotel meeting would dial down the prospect of an open revolt. "I was absolutely opposed to making trouble for the prime minister," Martin wrote. In fact, he said he wanted to calm his troops and avert a party crisis at the biennial meeting. This was either naive on his part or pure revisionism. In politics, the only prospect of a secret being kept is if fewer than two people are involved. A large gathering of political heavyweights was never going to be kept under wraps. Chrétien understood the foolishness of such an endeavour, once remarking that if something was secret you could find it in Maclean's and if it was top secret you had to pay five bucks to read it in *The Economist*.

Some who were in the Regal Constellation meeting said a PowerPoint presentation was delivered that concluded that Chrétien's position in the party was secure and that a mutiny was pointless. At the end of the meeting Liberal MP Joe Volpe was frustrated:

> Okay, let me get this straight. We've met here to talk about doing

nothing for a leadership campaign that isn't going to happen because the prime minister isn't going anywhere. Do me a favour. The next time you want to have a meeting about doing nothing for something that isn't going to happen, don't bother calling me.[32]

But at the same time the Martin camp was peddling three national public opinion polls that they said spelled bad news for Chrétien.[33] An Angus Reid poll, they claimed, showed that a majority of Canadians wanted Chrétien to retire. A Compass poll suggested that 40 per cent of Liberal voters wanted him to resign. In a Goldfarb poll, 45 per cent of respondents wanted Martin as Liberal leader to 37 per cent siding with Chrétien.

But Chrétien had his own poll conducted by EKOS Research Associates. Even though Martin outscored Chrétien 43 to 38 per cent on the issue of trustworthiness, the Liberal party continued to dominate in the polls. Chrétien could hardly feel threatened when 49 per cent of those polled indicated they would vote Liberal compared with just 19 per cent for the Canadian Alliance, 11 per cent for the NDP, 10 per cent for the Bloc Québécois and 9 per cent for the Progressive Conservatives. All the while, Chrétien's personal approval rating among Canadians remained high. Throughout Chrétien's ten years in office, his approval ratings averaged 54 per cent, and his disproval ratings 37 per cent. (By contrast, Brian Mulroney's approval ratings averaged 27 per cent, his disapproval numbers 65 per cent.)[34]

News of the hotel meeting did not remain a secret for long. Martin accused Chrétien of trying to make him appear disloyal by "torquing" the story of the meeting with reporters.[35] Goldenberg said Chrétien's team didn't know enough of what was going on behind the scenes to feed any information to the press. In any event, no torqueing was required. Historian Michael Bliss called it the strongest party rebellion against a sitting prime minister since 1896 when a hapless Sir MacKenzie Bowell spoke of his caucus as a "nest of traitors."[36]

When confronted by reporters to account for his role in the insurgency, Martin attempted an awkward and sheepish escape in what he described as "one of the most embarrassing moments I ever experienced in politics."[37]

When Chrétien arrived at the Liberal convention, he was greeted by young Liberals chanting "Four more years! Four more years!" During Chrétien's remarks at a plenary session, most of the delegates were on their feet cheering enthusiastically. The Martin supporters sat on their hands. John Manley said Martin's team missed their chance: "Had they put up banners that said thank you prime minister and praised him to the skies, he would have been gone at the end of his second term."

The lack of respect made Aline furious. While two terms as the wife of the prime minister was as much as she had bargained for, she wasn't about to let her husband get pushed out the door. She was overtaken by anger. Aline had been looking forward to a quiet retirement and had been travelling to Shawinigan on almost a weekly basis in 1998 to supervise the design and construction of the Chrétiens' new home. She was looking at residences in Ottawa that would allow her to stay close to her friends. Having been in politics for much of his working life, Chrétien was intent on a second career so that he and Aline would have a comfortable retirement.

The Regal Constellation uprising had the opposite effect of what Martin intended. Chrétien was prepared to leave, but not to be humiliated by his finance minister. Seeing the disrespect coming from the Martinites, Aline joined in the chants of "four more years." With her blessing, Chrétien quickly went into election mode:

> To be very frank, now that Aline had removed the only impediment to my staying, I was damned if I was going to let myself be shoved out the door by a gang of self-serving goons. By trying to force me to go they aroused my competitive instinct, ignited my anger, and inadvertently gave me the blessing I needed from Aline to fight for a third term. For that, ironically, I owed Paul Martin a great deal of thanks.

Richard Mahoney chaired the Martin meeting at the Regal Constellation. He said the entire episode was a mistake:

> We concluded that we couldn't push Mr. Chrétien out the door. We wanted our supporters to dial it down. It was naïve on our part to think we could put that many political people in a room and expect they would keep it a secret. Rather than dialing it down our supporters went in the opposite direction and openly challenged the prime minister and his team. The meeting was a mistake and another bad turn in the Chrétien-Martin relationship.

David Zussman believes that Martin's team may have gone further than their man might have wanted in holding the meeting. "There were moments when

Martin was simply not aware of what was happening around him. I'm not sure that he was the author of many of the things he was associated with but in the end that simply means he gave it away." Peter Donolo agreed, adding, "The extent to which the gang around him exerted control, and his passiveness with them, was bizarre." Martin never backed away from his team, and conceded, "I owe them a lot."[38]

Chrétien wrote that he wanted to fire Martin and to "fire the conspirators on his staff, and cancel the government contracts with his friends and advisors [at Earnscliffe]."[39] The senior staff at Earnscliffe, a government relations and lobbying firm that represented some of Canada's most important companies, were also elite members of Martin's leadership team. Martin claimed he relied on the Earnscliffe contingent to help him at Finance because an election promise to trim ministerial staffs had left him short of talent. Martin wrote that the Earnscliffe team was not paid by the government to work on his leadership campaign, but to provide advice to him as minister.[40] Indeed, Finance Department officials contend that members of the Earnscliffe team were integral to the policy development process, and, in some cases, had more clout than even the department's deputy minister. In a book that chronicled Martin's rise to prime minister, Susan Delacourt described Earnscliffe as an "adjunct" of the Department of Finance.[41]

In addition to government relations, Earnscliffe also had a research division. According to Delacourt, "you could go to one side of Earnscliffe to lobby for an item in the budget, fully aware the other side was deeply involved in preparing that budget." Earnscliffe commented that they had a "Chinese wall" between their two divisions. Reporters pursued the potential conflict but it was sufficiently complex that it never rose to the level of a scandal. One month after Martin was removed as finance minister, the new minister, John Manley, saw to it that Earnscliffe's presence at Finance was terminated. "Earnscliffe sat in on the budget preparation meetings. That was just not going to happen with me at Finance. Chrétien would have concluded I had lost my mind if this continued." Delacourt wrote that Earnscliffe then became a "temporary bunkhouse" for some of Martin's political staff who needed to find a new home after their boss was out of cabinet.[42]

CHRÉTIEN HELD A RARE meeting with Martin a few days after the dust-up in

Toronto. On the table Chrétien placed draft minutes that outlined a plot to oust the prime minister from office. Martin said the document was a forgery. By immediately refuting the authenticity of the document, Martin was affirming his familiarity with the event. Chrétien called Martin a liar. Goldenberg thought Martin was probably correct that the document was forged. "Some of the names in the document were wrong. But the relationship was so bad that we believed the memo was true." The relationship between the finance minister and the prime minister had become utterly dysfunctional.[43]

Chrétien wanted to dump Martin from cabinet. Beyond the disloyalty, Chrétien was worried that Martin was sufficiently preoccupied with his personal ambition that he was distracted from his duties as a minister. But Chrétien was talked out of it by his senior staff who thought that the financial markets would react badly. In time, Chrétien regretted taking their advice.[44]

Goldenberg thought he could keep Martin from doing serious damage and that when push came to shove Martin would remain loyal to the government. The Martin team continued to work with Goldenberg, but they never really trusted him and began to ridicule him behind his back.

While Martin had his hit squad, so did Chrétien. Martin contends that Chrétien's director of communications, Françoise Ducros, disparaged him to reporters.[45] Nonetheless, Martin was winning the public opinion war and a majority of Canadians said they wanted Chrétien to step down. All the while, the Liberal lead in public opinion polls under Chrétien remained strong.

IN THE SPRING OF 2000, the agriculture minister asked Martin for a billion dollars to support Canadian farmers. Martin was prepared to offer up $500 million while Chrétien suggested $700 million. When the caucus and the farming lobby complained that they were getting less than the billion dollars that was needed, Martin blamed Chrétien. Martin told caucus members that he had been in favour of the billion-dollar investment all along. Chrétien said that no prime minister could live with this type of situation for long.[46]

As far as *The Globe and Mail* was concerned, Martin was effectively running the federal government even before Chrétien called the November 2000 election. When it endorsed the Liberal party in that campaign, the *Globe* called the federal Liberal government the Paul Martin government. They added that Mr.

Chrétien loved power for its own sake and that he had to go. It was an unusual endorsement, written under the title "Why we recommend a vote for Paul Martin." Chrétien's place in history was decaying, the *Globe* wrote, tarnished by his ego and disrespect for the party's future: "Go now, and spare yourself the ignominy of being pushed."

After the November 2000 election, Chrétien offered to meet Martin to discuss his retirement plans, but Martin refused. Martin also turned down the opportunity to be part of a government announcement that commemorated the life of Pierre Elliott Trudeau. Martin's chief of staff told Goldenberg that it would not be good for the finance minister to be associated publicly with anything in Pierre Trudeau's memory.[47]

Chrétien wanted to change the dynamic and offered Martin the foreign affairs portfolio. Martin refused because he said he was doing more foreign policy at Finance than he could as minister of foreign affairs.[48]

When the cabinet was sworn in after the 2000 election, Jean Pelletier told Martin to bide his time and that there would be leadership convention before too long.[49] Pelletier said the same thing to senior public servants, which they used as their signal to prepare for a transition in leadership. But it didn't much matter what Pelletier said or Chrétien did. At that point, Martin had a firm grip on the Liberal party membership and a large chunk of the caucus was in his back pocket. His takeover was essentially complete and it was on his terms that the prime minister would be removed from office.

Ironically, Martin's ambition had delayed his rise to the top. Had he bided his time, kept his ambitions in check, and offered even slight praise to Chrétien he likely would have become prime minister in 2001. He would then have faced a divided conservative opposition and, according to many observers, would likely would have won one of the largest majority governments in Canadian history. As one senior government official observed, Martin would have had everything he wanted "had he not gone at it so hard." Instead, he instigated the overthrow of the prime minister and launched the civil war that fractured the Liberal party for the decade that followed. Goldenberg said there was no need for a mutiny because the captain was leaving of his own accord. Martin was using his power to push on a door that was already open. But the more he pushed, the more Chrétien resisted:

While preparing for his move into 24 Sussex, Martin had to deal with a host of Liberal MPs who thought they had earned, or been promised, a place in his cabinet. Chrétien was amused to hear that a "second-rate backbencher" had announced he was going to be transport minister.[50] Chrétien knew Martin could not fulfill all the promises he had made. When one group of Martin-friendly MPs of Italian descent came to Chrétien to complain about being referred to as the "pasta caucus" by another MP, Chrétien discerned that what they really wanted was a quick change in leadership. "You seem to have forgotten," Chrétien retorted, "who was the leader under whom you, and you, and you, managed to get elected. And let me tell you something. You all think you will be in cabinet after I am gone, but my successor will have to choose among you."

Martin suggested to some MPs who did not make it into the Chrétien cabinet that things would be different when he became prime minister. To one aspirant he said, "I know people will be looking to me for a fresh start, for fresh faces, for a new cabinet. I will be bringing fresh faces to cabinet."[51]

Chrétien had appointed some Martin loyalists to cabinet, including Maurizio Bevilacqua as minister of state for finance. But when Martin became prime minister, Bevilacqua was dumped from cabinet in retribution for his willingness to serve under Chrétien. A *Globe and Mail* report said Bevilacqua was punished for "pissing off the centre."[52] The centre in this reference was to the coterie of Martin advisors whom Bevilacqua criticized for damaging the party by openly disparaging Chrétien. In 2002, Bevilacqua told Martin that he would no longer deal with his advisors. Still, Bevilacqua showed his confidence in Martin by raising $200,000 for his leadership campaign.[53] Martin acknowledged that Bevilacqua had been with him from the beginning, "and I will never forget that." The only time Martin seemed to forget was on the day he chose his ministry.

As finance minister, Martin often saw matters that came before cabinet through the prism of his ascendancy to the leadership. And he sometimes used his powers to thwart the ambitions of his rivals and reward his supporters.

Having served in Chrétien's cabinet before becoming premier of Newfoundland and Labrador, Brian Tobin returned to Ottawa in 2000 to vie for the Liberal leadership when Chrétien resigned. He asked for an economic portfolio and Chrétien happily made him industry minister.

Paul Martin's team saw Tobin as their only serious threat. Richard Mahoney said that Tobin was a formidable player and a hustler and Chrétien's designated hitter in the campaign to take Martin down. Tobin told Mahoney, "I think you have this but if you leave the window open just a crack I'll squeeze in."

In the 2001 budget, Tobin sought funding to expand broadband coverage to rural Canadians. Just as the government electrified rural Canada at great cost in the early 1900s, Tobin wanted to do the same for the Internet. It was, he thought, an essential service as well as a matter of equity and fairness.

> The broadband agenda was already in place when I arrived at Industry Canada. It had formed part of the Liberal Party platform in the 2000 election. I received the report from the National Broadband Task Force that recommended that all Canadian communities be connected by broadband networks... Why would [Martin] hesitate to make a one-time investment of $1 billion to bring Canadians everywhere online?[54]

Tobin had sought $100 million to launch the broadband program, which was less than the $1 billion it would take to finish the job. It was reported that Paul Martin thought that delivering high-speed Internet would bolster Tobin's profile in rural communities across Canada. Tobin made his appeal for an investment directly to the prime minister. Chrétien made it clear to Tobin that the money was in the budget, "no ifs, ands, or buts." But the money wasn't there, or at least not over a timetable that Tobin thought was practical.[55]

> When I inquired about the cuts, the prime minister told me that his instructions had not been followed. My response to that bit of news was to say, 'Well, Prime Minister, if that is the case, you have an even larger problem than I have.'[56]

Martin claimed that the investment would have "cracked the fiscal framework," which was nonsense given that the operating surplus that year was $48 billion and the net surplus after interest costs was $8 billion. Martin made no reference to rural broadband in his budget, but included a $110 million investment over three years to build a high-speed research computer network to be used by smaller universities and community colleges.

Chrétien told Tobin he was prepared to overrule his finance minister and that the broadband program would be funded within days of the budget. But Tobin had decided his time in government had come to an end. Tobin said it was a "wow moment" for him:

> I was preaching the virtues of the policy and Martin simply said I wasn't going to get it. And he got away with it. Eddie was complicit but did not anticipate my reaction. By then it was too late. It was time to take stock of 22 years in public life. The prime minister tried to convince me to stay and that he would get the money and put in back in within days. But you should only get banged up the head once. When it happens it's time to move on. The Martin guys were focused on me because I was stirring up the leadership pot. But after I was gone I told the prime minister to watch out. Now that I wasn't around they would focus on him.

At about the same time that the ruckus between Martin and Tobin was playing out, it was revealed that the Finance Department had made an error in the calculation of federal tax payments to provinces. Martin wanted to negotiate a resolution, but federal-provincial relations were not in the finance minister's domain. Word came down from the Privy Council Office that Martin was usurping the prime minister's authority. In effect, the PCO, and, more likely, the PMO, accused Martin of trying to run the government by stealth. The objection, as Martin understood it, was that he was calling meetings of ministers to discuss major policy matters outside the formal PCO structure. Chrétien handed the file to John Manley to resolve. The issue only brought Martin and Chrétien closer to their breaking points.[57]

IT WAS AWKWARD TO have the sitting finance minister running for the leadership of his party. Martin was setting tax policy and making decisions that affected the profits of private sector companies at the same time as he was soliciting donations for his leadership campaign. One conflict came to light in March 2002 when a $25,000 cheque for Martin's leadership campaign from Calgary lawyer James Palmer was inadvertently sent to Liberal party headquarters. Palmer was under contract to the finance department to provide advice for the energy sector. The accidental disclosure led to Martin severing his relationship with Palmer. Martin, who made no reference to the incident in his memoirs, accused Chrétien's team of leaking the details of the misdirected cheque to the press.[58] Martin tried to downplay his personal connection to Palmer, saying that the advice he gave was to the department of finance.[59] But a key question remained unanswered: who else had contributed to Martin's campaign where a conflict of interest might exist?

On May 30, 2002, Chrétien issued an order at a cabinet meeting for all leadership aspirants to put their ambitions on hold. He said it was a distraction that was "destabilizing the government."[61] Allan Rock made a joke of it: "Do you hear that sound prime minister? It's the sound of my team laying down their tools all over Canada." John Manley recalled how Martin became nervous and stammered that he didn't know what the prime minister was talking about. "There is no one raising money for me," Martin professed. Eyes rolled and there were groans of disbelief around the table. At first, Manley thought Martin was joking, but he wasn't. "For me, it was a fundamental point where I knew I could never support Martin. He flat out lied to cabinet."

It incensed Martin to hear that accounts of the cabinet meeting were leaked to the press. While Chrétien was said to have taken Martin "to the woodshed," Martin told his staff "To hell he did."[62] Chrétien tried to calm the waters by saying, "Leave me alone and maybe I'll go."[63] It was a plea for respect and another indication that Chrétien was on his way out the door. But that wasn't enough for Martin.

MARTIN WAS SCHEDULED TO deliver remarks to the Canadian Federation of Municipalities in Hamilton in June 2002. He wanted to use the speech to present his vision for a "New Deal" in which municipalities would be given a broader and more stable tax base. These were themes that Martin wanted to pursue when he became prime minister.

Chrétien took note of the policy shift and asked PMO staff to obtain a change to the text of the speech. Martin called it censorship and told his senior staff member, Tim Murphy, to tell the Prime Minister's Office that not a single word would be changed. "This has never happened before," bellowed Martin, "and to hell with them."[64] It was not a policy fight per se. The issue, according to one of Martin's strategists, was that he was not prepared to accept the prime minister's direction.

Chrétien's team then instructed Martin to cancel another speech he was scheduled to give to the Labourers International Union. Again, Martin refused the order. Then Martin was asked to introduce Chrétien that weekend at a meeting of the Ontario wing of the federal Liberal party. He refused.

Chrétien's team leaked word of Martin's disloyalty, which led the press to hound Martin for a response. Martin's said that he was considering his options.[65] At that point there was no doubt what his options were. Having expressed a lack of confidence in the prime minister, either he had to quit the cabinet or lead a caucus mutiny to bring Chrétien down. Chrétien's only option at that point was to fire the openly rebellious Martin.

With Martin back at his farm in the Eastern Townships of Québec, Goldenberg sought to obtain a public declaration of loyalty to the prime minister and a commitment that he would faithfully serve the government. Goldenberg insisted that Martin call the prime minister. Martin replied that if the prime minister wanted to talk to him, he should pick up the phone and make the call himself.[66]

Sheila Copps thought that Martin had overstated his importance and was floating the notion that the government would be in disarray if he was ousted: "Martin knew his time in cabinet had come to an end, but he wanted to resign and create a crisis of confidence in the government that would cause Chrétien to resign." Manley thought the prime minister should have let the opposition have a go at Martin on Monday in question period so he could demonstrate his qualities of leadership, or lack thereof.

Martin must have known that the prime minister could not indulge him any longer. Chrétien had told his cabinet over the years that he didn't open letters of resignation, he accepted them. From the moment Martin said he was "looking at his options," a formal resignation was unnecessary. Martin knew he had days if not hours remaining as finance minister. Indeed, his political staff were in their offices over the weekend shredding whatever sensitive documents the law allowed.

John Manley was at the Meech Lake retreat chairing a cabinet committee that Sunday. He called Martin to tell him things had gotten out of control and that "you aren't looking good in this." Martin told Manley that it was over, that he was "done." Chrétien made numerous attempts to call Martin, leaving multiple messages, which Martin denied receiving. Eventually, a connection was made on Sunday afternoon. Chrétien said he accepted Martin's resignation and wanted to discuss a letter that would say the departure was by mutual agreement.

Chrétien called Manley and asked if he had a black suit at the ready. He was instructed to come to Rideau Hall with such haste that Judith Manley didn't have enough time to clean up from her gardening chores and be with her husband at the swearing-in ceremony. Manley wasn't entirely surprised to be asked to take over at finance. As Chrétien was to Trudeau, Manley was to Chrétien. Put in Chrétien's more colourful language: "I used you like Trudeau used me. When there is shit to shovel, I give you the shovel."

Martin heard he was officially out of cabinet on CBC Radio while in the car on his way back to Ottawa. Martin summed it up by saying, "I got quit." Chrétien's letter to Martin was more elegant: "It is with sadness that I can confirm that you are leaving the Cabinet."

Like a bad marriage that ends in divorce, by the time the split happened few people were surprised. The day after being sworn in, Manley gave a speech to a conference of international bankers in Montréal. Later that week he chaired a G8 finance ministers' meeting in Halifax. The financial markets did not react adversely to Martin's departure or Manley's appointment.

Manley delivered Chrétien's only budget not authored by Paul Martin. Manley said the budget was a "repair job" that dealt with long-festering blocks to economic growth, such as the tax on Canadian investments. Manley said that as he went around the world to attract investment he could see how stupid the tax on investment capital was: "It was saying don't invest in Canada." The government ended that year with a surplus of $9 billion. Operationally, the Chrétien government survived Martin's departure without skipping a beat.

MARTIN WAS OUT OF cabinet but remained in the Liberal caucus. Chrétien wanted to leave with dignity while Martin and his cabal were trying to kick him out the door. Chrétien had the government apparatus behind him, including the power to appoint cabinet ministers and deliver patronage posts. Martin had the Liberal party apparatchiks in his corner.

Having control of the party machinery meant that Martin could determine the rules around party conventions and the leadership selection process. This included the date when Chrétien would face a vote on his leadership. When pressed by a reporter with the question "When will you resign?" Chrétien's Yogi Berra-inspired response was, "When I quit."

Because Martin had the support of most Liberal MPs, he could bring Chrétien down by expressing no confidence in his leadership either inside caucus or more openly in the House of Commons. Even though Chrétien had won three successive majorities, he was now captive to Martin's dictates. The takeover was complete and the only question that remained was when Martin would be sworn in as prime minister.

With the Liberal party in disarray, Chrétien's personal popularity began to slip. In June 2002, a Globe and Mail/CTV poll revealed that, for the first time, more Canadians disapproved of Chrétien's performance than approved (49 per cent to 46 per cent). But the same poll indicated that a Chrétien-led Liberal party would still win a majority government. And Chrétien's approval rating still exceeded Liberal party support, which was at 42 per cent.[67]

To draw support away from Chrétien in caucus, Martin actively courted Liberal MPs with promises of cabinet posts, and, according to Sheila Copps, by helping them in their ridings with taxpayers' money:

> I remember one of my East Coast colleagues telling me he had promised to support Paul Martin in the 2003 leadership race in return for getting a road in his riding paved. That deal was sealed in 1999. That was the carrot. The stick was that if a Member of Parliament failed to come on board, they would be purged in their own riding in a nomination contest. When I was campaigning for the leadership I asked a Newfoundland and Labrador MP to support me. He said he would happy to but Paul Martin put $20 million into his riding for a road in return for his vote.

Eddie Goldenberg recalled an incident in which Martin traded federal tax dollars for support:

> In one of his last budgets Martin had inserted a $30-million item to support junior mining companies. The flow-through design of the policy was complicated so I said, 'Paul, what is this?' He responded 'I suppose you haven't had breakfast lately with Réginald Bélair, the MP from

Timmins-James Bay.' He defended the budget item saying the future of one-industry towns is going to be the single biggest policy issue of the 21sts century. I went back the next day and jokingly said to Paul, 'You are right. It will be the single biggest public policy of issue of the 21st century. You can't fix it with $30 million. Why don't we make it the centrepiece of your budget?' The reality was that Martin wanted the 12 delegates from that riding. He was very sheepish about it.

Beyond his friends in caucus, Martin had a force behind him that he called "The Board." This group included political assistants from Parliament Hill, organizers from across the country, and a host of government relations consultants. Martin described the board as a cadre of advisors who knew him well:[68]

> It was more than just a political organization. It was a network of close friends whose relationships had been forged through many political campaigns over many years ... At times, it also gave my opponents, inside and outside the party, a ready target to shoot at. Often this was presented in the form of an attack on Earnscliffe, the Ottawa firm where many of them worked from time to time. I think a fair examination of the record would show, however, that these attacks, which often insinuated conflicts of interest, were never backed up with even the flimsiest of evidence. I know these people very well, and they are as honest as they were loyal.[69]

The existence of The Board predates Martin and can be traced back to the 1984 Liberal leadership contest and the supporters of Don Johnson. This group believed Chrétien was not up to the job and that John Turner was not sufficiently "current." With Johnson out of the race they migrated to Turner, whom they saw through the 1986 leadership review vote. "The common theme for us in those days," said a Johnson supporter, "was that we didn't see Jean Chrétien as a leader we could get behind. When the 1990 leadership campaign came along we were looking for a modern candidate and Martin was it."

IN RESPONSE TO LOSING control of the party and a big chunk of caucus, Chrétien mused with his foreign affairs minister about leading the Liberal party into his fourth election. But Chrétien was being mischievous and didn't expect he would be taken seriously. When a staff member in the PMO asked

Chrétien if he would even consider a fourth term, he was unequivocal: "The most powerful force in politics is time for a change. When it hits it hits quickly and there is nothing you can do to turn it around. If we haven't done in ten years what we wanted to accomplish that's a problem for us."

To Chrétien's embarrassment, the *Hill Times* published a survey of Liberal MPs in June 2002 that showed 99 were behind Martin and only 48 were with Chrétien.[67/68] Then there was an open revolt at a caucus meeting in which several members, including Dan McTeague and Jim Karygiannis, told Chrétien he should leave while his dignity remained intact.[72] In response, Chrétien had his loyalists circulate a letter of support that most Liberal MPs were expected to sign. Only 55 per cent of them signed the letter, and that included members of cabinet who could not remain in place if they did not express confidence in their prime minister.[73]

Justice minister Anne McLellan was on the *Hill Times* list as a Martin supporter, but she said the publication never bothered to call her to ask where she stood. "Eddie Goldenberg called my chief of staff and told her that my name needed to come off the list." McLellan was distressed but it was indicative of the kind of atmosphere that had permeated the government and caucus:

> I was a Martin supporter if Mr. Chrétien decided to leave. My position, when asked by the press, was that as long as I was in Mr. Chrétien's government, my first and only loyalty was to the prime minister. The day I couldn't say that, was the day I would have resigned from his cabinet.

McLellan believed that Martin should have known the prime minister would have a harsh reaction to being taken down. She thought Chrétien deserved better:

> Some of Martin's people gave the "boss" little credit for having led us to three majority governments and for the good work that was done for the country — In fact, good work that Paul was central to. Mr. Chrétien deserved more respect than he was given. It was some of Martin's people who exacerbated the difficulties. They needed to be more patient and less conspiratorial. Even a perceived slight was the source of overreactions from some. I was busy enough managing complicated files and as the political minister for our government in Alberta. The internal leadership tensions did distract us from doing our jobs, at least at times.

Richard Mahoney said that what was most unfortunate was that the elements were there for the finance minister and prime minister to have a good relationship:

> They had a common purpose, common values, and a willingness to share power. But they lacked chemistry. Most Canadians would assume that as mature individuals that they would speak to one another, but they didn't. They needed surrogates to fill the gaps. No one is an angel in this piece. Chrétien felt he was undermined and disrespected. Martin did not feed his ego and did not say good things about him.

Martin did not understand that by pushing Chrétien into a corner he was damaging himself. Jeffrey Simpson, the national affairs columnist for *The Globe and Mail*, wrote in 2001 that it was inconceivable that the Liberal party would air its dirty linen in public: "Parties incapable of managing their internal affairs properly are viewed by voters as incapable of running those of the country."[74] But in 2002 the civil war played out in full public view. After he left cabinet, Sheila Copps alleges that Martin "issued a fatwa," calling on Liberal supporters to stop making donations to the party. She said he wanted to starve the Liberal party as long as Chrétien was leader.

Author and historian Peter C. Newman wrote that Chrétien treated his Parliamentary caucus like a servile retinue instead of the source of his power and that "it was Paul Martin's recognition of the difference that eventually allowed him to steal the party from under its leader."[75] Others commented that Brian Mulroney had enjoyed rock-solid caucus support even when his popularity ratings were in the basement, a feat Chrétien could not accomplish when his popularity levels ran above those of his party. Peter Donolo observed that Mulroney didn't have his second-in-command — Michael Wilson or Don Mazankowski — telling others that the prime minister was a loser and that they would have more clout after he was shown the door. In 1994, Martin's team began to pressure caucus members who were excluded from Chrétien's cabinet, saying: "If you don't sign up with us now you're out, you'll never be in. So don't dig your grave, you'd better come with us."[76]

Mitchell Sharp, sensing a potential disaster at the scheduled February 2003 leadership review vote, suggested to the press that Chrétien should be permitted a graceful exit. Of course, having a leadership review after winning a majority victory is an odd way to open up division within a party. John Rae observed that the review was a provision in the Liberal party constitution that put party above country. Having run both of his leadership campaigns, Rae was convinced Chrétien would win the review. "We prepared ourselves for that review, but it was going to be a battle." He said to Chrétien, "If we go into this you first have to make up your mind if you are going to run again. Why ask people to extend themselves if they don't think it affects their future."

Chrétien publicly downplayed Sharp's suggestion that it was time to go. At an event in New Brunswick to announce federal funding for a Trans-Canada Highway upgrade, Chrétien said he would not rule out the possibility of running for a fourth mandate.[77] "I have a mandate from the people of Canada, three majorities, and I have to do my job."

But it was not the February leadership review that was most pressing in August 2002; it was the caucus retreat in Chicoutimi to be held later that month. Tim Murphy, said that Liberal MPs would have to pay attention to what their constituents had been saying about the leadership of the party. By this, he meant that it was time for Chrétien to step aside. Montreal-area MP Nick Discepola said Chrétien should get out while he could: "My read of things is that he would be humiliated in a review vote. So why put the party through that?"

A senior Chrétien adviser thought that giving in to the Martin bullies would set a bad precedent: "The Martin strategy is to build things to such a crescendo that [Chrétien] just gives up and leaves. He won't do that. If there's a coup, if Chrétien's going to be toppled, there's going to be a lot of blood. This is intimidation. This is blackmail, and you do not give in to blackmail."[78]

Stéphane Dion described the leadership battle as a clash of personalities and ambition. Martin, he said, had been unable to identify a single policy dispute with Chrétien. Bill Graham, who had known Martin for much of his adult life, observed Martin's inclination to emotional and unproductive outbursts. Martin's staff became accustomed to these eruptions, which they called beatings.[79] Richard Mahoney described a horrible fight he had with Martin. "It deteriorated into a screaming match and I had never really had one before .... I thought we had a relationship-ending fight." Mahoney submitted his resignation the next day, which Martin refused. Martin biographer John Gray wrote that bureaucrats and political staff were subjected to explosions of frightening and frothing rages.[80] One family member recalled Martin becoming so enraged by a poor golf shot that he lodged his club into the upper branches of a tree, where it stayed for a full day.[81]

To the extent that personalities came into play, Martin's volatile temper was usually repressed when it came to his exchanges with Chrétien. Martin never raised his voice with Chrétien. That restraint may have limited the number of frank and authentic exchanges between the two men but it likely allowed the relationship to continue at a functional level for much of the time that Martin was in cabinet. Any beatings that were inflicted on Chrétien were left to Martin's friends and surrogates.

Ultimately, according to MP Reg Alcock, Martin's leadership ambitions froze the functioning of the government. "I think it's all done; I think it's over as far as the battle goes...Does [Chrétien] want to keep us in this type of mess for another few months or does he want to do what needs to be done and get us out of it and back to work?" Another MP, Joe Volpe, said any discussion about the future direction of the government was pointless as long as the leadership question remained unresolved. A Martin friend described a sense of entitlement that existed and that the longer that Chrétien held office "the more Paul was being cheated."[82]

Chrétien went to Chicoutimi hoping to talk about a refresh of the government's agenda, which included the Kyoto protocol, child poverty, and Aboriginal self-government. His opponents wanted to talk about how soon he would resign.

Martin backer Dan McTeague said one would have to be wilfully ignorant to deny that Liberals wanted a change in leadership.[83] But not all Liberal MPs and senators agreed. A list of 94 caucus members loyal to Chrétien was circulated to the press. The battle of attrition was not going Chrétien's way when four MPs asked that their names be removed from that list.[84] There were also those who wanted Chrétien to resign, but thought the public humiliation of the prime minister was in bad taste. "There is a lot of respect for the prime minister out there," said MP Derek Lee, "along with the desire for change. Those two feelings exist in almost every Liberal, each is divided on how to handle this."

After a rough first day at the caucus retreat, Chrétien concluded that the internal battles had gone on for too long and were doing damage to both the Liberal party and to the country. He told his caucus on August 21, 2002 that he would leave his office in February 2004:

For forty years the Liberal Party has been like a family to me. Its best interests are bred into my bones … This summer we have not been focusing on governing. We are not doing our job. Canadians don't like that. Liberals don't like that. I have reflected on the best way to bring back unity, to end the fighting, to resume interrupted friendships. I have taken into account my duty to protect for my successors the integrity of the office I hold from the Canadian people, and that office is non-negotiable. Here's my conclusion: I will not run again. I will fulfill my mandate and focus entirely on governing from now until February 2004, at which time my work will be done, and at which time my successor will be chosen.[85]

Don Boudria, who had been a Liberal MP since 1984 and was appointed by Chrétien to cabinet in 1996, called it the saddest day of his career. "Our country had prospered like never before, and our party's popularity was at an all-time high. Yet, none of this seemed to be good enough for those who wanted to see him leave."[86]

Moments before entering the caucus meeting, Chrétien had a note delivered to Martin to give him a heads up. "I'm going to make a statement that will bring unity back to the party."[87] In other words, the rancour and division promoted by Martin could come to an end. But some Liberal MPs loyal to Chrétien told reporters that Martin would become leader "over my dead body."[88]

While caucus members lined up to salute Chrétien and shake his hand, the Martin team kept their distance. While backbenchers and ministers flocked to the microphones to praise Chrétien, Martin waited almost four hours before reading a three-sentence statement: "I can tell you that none of us in the government would have enjoyed that success that we did without his support, without his leadership. Jean Chrétien is a man who has shown courage all his life. He is a man for whom I have the highest respect." Martin left the media scrum without taking a single question.

What took Martin so long to conjure up good words for Chrétien was that his team had to make a quick call on whether they would allow the prime minister the long, 18-month goodbye or whether they would short-circuit this timeline by forcing a vote on his leadership at the party convention in six months time. The risk to Martin in pulling this trigger was to expose his bully tactics and face a public backlash.

"I think the boss has laid a trap for them," said one Chrétien strategist. By not formally resigning in the moment, he circumvented Liberal Party rules would have required a leadership convention within 12 months. Chrétien said he would legally resign when it was appropriate. "Are they afraid I will stay?" he asked reporters. When pressed, Martin said he was prepared to operate within the time frame set by the prime minister. "It may be that not everybody heard what I said going into caucus this morning. But that's very clearly my position."

While Chrétien enjoyed being prime minister, his other motive in staying put for 18 months was to make it more difficult for Paul Martin. By 2004, Martin would be 65, a senior citizen. Among his potential rivals, John Manley would be 54, Sheila Copps 51, and Allan Rock 56. Manley would also have one or two federal budgets under his belt.

WITH ALL EYES FOCUSED on Martin, Chrétien reminded his caucus that there was no sure thing in politics. He recalled 1993 when the Tories thought they had a rising star and a sure bet in Kim Campbell. "She had a summer job" was Chrétien's way of saying that Martin might not be all he was cracked up to be.

Chrétien introduced rules that would require cabinet ministers to disclose the names, but not the amounts, of donors to leadership campaigns. Because Martin was out of cabinet, the rules did not apply to him. The amounts donated to Martin's leadership have never been disclosed, although Martin wrote that the surplus from his leadership bank account of $3.5 million was enough to retire the entire debt of the Liberal party that had accumulated under Chrétien.[89] And that surplus was in place even after Martin spent millions to win the leadership.

Sheila Copps, who was Chrétien's deputy prime minister, said running against Martin for the leadership in 2003 was the worst experience of her long political career. She said she dreaded reading the newspaper because Martin's forces were working overtime to leak stories to destroy her reputation. Copps said Martin wanted to win every single delegate, which included, at one riding meeting, creating a separate line for African-Canadian voters, ostensibly so they could help them with the voting.

John Manley was the other serious leadership candidate, but he dropped out of the race before the voting took place. Like Copps, he described the experience as horrible. He had no intention of running but did so after he concluded that Paul Martin was not a suitable prime minister:

> I felt that he was untrustworthy, that he had misled cabinet, that his behaviour was unacceptable. I don't like bullies. I did not want a prime minister like that. Someone had to stand up to him. Tobin had backed out, Rock had dropped out. Dhaliwal was considering it. I wanted more candidates because it would have meant more memberships. Chrétien said I would not win if I did not run and that it would be a shame to see this turn into an acclamation.

Manley focused on the leadership debates, largely because he thought he could expose Martin's vulnerabilities:

> Martin was a terrible debater. It was easy to get him riled up. He would get tongue tied. And he lied. On Canada-U.S. relations I said 'I won't have to call Brian Mulroney to get advice on Canada-U.S. relations like you did.' We knew he had and we heard the Martin team flipping out: 'Did he say he didn't talk, but he did.'

But when the debates were done, Manley had 19 per cent support and Copps was at 7. "It was not worth mortgaging my house and taking out a million-dollar loan," said Manley. "The money ran low and I wasn't going to the convention with handmade signs."

Manley had a strong personal reason to take Martin on. That's because Martin's team had taken on his son:

> He had won the presidency of the Liberal McGill Club, beating a Martin supporter along the way. That meant he would be a delegate at the leadership convention. A few weeks later the Liberal Party suspended the club because they claimed the membership list had too many names without postal codes. All the CEGEPS [colleges] with no history of Liberal Clubs were sending delegates but the 100-year-old Liberal McGill Club was denied. He asked me if the system was corrupt.

Martin's team, said Manley, couldn't win 99 to one. They had to win 100 per cent of the votes. "You can do what you want to do to me but don't burn my kid. That's just not acceptable."

Manley, who had raised $2.5 million for his leadership campaign, said that word in Liberal ranks was that Martin may have raised as much as $15 to $20 million. Manley tried to make the disclosure of campaign contributions an issue. Martin had infuriated Chrétien when he said he could not disclose the list of contributors, or the amounts, over fears that his donors would face retaliation from the prime minister.

To PREPARE FOR THE takeover of power, Martin developed a series of governance proposals on the "democratic deficit" that would lessen the power of the PMO and strengthen the authority of individual MPs. This included allowing parliamentary committees to choose their own chairs by secret ballot. Sensing division in Liberal ranks, the Canadian Alliance put forward a motion in support of the secret ballot in November 2002. Martin showed up in the House of Commons to support the Alliance motion. Chrétien opposed the resolution, fearing it would make it more difficult for women to become chairs. The vote was so important to Chrétien that his wife appeared in the gallery to watch the proceedings. In the end, 56 Liberals voted for the Alliance motion, which passed easily.

On the same November 2003 weekend that Martin was elected Liberal leader, he met with provincial premiers in a room below Taylor Field in Regina. They were there for Grey Cup weekend. He had not been sworn in as prime minister but was acting as if was already had the job. It angered Chrétien that Martin had violated a key tenet of Canadian democracy: that there was only one prime minister

A senior bureaucrat noted that the most important ingredient in the success of a transfer of power is the personal relationship between the incoming and outgoing leaders. The official concluded that the transition from Campbell to Chrétien in 1993 — from a Progressive Conservative to a Liberal — was done more professionally and positively than the transition in 2003 between two Liberals.

Martin had every reason to build unity in his party and should have made the healing of his rift with Chrétien his top priority. He could have praised Chrétien for his accomplishments and pledged to defend his legacy. He could have been gracious to Chrétien's supporters. He could have built a team of rivals of his own to strengthen the Liberal side to take on the newly united Conservative Party of Canada. But the damage that had been done was irreparable.

Allan Rock had a front-row seat for the Chrétien-Martin era. He said the relationship between the prime minister and finance minister worked well initially with the help of intermediaries. But there was a turning point:

> It was an overheated environment in which a lot of people with a lot of self-regard were competing for leadership when Jean Chrétien eventually left. Some of them were loyal to him and were prepared to patiently wait. Others wanted to push him out. The dynamic around Ottawa at the time was not healthy. Some thought the Liberal Party of Canada deserved to hold office as long as it wanted to. That thinking eventually led to our downfall and it led to the disunity of the party.

While Rock faults Martin, he also said it was unwise for Chrétien to have given Martin so much political room to manoeuvre:

> The prime minister had let control of the party get away from him. He would say, 'I'm not running to be the leader. I am the leader.' I told him he ought to have contested at every Liberal convention the election for key positions in the party. That whole apparatus ended up in the hands of a group that used it against him. It was used against me. I couldn't get membership forms when I was trying to sign up new members. The party was hijacked. And it was to the detriment of the party and the country. It was open to Jean Chrétien to deploy the group who were loyal to him to retain control of the party but he declined to do so. We were never dispatched to the front lines.

These were Chrétien's errors. Martin's fatal mistakes were also easy to identify:

- His team called Chrétien a traitor in the 1990 leadership campaign and then let that wound fester.

- He blatantly campaigned for the leadership before Chrétien declared his intent to leave.

- His supporters met at a Toronto airport hotel to openly plot how they would push Chrétien out the door.

Martin might have been forgiven for these transgressions had he allowed

Chrétien a dignified exit. But Martin and his team thought they didn't need Chrétien. They thought Liberal party support was due to their work and not Chrétien's. In fact, the Martinites were convinced that keeping their distance from Chrétien would increase their odds of winning the next election.

In the end, Chrétien's biggest challenge as prime minister was not the deficit or national unity but the putsch from within his own party. As much as he was a scrapper who never lost a political contest, he was unable to thwart the Martin-led mutiny.

Canadians have a powerful instinct when politicians lose sight of the public good and are focused on personal ambition. The former executive assistant to NDP leader Alexa McDonough, John Rainford, wondered about the impact the feud had on the country: "If the two camps used half the energy they poured into that self-serving war into, say, finding innovative solutions to Aboriginal housing, where would we be today?"

UNMET EXPECTATIONS

Normally the date when power is transferred to a new prime minister is not a source of controversy. This is especially true when the transition takes place within the same political party. But nothing involving Chrétien and Martin went according to script.

Martin was elected leader of the Liberal party on November 14, 2003. Chrétien said he didn't want to face the opposition in the House of Commons when he was not the leader of the party so he prorogued Parliament on November 12. When Eddie Goldenberg asked about the bills before Parliament that would die on the order paper, Chrétien cut him off: "If we haven't passed it in the previous 10 years it must not be all that important." Martin said he was annoyed, not so much that Parliament was prorogued but because he thought the decision was one he should have been able to make at his own convenience.[1]

Chrétien told the Clerk of the Privy Council that Martin could have the transition date of his choosing as long as he made his preference known in writing or in a public statement. Chrétien said he wanted Martin on the record so it could not later be said that a request had been refused.[2]

While Chrétien wanted to remain in office until February 2004, Martin wanted an earlier transition date. In a rare face-to-face meeting, Chrétien and Martin settled on December 12. This date allowed Chrétien to attend a farewell dinner in his honour hosted by Jacques Chirac in Paris and to be able to greet the premier of China. "I'll be gone the next day," Chrétien promised.[3]

In November of 2003 the auditor general's report on the sponsorship scandal was close to completion, but it would have to wait until Parliament was back in session before it could be tabled. In fact, had Martin called an election before Parliament resumed there would have been no auditor general's report to address.

A senior public servant said the timing of the release of the pending report had no effect on Chrétien. It was widely known that the report would reflect poorly on the government, but those advising cabinet thought it would make little difference who was prime minister at the time when the report came down.

Any suggestion that Martin could escape accountability from the findings of the report had it been released while Chrétien was prime minister was ludicrous. Besides, the same official confirmed that Martin was aware of the contents of the report and that nothing should have come as a surprise. His incoming finance minister, Ralph Goodale, had been fully briefed and almost every element in the report had been leaked to the press before Martin came to power.

Warren Kinsella, the top political staffer for the minister of Public Works, the departmental home of the sponsorship program, said that Martin not only knew about the workings of the program, he had lobbied for sponsorship projects and had corresponded with a least one of the ad executives at the centre of the controversy.[4] It was later revealed that Martin's team had previously fed damaging information about the sponsorship scandal to the leader of the Bloc Québécois.[5]

While Martin had no evidence that Chrétien was ducking the report, he raised that very prospect in his memoirs: "Whether it was out of a preoccupation about his legacy or bitterness towards me — and only [Chrétien] can answer that — he decided to take the steps that would delay its publication until after I replaced him at 24 Sussex."[6]

Chrétien said he did nothing to delay the release of the report and had no fear of the report. In fact, he said he had already acted to address policy and administrative deficiencies that had led to the sponsorship malfeasance. For example, he had passed an electoral reform package that substantially diminished corporate influence, tightened government procurement rules, put in place new guidelines for the ethical conduct of cabinet ministers and enhanced whistle-blower protection, eliminated Communications Canada, and handed over the files on the sponsorship program to the RCMP.

When the auditor general's report on the sponsorship program was tabled on

February 10, 2004, Martin had been prime minister for two months, which left him ample time to prepare a response. But Martin underestimated the firestorm the report set off in the media and with the public. Following public outrage, Martin asked a cabinet committee led by deputy prime minister Anne McLellan to consider the government's response. McLellan said that a number of meetings were held at which cabinet ministers expressed a range of views:

> Stephen Owen, the Minister of Public Works (where the program originated), felt strongly that there had to be a public inquiry. My colleagues from Québec felt a public inquiry would not lead to any greater insight into what happened but would exacerbate tensions that already existed in Québec. These were difficult meetings. On balance, the committee recommended an inquiry, but, few, including myself, thought that this was an ideal way forward.

McLellan also believes that there was no conspiracy on Chrétien's part to dump the auditor general's report on Martin's lap: "If Paul Martin's advisors believe that, then they are wrong."

Martin's camp initially thought the sponsorship scandal presented an opportunity to display their skill. One deputy minister told John Manley that at one cabinet committee meeting, there was talk about how the scandal was a difficult file to manage, but that Martin would "stoke the flames of the sponsorship mess and walk through the flames to show that he is a different kind of leader." Manley observed that Martin did walk through the flames but got third-degree burns along the way: "They knew what was in the auditor general's report. Instead of diminishing the scandal [Martin] inflated it."

Martin was encouraged by columnists and editorial writers to undertake a cleansing. "The new prime minister knows," wrote *The Globe and Mail*, "that after the ethically challenged years under his predecessor, Jean Chrétien, the Liberal government must persuade Canadians that the cronyism and boondoggles have ended."[7] Two weeks after the AG report was released, Martin boasted to his caucus that the Liberals were "ahead of the curve" on the scandal.[8]

Martin and his team had determined the conclusion they wanted from an inquiry. When the press conference was held to launch the Gomery Commission, the president of the Treasury Board, Reg Alcock, went out of his way to express his outrage, bowing his head to say, "I can't tell you how saddened I am by what

I've seen."[9] Not only was he pre-judging the outcome of the inquiry, it was a direct attack on Chrétien.

Martin thought that Chrétien had sabotaged what should have been his honeymoon period in office by not dealing with the auditor general's report himself. He returned the favour by accentuating the scandal and by blaming Chrétien for the fiasco. Martin even made his complaints known to foreign leaders. When Gordon Brown was taking over from Tony Blair as British prime minister a scandal was brewing about payments being made in exchange for government honours. Brown accused Blair of leaving him a "ticking time bomb" that would "wreck his leadership in the same way…Jean Chrétien had done to Paul Martin."[10]

Martin's complaints about the timing of the release of the auditor general's report came late in the process. He knew well before he was sworn in as prime minister that the report was coming but did nothing to stop it from landing in his lap.[11] In fact, his first attempt at damage control came the day after his cabinet was sworn into office.[12]

Despite the fraud that had been committed, Chrétien continued to defend the sponsorship program:

Perhaps there were a few million dollars that might have been stolen in the process. It is possible. But how many millions of dollars have we saved the country because we have re-established the stability of Canada as a united country? If somebody has stolen the money, they will face the courts. But I will not apologize to any Canadians.

Martin wanted Chrétien, then in retirement, to take responsibility. Martin said it was impossible to believe that there was no political direction in how the sponsorship money was spent. He spoke of a sophisticated cover-up and called the public servants the "mechanics" of the program, a term that evoked the Watergate scandal.[13] Martin wrote that Chrétien's time as prime minister was "marked by a scandal that was the fruit of mismanagement and malfeasance by others."

Despite the political consequences to the Liberal Party and the damage it caused to national unity, Martin said he has no regrets about calling a public inquiry. Martin admitted that the inquiry revived separatist parties in Québec, but he thought it was a price worth paying. This view was not unanimous. The cabinet was deeply divided, very much along geographical lines, on the issue of a public inquiry. "Few among my Québec ministers favoured a judicial inquiry," Martin acknowledged. "Ministers from the rest of Canada were mostly in favour."[14]

As much as Martin heaped blame on Chrétien, Canadians were not prepared to let the former finance minister off the hook. Martin was dumbfounded:

> I simply could not believe, emotionally and intellectually, that anyone thought I had anything to do with this mess ... I did not expect the level of criminality that was uncovered, nor the links back to the Liberal Party... If I had known all that, would I still have called the inquiry? The answer is yes.[15]

Chrétien agreed that no one in government was aware that crimes had been committed by a few rogue operatives and a corrupt civil servant. But he thought the inquiry was a colossal overreaction to unacceptable mismanagement.[16]

In the end, the sponsorship scandal damaged both Chrétien and Martin. A newly united Conservative Party of Canada made the scandal a key issue in the election that saw the Liberal majority government shrink to a minority on June 28, 2004.

CHRÉTIEN SET EXPECTATIONS LOW, then exceeded them. Martin's operatives, however, created the opposite effect. They were on political talk shows saying that no one in Canadian history was better prepared than Martin to become prime minister.[17] The editorial writers at *The Globe and Mail* remarked that Martin's grand ambitions for the country were a welcome attitude "after a decade of reactive, managerial leadership in Jean Chrétien's Ottawa."[18] Pollster Darrell Bricker of Ipsos-Reid said in 2003, "I don't see that [Martin] necessarily has any shortcomings. Right now, he is walking on water."[19]

Martin spoke with confidence about what his government would accomplish. "I want historians to look back and say that in this decade a Martin-led government essentially did what had to be done to make sure that when this huge catharsis that the world is going through is completed, Canada was one of the very countries that came out on top."[20]

But for Martin, being number one in government was far more difficult than being number two. Rather than enhance the role of individual MPs and parliamentary committees, as he had promised, he took more power into the Prime Minister's Office. And he took it upon himself to chair four of nine cabinet committees. As chair of the committee on Canada-US relations, Martin's presence undermined the foreign affairs minister. As chair of the committee on aboriginal issues, he weakened his Indian Affairs minister. He brought a national security adviser into the PMO, which put his public safety minister on a short leash. Three new secretariats were set up but were attached to the PMO under Martin's control.

Stephen Harper, who was later known for his stern prime ministerial authority, labelled Martin power-hungry: "The prime minister, his unelected aides and advisers in the PMO and his friends at Earnscliffe are the true holders of power, not the former backbenchers who are now members of the Paul Martin cabinet."

To assert his authority, Martin removed Chrétien loyalists from his midst. Despite being dropped from cabinet, Sheila Copps still wanted to run in the 2004 election. But she faced a challenge for the Liberal nomination in her riding from Martin loyalist Tony Valeri. While Valeri could argue that he was not challenging an incumbent because the boundaries of the riding had shifted in 2004, the reality is that he coveted the seat Copps expected to represent. The adjacent riding where he lived was tougher for a Liberal to win. With Martin's unspoken support, Valeri beat Copps for the Liberal nomination.[21] Copps had asked Martin to help her secure the nomination but he refused. Frank McKenna, a former New Brunswick premier who had planned to run in the 2004 federal election, got cold feet when he saw how Copps was treated. "I have too much respect for our party to engage in a bloodbath for a nomination."[22]

Martin also changed the face of the government by dumping 22 of Chrétien's 38 cabinet members. Allan Rock, who had served in Chrétien's cabinet from day one, became Canada's ambassador to the United Nations. Martin could not keep Manley in Finance because he had promised that portfolio to one of his supporters, Ralph Goodale.[23] Martin offered to make John Manley Canada's ambassador to the United States, which Manley was prepared to accept as long as he was given direct access to the prime minister and the cabinet committee on Canada-US relations. "Martin's team later spun it that I insisted on being given a cabinet-level rank which was not true," said Manley.

When Martin heard that Manley was going to call a press conference to announce he was retiring from politics, he panicked: "You have to tell them that
I offered to make you ambassador to Washington," Martin pleaded in a phone
call. Manley responded that it was not appropriate for him to say anything
about a diplomatic appointment for two reasons. First, Martin was not yet
the prime minister and the talk of appointments was premature. Second, it's
not how diplomacy works. Manley pointed out that before anything is said
about an ambassadorial appointment a government must first get agreement
from the host country. In addition, by declaring that Manley had rejected
the appointment, the ultimate ambassador would then be known as Martin's
second choice.

Brian Tobin said that Paul Martin's worst mistake as prime minister was allowing his desire to get even with Chrétien to take over:

> He flushed out anyone who had anything to do with Chrétien. That left
> a big chunk of the party sitting on their hands. He thought if Chrétien
> could win three majorities he would win at the level of Brian Mulroney.
> It was Martin's job to unite the party but he sustained the civil war after
> he had won. I was on the outside in the private sector and watched with
> a degree of shock that good people were being pushed aside.

Martin rescinded the appointment of Jean Pelletier, Chrétien's long-time chief
of staff, as chair of the board of VIA Rail. Chrétien called the move "an act of
petty revenge...abruptly and unjustly...for nothing more than making an off-
the-cuff remark to the press about a completely trivial matter."[24] Pelletier had
made inappropriate comments about Myriam Bedard, a former Olympic ath-
lete and a marketing officer for VIA Rail, saying that she was "a poor girl who
deserves pity, who doesn't have a spouse, as far as I know." Chrétien thought
it was a minor offence, particularly when taken in the context of Pelletier's
exemplary career in Ottawa and as the mayor of Québec City.

Pelletier racked up close to $500,000 in legal fees to fight his dismissal as
well as his portrayal by the Gomery Commission. The grief that Pelletier endured, according to Chrétien, may have hastened his death from cancer. Eddie
Goldenberg said Martin ruined the final five years of Pelletier's life. Chrétien
may forgive Martin for his ambition, said Goldenberg, but he will never forgive him for his attempt to humiliate Pelletier.

Martin also recalled Alfonso Gagliano as ambassador to Denmark. Gagliano, who was part of Chrétien's loyal Roman Guard and had served in his cabinet, was implicated in the sponsorship scandal. Chrétien said he always found Gagliano to be an honest, popular, and extremely hard-working person.[25] After Gomery concluded that Gagliano had lied about his role in the sponsorship scandal, Martin barred him from the Liberal party for life. It wasn't clear that he had the authority to do so, but no one came to Gagliano's defence. Martin was likely correct when he said, "Anyone who says that he was our best possible representative in that post at that time is being disingenuous.[26] Gagliano filed a $4.5 million lawsuit for defamation and wrongful dismissal against Martin and the federal government. The case was dismissed.

Martin also dumped Mississauga MP Carolyn Parrish from the Liberal caucus. Martin condemned her anti-American rhetoric, such as when she said, "Damn Americans; I hate the bastards." She later clarified her remarks, saying she didn't hate all Americans, just its sitting president, George W. Bush. She also appeared on a TV comedy show and stomped on a doll of President Bush. While Chrétien tolerated this nonsense from a backbench MP, Martin decided she did not belong on his team.[27] It did not help her standing with Martin that she had called the insiders of his team "sneaking, snivelling shitheads" following the meeting at the Regal Constellation Hotel that was focused on how to move Chrétien out of office.[28] She did not run in the 2006 election but she did support the Liberal candidate in her riding.

According to Sheila Copps, Martin thought he could sweep the country without the incumbent MPs who had been loyal to Chrétien on his team:

> Martin believed his own clippings. He thought he could replace MPs who were not sufficiently loyal to him without any risk to the party. Martin's team made a list of 30 MPs they wanted to take out through the nomination process. I was on the list and so was Stéphane Dion, who called me and asked what he should do. Martin's team was reported to have organized a takeover of the riding association of Chrétien cabinet minister Herb Dhaliwal when he was out of the country and his wife was dying of cancer. Susan Whelan was going to support me for the leadership but then wrote me a letter in 2003 to say she was going to support Martin because his team had told her if she supported me they were going to remove her as a Liberal candidate in the next election. Solid backbench MPs were targeted such as Bob Bertrand, the MP from

Pontiac-Gatineau-Labelle who had been elected in 1993, 1997, and 2000. He was caucus chair and thought he should remain neutral in the 2003 leadership race. He lost the Liberal nomination in 2004. Political staff were told if they supported any of the targeted MPs they would lose their job.

Jeffrey Simpson wrote that the distance Martin established from Chrétien was so profound that the Liberal party could well be renamed The Paul Martin Party.[29] Not surprisingly, few of those he had purged lifted a finger to help Martin in the 2004 election.

It DID NOT TAKE long for political observers to conclude that as prime minister, Paul Martin had a different leadership style from Jean Chrétien. Chrétien was instinctive while Martin was ponderous. Chrétien was decisive while Martin waffled. Chrétien believed that a prime minister cannot get bogged down in details while Martin enjoyed deep dives on every file he touched. Martin relied on analysis, argument, debate, focus groups, and polling to reach conclusions.[30] Chrétien, on the other hand, had a gut feel that guided him through difficult issues. Martin took his time and engaged in lengthy debate before deciding what to do. Chrétien was quicker to decide, fearing that deep analysis led to paralysis.

Chrétien's approach to being prime minister was to establish priorities, develop strategies, supervise crises, handle the toughest problems, and delegate as much as possible to his ministers.[31] Martin had difficulties in setting priorities, which came as a surprise to observers since he seemed to be so clearly focused as minister of finance.

One senior bureaucrat who served under both Chrétien and Martin found something to admire in the styles of both men:

> Chrétien was the chair of the board. He was strategic and political, always interested in the big picture and the bottom line. He was decision-oriented and had no difficulties saying no. Martin, on the other hand, was a policy leader. He wanted deep discussions and more engagement. It was easy for him at Finance because there was a clarity of purpose. It was more difficult for him as prime minister because the surplus gave him more options and he was not ready for it.

The most devastating criticism of Martin was delivered by the international magazine *The Economist*. After his first year in office it called him "Mr. Dithers," and concluded that Canada's top job was "too big" for Martin. His closest parallel, others said, was American president Jimmy Carter, who got so mired in the minutiae of policy that it was difficult to discern his government's overall direction. *The Economist* was not the first to suggest that Martin was a ditherer. Biographer John Gray wrote in 2003 that Martin was instinctively reluctant to accept what seemed easy and obvious.[32]

Martin conceded that he had a great many priorities and that he accepted that his agenda was too large for the political circumstances in which he found himself.[33] But Martin countered that his critics had it dead wrong about an inability to make decisions.

> When I became prime minister, I was accused of taking too long to make a decision, which gets me exactly wrong. I believe that you should take all the time available because it leads to a better outcome; but my weakness was and is to rush to a decision, not to worry about it…A leader needs to know where he or she wants to go but needs to consult widely before forging a path both for what can be learned and to rally support. Consultation works not just because it gives the folks at the top a fuller picture of the information and ideas available; it also helps to get buy-in where it is most needed. Some see listening as weakness. I don't … When I was prime minister, some people said the style was too consultative: that my job was to lead, not to listen. I don't believe that.[34]

Opposition MPs said that because everything was a priority for Martin, nothing was a priority. Indeed, when the Conservative Party launched its 2006 election campaign, it highlighted the fact that you could count its priorities on one hand.

One provincial premier described Martin as difficult to deal with because he could not decide or even have a private conversation to try to resolve problems. The premier found it unusual that Martin would not attend a meeting or be on a phone call without his entourage being present. Bureaucrats lamented that it was rare for a Martin speech to be delivered that had not gone through 35 drafts.[35]

Eddie Goldenberg observed that Martin's desire to avoid criticism and find the perfect solution to problems was paralyzing: "Martin was iffy on many issues.

If he was in a room with one hundred people and if 98 people agreed with him he would spend his time trying to bring the other two onside."

Brian Tobin thought Martin was not well suited to the times or the issues:

> It could be a good thing: take in advice, reflect on the options, and sleep on it. In another century, when things didn't move at the speed of light, that may have worked. But in this century, with the Internet and 24-hour news channel, things happen very quickly. You need to be able to move, not recklessly, but judiciously. Paul Martin was not able to make decisions at the speed that was needed. And when he did he would often change his mind.

John Manley also didn't believe Martin had the ability to make and hold decisions. He said Martin held few clear opinions because he wanted to please everyone he met: "I had one senior deputy tell me that he had been in a small group meeting when a clear decision was made between two binary options – there was black and white – and Martin chose black. By the time the deputy returned to his office a call had come in from one of Martin's aides to say the decision had been changed to white."

BECAUSE MARTIN WAS PERCEIVED to have been the architect of the government's policies in the Chrétien era, the business community expected continuity when he took over as prime minister. Thomas d'Aquino, the CEO of the Canadian Council of Chief Executives, spoke of Martin's exemplary credentials and said this boded well for the Canadian economy. But Peter Shawn Taylor of the *National Post* did a deep dive into Paul Martin's life and came to a different conclusion:

> Martin sees himself as a transformational leader, someone prepared and determined to leave the country a very different place than he found it. He will pick several 'great national objectives,' to use his term, and pursue them as relentlessly as he pursued his previous missions. And the result will be some noisy collisions. If you enjoyed the sleep-friendly Chrétien era, the Martin years are going to make a loud claim on your time ... his long-repressed preference for a busy central government and a desire to fulfil his father's activist legacy seem more likely to dominate the scene.[36]

Taylor discovered that those who knew Martin best, such as Toronto Liberal MP John Godfrey, expected the Liberal government would change course. "I think it will be a surprise to the business community that sees in him a fellow entrepreneur. He will take us down bold, new and exciting paths that go beyond simple, competent leadership. Conservative, middle-of-the-road business people don't necessarily want bold from government. But he knows that bold is important."[37]

Hugh Segal, a Conservative who Martin appointed to the Senate in 2005, came to the same conclusion:

> Martin desperately wants to be transformational. He will want his period to look like Pearson's: a time when seismic changes were seen to happen in the federal government and the country. The issue is not whether he is going to be a transformational leader, but whether he will be a successful one.[38]

After the 2004 election, Martin had a surplus and a please-everyone agenda. While he had spent his time in the finance department trimming spending and balancing the books, as a minority prime minister he was intent on spreading around the cash. Eddie Goldenberg said he couldn't say no to anyone and was good at writing blank cheques. For Aboriginals, it was the Kelowna Accord; for provinces, it was a health accord; for municipalities, it was a share of the federal gas tax. Tom Courchene, a Queen's University economist, said that Martin turned 180 degrees when he went from finance minister to prime minister, running his government "as an open bar.[39]

Martin had struck a politically-useful friendship with the rock star Bono that he cemented by promising to top up foreign aid. But when Martin hesitated to meet Bono's expectations, the relationship soured. Bono said he was crushed: "I felt as a former finance minister he would be able to make the numbers work ... I'm mystified actually by the man."[40]

In the days before the 2004 election, *The Economist* foretold the result: "The trouble is, his brief tenure as prime minister has been singularly ineffective. His advisers have been good at only one thing: knifing their fellow-Liberal rivals in the back ... Otherwise, Mr. Martin has been a bumbling and hesitant chief executive, trying to placate all voters. During the campaign, he has often seemed tired."[40]

Martin admitted that he often made things up on the fly. For example, when municipalities wanted federal dollars, they simply had to show up at the right time:

> On the same day as my second throne speech, October 5, 2004, there was a meeting of Canada's 22 big-city mayors in Ottawa. I decided that I should invite them to 24 Sussex for an informal get-together over drinks …. The ideas were flying around … so I got their attention and said we should have a collective bull session right there. Some of the mayors were standing, some were sitting on the spiral staircase leading up to the second floor … then I offered them a place at the national table – literally. We moved into the dining room, crowded around the big table, ordered more food and drink, and away we went for hours.[42]

Martin had made a promise to televise meetings that he held with provincial premiers. But when they ganged up on him — demanding a flat 25 per cent contribution to health care — it was more than Martin could handle. As he did with the mayors, he went behind closed doors at 24 Sussex to work out a generous deal over pizza that included a 6 per cent escalation clause at a time when inflation was running at 2 per cent.

It was also ad hoc thinking that led to the appointment of Canada's 27th governor general. As Adrienne Clarkson's term was coming to an end, Martin had to recommend a replacement to the Queen. Martin did not have a list of candidates in mind or the criteria he would use for his decision. When a staff member floated the idea that Michaëlle Jean, a Radio-Canada journalist could be a possibility, Martin was instantly intrigued. Jean had come a long way after immigrating to Canada from Haiti with her family in 1968. Martin said he was drawn to the idea, in part because of Jean's intelligence and poise, but also because she would be a "fitting symbol to ourselves and the world." Martin invited Michaëlle Jean and her husband Jean-Daniel Lafond to his farm for a visit. What was supposed to be a one-hour chat became a marathon conversation.[43] The appointment was made, but it was not without controversy. Michaëlle Jean ended up relinquishing her dual citizenship with France and her husband felt compelled to disavow his past association with Québec separatists. Derek Burney was stunned that the vetting for the position was so lacklustre: "The premier of Québec, Jean Charest, was never consulted. He could have warned Martin about the pitfalls, that her husband had been a separatist. There was no security vetting — nothing.

MARTINITES BELIEVED THEIR MAN was the reason why Jean Chrétien won three elections. They thought the economic and fiscal turnaround was their doing. The big ideas were theirs too. Martin's supporters considered Chrétien an intellectual lightweight, incapable of accomplishing anything without the acquiescence of the Martin people.[44] Imagine, they thought, how high Liberal numbers would go with their man at the helm. So overwhelming was Martin's intellect and ability, they thought that they not only didn't need Chrétien to succeed, they didn't need any of his supporters.

But Martin overplayed his hand and was the architect of his own demise. He kept the civil war in the Liberal party alive and unceremoniously jettisoned many capable cabinet ministers and political aides. He called a public inquiry that exposed illegality, but also came at a steep price that included harm to himself, political divisions within his party, and damage to our national unity. The Commission also cost taxpayers $60 million.[45] Martin admitted that the inquiry made it difficult to govern but defended his decisions on other grounds: "Politically, you can debate it," Martin noted, "But from a moral imperative, I don't think you can." It's true that Martin's decision to call a public inquiry into the sponsorship scandal has left a reminder that will resonate for decades to come that a high political price is paid for mismanagement and malfeasance.

Chrétien's patience was certainly tested by the comments Martin made about him. And at a speech before the Commonwealth Foundation in London in March 2004, Chrétien fought back: "In life and politics, I am someone who believes in solving problems, in accentuating the positive … in defending institutions … especially defending them against the armchair critics who would only notice faults. Fault-finding is very easy. But it is paralyzing. It saps confidence and trust. I am not a fault-finder. I am a doer."[46]

Ultimately, *The Globe and Mail* had to concede that while Paul Martin was a decent and honourable man, he was not up to being prime minister: "Sadly there has been more hope than achievement … there had long been a sense of drift."[47] Historian Michael Bliss wrote that Martin was a policy wonk who was long on talk and short on execution: "Short, too, on political common sense: It takes profound ham-handedness, stupidity really, to turn Sheila Copps into a victim and lose Hamilton, and to make Jean Lapierre your Québec lieutenant. Perhaps Jean Chrétien, for all his faults, did have the measure of Paul Martin."[48]

In the political world, Martin will be remembered for his strong policy intellect and for helping to steer the country from deficit to surplus as minister of finance. He will also be remembered for leading a mutiny that removed Jean Chrétien from office and for not living up to the expectations that he and his team set for his time as prime minister. A 2011 *Maclean's* survey ranked Martin second to last among 17 elected prime ministers. Only Joe Clark ranked lower.

But many Liberals today are grateful that Martin's impatience and ambition got the better of him. Had Martin been more respectful of Chrétien — and more strategic in his calculations — he likely would have taken over as the leader in 2000 and would have trounced a divided conservative movement in a 2001 election. That would have put Martin in power when George W. Bush and Tony Blair applied pressure on Canada to join in the Iraq war. Key Liberals believe Martin would not have been able to resist the pressure to follow America's lead. But because he had so antagonized Chrétien, Martin never got to make that call.

The enduring lesson that Martin and other ambitious politicians need to learn is that pushing a duly elected and popular prime minister out the door is unlikely to end well. And that being prime minister is much more difficult than being a minister of the Crown.

The official portraits of Chrétien and Martin hang side by side in the Centre Block of Parliament. Fittingly, in between the two portraits is a stone column.

CONCLUSION

A GREAT PRIME MINISTER

Jean Chrétien loved politics, and not just for the glory: "There was the sheer fun of it, too: the personal thrill of the sport."[1] On his last foreign trip as prime minister, a reporter asked him what made for a good politician. His response: "The one who wins."[2] And win he did, going 12–0 when running for Parliament and 3–0 in elections as party leader.

To Chrétien, politics was about being able to skate on thin ice: "You never know when you're going to fall into a hole and disappear forever."[3] It wasn't all footwork. He said he had to learn to walk with his back against the wall and his elbows held high.[4] He was as popular when he left 24 Sussex Drive as when he had arrived ten years earlier; that puts him in rare company.

Chrétien said he was content to be known as a competent prime minister. By his own account, he more than met this measure of success. When he came into office, Chrétien thought Canada was exhausted, demoralized, and fractured:

> The federal, provincial and municipal governments were virtually bank-rupt, and their combined debt was greater than the country's total GDP. Unemployment was stuck at 11.4 per cent. Our interest rates seemed permanently fixed higher than U.S. rates, despite our lower inflation rate, and many of our best scholars were leaving for greener pastures.[5]

He didn't blame all the nation's ills on the nine years of Progressive Conservative rule but said that the recession in the early 1990s was deepened by a restrictive monetary policy and the country's failure to adapt to the realities of globalization and rapidly changing technology.

Chrétien said his three priorities as prime minister were keeping Canada unit-ed in the face of a separatist threat in Québec and a sense of alienation in

Western Canada, reducing the federal deficit, and lessening the influence of the United States on Canada. On the day he left office, Chrétien assessed the state of the nation: "The economy is booming, separatism has been checked, we're not at war in Iraq, but we do have one terrible problem. We don't know what to do with our surpluses."[6]

Despite Chrétien's electoral dominance and notable accomplishments, opinion leaders were stingy with praise when he retired. The Liberal-friendly *Toronto Star* wrote that Chrétien's virtue was that he was a pragmatist who brought a decade of prosperity, stability, and relatively good government. The Star observed that Chrétien's critics forget that progress is not a smooth, steady process: "Nations periodically need time to consolidate their gains, to repair and renew themselves for the next leap forward, and Chrétien has prepared the country well for the next major advance."[7]

The Globe and Mail concluded that Chrétien would be remembered for cleaning up a fiscal mess, but also for the near disintegration of the federation during the referendum and for lurches in policy that reflected a mind with a short attention span. What was lacking under Chrétien, wrote the *Globe*, was a considered vision of what Canada should be.[8] The editorialists hoped that under Paul Martin the country would aim higher: "Certainly, the people are primed for a leader who will represent them to the future ... The country aches for vision. It itches for action."[9]

Some of Canada's leading academics and historians were similarly unimpressed. Michael Bliss, author of *Right Honourable Men: The Descent of Politics from Macdonald to Chrétien*, concluded that Chrétien left his successor a united and prosperous country but that he was not a great prime minister and was not even one of the very good ones. He wrote that Chrétien left an unusually small mark on the country where policymaking was made at times in a vacuum by the vacuous.[10] He had an easy ride in office, wrote Bliss, and faced weak opponents that let him act like a street fighter who took on all the women and children on the block.[11] Bliss's ultimate assessment was that Chrétien government was, "moderately competent and only moderately corrupt."[12]

Jack Granatstein and academic Norman Hillmer assembled 26 academics, historians, and political scientists to inform their 1999 book *Prime Ministers: Ranking Canada's Leaders*. The book's timing did not cover the last four of the ten years Chrétien held office so the prime minister's decision to keep Canada out of the war in Iraq war was not factored into this assessment. They wrote that Chrétien was cautious and conservative by temperament, governing from the middle while avoiding the hard choices whenever possible. They thought Chrétien had no great abiding vision of the country but that he made very few mistakes.[13] For the period in question, the panel put Chrétien in the average category.

When *Maclean's* magazine first assembled a panel to rate Canadian prime ministers in 1997, Chrétien ranked ninth. The editors called this surprising given that he had nearly presided over the end of Canada with a lacklustre performance in the 1995 Québec referendum campaign. When the survey was repeated in 2011, Chrétien had moved up to sixth place.

It didn't help Chrétien's standing that he was seen within the Liberal party establishment as being unworthy of the brand. Lester Pearson had won the Nobel Prize. Pierre Trudeau quoted Plato. John Gray wrote that Liberals saw themselves as intellectuals and sophisticates. "They talked a great deal and in glowing terms about the common people, but they weren't sure they wanted to be led by one of them.[14] One of Pierre Trudeau's key advisors, Jim Coutts, commented that Chrétien had a common touch but that he had turned away from the traditional Liberal social conscience. He had a passion for winning elections, noted Coutts, but not the purpose that was required to advance society.[15]

JEAN CHRÉTIEN'S 2007 PRIME ministerial memoir gave the nation's opinion leaders and scribes a fresh opportunity to review his record. Peter C. Newman, a Lifetime Achievement Award winner from the Canadian Journalism Foundation, wrote that the book offered more evidence that Chrétien had no vision or narrative arc for where he wanted to take Canada:

> This memoir faithfully records the events of his baleful interregnum – an extended, listless March break between the reigns of Brian Mulroney and Stephen Harper. It was a time out of joint … Nothing was resolved; less was settled … [mostly] this volume chronicles the old stag's stunning ability to evade criticism…Chrétien's stewardship was devoid of defining legacies or memorable quotes.

Not satisfied to just diminish his record, Newman, like so many of Chrétien's establishment critics, went after the former prime minister for his lack of sophistication and unworldly ways:

> [Chrétien] disgorged disconnected words instead of marshalled ideas...
> He turned incoherence into an art form...Canadians watched in horror
> or wonderment as Chrétien transformed the country from a one-par-
> ty state into an elected dictatorship whose operational code demand-
> ed loyalty to him, personally, that was so blind that even most faithful
> Liberals could not stomach it. The first Liberal PM to be overthrown by
> his own party.[16]

Finally, Newman went after Chrétien because he did not look the part. In his
public appearances, Newman charged, it was sometimes difficult to distinguish
the prime minister from his bodyguards, "except that Chrétien was rougher with belligerent bystanders." It was reminiscent of what key Tory strategist
Dalton Camp once said of Chrétien: that he looked like the guy who drove the
getaway car.

To his critics, what Chrétien looked like and how he spoke mattered as much
or more than what he said and what he did. Indeed, over his career, Chrétien
has been diminished more on style than on substance. But this criticism
raises the question: if he did not have the temperament or brains or looks
or linguistic skills to succeed in the top job, then how did he win so many
elections? Chrétien is the only Canadian prime minister to have won three
successive majorities without ever suffering a defeat. His critics attribute it to
luck, but that doesn't explain how Chrétien maintained his approval ratings
throughout his time in office. The evidence shows that Chrétien won not because of luck, but skill. He won because people liked him and he delivered
good results for Canada.

All great prime ministers have one or two legacy initiatives. Macdonald forged
a country from ocean to ocean. Laurier expanded our horizons and kept
Canada united. Mackenzie King steered the country through a world war.
Trudeau created the Charter of Rights and Freedoms. Mulroney launched free
trade and the GST.

Jean Chrétien has not one or two significant legacies, but four.

1. Canada went from being a financial basket case to an international
    role model of economic management. Chrétien's decisive leader-
    ship in eradicating a crippling deficit and in creating the conditions

that led to stellar economic growth can be matched by few other prime ministers. The case for putting Canada's fiscal house in order could not have been demonstrated more clearly than by how the country used its financial strength to deftly manage the worldwide economic crisis of 2008

2. He kept Canada out of the Iraq war. The events that followed Chrétien's time in office have only amplified the importance of that decision. All that Chrétien feared would happen has happened. When 1,000 Canadians were asked in 2007 to name Canada's greatest achievement of all time in foreign policy, the decision not to participate in the Iraq war came out on top. It was Chrétien's determination to stay out of the Iraq war that cements his legacy as one of the great world leaders of his day. And his decision established a doctrine that Canada could trade freely with the United States without always having to follow American foreign policy.

3. He dealt a fatal blow to Québec separatists with the passage of the Clarity Act and by his reforms to federal-provincial arrangements. His inaugural speech in the House of Commons in 1963 was about national unity and it remained the cause of his political life over the 40 years that followed. He wrote that it hurt him and his family to be vilified in his home province, but that nothing gave him greater satisfaction than to have earned the respect of the people of Québec.[17] Even western Canadians came to appreciate how Chrétien managed the nation's finances and that he did not intervene in areas of provincial jurisdiction. When Chrétien left office, Canada was a more united and stable country than at any point in the previous 50 years. Since then, unity has continued to strengthen from the foundation that Chrétien laid.

4. He transformed Canada's intellectual infrastructure, turning what had become a brain drain into a brain gain. Chrétien addressed a creeping decline in research and education by establishing the Canadian Foundation for Innovation, the Canadian Institutes of Health Research, the Canada Research Chairs, and the Canada Millennium Scholarship Foundation. These investments enabled leading Canadian research talent to do world-class work in their home country.

Chrétien made mistakes. He was old-school in how he sprinkled government money around the country to gain political favour. The sponsorship scandal was ill-conceived and mismanaged. The gun registry fired blanks. He also let Paul Martin take control of the Liberal party without putting up much of a fight. But his decisions on the issues that mattered most to Canadians and their quality of life have been proven to be prescient.

WHAT IS IRONIC ABOUT Chrétien's success is that he was often held in higher esteem by Canadians than those in his own party. Despite having delivered three majority governments, his political skills did not become evident within Liberal ranks until after he left office. The Liberals, who had been riding high in the polls when Paul Martin took over, were reduced to a minority government six months after Chrétien's departure. Within two years they were out of office.

The evidence shows that Chrétien won elections because of the street-smart qualities that many masterminds within the Liberal party openly mocked. To learn the lessons from the Chrétien era, it is important to understand what he knew about leadership that others failed to appreciate or grasp.

Among his leadership qualities and approaches, four were critical to his success:

1. He led with his own brand of populism.

2. He was inherently optimistic about Canada.

3. He kept his eye on the most important issues and did not get mired in detail.

4. He was a problem-solver, not an ideologue.

JEAN CHRÉTIEN WAS A populist. To his critics, Chrétien's populism was his excuse not to think deeply about the issues. Populism, they said, allowed Chrétien not to have a vision, not to look ahead, a way to skirt complex problems by offering simplistic solutions. But being a populist was essential to Chrétien's success as a prime minister.

His critics said that all Chrétien wanted to do was win elections and that he was unwilling to spend his political capital for a good cause. Peter C. Newman wrote that Chrétien's policies and principles were not Liberal per se but could be summed up in two words: whatever works. A friendlier perspective offered by the *New York Times* described Chrétien as a leader who was short on panache and vision and long on prudence and street smarts.[18]

But the thinking among the established policy leaders in the country was that Chrétien would not strain his approval ratings by doing the sort of heavy lifting that his predecessor undertook to implement the GST, for example. Indeed, in 1993 Chrétien campaigned to scrap the much-needed tax in order to win votes. But Chrétien's brand of populism was not simplistic and was never destructive. He did not appeal to people's fears or prejudices. His populism was grounded in optimism and faith in the judgment of the Canadian people. It was not because of ideology that Chrétien cut deeply into government programs and sliced the military budget. He did it because he knew that Canadians trusted him to eliminate the deficit.

His task as a politician, Chrétien said, was not to impose his views on voters but to understand and extract their wisdom. Since Canadians had no burning desire to change the constitution, neither did he. With this view, he was channelling Sir John A. Macdonald, who once said, "If there is one thing to be avoided it is meddling with the constitution of the country, which should not be altered till it is evident that people are suffering from the effects of the constitution as it actually exists."

Jean Charest said Chrétien understood what Canadians expected of him: "He knew the country was exhausted from Meech Lake, the GST, and the recession. He understood he was to be a transactional prime minister and not a transformational prime minister. He was content to fix the problems that were before him. He may have been lucky with his timing, but he made the most of it."

Being a populist also relieved Chrétien of any pretensions he may have had. Making friends with George W. Bush meant far less to Chrétien than having the trust of ordinary Canadians. He spoke to a factory worker in the same manner as he would to the Queen. He took pride in coming from Shawinigan. To be called "small-town cheap" by Justice Gomery for handing out free golf balls emblazoned with the prime minister's logo could have been taken as a compliment. He was proud of his small-town roots. Some world leaders might prefer to hand out elaborate fountain pens as gifts but what's wrong with being cheap when most Canadians live pay cheque to pay cheque.

Being a populist was an image Chrétien cultivated. That's why he hid from view his taste in literature and music, interests most Canadians might associate with the glittering class. John Manley recalled meeting Chrétien at 24 Sussex where the prime minister greeted him at his desk: "Listen to this passage in French," said Chrétien. "That's Voltaire." Manley asked if he knew how many Canadians thought of le petit gars de Shawinigan sitting in his office on a Thursday morning reading Voltaire? "Not too many because they would never vote for me, Goddamn it!" Wayne Wouters remembered delivering briefing material to 24 Sussex Drive and marvelled that Chrétien was watching a baseball game with the sound turned off, had symphony music playing in the background, and was deep into his briefing notes. Gilles Duceppe, then the leader of the Bloc Québécois, tried to expose the real Chrétien when he told the *New York Times* in 2000 that the prime minister was the little guy from Ottawa who disguised himself as the little guy from Shawinigan. In many ways, Chrétien was not who Canadians thought he was. He thought and read more deeply than many appreciated, his tastes more refined than many imagined.

Perhaps the most intriguing element of Chrétien's populism is that he rarely gave anything away to increase his approval ratings. In many instances, he reduced the scope of government programs and scaled back public services. For Chrétien, the good of the country came before easy wins for his party. In fact, his political staff said he was not particularly political or partisan. This may explain why his biggest challenge came not from the electorate but from within his own party. To his detriment, Chrétien was much more focused on his relationship with ordinary Canadians than he was with the inner workings of the Liberal Party.

Chrétien's instincts told him that tooting his own horn or seeking to be the centre of attention would cost him votes. Unlike most politicians, he shunned the limelight. He thought voters would conclude that he was not doing his job if they saw him on television every night. He did not seek attention in a crisis and often downplayed the seriousness of events. Chrétien told CBC journalist Don Newman not to expect many interviews, adding that Pierre Trudeau and Brian Mulroney were always in the middle of things but they ended up being hated.[19] It's not an accomplishment, he said, for a prime minister (or president of the United States) to be in the news a lot.[20]

Some might think that public opinion polls would be a populist's best friend. But Chrétien didn't need them. His insights came from decades of travelling the country and from visiting its many communities. He had an instinct for what Canadians were thinking, which he fine-tuned by regularly calling people in his riding and elsewhere. Chrétien didn't ask them about his problems but about what they were discussing with their neighbours. An even more accessible group was the prime minister's RCMP security detail. He enjoyed a casual relationship with his protectors and would routinely ask them what he should do, including on serious issues such as the Iraq war. Ministers and government officials marvelled at how Chrétien could predict the findings of a poll before it was even commissioned. The only question he would routinely ask his staff was about the price of milk, just in case the topic came up in a public forum.

Like all great leaders, Mr. Chrétien was grounded with a strong sense of place. He knew where he came from and he did not try to be something that he was not. He was a product of a working-class family from Shawinigan. He came from the riding of La Mauricie, a place, he said, where fun mixes with politics and where you can't put on airs.[21] He was a family man who lived a traditional lifestyle with conservative habits. He did not flaunt his wealth.

Lawrence Martin wrote that after ten years in office, the prime minister was still a misfit for the job: "It was as if he had been taken straight from the factory floor and plunked down under the chandeliers." That assessment could not have made Chrétien any happier.

JEAN CHRÉTIEN WAS INHERENTLY optimistic about Canada. Many populist politicians come with a chip on their shoulders and a mean streak. But Chrétien was a cheerleader for his country. Newspaper reporters would roll their eyes when Chrétien spoke of his love for Canada and how it was the best country in the world, as he did in most speeches. Many thought his cheerleading was trite and demeaning. But Chrétien concluded every speech with the same positive refrain, "Vive le Canada."

Chrétien was not the first prime minister to speak in such patriotic tones. Of the 19 who preceded him in office, Chrétien was most like Sir John A.

Macdonald. Bob Rae said that Chrétien, like Macdonald, had a gift for political leadership that resonated with the public: "His ability to strike a chord with Canadians and develop a sense of affection from Canadians is unique and strong. Few prime ministers can match that." Macdonald and Chrétien shared other traits. Both were great competitors. Both were decisive. Both were engaging storytellers. Both could make us laugh. Both possessed a basic decency that Canadians appreciated. Both placed national unity above all other issues. Both had an abiding and fervent love of Canada.

Laurier had optimism in abundance but lacked Chrétien's sense of humour. Borden, Bennett, and Mackenzie King could be gruff and dour. Diefenbaker had wit and could tell a good story but his rabid partisanship gave him a harsh edge. Pearson was joyful and positive, but could not match Chrétien's people skills. Pierre Trudeau could do many things, but telling a story or cracking a joke were not in his repertoire. Mulroney was optimistic and cheerful and had charm in abundance. He even had small-town roots. But his desire to rub shoulders with the powerful and mighty distanced him from the people.

Allan Rock said the prime minister was an instinctively good reader of people and issues. Far from his reputation as a pugilist, Rock said Chrétien was inherently courteous and respectful of people. Among American presidents, Chrétien said he was impressed by Ronald Reagan's congenital optimism and his capacity for making Americans feel proud and confident. If people are worried or depressed, Chrétien argued, they won't build for the future. Chrétien convinced us there were no problems that we could not fix. But his approach was not to persuade Canadians with intellectual arguments or economic theories. His view was that the public was moved more by mood than by logic, more by instinct than reason, more by results than boastfulness. Canadians liked the fact that Chrétien took his job more seriously than he did himself.

It's revealing that when Chrétien identifies with other politicians, it is American president Harry Truman comes to mind. Both Truman and Chrétien were decisive, orderly, plain-spoken, likeable, buoyant, and universally underestimated. Both were faintly praised on leaving office. But both have seen their stock rise in time. Of Truman, Sir Winston Churchill said, "I must confess, sir. I held you in very low regard ... I misjudged you badly." We could say the same for Chrétien, although Canadian opinion leaders remain slow to convert their criticism to praise.

Because Chrétien's government had overcome some festering national problems, his optimism made sense to Canadians. He made them feel better
about their country. While the editorial writers at *The Globe and Mail* offered
Chrétien faint praise on his retirement, they added this about the country:
"Today, Canadians blessed with the quiet confidence and resilience that comes
from having survived two severe recessions in the 1980s and 1990s and a brutal fiscal reckoning, are not just prepared to meet their future but desirous of
it."[22] What greater contribution could a prime minister make to his country
than embedding in our spirit a sense of confidence that there are no limits to
what can be accomplished?

Allan Rock added that while Chrétien might not have been the most eloquent
and articulate speaker, he was nonetheless inspirational:

> The alchemy that comes from a leader inspiring people, setting out
> a goal, even if he doesn't have a blueprint as to how it's going to be
> achieved but touches them in a way that is almost spiritual, summons
> their help, identifies the cause, persuades them that it's worthwhile, and
> inspires them to make the effort necessary to achieve it. That's political
> leadership and it's a wonderful thing to see when it happens.

JEAN CHRÉTIEN SAW THE big picture and did not get mired in details. He had
a knack for quickly boiling issues down to their essence, trusting the instincts
that he had garnered from his 30 years in public life before becoming prime
minister. He had little need for lengthy debate and was rarely stumped on how
to handle an issue. Lawrence Martin wrote that Chrétien had a fast-food mind
in that he would ask for the facts, digest them immediately, and decide.

Allan Rock said Chrétien did not get drawn into long discussions at the cabinet table and wanted his two cabinet committees to carry the load:

> He made it clear that by the time matters arrived at the big cabinet ta-
> ble — where 30 of us were present — that he would want all issues to
> have been resolved in committee. If anyone raised their hand to raise a
> concern he would respond by sending the matter back to the respective
> committee. 'Bring it back here when it is resolved and your question
> has been answered,' he would say. So no one would raise their hand
> because they knew it would set back the matter for months. His office

was represented at those committees so he knew what was going on. If he felt he had to assert his authority he would. But when it got to the big table he did not want to hear the rehashing of issues that took place in committees. Once regular business was dealt with he would put other issues before cabinet when he wanted their views.

Extended debates, Chrétien thought, did not necessarily produce better answers. As a minister, he was once given an opportunity to chair a cabinet meeting when Pierre Trudeau had stepped out of the room. Chrétien proceeded to power through each agenda by simply asking "Are we agreed?" as each item was introduced. When Trudeau returned, he felt the need to relitigate each of the items that Chrétien had already disposed of. Chrétien saw how lengthy interventions by ministers had perturbed Pierre Trudeau, but that Trudeau was loath to cut someone off. Even while in Trudeau's cabinet, Chrétien interceded and would pass along a note to a verbose minister: "Shut up. The boss is annoyed."

Chrétien's need for order and timeliness were legendary. Punctuality, he often said in reference to a short story by P.G. Wodehouse, was the politeness of princes.[23] Unlike most politicians, Chrétien stuck to a schedule and was late only once for a cabinet meeting: because he was on the phone with the president of the United States.

Chrétien connected his need for orderliness and punctuality with his inclination to be decisive:

> The truth is, I hate seeing reports and correspondence piled up around me. For me, order leads to decisiveness. Most people keep documents on their desk because they don't know what else to do with them. Trying to keep a clean desk is an incentive to make a decision, even if that decision is only to put a folder away in the proper drawer.[24]

Chrétien told his ministers that lengthy meetings were synonymous with a poor use of time. "If we stay here late," Chrétien cautioned, "the press outside the room will speculate that we are dealing with a crisis when we are not … I don't want ministers spending all day in cabinet and cabinet committee meetings."[25] He said cabinet meetings weren't graduate seminars for discussion groups; they were a place to make decisions. At first, foreign affairs minister Bill Graham struggled with the meaning of the hand gestures Chrétien was making in cabinet. "You're not a professor now," Graham was told. "We're not here in cabinet to talk a lot. We're here to get things done."

Cabinet ministers who chewed up time by complaining about government decisions were punished. At a retreat in 1995, Chrétien warned his ministers that those who protested spending cuts would see their budgets chopped by an additional 25 per cent.

Brian Tobin said few decisions were set aside and that Chrétien was prepared to live with the fact that he might not bat a thousand. The benefit was that there was no bottleneck at the top that jammed things up. Tobin also knew that if you went to see Chrétien and you wanted to come back, you brought in only a single sheet of paper. When Chrétien was in Trudeau's cabinet, a fellow minister, Bob Kaplan, told him a note was coming from his department on suspected war criminals. Chrétien tore off a corner of a page from a pad of paper and said: "Put it on this."

Chrétien felt that his restriction on memo length was only a problem for those who didn't know what they were talking about.[26] But he did tell his colleagues and government bureaucrats to attach whatever supplementary information they thought necessary in an appendix. By demanding that bureaucrats and ministers summarize their material, Chrétien was signalling his confidence that they could do their homework. He did not want to run their departments and make their decisions for them. He wrote that he never lost sleep over things he could not control.

Chrétien wanted the PMO to be a strategic player, not a micro-manager.[27] "He didn't want to be called with problems," said cabinet minister Don Boudria. "If you called him for help or direction he might conclude you didn't know what you were doing." Even though his staff and ministers frequently referred to Chrétien as "The Boss," his style in managing cabinet was less managerial and more chair of the board.

Chrétien worked under two prime ministers and saw strengths and weaknesses in how each managed cabinet. Under both Pearson and Trudeau, he witnessed a decision-making approach that left almost all the power in the hands of the prime minister. He recalled that there were relatively few votes in the cabinets he served, and even then, hands might only be raised over trivial matters such as whether smoking in the room would be permitted.[28] Pearson resolved heated debates at the cabinet table by reserving decisions for himself. Trudeau would remind everyone at the table where the power really lay by saying, "It's 18 to 12, and the 12's have it."[29] In other words, sometimes he counted the votes and other times he weighed them.

Chrétien was determined to download power from the PMO to the offices of ministers and then from their offices into the hands of the professional bureaucracy. He said he was bothered by the trend that had developed under Mulroney in which ministers built up large political offices headed by a chief of staff who competed with the deputy minister for power. Mitchell Sharp told Chrétien that the bigger the staff, the smaller the minister.[30] Chrétien told a collection of deputy ministers the day he was sworn in as prime minister that the era of 25-year-old kids telling you what to do is over: "I have been around long enough to know that when you do well that we do well."

But that did not mean Chrétien's PMO was run with a light touch. His chief of staff, Jean Pelletier, was mayor of Québec City for 12 years. Pelletier had a deft and firm hand, which earned him the nickname "The Velvet Executioner." Chrétien said Pelletier was disciplined, well organized, and as hard as nails. "He ran a very tight ship — and a tight-lipped ship. He neither wanted nor needed to be in the news."[31]

Chrétien wanted to get out of the way of the day-to-day functioning of government and reduced the number of permanent cabinet committees from more than a dozen to only two: economic policy and social policy.[32]

I saw myself as the head of the team of ministers charged with the management of their own departments. I had no intention of breathing down their necks, looking over their shoulders, or interfering with their officials as long as everything was functioning smoothly. Nor did I expect them to come running to me with every little problem.[33]

But Chrétien also reserved for himself the right to change any decision made by one of his ministers. This stems from the prime minister's power to appoint and dismiss cabinet ministers at will. There was no formal vote in cabinet, Chrétien said, "because everybody knows exactly who has the last word.[34] When one official from the Defence Department questioned whether a decision could be taken with so few ministers present, Chrétien gave him a lesson on cabinet government: "He went into the other room – he was alone," said a senior minister. "He returned and said I am the cabinet and I have decided."

Though he was known to cut off discussion in cabinet, Chrétien did not want his ministers to blindly follow directions from the Prime Minister's Office. "Just because my staff calls you," Chrétien said, "doesn't mean they are speaking for me. If I need to tell you something I will. Don't take directions from my staff."

Chrétien ran only a few key priorities and issues from the centre. These were areas that cut across departments such as government finances and national unity. Chrétien would also involve himself in a political crisis if it reflected on the government. Because he didn't dive into the details, Chrétien was ridiculed by columnists as someone with a short attention span or, worse, a simpleton who refused to read more than a single-page memo. But Chrétien understood that the fine print is not where political leadership is exercised.

JEAN CHRÉTIEN WAS A problem solver, not an ideologue. He was certainly not one to let political ideology stand in the way of a potential resolution to a problem. It didn't bother Chrétien if his solutions were theoretically contradictory or inconsistent. To the frustration of his opponents, he didn't hesitate to change past positions when dealing with new circumstances, new evidence, or unexpected events. His conversion to free trade was not based on ideology but because the data showed it was working for Canada. He was not an advocate for Milton Friedman's theories on economic order, but he nonetheless reduced the size of government more than any other prime minister.

Despite coming to office with more experience around the cabinet table than any of his predecessors, Chrétien had few fixed policy prescriptions in mind. Rather, he had instincts. He was fiscally conservative by nature. He believed that Canada was the best protector of the French language and culture in North America. He was a multilateralist, in part to ensure Canada did not get absorbed into the vortex of the United States any more than it already was.

Chrétien cared about kitchen-table issues and did not get sucked into arguments about economic theories or artificial abstractions. His international forays were not about international peace; they were Team Canada trade missions. When he cut back on employment insurance he knew it would cost him some seats in Atlantic Canada. But he also knew that Canadians generally didn't like it that people were being paid to, as he said, stay at home and drink beer. It wasn't ideology that caused Chrétien to bristle at the thought that the able-bodied were taking from the state. He reflected what most hard-working Canadians thought: that sympathy is not for the lazy.

Chrétien's personal qualities adapted well to unforeseen circumstances. Never was that more important than when Canada was asked to join in the Iraq war. Chrétien could not be bullied and he refused to surrender his instincts and his judgment to others. He simply could not be intimidated. And his instincts were rarely wrong. As he suspected, Saddam Hussein was not hiding weapons of mass destruction. And as he also suspected, the region did not flourish as a peaceful democracy after the Iraq war ended. By being on the right side of history, Chrétien saved the lives of many Canadian soldiers. By giving little heed to the accepted dogma, Chrétien made each call on its own merits.

JEAN CHRÉTIEN CONSISTENTLY PROVED his critics wrong. For a man who was thought to be unserious, he was as clever and cunning as the metaphorical fox. It was only after Paul Martin was prime minister that the Liberal establishment realized why the party had won three successive elections under Chrétien.

Contemporaries consistently underestimated his intelligence and his instincts for making the right call on the tough issues. Political commentators misjudged Chrétien's grasp of the big picture and his direction for the country. After demonizing Chrétien, Québec nationalists could not reconcile themselves to the reality that he gave their province new tools to protect the French language and culture.

Chrétien was the right leader for the times. He fixed problems. He made difficult and controversial decisions that time has proven prescient. He succeeded where others had failed. The country thrived under Chrétien.

He deserves his place in Canada's history books, not just for his electoral success and his time in office, but for a remarkable record of accomplishment. He may have been le petit gars de Shawinigan, but Jean Chrétien was also one of Canada's great prime ministers.

END

AUTHOR'S NOTES

Books of this sort are labours of love. And that love, for me, is Canada.

Thankfully, I am not alone in my desire to contribute to a better understanding of where our country has succeeded and where we have fallen short of the mark. Among those who lent me a helping hand are Dany Horovitz, Jordan Fraser, Cam Rufelds, Rob Collins, John Rainford, Graham Fraser, Barbara Uteck, Ian Hamilton, Jeffrey Simpson, Lawrence Martin, Mark Goetz, Serge Blais, and Peter O'Neil. John Usborne not only dissected every word, he is the creative genius behind putting fox in the title. As always, one of my best sources of information is the Ottawa Public Library.

I conducted over 50 interviews for this book. Their contributions are evident in the quotes that are not otherwise included in the 740 endnotes. While the large majority of those interviewed went on-the-record, some preferred to remain anonymous.

I was rejoined on this book by copyeditor extraordinaire, Gilian Scobie. Lisa Georges created the stunning cover design and did a spectacular job on the pages. (Reformatting graphs and endnotes is not as easy as you might think). Having covered much of Jean Chrétien's career, including being his Official Photographer, Jean-Marc Carisse generously scoured his archives and selected the perfect cover photo.

My editor, Mark Sutcliffe, not only helped to clarify and brighten the text but sharpened the book's focus to make it a more exciting read. It was a joy to have his critical eye oversee this project.

Of course, none of this work would have been possible with the patience and support of my family. Marian has learned that I don't hear much of what's going on around me when my mind is focused on my work. My children – Nathaniel, Charlotte, Megan and Michael — have yet to develop my passion for Canadian history, but there's hope. They are nonetheless grateful that while my interest has been consumed by more recent history I have spent less time talking about Sir John A. Macdonald at the dinner table.

The book is dedicated to my friend and model parliamentarian, Mauril Belanger, who passed away in 2016 from ALS.

BIBLIOGRAPHY

Black, Conrad. *Rise to Greatness: The History of Canada From the Vikings to the Present*. Toronto: McClelland & Stewart, 2014.

Blair, Tony. *A Journey: My Political Life*. New York: Alfred A. Knopf, 2010.

Bliss, Michael. *Right Honourable Men: The Descent of Politics from Macdonald to Chrétien*. Toronto: Harper Collins, 1994.

Bouchard, Lucien. *On the Record*. Toronto: Stoddart Publishing, 1992.

Chrétien, Jean. *My Years as Prime Minister*. Toronto: Alfred A Knopf, 2007.

Chrétien, Jean. *Straight from the Heart*. Toronto: Key Porter Books, 1985.

Clarkson, Stephen. *The Big Red Machine: How the Liberal Party Dominates Canadian Politics*. Vancouver: University of British Columbia Press, 2005.

Cohen, Andrew. *A Deal Undone: The Making and Breaking of the Meech Lake Accord*. Vancouver: Douglas and McIntyre, 1990.

Clinton, Bill. *My Life*. New York: Alfred A. Knopf, 2004.

Copps, Sheila. *Worth Fighting For*. Toronto: McClelland & Stewart, 2004.

Crowley, Brian. *Fearful Symmetry: The Fall and Rise of Canada's Founding Values*. Toronto: Key Porter Books, 2009.

Delacourt, Susan. Juggernaut: *Paul Martin's Campaign for Chrétien's Crown*. Toronto: McClelland & Stewart, 2003.

English, John. *Just Watch Me: The Life of Pierre Elliot Trudeau*. Toronto: Alfred A. Knopf, 2006.

Frum, David. *The Right Man: An Inside Account of The Bush White House*. New York: Random House, 2005.

Goldenberg, Eddie. *The Way it Works: Inside Ottawa*. Toronto: McClelland & Stewart, 2006.

Graham, Bill. *Call of the Wild: A Political Memoir*. Vancouver: On Point Press, a UBC Press imprint, 2016.

Granatstein, Jack and Norman Hillmer. *Prime Ministers: Ranking Canada's Leaders*. Toronto: HarperCollins Canada, 1999.

Granatstein, Jack. *Who Killed the Canadian Military?* Toronto: Harper Festival, 2004.

John Gray, *Paul Martin: The Power of Ambition*. Toronto: Key Porter Books, 2003.

–– *Paul Martin: In the Balance*. Toronto: Key Porter Books, 2004.

Harder, Lois and Steve Patten. *The Chrétien Legacy: Politics and Public Policy in Canada*. Montreal & Kingston: McGill-Queen's University Press, 2006.

Hébert, Chantal, and Jean Lapierre. *The Morning After: The 1995 Quebec Referendum and the Day that Almost Was*. Toronto: Knopf Canada, 2014.

Hillier, Rick. *A Soldier First: Bullets, Bureaucrats and the Politics of War*. Toronto: HarperCollins, 2010.

Johnson, William. *Stephen Harper and the Future of Canada*. Toronto: McClelland & Stewart, 2005.

Kinsella, Warren. *The War Room: Political Strategies for Business, NGOs, and Anyone Who Wants to Win*. Toronto: Dundurn Press, 2007.

Lang, Eugene and Janice Gross Stein. *The Unexpected War: Canada in Kandahar*, Toronto: Viking Canada, 2008.

Litt, Paul. *Elusive Destiny: The Political Vocation of John Napier Turner*. Vancouver: University of British Columbia Press, 2011.

Manning, Preston. *Think Big: My Adventures in Life and Democracy*. Toronto: McClelland & Stewart, 2002.

Martin, Lawrence. *Iron Man: The Defiant Reign of Jean Chrétien*. Toronto: Penguin Canada, 2004.

Martin, Lawrence. *Jean Chrétien, Will to Win*. Toronto: Lester Publishing, 1995.

Martin, Paul. *Hell or High Water: My Life in and out of Politics*. Toronto: McClelland & Stewart 2008.

May, Elizabeth. *Who We Are: Reflections on my Life and Canada*. Vancouver: Greystone Books, 2014.

Milnes, Arthur. *Canada Always: The Defining Speeches of Sir Wilfrid Laurier*. Toronto: Penguin Random House, 2016.

Mulroney, Brian. *Memoirs: 1939–1993*. Toronto: McClelland & Stewart, 2007.

Newman, Peter C. *The Secret Mulroney Tapes: Unguarded Confessions of a Prime Minister*. Toronto: Random House Canada, 2005.

Newman, Don. *Welcome to the Broadcast: A Memoir*. Toronto: HarperCollins, 2013.

Olsen, Lynne. *Those Angry Days: Roosevelt, Lindbergh, and America's Fight Over World War II, 1939–1941*. New York: Random House, 2013.

Radwanski, George. *Trudeau*. Toronto: Macmillan of Canada, 1978.

Savoie, Donald J. *Governing from the Centre: The Concentration of Power in Canadian Politics*. Toronto: University of Toronto Press, 1999.

Sharp, Mitchell. *Which Reminds Me: A Memoir*. Toronto: University of Toronto Press, 1994.

Simpson, Jeffrey. *The Friendly Dictatorship*, Toronto: McClelland & Stewart, 2001.

Southam, Nancy. *Pierre: Colleagues and Friends Talk about the Trudeau They Knew*. Toronto: McClelland and Stewart, 2005.

Stoffman, Daniel. *Who Gets In: What Wrong with Canada's Immigration System and How to Fix It*. Toronto: Macfarlane Walter & Ross, 2002.

Tobin, Brian. *All in Good Time*. Toronto: Penguin Canada, 2002.

Trudeau, Pierre. *Memoirs*. Toronto: McClelland & Stewart, 1993.

Tuns, Paul. *Jean Chrétien: A Legacy of Scandal*. Jordan, ON: Freedom Press, 2004.

Wells, Paul. *The Longer I'm Prime Minister: Stephen Harper and Canada, 2006*. Toronto: Random House Canada, 2013.

Woodward, Bob. *Plan of Attack*. New York: Simon & Shuster, 2004.

INDEX

OTHER BOOKS BY BOB PLAMONDON

BLUE
THUNDER

THE TRUTH ABOUT **CONSERVATIVES**
FROM **MACDONALD** TO **HARPER**

FROM THE AUTHOR OF **FULL CIRCLE**

BOB PLAMONDON

FULL CIRCLE

DEATH AND RESURRECTION IN
CANADIAN CONSERVATIVE POLITICS

BOB PLAMONDON
FOREWORD BY **LAWRENCE MARTIN**

"Finally!"   "Powerful"
— DAVID FRUM   — LAWRENCE MARTIN

THE TRUTH
ABOUT
TRUDEAU

BOB PLAMONDON

ENDNOTES

"Goddamn Chrétien"

[1] Paul Martin, *Hell or High Water: My Life in and out of Politics*, 132.

[2] John Gray, *Paul Martin: The Power of Ambition*, 153.

[3] Taylor, "Not Exactly as Advertised," *National Post*; Don Mills, Ont., 01 Oct 2003: 48.

[4] "Lessons from Canada's 'Basket Case' Moment," Reuters, *National Post*, November 21, 2011.

[5] Ibid.

[6] Jean Chrétien, *My Years as Prime Minister*, 67.

[7] E. Kaye Fulton, "A Very Private Lady," *Maclean's*, April 18, 1994.

[8] Eddie Goldenberg, *The Way it Works: Inside Ottawa*, McClelland & Stewart, Toronto, ON., 2006, 147.

[9] Chrétien, *My Years as Prime Minister*, 68.

[10] P. Martin, *Hell or High Water*, 151.

[11] Ibid., 182.

[12] Gray, *Power of Ambition*, 170.

The Fox and the Badger

[1] Lawrence Martin, *Chrétien, The Will to Win*, 13.

[2] Jean Chrétien, *Straight from the Heart*, 16.

[3] Chrétien, *My Years as Prime Minister*, 15.

[4] Jack Granatstein and Norman Hillmer, *Prime Ministers: Ranking Canada's Leaders*, 215.

[5] Ibid., 101.

[6] L. Martin, *Will to Win*, 136.

[7] Chrétien, *Straight from the Heart*, 25

[8] Chrétien, *Straight from the Heart*, 51

9   Mitchell Sharp, xii.

10   Ibid., 142.

11   Chrétien, *Straight from the Heart*, 37.

12   Ibid., 28.

13   Ibid., 32.

14   Ibid., 49.

15   L. Martin, *Will to Win*, 314.

16   Ibid., 320.

17   Granatstein and Hillmer, 215.

18   Aileen McCabe, "Chrétien Blew His Chance to Leave Serious Legacy of Social Change, Coutts says," *CanWest News* [Don Mills, ON] 11 Nov 2003: 1.

19   Taylor, "Not Exactly as Advertised," *National Post*; Don Mills, Ont., 01 Oct 2003: 48.

20   "Jean Chrétien v Paul Martin: Now It's Really War," *The Economist*, June 6, 2002.

21   P. Martin, *Hell or High Water*, 69.

22   Ibid., 35.

23   Ibid.

24   Ibid., 39.

25   Ibid., 51.

26   Ibid., 55.

27   http://www.cbc.ca/archives/entry/no-ordinary-candidate, accessed September 19, 2016.

28   P. Martin, *Hell or High Water*, 77.

29   Ibid., 81.

30   Ibid., 72.

31   Ibid., 80.

32   Ibid., 76.

33   Susan Delacourt, *Juggernaut: Paul Martin's Campaign for Chrétien's Crown*, 33.

34   Peter Maser, "Liberal Star; Paul Martin Jr. Has Brains and Heart," *Ottawa Citizen*, 25 Nov 1988: A9.

Meech Lake

1   Chrétien, *My Years as Prime Minister*, 114.

2   Ibid., 115.

3   Chrétien, *Straight from the Heart*, 150.

4 Ibid., 128.

5 L. Martin, *Will to Win*, 304.

6 Chrétien, *My Years as Prime Minister*, 392.

7 Brian Mulroney, *Memoirs: 1939–1993*, 739.

8 Ibid

9 P. Martin, *Hell or High Water*, 88.

10 Gray, *Power of Ambition*, 96.

11 P. Martin, *Hell or High Water*, 90.

12 Ibid., 91.

13 Chrétien, *My Years as Prime Minister*, 120.

14 P. Martin, *Hell or High Water*, 90.

15 Delacourt, 55.

16 Peter C. Newman, *The Secret Mulroney Tapes: Unguarded Confessions of a Prime Minister*, 127.

17 Lucien Bouchard, *On the Record: Lucien Bouchard*, Stoddart Publishing, Toronto, 1992, 235.

18 Chrétien, *My Years as Prime Minister*, 120.

19 L. Martin, *Iron Man: The Defiant Reign of Jean Chrétien*, 26.

20 Newman, *The Secret Mulroney Tapes*, 157 and 357.

21 Chrétien, *My Years as Prime Minister*, 122.

22 Ibid., 123.

23 Ibid., 119.

24 Ibid., 4.

25 Ibid., 124.

26 Chantal Hébert, "Elijah Harper Another Brick in Liberal Wall," *Ottawa Citizen*; Ottawa, Ont., 27 Mar 1993: A10.

1995 Referendum

1 Chrétien, *My Years as Prime Minister*, 115.

2 Ibid., 132.

3 "Unwitting Separatist Ally," *The Gazette; Montreal*, Que., 23 Sep 1995: B.4.

4 Hébert and Lapierre, 171.

5 Ibid., 249.

6 Chrétien, *My Years as Prime Minister*, 134.

7 Ibid., 135.

8 Ibid., 136.

9 Ibid., 134.

[10] L. Martin, *Iron Man*, 118.

[11] Ibid., 121.

[12] Hébert and Lapierre, 251.

[13] L. Martin, The *Will to Win*, 51.

[14] Chrétien, *My Years as Prime Minister*, 137.

[15] Ibid., 129.

[16] Ibid., 145.

[17] Hébert and Lapierre, 143.

[18] Douglas Jehl, "Clinton, In Talk to Canadian, Opposes Separation," *The New York Times,* February 24, 1995.

[19] Ibid., 141.

[20] Goldenberg, 197.

[21] Ibid., 206.

[22] "Edward Greenspon, Federalists Want to be Agents of Change," *The Globe and Mail*, Toronto, ON, 02 Nov 1995: A6.

[23] Peter Salmon, "Trudeau Out of Power Still Weaves a Spell," *Times-Colonist*; Victoria, B.C., 19 Nov 1995: 1.

[24] L. Martin, *Iron Man*, 124.

[25] Chrétien, *My Years as Prime Minister*, 144.

[26] Ibid.

[27] Ibid., 148.

[28] Goldenberg, 205.

[29] Ibid., 212.

[30] Ibid., 211.

[31] Ibid., 213.

[32] P. Martin, 173.

[33] Brian Tobin, 143.

[34] Chrétien, *My Years as Prime Minister*, 150.

[35] Hébert and Lapierre, 115.

[36] "Mr. Bouchard Takes Centre Stage," *The Gazette; Montreal*, Que., 11 Oct 1995: B.2.

[37] Jeffrey Simpson, "The Most Powerful Voice for Secession Utters an Appealing Message," *The Globe and Mail*, Toronto, ON, 13 Oct 1995: A18.

Clarity

[1] Goldenberg, 223.

[2] Chrétien, *My Years as Prime Minister*, 152.

3 William Thorsell, "What Makes Chrétien Rage?" *The Globe and Mail*, Toronto, ON., 24 Oct 1998: D6.
4 Chrétien, *My Years as Prime Minister*, 268.
5 Edison Stewart, "Reform has Option for Quebecers," *Toronto Star*, 01 Dec 1995: A.21.
6 Chrétien, *My Years as Prime Minister*, 270.
7 "A Good Deal on Social Union: Ottawa and the Provinces have Reached a Compromise that will Benefit Canadians," *The Globe and Mail*, Toronto, ON., 06 Feb 1999: D.6.
8 Chrétien, *My Years as Prime Minister*, 154.
9 Ibid., 156.
10 "Plus ca change," *Ottawa Citizen*; Ottawa, Ont., 29 Jan 1996: A.6.
11 Goldenberg, 251.
12 Robert McKenzie, "Dion gets a Rough Ride in Quebec," *Toronto Star*; Toronto, Ont., 28 Jan 2000: 1
13 "Supreme Danger," *Ottawa Citizen*; Ottawa, Ont., 27 Feb 1996: A.10.
14 Chrétien, *My Years as Prime Minister*, 163.
15 Ibid., 165.
16 Ibid., 167.
17 Hébert and Lapierre, 142.
18 Delacourt, 152.
19 P. Martin, *Hell or High Water*, 174.
20 Chrétien, *My Years as Prime Minister*, 169.
21 Goldenberg, 254.
22 Scott Reid, "Clear Question? Harper was There," *National Post*; Don Mills, Ont., 02 Dec 1999: A18.
23 http://legisquebec.gouv.qc.ca/en/ShowDoc/cs/E-20.2, accessed August 14, 2017.
24 Chrétien, *My Years as Prime Minister*, 172.
25 L. Martin, *Iron Man*, 247.
26 Chrétien, *My Years as Prime Minister*, 171.
27 Conrad Black, 956.
28 Michael Bliss, *Right Honourable Men: The Descent of Politics from Macdonald to Chrétien*, 320.
29 Lawrence Martin, "Chrétien Realizes His Dream," *Times-Colonist*, 03 July 2000: A6.

Deficit Slayer

[1] Chrétien, *My Years as Prime Minister*, Alfred A. Knopf (A Ron Graham book), Toronto, ON. 52

[2] "Lessons from Canada's 'Basket Case' Moment," *National Post*, November 21, 2011.

[3] "To put the Liberals on a Leash," *The Globe and Mail*, Toronto, ON, 20 Oct 1993: A22.

[4] Chrétien, *My Years as Prime Minister*, 51.

[5] Bill Curry, "GST Killed Off Deficit, Mulroney Maintains," *The Globe and Mail*, Toronto, Ont., 15 Sep 2007: A.4.

[6] Bliss, 317.

Dr. No

[1] William Johnson, "Cabinet Change PM's Last Hope, Liberals Believe." *The Globe and Mail*, Toronto, Ont., 16 Sep 1976: 1.

[2] L. Martin, *The Will to Win*, 240.

[3] Budget speech, April 10, 1978, delivered by Jean Chrétien, accessed April 1, 2013, http://www.parl.gc.ca/parlinfo/Documents/Budgets/English/1978-04-10.pdf.

[4] Chrétien, *My Years as Prime Minister*, 54.

[5] Edward Greenspon and Anthony Wilson-Smith, 2.

[6] "Shine off Mulroney's Flying 'Taj Mahal' as it Dives to Cargo Role," *Times-Colonist* [Victoria, BC] 02 Dec 1994: 1.

[7] Jack Aubry, "Flying `Taj Mahal' now a `Winnebago'," *Edmonton Journal*; Edmonton, Alta., 13 Nov 1997: A.10.

[8] Chrétien, *My Years as Prime Minister*, 53.

[9] Ibid., 86.

[10] Ibid., 239.

[11] Ibid., 29.

[12] "When the Party's Over," *The Globe and Mail*, Toronto, ON., 26 Oct 1993: A30.

[13] William Johnson, 209.

[14] Preston Manning, 101.

[15] "Judging the Budget: Few Loud Boos, Few Real Cheers," *The Globe and Mail*, Toronto, Ont., 24 Feb 1994: A2.

[16] Gray, *Power of Ambition*, 112.

[17] "A Year On, Time to Govern," *The Globe and Mail*, Toronto, Ont., 25 Oct

1994: A23.

[18] John Fund, "Bankrupt Canada?" Editorial, *Wall Street Journal*, January 12, 1995.

[19] "Lessons from Canada's 'Basket Case' Moment," *Financial Post-Reuters*, November 21, 2011.

[20] Bank of Canada, Data and Statistics Office: Covered Differentials: Canada–United States 3-month Treasury Bills.

[21] P. Martin, *Hell or High Water* ,148.

[22] Donald J. Savoie, *Governing from the Centre: The Concentration of Power in Canadian Politics*, 178.

[23] Gray, *Power of Ambition*, 152.

[24] P. Martin, *Hell or High Water*, 137.

[25] L. Martin, *Iron Man*, 107.

[26] Derek Ferguson, "Manning Says Cuts Don't Go Far Enough," *Toronto Star*, 28 Feb 1995: A11.

[27] Michael Den Tandt, "Not a Bad Budget - If It Sets a Pattern," *Kingston Whig-Standard*, 28 Feb 1995: 6.

[28] "Mr. Martin Has Decided to Act," *The Globe and Mail*, Editorial, February 28, 1995, A 24.

[29] Goldenberg, 118.

[30] Pierre Trudeau, *Memoirs*, 199.

[31] Chrétien, *Straight from the Heart*, 177.

[32] Trudeau, *Memoirs*, 200.

[33] Jeffrey Simpson, "What He Leaves Behind," *The Globe and Mail*, Toronto, ON, 01 Nov 2003: F10.

[34] Goldenberg, 119

[35] Ibid., 59.

[36] Delacourt, 94.

[37] Chrétien, *My Years as Prime Minister*, 78.

[38] P. Martin, *Hell or High Water*, 177.

[39] Chrétien, *My Years as Prime Minister*, 80.

[40] Ibid., 78.

[41] Sheila Copps, *Worth Fighting For*, 175.

[42] "National Health Expenditure Trends, 1975 to 2015," Canadian Institute for Health Information, October 2015, 8.

[43] https://www.fraserinstitute.org/studies/end-of-the-chretien-consensus.

[44] Public Accounts of Canada, Part ll, under the Department of Canadian Heritage.

45 Joan Bryden, "Anatomy of a Political Disaster: Liberal Strategists are Still Trying to Figure Out How They Went So Wrong," *Calgary Herald*; Calgary, Alta., 22 Jan 2000: A14.

46 Kathryn May, "A Stunning Reversal: Minister Misjudged Public Opposition to NHL Deal," *Ottawa Citizen*, Ottawa, Ont., 22 Jan 2000: A1 / FRONT.

Brain Gain

1 Chrétien, *My Years as Prime Minister*, 260.

2 P. Martin, *Hell or High Water*, 183.

3 For a full collection of the CFI Annual Reports, see: http://www.innovation.ca/en/AboutUs/PublicationsandReports/AnnualReportArchives.

4 P. Martin, *Hell or High Water*, 186.

5 Scott Feschuk, "Chrétien Pledges to Establish Scholarship Fund Endowment Estimated at $1-billion to Help Needy, Achieving Students Starting in 2000," *The Globe and Mail*; Toronto, Ont., 25 Sep 1997: A.4.

6 Goldenberg, 362.

7 P. Martin, *Hell or High Water*, 187.

8 Jeffrey Simpson, "There's at Least One Chrétien Legacy: Universities," *The Globe and Mail*, Toronto, Ont., 09 Nov 2002: A21.

9 Simpson, "What He Leaves Behind.

10 "Zachary Spicer, "The Rise and Fall of the Ministry of State for Urban Affairs: A Re-Evaluation," *Canadian Political Science Review*, Vol. 5, No. 2, 2011, 117–26.

11 "Bench Strength MPs to Watch for from the Opposition Ranks: An Inside Track on Bloc, Reform, NDP and Tory Members Who Represent Their Parties' Best Hopes," *The Globe and Mail* [Toronto, ON] 15 Jan 1994: D.5.

12 James Travers, "Liberal Feud Shapes Manley Budget," *Toronto Star*, 18 Feb 2003: A01.

13 House of Commons, Hansard, May 6, 2002.

Tax Avoidance

1 Goldenberg, 31.

2 Gray, *Power of Ambition*, 106.

3 "PM Says He Knew GST Would Be Unpopular; Was elected to Make the Hard Decisions, PM Tells Radio Hotline Listeners," *Edmonton Journal*, 23 Oct 1990: A1/FRONT.

[4] P. Martin, *Hell or High Water*, 156.

[5] Ibid., 157.

[6] Delacourt, *Juggernaut*, 103.

[7] Gray, *Power of Ambition*, 116.

[8] Goldenberg, 59.

[9] Ibid., 188.

Pension Accord

[1] 2012 SCC 71, Professional Institute of the Public Service of Canada v. Canada (Attorney General).

[2] *Canwest News Service*, February 27, 2007.

[3] Chrétien, *My Years as Prime Minister*, 201.

[4] Ibid., 202.

[5] P. Martin, *Hell or High Water*, 163.

[6] http://www.osfi-bsif.gc.ca/eng/oca-bac/ar-ra/cpp-rpc/pages/cpp26.aspx-#Toc-1e, accessed April 14, 2016.

The Loonie

[1] P. Martin, *Hell or High Water*, 192.

[2] L. Martin, *Iron Man*, 204.

[3] Chrétien, *My Years as Prime Minister*, 55.

[4] Jonathan Ferguson, "Chrétien says He'd Make Crow Follow Orders on Inflation Policy," *Toronto Star*, Toronto, ON, 23 Nov 1991: A18.

[5] Shawn McCarthy, "Top Banker John Crow Put On Trial in Election," *Toronto Star*, Toronto, ON, 10 Sep 1993: A1.

[6] Chrétien, *My Years as Prime Minister*, 56.

[7] P. Martin, *Hell or High Water*, 112.

[8] "Agendas, Real and Political (II)," *The Globe and Mail*, Toronto, ON., 30 Oct 1993: D.6.

[9] P. Martin, *Hell or High Water*, 116.

[10] Terrance Wills, "That Sinking Feeling: Jean Chrétien's Personal and Political Style Has Always Been Laid Back. But his seeming "don't-worry, be-happy" attitude on the fading loony could backfire, becoming a permanent fixture in the public mind and damaging his long-running popularity," *The Gazette; Montreal*, Que., 01 Aug 1998: B1. [This title could be shortened.]

[11] Chrétien, *My Years as Prime Minister*, 76.

[12] "Andrew Duffy, Liberals Stole Central Bank's Power: Crow: In memoir, Former Governor Says Government Controls Monetary Policy," *Ottawa Citizen*, Ottawa, ON, 20 Nov 2002: A3.

Job, Job, Jobs

[1] Brian Crowley, *Fearful Symmetry: The Fall and Rise of Canada's Founding Values*, Key Porter Books, Toronto, ON., 2009, 212.

[2] "PM's UI Plan Smacks of 1930's Work Camps, B.C. Union Leaders Say," *The Gazette* [Montreal, Que] 28 Dec 1993: B1.

[3] Chrétien, *My Years as Prime Minister*, 71.

[4] "PM says Canada Can't Pay People to Drink Beer," *Ottawa Citizen*, Ottawa, ON., 21 Apr 1994: A5.

[5] "Small Issues, Big Headlines," *The Globe and Mail*, Toronto, Ont., 26 Apr 1994: A22.

[6] Paul Tuns, *Jean Chrétien: A Legacy of Scandal*, Freedom Press, Jordan, ON., 2004, 43.

[7] Gray, *Power of Ambition*, 159.

[8] Valerie Lawton, "Critics Condemn EI Reform Plans; Liberals Deny Move is Part of Election Strategy," *Toronto Star*, 29 Sep 2000: A19.

[9] Robert Fife, "Cabinet Rift Over Looser EI Rules: Martin, Manley and Axworthy stand against PM's Plan," Ottawa Bureau Chief, *National Post*, 21 Sep 2000: A1.

Canada's Most Conservative Prime Minister

[1] L. Martin, *Iron Man*, 427.

[2] Paul Wells, 296.

[3] Jeffrey Simpson, *The Friendly Dictatorship*, 32.

[4] Ibid., 76–7.

[5] Tobin, 72.

[6] "Where Paul Martin Should Lead Canada (1)," Editorial, *The Globe and Mail*, December 13, 2003, 22.

[7] Thomas Walkom, "Jean Chrétien and the Paradox of the Liberals: Liberal Politicians are a Strange Breed. They build Useful Social Institutions. Then They Destroy Them," *Toronto Star*, Jan. 22, 2014.

[8] "Lessons from Canada's 'Basket Case' Moment," *National Post*, November 21, 2011.

[9] "Tom Velk and Al Riggs, Brian Mulroney and the Economy Still the Man to

Beat," McGill University, undated paper accessed August 19, 2017, https://mcgill.ca/economics/files/economics/still_the_man_to_beat.pdf

10 Eric Beauchesne, "Canadian Living Standards Rose By Nearly 30 per cent under the Chrétien Government – More Than Double the Increase under the Former Mulroney Government, Says Economist," *CanWest News*, Don Mills, ON., 24 Nov 2003: 1.

11 Michael Bliss, "A Great Minister, an Imperfect PM: Now He Becomes Yesterday's Man," *National Post*; Don Mills, Ont., 22 Aug 2002: A6.

The Clinton Years

1 Chrétien, *My Years as Prime Minister*, 332.

2 Lois Harder and Steve Patten, 124.

3 Ibid, 84.

4 Chrétien, *My Years as Prime Minister*, 265.

5 Ibid., 101.

6 Ibid., 87.

7 Bill Clinton, *My Life,* 2004, 646.

8 Chrétien, *My Years as Prime Minister*, 96.

9 Ibid., 82.

10 Arthur Milnes, *Canada Always: The Defining Speeches of Sir Wilfrid Laurier*, 494.

11 Chrétien, *My Years as Prime Minister*, 83.

12 Goldenberg, 53.

13 Chrétien, *My Years as Prime Minister*, 84.

14 "Free Trade and Chrétien's Legacy," *National Post*; Don Mills, Ont., 02 Feb 2001: A15.

15 Goldenberg, 54.

16 The letters were from the President of the United States, which did not go to Congress for approval (per Bill Graham, interview on *The Current* [CBC] on March 31, 2106).

17 Chrétien, *My Years as Prime Minister*, 85.

18 Ibid., 99.

19 Harder and Patten, 134.

20 Global Affairs Canada, http://www.international.gc.ca/trade-agreements-accords-commerciaux/agr-acc/nafta-alena/facts.aspx?lang=eng.

21 Tobin, 153.

9/11

1 David Collenette, "David Collenette on 9/11: The Former Transport Minister on Deciding Who To Ground and Who Could Fly on Sept. 11, 2001, *Maclean's*, September 7, 2011.

2 Lynne Olsen, *Those Angry Days*, 425.

3 After 9/11, the regulations were amended to provide clarity over decision-making power in such a crisis.

4 Chrétien, *My Years as Prime Minister*, 295.

5 Ibid., 296.

6 Goldenberg, 261.

7 Chrétien, *My Years as Prime Minister*, 297.

8 David Frum, *The Right Man: An Inside Account of The Bush White House*, 149.

9 Ibid., 150.

10 Goldenberg, 279.

11 Chrétien, *My Years as Prime Minister*, 299.

12 Bill Graham, Chrétien's foreign minister, recalled a "hopeless" meeting with Hillary Clinton where he was unsuccessful in persuading her that there was no Canadian connection. (Interview on CBC, *The Current*, March 31, 2016).

The Early Bush Years

1 http://ipolitics.ca/2015/12/03/Chrétien-on-canada-u-s-relations-the-zingers-and-the-digs/.

2 Robert Russo, "Chrétien, Bush Hit It Off," *Kingston Whig-Standard*; Kingston, Ont., 06 Feb 2001: 9 / FRONT.

3 Chrétien, *My Years as Prime Minister*, 289.

4 Ibid., 292.

5 Ibid., 364.

6 Chris Hall, CBC News, accessed February 26, 2015, http://www.cbc.ca/news/politics/in-the-conservative-war-on-terror-the-first-casualty-is-parliament-1.2972506.

7 Chrétien, *My Years as Prime Minister*, 301.

8 L. Martin, *Iron Man*, 397.

9 "Stop Cringing, Please," *Ottawa Citizen*, 13 Sept. 2002: A18.

10 Shawn McCarthy, "PM's Sept. 11 Remarks 'Disgraceful,' Mulroney Says," *The Globe and Mail*, Toronto, Ont., 13 Sep 2002: A1.

[11] Bill Graham, *Call of the Wild: A Political Memoir*, 276.

[12] http://www.global-economics.ca/border_post911.pdf, Accessed March 12, 2016.

Yes to Afghanistan

[1] http://www.forces.gc.ca/en/operations-abroad-past/cafla.page National Defence website, the Canadian Armed Forces Legacy in Afghanistan.

[2] Rick Hillier, *A Soldier First: Bullets, Bureaucrats and the Politics of War*, 159.

[3] Eugene Lang and Janice Gross Stein, 41.

[4] Ibid., 101.

[5] http://www.nato.int/sfor/coms-sfor/prevcomm.htm.

6 Hillier, 244.

[7] In the Battle of Medak Pocket in the former Yugoslavia, Canadians were involved in a combat mission, using fire to push back a Croatian force. But there was no declaration of war in that instance.

[8] Lang and Gross Stein, 41.

[9] David Pugliese, "Girlfriend's Study An Insult, Sick Soldier Says: Eggleton's Former Lover Not Qualified To Write Paper On Post-Traumatic Stress, Sufferer Argues," *Ottawa Citizen*, 27 May 2002: A8.

[10] Tim Harper, "Ex-girlfriend Talks of Broken Heart as Eggleton Dumped," *Canadian Press NewsWire*, Toronto, ON., 27 May 2002.

[11] Tim Harper and Les Whittington, "Eggleton Gets Boot in Surprise Shuffle; PM scrambles to Crush Growing Ethics Scandal," *Toronto Star*, 27 May 2002: A0.

[12] Lang and Gross Stein, 40.

[13] Ibid., 60, 62.

[14] Ibid., 49.

[15] Bill Graham interview on CBC, *The Current*, March 31, 2016.

[16] Hillier, 311.

[17] Lang and Gross Stein, 56.

[18] David Olive, "Martin Serves Platter of Waffles," *Toronto Star*, 05 Dec 2002: B01.

[19] Lang and Gross Stein, 71.

[20] Ibid., 263.

[21] Ibid., 267.

[22] Jack Granatstein, *Who Killed the Canadian Military?*, 171.

[23] Hillier, 272.

24 Ibid., 133.

25 Chrétien, *My Years as Prime Minister*, 305.

26 "Canada Must Reclaim Its Role as a World Leader," *The Globe and Mail*, Sep. 12, 2015.

No to Iraq

1 Tim Harper, "Canada May Join the Growing Multinational Military Effort in the Middle East, Prime Minister Brian Mulroney Says," *Toronto Star*; Toronto, Ont., 09 Aug 1990: A16.

2 Howard Ross, Kevin Cox, "PM Orders Jet Squadron to Persian Gulf CF-18s to Protect Canadian Ships Enforcing Blockade; $75-million Further Aid Approved," *The Globe and Mail*; Toronto, Ont., 15 Sep 1990: A.1.

3 "Clark Trying to Play `Rambo:' Chrétien; Canada Shouldn't Become a `Yes Man' for the U.S., He Says," *The Gazette; Montreal*, Que., 25 Nov 1990: A8.

4 Edison Stewart, "Chrétien says PM 'Rolls Dice with Lives," *Toronto Star*, 16 Jan 1991: A1.

5 Edison Stewart, "Chrétien Emerges Battle-Scarred from War Vote," *Toronto Star*, Toronto, Ont, 23 Jan 1991: A14.

6 Harder and Patten, 136.

7 Chrétien, *My Years as Prime Minister*, 306.

8 Ibid., 307.

9 Ibid., 308.

10 Ibid., 309.

11 Ibid., 310.

12 Louise Elliott, "Sparks Fly Over Bush a 'Moron' Talk," *Kingston Whig-Standard*; Kingston, Ont., 23 Nov 2002: 13 / Front.

13 Chrétien, *My Years as Prime Minister*, 311.

14 Lang and Gross Stein, 111.

15 L. Martin, *Iron Man*, 413.

16 Chrétien, *My Years as Prime Minister*, 311.

17 William Johnson, 323.

18 "Proof Will Come Too Late," *National Post*; Don Mills, Ont., 10 Sep 2002: A19.

19 Chrétien, *My Years as Prime Minister*, 312.

20 Graham, 297.

21 Chrétien, *My Years as Prime Minister*, 312.

22 Bliss, *Right Honourable Men*, 326.

23 Ibid., 65.

24 Hillier, 262.

25 Lang and Gross Stein, 76.

26 Bob Woodward, *Plan of Attack*, 373.

27 Chrétien, *My Years as Prime Minister*, 315.

28 Bruce Wallace, Chrétien is Odd Man Out with Bush, Blair: Two PMs Manage 'Special Relationship' with United States in Very Different Ways," *Ottawa Citizen*, 05 Apr 2002: A14.

29 Ibid., 315.

30 Graham, 307.

31 http://www.wsj.com/articles/SB104881540524220000, accessed August 1, 2016.

32 Ted Morton, "Triple-E -- or Else," *National Post*, May 22, 2003.

33 Graham, 304.

34 Lang and Gross Stein, 90.

35 Chrétien, *My Years as Prime Minister*, 316.

36 "Mulroney Would've Helped 'Old Friends' in Iraq War," CBC News. Posted: May 09, 2003 9:54 PM ET Last Updated: May 09, 2003.'

37 "Clifford Krauss, Canadian Candidate Suggests an Effort to Mend Ties with U.S.," *The New York Times*, May 4, 2003.

38 Gray, *Power of Ambition*, 233.

39 Delacourt, 325.

40 Zev Singer, "It's Time to Back War," *Ottawa Citizen*; Ottawa, Ont., 23 Mar 2003: A4.

41 Clifford Krauss, "New Prime Minister is Steering Canada Cautiously to the Right," *The New York Times*, December 20, 2003.

42 "The Struggle for Iraq: The Reconstruction; Canadians to Bid on Iraq Projects," *The New York Times*, January 14, 2004.

43 Chrétien, *My Years as Prime Minister*, 319.

44 Tony Blair, *A Journey: My Political Life*, 309.

45 "Canada's Iraq Policy: Inconsistency Ho!," *The Globe and Mail*. Toronto ON., 19 March 2003, A22.

46 "Chrétien Needs His Own Reality Check," *Sudbury Star*; Sudbury, Ont., 14 Apr 2003: A8.

47 "A War that Must Be Won: There's Much More at Stake than Removing Saddam Hussein," *Ottawa Citizen*; Ottawa, Ont., 20 Mar 2003: A20.

48 "The PM; Wrong to Follow UN on Iraq," Windsor Star; Windsor, Ont., 19 Mar 2003: A6.

49 Don Martin, "The Prime Minister's Moment of Truth," *National Post*, Don Mills, ON., March 18, 2003, A16.
50 Peter Donolo, "Why Jean Chrétien was Right to Stay Out of Iraq," *The Globe and Mail*, Toronto, ON, 21 Mar 2006: A21.

Turbot War
1 Tobin, 82.
2 Ibid., 87.
3 Ibid., 91.
4 Ibid., 130.
5 Ibid., 115.
6 Ibid., 109.
7 Ibid., 117.
8 Ibid., 118.
9 Ibid., 121.
10 "More Fish Foolishness," *The Globe and Mail*, Toronto, Ont., 05 May 1995: A20.
11 Tobin, 5.
12 Ibid., 127.
13 Ibid., 130.
14 Ibid., 132.
15 Ibid., 136.
16 Ibid., 135.

Liberal Traditions
1 Granatstein, 191.
2 Bliss, *Right Honourable Men*, 324.
3 Jean Chrétien speech at Library and Archives Canada, May 18, 2016.
4 http://www.cnn.com/2009/POLITICS/11/24/us.landmines/index.html.
5 David T. Jones, "Canada and the US in the Chrétien Years: Edging Toward Confrontation," Policy Options, November 2, 2001.
6 Chrétien, *My Years as Prime Minister*, 337.
7 http://www.globalresearch.ca/the-international-criminal-court-icc-will-not-prosecute-tony-blair-others-are-planning-to/5534046, accessed August 10, 2016.
8 L. Martin, *Iron Man*, 92.
9 Chrétien, *My Years as Prime Minister*, 291.

10 Ibid., 328.

11 "David Filipov, Here are 10 Critics of Russian President Vladimir Putin who Died Violently or in Suspicious Ways," *Washington Post*, March 24, 2017.

12 Cétien, *My Years as Prime Minister*, 92.

13 Goldenberg, 79.

14 Ibid., 159.

15 "Mocked in Cuba," *The Gazette*, Montreal, Que., 04 May 1998: B2.

16 Chrétien, *My Years as Prime Minister*, 284.

17 Ibid., 348.

18 L. Martin, *Iron Man*, 275.

19 http://news.nationalpost.com/full-comment/chris-selley-on-canadian-politicians-going-to-israel-our-glory-days-as-honest-broker.

20 "Chrétien trip; Words Without Wisdom," *The Windsor Star*; Windsor, Ont.,19 Apr 2000: A8.

21 Chrétien, *My Years as Prime Minister*, 353.

22 Norman Webster, "Truth is No Defence in Mideast: It's Not What Chrétien's Been Saying That's Stupid, It's the Fact that He's Been Saying It," *The Gazette*, Montreal, Que., 15 Apr 2000: B7.

23 Chrétien, *My Years as Prime Minister*, 327.

24 P. Martin, *Hell or High Water*, 199.

25 Graham, 257.

26 P. Martin, *Hell or High Water*, 216.

27 Heather Scoffield, "Canada Seeks Allies for Debt Relief Plan: Martin Not Ready to Go It Alone to Cut Payments from Poorest Countries," *The Globe and Mail*, Toronto, ON, 26 Sep 2000: B5.

28 P. Martin, *Hell or High Water*, 215.

29 Chrétien, *My Years as Prime Minister*, 360.

Decade of Darkness

1 Bruce Campion-Smith, "General Draws Liberal Fire," *Toronto Star*, February 17, 2007

2 Hillier, 114

3 Chrétien, *My Years as Prime Minister*, 304.

4 Ibid., 303.

5 NATO statistics: http://www.nato.int/nato_static_fl2014/assets/pdf/pdf_1999_12/20100614_p99-152e.pdf accessed January 12, 2017.

6 Hillier, 114.
7 Granatstein, 175.
8 Hillier, 129.
9 Ibid., 122.
10 Ibid., 123.
11 Ibid.
12 Granatstein, 197.
13 Hillier, 203.
14 Granatstein, 189.
15 Hillier, 257.

Misfire

1 Chrétien, *My Years as Prime Minister*, 209.
2 Kenneth Whyte, "Allan Rock," Saturday Night, (Nov 1995): 18-19.
3 "The Rock Prescription," *The Windsor Star*; Windsor, ON, 01 Dec 1994: A6.
4 "Implementing the Firearms Act," CBC News. October 20, 2011. http://www.cbc.ca/news/canada/timeline-the-gun-registry-debate-1.786548, Retrieved October 20, 2011.
5 Marta Gold, Alberta Considering Court Challenge to National Gun Registry; What's a Registry? *Edmonton Journal*, 24 Nov 1995: A.3.
6 "Public Safety will be At Risk if Gun Registry is Dismantled," *Toronto Star*, 10 April 2009: A23.
7 Chrétien, *My Years as Prime Minister*, 209.
8 Eric Mayne, "We Don't Want Your Guns, PM Tells U.S.: Chrétien Slams Charlton Heston in Anti-Guns Speech," *Ottawa Citizen*; Ottawa, Ont., 08 May 1999: A6.
9 http://www.statcan.gc.ca/pub/11-630-x/11-630-x2015001-eng.htm.
10 See, for example, 2014 crime stats http://www.statcan.gc.ca/pub/85-002-x/2015001/article/14211-eng.htm.
11 http://www.statcan.gc.ca/pub/11-630-x/11-630-x2015001-eng.htm.
12 Sheila Fraser, Auditor General of Canada, December 3, 2002.
13 House of Commons, Hansard, November 28, 2002.
14 "Trudeau's Gun Registry Realism a Welcome Surprise," *Telegraph-Journal* [Saint John, N.B] 13 Dec 2012: A.11.

Kyoto Bound

1 Mulroney was voted Canada's greenest prime minister in a 2006 survey of business and environmental leaders led by *Corporate Knights* magazine.

[2] Library and Archives Canada, https://www.collectionscanada.gc.ca/pri-meministers/h4-3506-e.html, accessed June 21, 2016.

[3] Chrétien, *Straight from the Heart*, 70.

[4] "Copps Waffles on Promise to Slash Greenhouse Gasses," *The Windsor Star* [Windsor, ON] 31 Oct 1994: A2.

[5] Public Accounts, Government of Canada (1993 and 1998). While there was some reprofiling of the department's activities, actual spending in the department of the environment fell from $1.1 billion to $558 million. The 48 per cent cut was over Chrétien's first term in office.

[6] "Copps Shows New Feistiness as Environment Minister," *Canadian Press NewsWire* [Toronto] 09 July 1995.

[7] Jean Charest, "Kyoto Summit: Will Canada Clean Up Its Act?" *The Globe and Mail*, 27 Nov 1997: A.27.

[8] Elizabeth May, Who We Are: Reflections on my Life and Canada, 49.

[9] Chrétien, *My Years as Prime Minister*, 387.

[10] Dennis Bueckert, "Chrétien Stirs Delight and Fury with Pledge to Send Kyoto Pact to Parliament," *Canadian Press NewsWire* [Toronto, ON.] 02 Sep 2002.

[11] Peter Calamai, "Most Still Support Ratifying Kyoto Pact; National Backing for Climate Accord Down Since May Just 40 per cent of Albertans Want It Passed," *Toronto Star*, 06 Dec 2002: A06.

[12] Kate Jaimet, "PM Gave Go-Ahead to Kyoto Treaty Based on 'Gut Feeling,'" *Times-Colonist* [Victoria, B.C] 19 Dec 2002: A3.

[13] Chrétien, *My Years as Prime Minister*, 388.

[14] Les Whittington and Andrew Chung, "Martin Wants Kyoto Pact Delay; Preferable to Wait for a Consensus. Sets Stage for Clash with PM on Vote," *Toronto Star*, 19 Nov 2002: A01.

[15] "Peter Calamai and Les Whittington, "Martin Attacks Chrétien on Kyoto; Climate-change Strategy Flawed, Commons Told. Two Ministers Rise to Defence of Absent PM," *Toronto Star*, 03 Dec 2002: A01.

[16] May, 50.

Immigration

[1] Joan Bryden, "Chrétien Warns of More Shuffling if He Wins Upcoming Federal Vote," *The Vancouver Sun*, 08 July 1993: A4.

[2] "Canada's Proposed Changes to the Immigration Policy," *CTV National News*-CTV Television, 01 Nov 1994.

3 Afrif Noorani, Cynthia Wright, "They Believed the Hype: The Liberals were Elected as the Friend of the Immigrant: a Year Later, they're Fanning the Flames of Crime Hysteria with Their New Pals, the Tabloids and Preston Manning," *This Magazine*, (Dec 1994/Jan 1995): 29–32.

4 Allan Thompson, "Immigration Force Could Set Up Snitch Line: Marchi," *The Gazette* [Montreal, Que] 12 July 1994: B1.

5 http://open.canada.ca/data/en/
dataset/8c0cbfcb-4ea4-44ed-a58a-3fbc9edd8381.

6 David Vienneau, "Time For Healing, Chrétien Tells Nation," *Toronto Star*, 31 Oct 1995: A.9.

Indigenous Affairs

1 Chrétien, *Straight from the Heart*, 62.

2 Ibid.

3 For the sake of clarity and convenience, the term "Indigenous" is taken throughout this work to include Aboriginal, First Nations, Inuit, and Métis people.

4 L. Martin, *Will to Win*, 200.

5 Ibid., 226.

6 Jack Aubry, "Native Leaders Rejecting Irwin Self-Government Plan," *Edmonton Journal*. 13 May 1995: A.8.

7 Goldenberg, 147–8.

8 Chrétien, *Straight from the Heart*, 65.

9 http://www.aadnc-aandc.gc.ca/eng/1345816651029/1345816742083.

Same-sex marriage

1 Graham, 407.

2 Campbell Clark, "Civil Union" Option Martin Says," *The Globe and Mail*, Aug. 20, 2003.

3 L. Martin, *Iron Man*, 422.

4 Alexander Panetta, "MPs Vote Down Alliance Motion to Preserve Traditional Definition of Marriage," *Canadian Press NewsWire* [Toronto] 17 Sep 2003.

5 Gray, *Power of Ambition*, 227.

6 "Supreme Court Simply Affirms Reality," *The Gazette; Montreal*, Que., 10 Dec 2004: A26.

7 "Canada's NEW SPIRIT - Exciting times, BUT MUCH UNFINISHED BUSINESS, in the NOrth," *The Economist*, September 25, 2003.

Shawinigate

1 Thorsell, "What Makes Chrétien Rage?" *The Globe and Mail*, Toronto, ON, 24 Oct 1998: D6.

2 Chrétien, *My Years as Prime Minister*, 185.

3 Ibid., 188.

4 https://www.wsws.org/en/articles/2001/04/chre-a10.html.

5 Chrétien, *My Years as Prime Minister*, 217.

6 Simpson, 43.

7 Chrétien, *My Years as Prime Minister*, 218.

8 L. Martin, *Iron Man*, 313.

9 Goldenberg, 283.

10 Chrétien, *My Years as Prime Minister*, 220.

11 Graham Green, "Double Standard," *Ottawa Citizen* [Ottawa, ON] 01 June 2002: B1.

12 "Asper Promises a Free Press: Citizen's Reporting Violated Journalistic Principles, CanWest President Says," *Ottawa Citizen* [Ottawa, ON] 21 June 2002: A1.

13 "Liberals Deny Role in Firing Citizen Publisher: Russell Mills: Opposition Tries to Link Dismissal to Editorial Calling for PM's Resignation," *National Post*,18 June 2002: A2.

14 Jeffrey Simpson, "What the Mills Affair Reveals about the PM, Aspers," *The Globe and Mail*, Jun. 18, 2002.

15 Mitchell Sharp had an office next to Eddie Goldenberg and they shared the same secretary. Goldenberg recalled that Sharp kept her busier than I did: "He demonstrated the importance of institutional memory. On any given issue, he could recall what Mackenzie King or St. Laurent did and why."

16 Chrétien, *My Years as Prime Minister*, 41.

17 L. Martin, *Iron Man*, 399.

18 Tobin, 242.

A Billion-Dollar Boondoggle?

1 Andrew McIntosh, "Auditor-general to Probe Federal Job-Creation Fund: Audit will Determine Whether Grants were Handed Out Properly," *National Post*, Don Mills, ON, 19 June 1999: A1.

2 Andrew McIntosh, "I Haven't Touched Secret Jobs Fund, Stewart Insists:

Reform MP Blasts Minister's 'Disturbing Discrepancies'" *National Post*; Don Mills, ON, 19 Nov 1999: A7.

3 Peter Foster, "What We Need is a Witch Hunt," *National Post*, 21 Jan 2000: C07.

4 Joan Bryden, Kathryn May, "I'll Clean House: Embattled Minister Willing to Fire Bureaucrats, Alert Police Over Financial Fumbling at Human Resources Department," *The Gazette* [Montreal, Que] 29 Jan 2000: A12.

5 Robert Fife, "PM Rescues Floundering Stewart: Spin Doctor Calls Out Chrétien to Save Minister Under Siege Over Grant Scandal," Ottawa Bureau Chief, *National Post*, 02 Feb 2000: A1, A2.

6 Excerpt from Hansard, May 16, 2000, http://www.parl.gc.ca/HousePublications/Publication.aspx?DocId=2332220&Mode=2&Parl=36&Ses=2&Language=E.

7 Daniel Leblanc, "Liberal MP Lashes Out at Ottawa's Jobs Scheme: Controversial Grants Handed Out Arbitrarily, Gallaway Charges," *The Globe and Mail* [Toronto, ON] 30 Nov 1999: A.1.

8 "Daniel Leblanc, Liberals Defend Grants in Chrétien's Riding: Government Handouts," *The Globe and Mail* [Toronto, Ont] 17 Dec 1999: A.13.

9 L. Martin, *Iron Man*, 228.

10 "Joan Bryden, "Mismanaged Funds are No Political Scandal: PM," *The Gazette* [Montreal, Que] 01 Feb 2000: A9.

11 http://www.oag-bvg.gc.ca/internet/English/parl_oag_200010_11_e_11198.html#0.2.0AKH9E.78C5D1.75Z72G.Q4.

12 Kevin Dougherty, "No 'Shovelgate' Here: Federal Largesse a Plus in Chrétien's Home Riding," *The Gazette* [Montreal, Que] 25 Oct 2000: A1.

13 Daniel Leblanc, "Quebec Liberals Paid to Silence Bagman, Trial Told," *The Globe and Mail*, October 8, 2016.

14 Jack Aubry, "Shawinigate Figure Ordered to pay $10,000: Paul Lemire Fined, Confined to His Home for Defrauding Funds," *Star-Phoenix* [Saskatoon, Sask] 10 Jan 2002: B7.

15 Graham Fraser, "PM Can Act to Restore Government Morale," *Toronto Star*; Toronto, Ont., 17 Dec 2000: A09.

Sponsorship

1 Chrétien, *My Years as Prime Minister*, 157.

2 Ibid., 160.

3 Goldenberg, 239.

[4] According to the Gomery Report, Phase l, "Mr. Pelletier bypassed the normal methods of administration of government programs, and effectively eliminated the oversight that would have been provided by Mr. Quail and his department." 74.

[5] Chrétien, *My Years as Prime Minister*, 161.

[6] Ibid.

[7] Elizabeth Thompson, "Scathing Auditor's Report Orders Probe of Contracts; 'Senior Public Servants Broke Just About Every Rule in the Book'," *The Windsor Star*, 09 May 2002: A1.

[8] Daniel LeBlanc, "Ottawa Can't Find $550,000 Report," *The Globe and Mail*, Toronto, Ont., 11 Mar 2002: A1

[9] http://www.oag-bvg.gc.ca/internet/English/osh_20040219_e_23407.html#os1, accessed February 19, 2006.

[10] Gomery Report: Phase l, 74.

[11] Randy Boswell, "Chrétien's Legacy Not So Bright," *Kingston Whig-Standard*, Kingston, Ont., 02 Nov 2005: 15.

Friends and Relations

[1] L. Martin, *Will to Win*, 65.

[2] Ibid., 89.

[3] Jack Aubry, "Chrétien Says Wife Wanted Him to Quit," *Calgary Herald*; Calgary, Alta., 23 Dec 2000: A6.

[4] Chrétien, *My Years as Prime Minister*, 28.

[5] Ibid., 244.

[6] Ibid., 245.

[7] Bauch, "What is It About Jean Chrétien that Quebecers Hate?" *The Gazette*, Montreal, Que., 21 Aug 1993: B1/BREAK.

[8] Norman Webster, "No Clodhopper," *The Gazette*, Montreal, Que., 08 Jan 1993: B5.

[9] David Vienneau, "Tough to Praise PM, McLaughlin Says," *Toronto Star*, 25 Feb 1993: B8.

[10] Chrétien, *Straight from the Heart*, 123.

[11] Jeff Heinrich, "German Magazine Says Lobbyist Paid Millions in Airbus Sale," *The Gazette* [Montreal, Que] 21 March 1995, 3.

[12] Andy Riga, "Mulroney Lashes Back; Federal Government, RCMP Sued Over Airbus Allegations; Aftermath of the Airbus Sale," *Edmonton Journal* [Edmonton, Alta] 19 Nov 1995: A.1.

13 Chrétien, *My Years as Prime Minister*, 228.

14 Ibid., 230.

15 L. Martin, *Iron Man*, 152.

16 Goldenberg, 275.

17 "Black Aims for Seat in House of Lords: Press Baron will be Appointed a Life Peer This Month, Sources Say," *The Globe and Mail*, Toronto, ON., 08 June 1999: A1.

18 Andrew Duffy, "Manning Rises to Black's Defence: Liberals' Decision to Block Peerage Called `An Unnecessary Slight,'" *Ottawa Citizen*; Ottawa, Ont., 22 June 1999: A1 / FRONT.

19 Ibid., 225.

20 Granatstein and Hillmer, 227.

21 Chrétien, *My Years as Prime Minister*, 13.

22 Chrétien, *Straight from the Heart*, 202.

23 Milnes (editor), 494.

24 Jean Chrétien speech at Library and Archives Canada, May 18, 2016.

25 Nancy Southam, Pierre: Colleagues and Friends Talk about the Trudeau They Knew, McClelland & Stewart, Toronto ON., 2005, 195.

26 Chrétien, *Straight from the Heart*, 199.

27 Chrétien, *My Years as Prime Minister*, 283.

28 "Not Interested in Next Election, Justin Trudeau Says: 'I'm Not Going Anywhere Near Politics,'" *Edmonton Journal*, 03 Dec 2003: A11.

29 Robert Fife, "Martin Tightens Purse Strings with Freeze on Capital Spending," *Edmonton Journal*, 17 Dec 2003: A2.

30 "Richard Cleroux, Trudeau says Mirabel Airport Will Have Torontonians on Their Knees," *The Globe and Mail*, October 6, 1971, A1.

31 John English, Just Watch Me: The Life of Pierre Elliot Trudeau, 468.

32 L. Martin, *Will to Win*, 177.

33 Chrétien, *Straight from the Heart*, 20.

34 L. Martin, *Will to Win*, 92.

35 Goldenberg, 87.

36 Ibid., 89.

37 "New Session Promises to be Sad Spectacle," *The Gazette*; Montreal, Que., 15 Sep 2003: A22.

38 Susan Delacourt, "Rivals, Allies Alike Fete Former PM," *Toronto Star*; Toronto, ON, 22 Jan 2014: A.4.

39 Joan Bryden, "Old Political, Leadership Rivals Unite to Pay Tribute to Jean Chrétien," *Waterloo Region Record*, Jan. 20, 2014.

40 Joan Bryden "Jean Chrétien's Star-Studded 80th Birthday Tribute Sees Justin Trudeau to Stephen Harper Praising the Former PM," *The Canadian Press*, January 22, 2014.

Risky Business

1 Chrétien, *My Years as Prime Minister*, 197.
2 Goldenberg, 224.
3 L. Martin, *Iron Man*, 139.
4 Chrétien, *My Years as Prime Minister*, 178.
5 "We Blew It, Mounties Concede," *Times-Colonist*, Victoria, B.C, 07 Nov 1995: 1.
6 Leonard Stern, "RCMP Report Pinpoints Weaknesses in Guarding Chrétien; New Orders for PM's Protectors" *Edmonton Journal*, 14 Dec 1995: A.3.
7 Sue Yanagisawa, "We Didn't Think It Could Happen Here: RCMP Commissioner," *Kingston Whig-Standard* [Kingston, On.] 15 Dec 199 5: 3.
8 Chrétien, *Straight from the Heart*, 30.
9 L. Martin, The *Will to Win*, 113.
10 Ibid., 3.
11 "Prime Minister Should Apologize," *The Gazette;* Montreal, Que., 17 Feb 1996: B.4.

Winning

1 Chrétien, *My Years as Prime Minister*, 107.
2 Ibid., 216.
3 Chrétien, *Straight from the Heart*, 199.
4 L. Martin, *The Will to Win*, 324.
5 Granatstein and Hillmer, 216.
6 Mulroney, 293.
7 Granatstein and Hillmer, 218.
8 L. Martin, *The Will to Win*, 357.
9 Tobin, 71.
10 Benoit Aubin, "My Mind was Made up to Quit: Chrétien; He Refuses to Blame Turner, but Leaves Door Ajar for Return," *The Gazette*, Montreal, Que, 28 Feb 1986: A7.
11 This includes 200,000 hardcover and 100,000 softcover books.
12 "Leaked Survey Hurting Turner Angers Liberals," Canadian Press, *Toronto*

Star, 06 Sep 1986: A12.

13 L. Martin, *Iron Man*, 51.

14 "Free Trade Touchy Topic in Chrétien-Bush Talks," *The Windsor Star*, Windsor, Ont., 15 Feb 1992: D15.

15 L. Martin, *Iron Man*, 44.

16 Goldenberg, 47.

17 Bauch, *The Gazette*, B1/BREAK.

18 Chrétien, *My Years as Prime Minister*, from a photo opposite page 120.

19 L. Martin, *Iron Man*, 55.

20 "Terrance Wills, Chrétien Lectures Liberal 'Crybabies'" *The Gazette*, Montreal, Que., 18 Mar 1993: A1.

21 Mulroney, 676.

22 Chrétien, *My Years as Prime Minister*, 232.

23 Warren Kinsella, *The War Room: Political Strategies for Business, NGOs, and Anyone Who Wants to Win*, 191.

24 Chrétien, *My Years as Prime Minister*, 11.

25 Ibid., 31.

26 Bliss, 314.

27 Ibid., 327.

28 Chrétien, *My Years as Prime Minister*, 207.

29 Ibid., 204.

30 Ibid., 206.

31 Ibid., 204.

32 http://www.cbc.ca/news/canada/doris-day-petition-hits-the-mark-1.209426, accessed October 12, 2016.

33 Chrétien, *My Years as Prime Minister*, 279.

34 Kinsella, 144.

35 Chrétien, *My Years as Prime Minister*, 285.

36 P. Martin, *Hell or High Water*, 246.

37 Goldenberg, 384.

38 Robert Fife and Anne Dawson, "Canada Moves to the Right," *Edmonton Journal*, 13 Dec 2003: A1.

Mutiny

1 P. Martin, *Hell or High Water*, 83.

2 Chrétien, *My Years as Prime Minister*, 57.

3 P. Martin, *Hell or High Water*, 82.

4 Goldenberg, 21

5 Delacourt, 63.

6 "A Very Bitter Defeat for Paul Martin," CBC Archives, http://www.cbc.ca/
   archives/entry/a-very-bitter-defeat-for-paul-martin, accessed October 27.

7 "Into the Final Stretch," *Maclean's Magazine*, May 14, 1990, 22.

8 "A Very Bitter Defeat for Paul Martin," CBC Archives, http://www.cbc.ca/
   archives/entry/a-very-bitter-defeat-for-paul-martin, accessed October 27.

9 Gray, *Power of Ambition*, 98.

10 P. Martin, *Hell or High Water*, 94

11 Goldenberg, 25.

12 Chrétien, *My Years as Prime Minister*, 27.

13 "Martin Matriarch Wit Intact Until the End," *Times-Colonist*; Victoria, B.C.
   [Victoria, B.C] 14 Nov 1993: 1.

14 P. Martin, *Hell or High Water*, 185

15 Goldenberg, 131.

16 Delacourt, 124.

17 Ibid., 149.

18 Goldenberg, 126.

19 Simpson, 35.

20 Bliss, 327.

21 Goldenberg, 138.

22 Chrétien, *My Years as Prime Minister*, 371.

23 Ibid., 254.

24 P. Martin, *Hell or High Water*, 223.

25 Graham, 126.

26 Ibid., 212.

27 Delacourt, 221.

28 Graham, 212.

29 Ibid., 213.

30 Chrétien, *My Years as Prime Minister*, 257.

31 Delacourt, 158.

32 Andrew Duffy, "Poll Suggests Voters Want Chrétien Gone," *Kingston Whig-
   Standard* [Kingston, Ont] 18 Mar 2000, 15.

33 Eric Grenier of 308.com: http://www.threehundredeight.com/2015/01/ap-
   proval-ratings-of-five-prime-ministers.html, accessed March 1, 2017.

34 P. Martin, *Hell or High Water*, 224.

35 Bliss, 333.

36 P. Martin, *Hell or High Water*, 224.

[37] Delacourt, 175.

[38] Chrétien, *My Years as Prime Minister*, 259.

[39] P. Martin, *Hell or High Water*, 119–20.

[40] Delacourt, 87.

[41] Delacourt, 256.

[42] P. Martin, *Hell or High Water*, 228.

[43] Chrétien, *My Years as Prime Minister*, 259.

[44] P. Martin, *Hell or High Water*, 222

[45] Chrétien, *My Years as Prime Minister*, 378.

[46] "Why We Recommend a Vote for Paul Martin," *The Globe and Mail*, Toronto, Ont., 25 Nov 2000: F6.

[47] Chrétien, *My Years as Prime Minister*, 372.

[48] Goldenberg, 23.

[49] P. Martin, *Hell or High Water*, 228.

[50] Ibid., 228.

[51] Chrétien, *My Years as Prime Minister*, 376.

[52] Delacourt, 133.

[53] Jane Taber, "The Day a Close Friend Walked Out On the PM," *The Globe and Mail*, December 20, 2003.

[54] Ibid.

[55] Tobin, 249.

[56] Ibid., 252.

[57] Ibid.

[58] P. Martin, *Hell or High Water*, 231.

[59] L. Martin, *Iron Man*, 363.

[60] Joan Bryden, "Chrétien Studies Rules for Challengers: Ethics Counsellor Has Drafted Set of Guidelines.", *Calgary Herald*; Calgary, Alta., 16 Apr 2002: A8.

[61] P. Martin, *Hell or High Water*, 231.

[62] Ibid., 232.

[63] Susan Delacourt, "For Mr. Chrétien, Spite Makes Right," *Ottawa Citizen* [Ottawa, ON] 30 May 2002: A18.

[64] P. Martin, *Hell or High Water*, 234.

[65] Ibid., 235.

[66] Ibid.

[67] Shawn McCarthy, "PM's Popularity at Record Low, Poll Shows," *The Globe and Mail*, Jun. 07, 2002, A1.

[68] P. Martin, *Hell or High Water*, 242.

69 Ibid., 243.

70 Jane Taber, "Liberal MPs Checking the List of Loyalties: Ever-shifting Survey Reveals Who Supports Chrétien or Martin," *National Post*, Don Mills, ON, 10 July 2002: A6.

71 Tim Naumetz, "MPs Switch Allegiance to Chrétien: Minds Changed after Pressure from PM, Ministers: Critics," *Ottawa Citizen*, 10 July 2002: A4.

72 L. Martin, *Iron Man*, 383.

73 Ibid., 387.

74 Simpson, 125.

75 Peter C. Newman, "What Scandal?" *The Globe and Mail*, Toronto, On., 20 Oct 2007: D6.

76 Gray, *Power of Ambition*, 181.

77 'I'll Decide When It's Time,' Chrétien Insists: PM Refutes Reports that He's Looking for a Graceful Exit: Will He Stay or Will He Go Now?; *Edmonton Journal*, 15 Aug 2002: A6.

78 Joan Bryden, "Chrétien Fears Setting Bad Precedent: 'Since it is Clearly a Clash of Personalities, We Should Not Remove the Prime Minister': Liberal Infighting: PM's Supporters Say He Will Not Give in to Pressure to Retire," *National Post*, 17 Aug 2002: A6.

79 Gray, 137.

80 Ibid., 163.

81 Ibid., 139.

82 Ibid., 183.

83 Jim Brown, "Chrétien, Detractors Square Off at Liberal Caucus This Week in Chicoutimi"
Canadian Press NewsWire [Toronto] 18 Aug 2002: n/a.

84 Elizabeth Thompson, "Count Us Out, Mps Say: Pro-Chrétien List Loses Four," *The Gazette* [Montreal, Que] 20 Aug 2002: A1.

85 L. Martin, *Iron Man*, 390.

86 Don Boudria, *Busboy: From Kitchen to Cabinet*, Optimum Publishing International Inc., 2005. 282.

87 Joan Bryden, *Leadership Race Begins as PM Plans 2004 Exit: Liberal Leader Hopes to Stem Infighting*, [Final Edition], Calgary Herald [Calgary, Alta] 22 Aug 2002: A1 / FRONT.

88 Joan Bryden, "PM to Leave in 2004: Decision Made On Weekend, Only Closest Aides Knew His Plans," *Edmonton Journal*; Edmonton, Alta., 22 Aug 2002: A1 / FRONT.

89 P. Martin, *Hell or High Water*, 243.

Unmet Expectations

1. John Gray, *Paul Martin: In the Balance*, 252.
2. Chrétien, *My Years as Prime Minister*, 401.
3. Ibid., 400.
4. Kinsella, 222.
5. Martin Patriquin, "The Coderre Treatment," *Maclean's*, September 22, 2014, 22
6. P. Martin, *Hell or High Water*, 278.
7. "Where Paul Martin Should Lead Canada (3)," Editorial, *The Globe and Mail*, December 16, 2003, A 20.
8. Gray, In the Balance, 269.
9. Susan Delacourt, Les Whittington, and Tonda MacCharles, "Your Money, Their Friends; Martin moves: Inquiry Ordered, Gagliano Fired RCMP Probing 13 Sponsorship Program Cases," *Toronto Star* [Toronto, ON] 11 Feb 2004: A01.
10. Blair, 600.
11. Susan Delacourt, "Chrétien, Martin Plan Early Handoff; Key Bills Die as Parliament Ends to Reopen Under New Leader," Jan. 12, *Toronto Star*, 13 Nov 2003: A01.
12. Jack Aubry, "RCMP Estimates Sponsorship Probe at $2.5 million," *Times-Colonist* [Victoria, B.C] 21 Dec 2003: A3.
13. L. Martin, *Iron Man*, 442.
14. P. Martin, *Hell or High Water*, 279.
15. Ibid., 281–2.
16. Goldenberg, 221.
17. P. Martin, *Hell or High Water*, 449.
18. "Where Paul Martin Should Lead Canada (2)," Editorial, *The Globe and Mail*, December 15, 2003, A 16.
19. Taylor, "Not Exactly as Advertised," *National Post*; Don Mills, Ont., 01 Oct 2003: 48.
20. Gray, *Power of Ambition*, 238.
21. "Copps Victim of a Setup," The Province [Vancouver, B.C] 10 Mar 2004: A8.
22. Gray, *In the Balance*, 256.
23. P. Martin, *Hell or High Water*, 251
24. Chrétien, *My Years as Prime Minister*, 371.

25 Ibid., 374.

26 P. Martin, *Hell or High Water*, 282.

27 Ibid., 375.

28 Delacourt, 161.

29 Jeffrey Simpson, "It's His Party and You Can Cry if You Want To," *The Globe and Mail*, December 3, 2003, A25.

30 Ibid., 111.

31 Chrétien, *My Years as Prime Minister*, 7.

32 Gray, *Power of Ambition*, 88.

33 P. Martin, *Hell or High Water*, 259.

34 Ibid., 46.

35 Gray, *Power of Ambition*, 127.

36 Taylor, "Not Exactly as Advertised," *National Post*, Don Mills, Ont., 01 Oct 2003: 48.

37 Ibid.

38 Ibid.

39 L. Ian MacDonald, "As Prime Minister, Paul Martin Ran His Government like an Open Bar," *The Gazette* [Montreal, Que] 27 Feb 2006: A25.

40 Mike Blanchfield, "Bono 'Crushed' by Martin's Broken Promise," *Ottawa Citizen*, Ottawa, ON, 26 Nov 2005: A6.

41 "How to Squander an Inheritance; Paul Martin Lost the Campaign, Even if he Wins the Election," *The Economist*, June 24th 2004.

42 P. Martin, *Hell or High Water*, 310.

43 Ibid., 410.

44 Gray, *Power of Ambition*, 180.

45 Daniel Leblanc and Jeff Sallot with a report from Brian Laghi, "Gomery Cost Soars," *The Globe and Mail*, Feb. 01, 2005.

46 "John Ibbitson, "Chrétien Assails Martin in a Most Diplomatic Tone," *The Globe and Mail*, Toronto, On., 30 Mar 2004: A1

47 "Paul Martin's Legacy," Editorial, *The Globe and Mail*, Toronto, On., 25 Jan 2006: A20.

48 Michael Bliss, "An Unenviable Win: Paul Martin's Victory Will Be Short-Lived and Unsteady at Best," *National Post*; Don Mills, ON. 29 June 2004: E1 Front.

A Great Prime Minister

1 Chrétien, *My Years as Prime Minister*, 406.

2 Paul Wells, *The Longer I'm Prime Minister*, 2006-, 405.

3 Chrétien, *My Years as Prime Minister*, 405.

4 "Anthony Depalma, "Just Blunt, or a Bully: Canada Divided on Leader," *The New York Times*, October 28, 1998.

5 Chrétien, *My Years as Prime Minister*, 4.

6 Ibid., 404.

7 "Chrétien's Legacy is a Stable Country," *Toronto Star* [Toronto, ON] 12 Dec 2003: A34. [editorial?]

8 "Where Paul Martin Should Lead Canada (1)," Editorial, *The Globe and Mail*, December 13, 2003, 22.

9 Ibid.

10 Bliss, *Right Honourable Men*, 335.

11 Ibid., 315.

12 Ibid.

13 Granatstein and Hillmer, *Prime Ministers*, 227.

14 Gray, *Power of Ambition*, 173.

15 Aileen McCabe, "Chrétien Blew His Chance to Leave Serious Legacy of Social Change, Coutts Says," *CanWest News* [Don Mills, Ont] 11 Nov 2003: 1.

16 Peter Newman, "What Scandal?" *The Globe and Mail*, Toronto, On., 20 Oct 2007: D6.

17 Lawrence Martin, *Iron Man*, 438.

18 Clyde Farnsworth, "New Canadian Chief Winning Applause," *The New York Times*, January 23, 1994.

19 Don Newman, *Welcome to the Broadcast: A Memoir*, Harper Collins, 2013, 340.

20 Scott White, "PM Named Top Newsmaker of '98: National News Media Select Chrétien First, Conrad Black Second," *Ottawa Citizen*; Ottawa, ON, 26 Dec 1998: A4.

21 Bauch, *The Gazette*, B1/BREAK.

22 "Where Paul Martin Should Lead Canada (1)," Editorial, *The Globe and Mail*, December 13, 2003, 22.

23 Chrétien, *My Years as Prime Minister*, 103.

24 Ibid., 105.

25 Goldenberg, 99.

26 Chrétien, *My Years as Prime Minister*, 105.

27 Goldenberg, 73.

28 Chrétien, *Straight from the Heart*, 53.

[29] George Radwanski, *Trudeau*, 169.

[30] Chrétien, *My Years as Prime Minister*, 38.

[31] Ibid., 18.

[32] Ibid., 32.

[33] Ibid., 33.

[34] Ibid., 35.